PSYCHOPATHOLOGY
in the
WORKPLACE

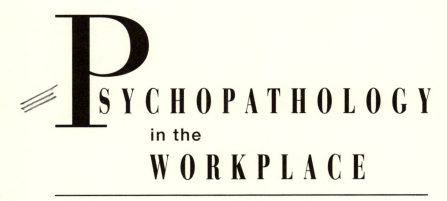

PSYCHOPATHOLOGY
in the
WORKPLACE

Recognition and Adaptation

edited by
Jay C. Thomas • Michel Hersen

BRUNNER-ROUTLEDGE
NEW YORK AND HOVE

Published in 2004 by
Brunner-Routledge
29 West 35th Street
New York, NY 10001
www.brunner-routledge.com

Published in Great Britain by
Brunner-Routledge
27 Church Road
Hove, East Sussex
BN3 2FA
www.brunner-routledge.co.uk

Library of Congress Cataloging-in-Publication Data

Psychopathology in the workplace : recognition and adaptation / Jay C. Thomas and Michel Hersen, editors.
    p. cm.
Includes bibliographical references.
    ISBN 0-415-93379-X (hbk.)
1. Industrial psychiatry. 2. Psychology, Pathological. 3. Employees--Mental health. 4. Work--Psychological aspects. I. Thomas, Jay C., 1951- II. Hersen, Michel.

RC967.5 P785 2004
616.89--dc22   2003024666

Contents

PART III *Environmental and Managerial Interventions*

About the Editors

Jay C. Thomas, ABPP, is Director of the Counseling Psychology program at Pacific University, Portland, Oregon, USA. He received his Ph.D. from the University of Akron in Industrial and Organizational Psychology and holds a diploma from the American Board of Professional Psychology in that specialty. He worked several years as a consultant and in private practice before he joined Pacific's School of Professional Psychology teaching statistics, research methods, program evaluation, and courses in organizational behavior and career development. His research interests include program evaluation, methodology for field studies, outcome research, and integrating findings and concepts across I/O and clinical/counseling psychology. He is co-editor with Michel Hersen of *Understanding Research in Clinical and Counseling Psychology* (2004, Erlbaum), the *Handbook of Mental Health in the Workplace* (2002, Sage Publications), editor of the *Comprehensive Handbook of Psychological Assessment- Volume 4, Industrial and Organizational Assessment* (2004, John Wiley and Sons), and has published several papers in I/O psychology, program evaluation, and mental health.

Michel Hersen (ABPP, State University of New York at Buffalo, 1966) is Professor and Dean, School of Professional Psychology, Pacific University, Forest Grove, Oregon. He completed his post-doctoral training at the West Haven VA (Yale University School of Medicine Program). He is Past President of the Association for Advancement of Behavior Therapy. He has co-authored and co-edited 139 books and has published 224 scientific journal articles. He is co-editor of several psychological journals, including *Behavior Modification, Aggression and Violent Behavior: A Review Journal, Clinical Psychology Review, Journal of Family Violence, and Journal of Developmental and Physical Disabilities,* and Editor-in-Chief of the *Journal of Anxiety Disorders* and *Clinical Case Studies*, which is totally devoted to description of clients and patients treated with psychotherapy. He is Editor-in Chief of the four-volume work entitled: *Comprehensive Handbook of Psychological Assessment* and the two-Volume work entitled: *Encyclopedia of Psychotherapy.* He has been the recipient of numerous grants from the National Institute of Mental Health, the Department of Education, the National Institute of Disabilities and Rehabilitation Research, and the March of Dimes Birth Defects Foundation. He is a Diplomate of the American Board of Professional Psychology, Fellow of the American Psychological Association, Distinguished Practitioner and Member of the National Academy of Practice in Psychology, and recipient of the Distinguished Career Achievement Award in 1996 from the American Board of Medical Psychotherapists and Psychodiagnosticians. Finally, at one point in his career, he was in full-time private practice and on several occasions he has had part-time private practices.

List of Contributors

Drew A. Anderson
University at Albany, State University
of New York

Kristen G. Anderson
University of California, San Diego

David O. Antonuccio
University of Nevada School of
Medicine

Melanie E. Bennett
University of Maryland School of
Medicine

Gary R. Birchler
University of California, San Diego

Elisa Bolton
New Hampshire–Dartmouth Psychiatric
Research Center

Seth A. Brown
University of Northern Iowa

Andrea B. Burns
Florida State University

Mandy Davies
Pacific University

Brad C. Donohue
University of Nevada, Las Vegas

William Fals-Stewart
State University of New York, Buffalo

John P. Forsyth
University at Albany, State University
of New York

Jon Frew
Pacific University

Tiffany K. Fusé
University at Albany, State University
of New York

Eileen Gambrill
University of California, Berkeley

Charles J. Golden
Nova Southeastern University

Zarabeth L. Golden
Nova Southeastern University

Dana R. Holohan
Salem VA Medical Center

Leslie E. Horton
Duke University Medical Center

Thomas E. Joiner, Jr.
Florida State University

Maria Karekla
University at Albany, State University
of New York

Megan M. Kelly
University at Albany, State University
of New York

Daniel W. King
VA Boston Healthcare System and
  Boston University School of Medicine

Lynda A. King
VA Boston Healthcare System and
  Boston University School of Medicine

Gerald Lewis
COMPASS

Jennifer D. Lundgren
University at Albany, State University
  of New York

Thomas R. Lynch
Duke University Medical Center

Douglas G. McClure
Employee Assistance Services
  Enterprises

Susan R. McGurk
Mount Sinai School of Medicine

Terry Michael McClanahan
The Permanente Medical Group, Inc.

Rachel G. Morier
University at Albany, State University
  of New York

Kim T. Mueser
Dartmouth Medical School

Jeremy W. Pettit
University of Houston

Leah Toney Podratz
Shell Oil Company

Mayumi Purvis
University of Melbourne

Natalie Sachs-Ericsson
Florida State University

Benson Schaeffer
Pacific University

Nadia E. Stellrecht
Florida State University

Marilyn J. Strada
University of Nevada, Las Vegas

Claire A. Stewart
Deakin University

Lois E. Tetrick
George Mason University

Tony Ward
Victoria University of Wellington

Thomas A. Widiger
University of Kentucky

Preface

O ur book will fill a unique niche. In recent years there has been widespread recognition that many people who experience psychopathology are in the workforce, that it is important for these individuals' recovery that they remain in the workforce, and that it is in employers' best interest to keep such individuals employed. This recognition is bringing modification in practice, yet there are few resources for students to use to learn how to deal with this manifestation of psychopathology in the workplace. Therefore, with *Psychopathology in the Workplace: Recognition and Adaptation* we provide students in psychology, psychiatry, counseling, social work, and human resources with the background knowledge they need to contribute to this new aspect of practice.

We divided the book into three parts. Part I, Overview, provides the foundation of the interface of psychopathology and the workplace and presents a model of psychopathology, work, and life stressors, and the basics of assessing psychopathology. Part II, Categories of Dysfunction, describes the major forms of psychopathology that are most likely to be found in the workplace. The forms are livened with an actual case illustration. Each chapter in Part II follows the same general format to ensure cross-chapter consistency. Part III, Environmental and Managerial Interventions, consists of chapters that detail actions that organizations can take to accommodate persons with mental health needs, strategies to motivate and lead employees, and techniques to promote positive mental health. With twenty-one chapters, the book can stand alone in a one-semester course or may be used as an adjunctive text for general psychopathology.

Preparing this book was an enjoyable adventure over the past couple of years. Its development was enhanced through the efforts of several people to whom we owe our sincere thanks. Johan Rosqvist and Garen Weitman provided cases, and Katie Winder provided economic data for Chapter 1. Our graduate students Alison Brodhagen, Tamara Tasker, and Cynthia Polance were extremely helpful in gathering information for the indices. We thank Dr. George Zimmar, our editor at Brunner-Routledge, for understanding the value and the need for this project. Finally, Carole Londerée was a superlative editorial assistant throughout this project, reminding us all of the important deadlines that we needed to meet. We are most grateful to her.

Jay C. Thomas
Portland, Oregon

Michel Hersen
Forest Grove, Oregon

Part I

Overview

1

Introduction

JAY C. THOMAS
Pacific University

Henry[1] is a man in his mid-30s. He is a wine expert and works for a company that distributes fine wines. Henry's job involves calling on customers, such as restaurants and caterers, delivering wines by the case, and having the customer sample wines for possible resale. He is expected to engage in a good deal of socializing with customers and others in the food and beverage industry and to attend charity auctions, golf tournaments, and similar events. Because Henry's company is very small and he is involved with the management of the firm, he must attend several critical meetings each week. Henry is very good at his job except for one problem, which now interferes with his ability to perform most of his important work functions.

Sometimes Henry's heart seems to race and he feels as if he is having a heart attack. He has been to the hospital emergency room (ER) several times, and he has had his coronary health thoroughly examined, with no finding of disease. Still, he panics whenever he feels his heart racing. He is so afraid of setting off an episode that he avoids all types of physical exertion. Consequently, he has gained a lot of weight, which, ironically, puts him at much greater risk of developing cardiac disease. In the past several months, Henry's anxiety over his panic attacks has progressed to the point that he now frequently believes himself to be suffering from many other medical conditions. For example, one day he saw an advertisement on the side of a bus for a stroke medication. He immediately interpreted his slight headache as the beginnings of a stroke, so he went to the ER instead of going to work. An ache in his side or arm may be cancer and a cold may be pneumonia. Henry no longer finds it easy to call on customers, and carrying a case of wine is out of the question. Social events are too taxing, so he quit attending them. He actually left several business meetings to seek medical attention. His medical leave from work is long since exhausted, and the company's health insurance rates are increasing because of his extreme overuse of benefits. Henry's customers are

---

[1] This is an actual case treated by my colleague Johan Rosqvist.

complaining about poor service, and his co-workers and employer are tired of covering for him. Although a valued employee, Henry is about to lose his job because of his hypochondriasis and panic attacks.

Pat is a sergeant in the county sheriff's office.[1] Two years ago Pat's good friend and colleague Lieutenant Howard Brown was shot in the head while responding to a domestic disturbance. Lieutenant Brown is unable to speak clearly or walk without help and will never return to his job. Pat was supposed to take the call but was tied up in a traffic enforcement stop when the dispatch came. Lieutenant Brown covered the call as a favor. Now Pat and her spouse worry that the same thing could happen to her, and Pat feels guilty that Lieutenant Brown was wounded in her place. Now she has mixed feelings about responding to the dispatcher's call: a heightened sense of duty and fear. Sometimes after a shift she goes home and shakes for an hour and finds it hard to talk to her husband about work. Pat's husband wants her to leave her job and get out of police work.

Francesca works in an office supply store, part of a nationwide chain. She runs a small department that makes copies and performs simple printing jobs, such as business cards. She thought she was getting a "normal" job in which she would work 40 hours a week and leave her work behind when she was off duty.[2] She has three children, whose ages range from 3 to 11 years. Her ex-husband used to take care of their children on alternate weekends and would pick them up from day care or school and watch them on those days when she had to work late. He also was the one who took the older children to swimming lessons and to soccer and baseball practice. Four months ago, just as Francesca's employer was facing increasing competition and requiring more and more overtime and weekend work, her ex-husband's National Guard unit was called up for extended service in Afghanistan. He will be gone at least a year, and Francesca's employer sees no end to the increased work demands. Her boss says she cannot hire additional workers without approval from the head office and there is not a chance of that happening. Francesca is making more money than she ever imagined, but the strain of overworking, plus caring for her children and her house, has her feeling depressed, anxious, and full of resentment.

When Gary was 20 years old, his symptoms were diagnosed as schizophrenia. His personal appearance is slovenly (his hair is matted into dreadlocks and he wears dirty clothes), and he often has a vacant stare. He experiences auditory delusions and sometimes talks back to them. He is employed as a groundskeeper in a park. His duties involve mowing the lawn, raking leaves, emptying the garbage, and performing similar chores. So far, his performance on these tasks has been satisfactory. However, sometimes while working he stops and stares off for minutes at a time. Other times young children think that his talking is directed to them and they get scared. His appearance makes him seem threatening. Gary is not aggressive or assertive, and his response to aggression is to back off. His psychiatrist prescribed medication, and when Gary takes it as prescribed his most obvious symptoms disappear. However, Gary dislikes the medication because of the side effects (including gaining a great

---

[1] To protect confidentiality we modified this case from one presented by Garen Weitman in my organizational behavior class.

[2] Francesca's story and the following story about Gary are slightly changed to protect their identities.

deal of weight) and because he wants people to know "the real me." Many families with young children use the park, and Gary's strange appearance and mannerisms scare some away. Parents have been complaining about him, and some worry that he will hurt the children because he is "obviously crazy."

These four cases illustrate some of the issues of psychopathology in the workplace; similar cases can be found in any industrialized country in the world. Work can be stressful, and employers can be very demanding because of the demands of the marketplace. In such an environment people with mental disabilities, cognitive or emotional strain, or other impairments are at an extreme disadvantage. Historically, the employer's solution was simply to terminate the employee, if possible. Certainly, people with a history of psychopathology would not be hired if the employer could find any other alternative. Times, however, have changed and are continuing to change rapidly. Laws, such as the Americans with Disabilities Act of 1990 (ADA), limit the employer's ability to discriminate against those people with disabilities who can perform the essential functions of a job. Highly trained employees such as Henry and Pat may be too expensive to replace, unless as a last resort.

Demographers and labor economists believe that, in spite of many companies moving jobs overseas, there may be a shortage of workers in the U.S. economy over the next several years (Fullerton, 1997, 1999; Olsen, 1994). The country cannot afford to have people, who can be productive, being idle because of an accommodable or treatable mental condition. Such conditions are common in U.S. society, with National Institute of Mental Health (NIMH) data indicating that more than 22 percent of Americans older than age seventeen years have a diagnosable mental disorder in any given year (NIMH, n.d.). Throughout the world mental illness is second only to cardiovascular disease in disease burden (NIMH, n.d.). It is also well established that people with mental disorders have lower rates of participation in the workforce, with rates for people with psychoses, such as schizophrenia, being among the lowest and rates for people with anxiety disorders being somewhat below that of the general population (Yelin & Cisternas, 1997). There are many barriers to getting people experiencing psychopathology into the workforce. Moffitt and Winder (2003) examined data from the Three-City Study, a large longitudinal project concerned with welfare-to-work transition, and found that, compared with other study participants, those participants with identifiable mental health concerns were more likely to enter welfare rolls and less likely to leave welfare by finding a job. There is a large pool of potential workforce entrants among those people experiencing psychopathological conditions, and it may be to the advantage of employers and society to find methods of effectively tapping it.

Integrating people with mental disorders into the workplace is apt to be difficult without due consideration of the work environment, particularly of the social environment. Jeff Hite and I have argued that research in the past half century of organizational theory has resulted in organizational designs and practices in which people with psychopathological conditions are unlikely to be either successful or comfortable (Thomas & Hite, 2002). Modern organization design, with its flat hierarchies, team emphasis, goal setting, fast pace, accountability, the need for flexibility and continual change, and high-stress conditions puts a premium on the possession of excellent interpersonal skills and coping strategies, initiative, and other characteristics that often are muted by psychopathology. The need for employees with these skills creates a challenge for those people who are responsible for managing organizations, therapists, job coaches, and individuals with mental disorders who wish to hold or retain a responsible job. They must find creative ways to achieve the objectives implied by system and organizational design and to minimize the environmental factors that encourage failure. Job accommodation cannot be a cookie-cutter approach but must be accomplished by using an understanding of the individual's condition, the working situation, and the organizational environment.

The common saying "This job is driving me crazy" should be a reminder that sometimes it is the work environment or conditions that contribute to a person's mental distress. "Job stress" has entered the popular lexicon, and it is popularly considered to be at fault for many problems faced by individuals, including depression, violent behavior, heart disease, divorce, and, in Japan, karoshi, or death from overwork. A recent MSNBC series presented examples and expert opinions supporting these ideas (Weaver, n.d., with links to other episodes of the series). Professionals need to go beyond popular portrayals and examine the scientific bases for these assertions. In later chapters in this book we will present some of the research that can sustain or reject such claims.

A majority of clinicians are interested in treating psychopathology and, to a much lesser extent, in adapting environments that allow their clients the best chance of success. The "client's work" refers to something that goes on in the treatment session, not what the client does for a living. For some reason the notion that clients may have or wish to have a job not only as a means of survival but also as a way to establish relationships with others, a sense of self-esteem and self-efficacy, and meaning in their life has not received the attention it deserves in the clinical literature. For example, a recent, comprehensive, four-volume compendium of psychotherapy does not contain index references to terms such as *job, employment,* or *work* (Kaslow, 2002). The same is true of Barlow's (2002) comprehensive and authoritative book on anxiety, although Beckham and Leber's (1995) *Handbook of Depression* includes one chapter that considers some aspects of the workplace and their influence on the development and maintenance of the disorder (Brems, 1995). Programs in clinical and counseling psychology often include education and training about the family, schools, and other important milieus but rarely cover the workplace. There are many therapies that have been shown empirically to result in positive changes, but even in the best of studies one-fourth to one-third of clients fail to improve (Thomas, 2002). In preparing this book, we had the objective of training therapists to be better prepared to understand the client's work life and to be more able to use that understanding to effect change on the job.

Managers and human resource professionals are less concerned with treatment of mental disorders than clinicians are. Their attention is concentrated on having a smoothly operating, productive workplace. In recent years there has been a reawakening interest in dysfunctional behavior in the workplace (e.g., Giacalone & Greenberg, 1997; Lowman, 1993; Vardi & Weitz, 2004). Lowman's book, in particular, is an excellent resource for the clinician, although it concentrates on changing the individual rather than including adaptation and accommodation as other treatment options. Often, authors are interested in personality processes, as they may result in undesirable behavior at work—an important perspective but one that necessarily leaves out the purposeful or inadvertent dysfunctional behavior related to other forms of psychopathology. We have found it helpful for people in management positions to obtain an understanding of the more common forms of psychopathology and their genesis and treatment and their potential impact at work. So armed, these managers can participate more meaningfully in recognizing the need for adapting a mentally disabled employee's work in appropriate ways.

In conclusion, it is a priority that people with mental disorders be able to work successfully, to hold a job, and to contribute economically to society and to their own support. At the same time employers need to be able to change the organizational systems whose design works against people with mental disorders to an environment that allows for success while keeping up with productivity demands and competing effectively against other organizations. These goals are to a large degree antagonistic and meeting them requires that clients, therapists, and management work together to understand each other's situation, objectives, and presses. Few areas of psychology and management require the breadth of knowledge, critical thinking, and creativity that working with psychopathology in the workplace does. The reader is invited to enter this challenging and potentially rewarding arena.

References

Barlow, D. H. (2002). *Anxiety and its disorders: The nature and treatment of anxiety and panic* (2nd ed.). New York: Guilford.

Beckham, E. E., & Leber, W. R. (Eds.). (1995). *Handbook of depression* (2nd ed.). New York: Guilford.

Brems, C. (1995). Women and depression: A comprehensive analysis. In E. E. Beckham & W. R. Lever (Eds.), *Handbook of depression* (2nd ed., pp. 539-566). New York: Guilford.

Fullerton, H. N. (1997). Labor force 2006: Slowing down and changing composition. *Monthly Labor Review, 120*(11), 23-38.

Fullerton, H. N. (1999). Labor force participation: 75 years of change, 1950-98 and 1998-2025. *Monthly Labor Review, 122*(12), 3-12.

Giacalone, R. A., & Greenberg, J. (Eds.). (1997). *Antisocial behavior in organizations.* Thousand Oaks, CA: Sage.

Kaslow, F. W. (Ed.). (2002). *Comprehensive handbook of psychotherapy* (Vols. I-IV). New York: John Wiley.

Lowman, R. L. (1993). *Counseling and psychotherapy of work dysfunctions.* Washington, DC: American Psychological Association.

National Institute of Mental Health. (n.d.). *The impact of mental illness on society.* Retrieved from http://www.nimh.nih.gov/publicat/burden.cfm.

Moffitt, R., & Winder, K. (2003). *The correlations and consequences of welfare exit and entry: Evidence from the Three-City Study* (Three-City Working Paper 03-01). Baltimore: Johns Hopkins University. Retrieved from www.jhu.edu/~welfare.

Olsen, R. J. (1994). Fertility and the size of the U.S. labor force. *Journal of Economic Literature,* 32 (March), 60-100.

Thomas, J. C. (2002, November). *Understanding non-response: What other disciplines can teach us*. Paper presented at Association for Advancement of Behavior Therapy, Reno, NV.

Thomas, J. C., & Hite, J. (2002). Mental health in the workplace: Toward an integration of organizational and clinical theory, research, and practice. In J. C. Thomas & M. Hersen (Eds.), *Handbook of mental health in the workplace* (pp. 3-14). Thousand Oaks, CA: Sage.

Vardi, Y., & Weitz, E. (2004). *Misbehavior in organizations: Theory, research, and management*. Mahwah, NJ: Lawrence Erlbaum.

Weaver, J. (n.d.). *Job stress, burnout on the rise*. Retrieved from http://www.msnbc.com/news/952425.asp.

Yelin, E. H., & Cisternas, M. G. (1997). Employment patterns among persons with and without mental conditions. In R. J. Bonnie & J. Monahan (Eds.), *Mental disorder, work disability, and the law* (pp. 25-51). Chicago: University of Chicago Press.

2

Overview of Models of Psychopathology

THOMAS A. WIDIGER

University of Kentucky

*T*he American Psychiatric Association's (APA) *Diagnostic and Statistical Manual of Mental Disorders–Fourth Edition–Text Revision* (*DSM-IV-TR*) (APA, 2000) is the authoritative guide in the United States for the diagnosis and classification of psychopathology. If one wishes to determine whether a person has a mental disorder or under what circumstances a particular behavior pattern (e.g., drug usage, homosexual activity, failure to complete occupational responsibilities, or deficits in attention) is considered to be a mental disorder, one would consult the *DSM-IV* (Frances, First, & Pincus, 1995).

However, there is not a single authoritative model for understanding the etiology and pathology of these mental disorders. Nevertheless, there are models of psychopathology that have substantial theoretical and empirical support. Presented in this chapter are eight alternative perspectives for understanding the etiology and pathology of mental disorders: (1) neurobiological, (2) sociobiological, (3) psychodynamic, (4) behavioristic, (5) cognitive, (6) interpersonal and systems, (7) humanistic, and (8) anthropological. Next, I describe each perspective and provide historical and current illustrations.

NEUROBIOLOGICAL PERSPECTIVE

We have perhaps left the decade of the study of the brain (Judd, 1998) to enter a decade of the study of brain disease (Hyman, 1998). Psychiatry originally distinguished itself from neurology by providing psychological models for the etiology and pathology of disorders that were not, at that time, being effectively understood or treated by neurologists (Stone, 1997). Psychiatry is now shifting back toward neurology. Mental disorders consist of maladaptive cognitions, feelings, and behaviors. Neurobiological models of psychopathology reduce or explain these symptoms as dysregulations along neurochemical pathways within the central (and peripheral) nervous system. As expressed by a recent director of the National Institute of Mental Health (NIMH), "Mental illnesses are real, diagnosable, treatable brain disorders" (Hyman, 1998, p. 38).

All normal human behavior, from moving a leg to thinking about a business deal, depends on smooth and organized activity among the neurons within the nervous system. Dysfunction can occur for a wide variety of reasons. Dysregulation along neurochemical pathways can occur because of excessive or inadequate release of particular neurotransmitters, because of inordinately or inadequately sensitive receptor sites, because of inordinately or inadequately functioning reuptake sites, or because of excessively active or inactive neuromodulators. The nature of the symptoms that result also depends on the connections or pathways that are affected.

Even disorders that have been understood in the past as being largely the result of environmental events are now being interpreted as being largely the result of a neurochemical pathology (Widiger & Sankis, 2000). For example, the diagnosis of post-traumatic stress disorder (PTSD) used require that the stressor be an event that was outside the range of usual human experience and be markedly distressing to most anyone. This requirement was consistent with the theory that the disorder was largely due to the horrific nature of the stressor (e.g., any normal person might respond with PTSD symptoms). However, "studies of the prevalence, course, and comorbidity of PTSD have raised issues regarding the role of the stressor as the true etiologic factor in the development of this disorder" (Yehuda & McFarlane, 1995, p. 1705). Yehuda and her colleagues suggest that occurrence of PTSD might say more about a biological disposition than the psychological significance of the event. Yehuda (1998) suggest that a qualitatively distinct set of biological alterations occur in persons who develop the symptoms of PTSD. A purportedly normal response to stress would involve increased adrenocortical activity and ultimately pituitary hyporesponsivity, but the hypothalamic-pituitary-adrenal system appears to become more sensitized in cases of PTSD, manifested by a decreased cortisol release and an increased (rather than decreased) negative feedback inhibition. "This disruption may lead to alterations in the processing of traumatic memories. Indeed, low cortisol enhances the memory-potentiating effects of catecholamines in the central nervous system" (Yehuda et al., 1998, p. 858).

"For all our major disorders ... the situation is one in which genes, acting at different times in brain development in different locations in the brain, interact with epigenetic and environmental influences to produce vulnerabilities to mental disorders" (Hyman, 1998, p. 37). No event in life that has a lasting impact on psychological functioning would fail to have a significant neurophysiological representation. "Each and every thought, impulse, affect, perception, and motivation is isomorphic with a commensurate pattern of brain activity" (Ilardi & Feldman, 2001, p. 1072). Any lasting effect of a traumatic, abusive, or otherwise harmful psychological experience might then be reducible to a neurophysiological pathology or lesion. For example, a disorder might be traced to a history of being sexually abused (Ornduff, 2000). Even if this abuse was perpetrated on someone with little to no genetic vulnerability, the eventual occurrence of psychopathology might still be reduced to a neurophysiological brain disease. "Alterations in gene expression induced by learning give rise to changes in patterns of neuronal connections ...

[that] are responsible for initiating and maintaining abnormalities of behavior that are induced by social contingencies" (Kandel, 1998, p. 460). Being shot in the head is also a psychosocial event, but the illness that results from this event that is treated by a physician is a medical, brain pathology. Similarly, a child being repeatedly told that he or she is a worthless unlovable person has endured a series of psychosocial events, but the illness that results from this experience (e.g., dysregulation along serotonergic pathways) might also be a medical, brain disease.

SOCIOBIOLOGICAL AND EVOLUTIONARY BIOLOGICAL PERSPECTIVE

A fundamental assumption of sociobiological models of psychopathology is that the human brain includes specialized mechanisms developed through natural selection over vast periods of time that have increased the likelihood of the survival of a particular species, tribe, or individual (Durrant & Ellis, 2003; Tooby & Cosmides, 1990). Most of these mechanisms continue to have adaptive value. However, some mechanisms that had the effect of increasing the likelihood of survival in our ancestral past could be maladaptive within modern society (Buss, Haselton, Shack-elford, Bleske, & Wakefield, 1998).

Seligman (1971) provided one of the earliest sociobiological models of psycho-pathology. Anxiety, like physical pain, is a very unpleasant experience that is difficult to ignore. However, it is precisely this quality that provides its adaptive value. Physical pain alerts us to the potential existence of a life-threatening lesion, disease, or injury. Anxiety likewise alerts us to the potential existence of threats to our safety and security. Some persons may have inherited an innate preparedness to be fearful toward certain things that were life threatening throughout much of our genetic history but are no longer a meaningful threat. For example, persons tend to be phobic of a particular set of objects and situations, such as heights, spiders, rats, darkness, snakes, water, and enclosed places (Barlow, Pincus, Heinrichs, & Choate, 2003). Seligman (1971) hypothesized that an innate disposition to be fearful of these stimuli might have had a compelling survival value in the long years of our ancestral hunter-gatherer past. It is maladaptive and irrational to become intensely anxious when looking out the window of a tall building or an airplane, but the only comparable situation in the Pleistocene hunter-gatherer period was when a person perhaps stood at the edge of a cliff. Persons for whom this situation aroused intense feelings of anxiety would have been more likely to avoid this life-threatening behavior and to have offspring who would maintain this genetic disposition. Those people who lacked the genetic disposition would have been more likely to have fallen off cliffs and, as a result, have fewer offspring (Buss et al., 1998).

Evolutionary models also have been developed for other forms of psychopathol-ogy. Perhaps the most has been written about the potential adaptive value of depres-sion. The fact that depression is a universal phenomenon that has been present throughout the history of our species does imply that it might have some survival value. Researchers have proposed alternative hypotheses. One suggestion is that depression acts as a signal to others that the person is in need of support and help.

Anxiety is a signal to the self that danger is present; depression is perhaps a signal to others that a major loss has occurred. Tearful, panicked crying is a hardwired signal to caregivers that is relied on heavily by infants to indicate a need for protection, care, or nurturance (Lummaa, Vuorisalo, Barr, & Lehtonen, 1998). Not only is this signal difficult to ignore but it also would have served as a good location device in the days when infants might have crawled off into the prairies, fields, forests, and jungles of the hunter-gatherer days.

An alternative evolutionary model is that depression is a mechanism through which a person disengages from a failing (unreachable) goal or activity (Nesse, 2000). Positive and negative moods regulate the allocation of effort and resources invested in various activities. Elevations in mood stimulate a person to engage in the pursuit of a goal; depression might be a mechanism that facilitates the complementary disengagement. Lack of energy, pessimism, hopelessness, fatigue, and loss of initiative are fundamental symptoms of depression that might be largely natural adaptive expressions of disengagement. There are times in which it is adaptive to keep trying, but there also are times when it is realistic to give up and to accept a defeat or loss, as any further engagement will entail only a wasted effort and the loss of additional resources.

PSYCHODYNAMIC PERSPECTIVE

Psychodynamic theory was the predominant perspective in psychiatry for much of the first half of the twentieth century (Stone, 1997). Credit for the substantial impact and importance of this perspective can be traced to the innovative brilliance of one particular person: Sigmund Freud. Many of Freud's original hypotheses have been discredited (Crews, 1996), but this reflects in large part the natural growth of any body of knowledge. "To reject psychodynamic thinking because Freud's instinct theory or his view of women is dated is like rejecting modern physics because Newton did not understand relativity" (Westen, 1998, p. 334). Current psychodynamic theory is not concerned with penis envy or psychosexual fixations; these were not even the major contributions of Freud. Freud was innovative in his rich development of a perspective that was at the time receiving inadequate appreciation, that psychopathology reflects, at least in part, unconscious psychological conflicts (Cooper, 1998; Gabbard, 2000; Westen, 1998). Freud placed particular emphasis on conflicts involving primitive sexual and aggressive impulses. Contemporary clinicians emphasize instead conflicts regarding self-esteem, intimacy, and interpersonal relatedness.

These conflicts are believed to develop through a traumatic or sustained history of pathogenic childhood experiences. How one, as an adult, views oneself and other persons is said to be a symbolic representation of how one was treated by the significant persons' of one's past, notably one's parents (Gabbard, 2000; Westen, 1991). It is difficult to imagine a relationship ever being as significant as one's relationship with one's parents. For Freud, growing up with one's parents is analogous to being raised by God. In fact, Freud (1933) suggested that God is a symbolic representation of one's parents. They are their child's creator and, for the child, they are all powerful and all knowing. Much of what one initially understands about oneself, other persons, and life in general is obtained in the context of this close, intense, and sustained initial relationship of life. If parents convey to their child generally unconditional love, value, and regard, the child may incorporate (introject) these feelings as a positive self-confidence, self-regard, and self-worth. If the relationship is negative, devaluing, or markedly inconsistent, conflicts in self-image and self-esteem may occur.

These cognitive schemas are not simply a matter of social learning. Their development is a dynamic, motivated process. The child is actively trying to adapt to the pain, demoralization, dysphoria, or confusion that is generated by the psychological, and at times even physical and sexual, abuse by the creator, nurturer, and protector. Recognizing that one's parents are indifferent, devaluing, or even abusive can be very difficult; therefore, the child may avoid being fully aware of this knowledge through denial, repression, or even dissociation.

The dissociative disorders are among the most controversial diagnoses within the *DSM-IV* (Frances, First, & Pincus, 1995), but the prevailing research does suggest that many persons display dissociative phenomena in response to severely stressful and traumatic events (Cardena, Butler, & Spiegel, 2003). For example, one of the symptoms of PTSD is a depersonalization or derealization in which the person experiences life in a flat, affectless, and empty manner. Nothing appears to have any meaning, value, or purpose. This "emotional anesthesia" is at times experienced during a traumatic event (e.g., rape or combat), and some persons continue to have uncontrollable episodes of derealization after the event. From the psychodynamic perspective, derealization is a defense mechanism a person uses to avoid experiencing or appreciating the actual fright, terror, or horror. The allowance of any emotion increases the potential for opening floodgates of overwhelming despair, and so the tap of emotion remains tightly shut.

Another well-established symptom of PTSD is amnesia, or the inability to remember important aspects of an event that cannot be attributed to simply normal forgetfulness. A highly controversial issue is whether some persons who have been sexually abused as children and have repressed all memory of this abuse can later recover the memories in adulthood. There are data to suggest that some of these purportedly recovered memories have in fact been suggested or implanted during the course of psychological treatment (Loftus & Ketcham, 1994). However, there also is compelling evidence to indicate that some persons who have experienced significant sexual abuse during childhood fail to remember this experience and that this failure might be due to an active effort to avoid facing or addressing the anxiety, despair, and pain that would often be associated with this abuse (Williams & Banyard, 1997).

Physical abuse and sexual abuse are associated with a wide variety of psychological disorders, but psychodynamic clinicians suggest that this might only be the tip of the iceberg. Abuse can be psychological, as well as physical or sexual, in the form of disinterest, denigration, neglect, disparagement, infantilization, devaluation, idealization, and other potentially pathogenic ways of relating to a child who is dependent on a parent for his or her self-image and understanding of others (Ornduff, 2000). For example, children may learn that the attention and interest of a parent is contingent largely on achievements or successes (e.g., the father who provides time for his son only when the son demonstrates that he is worthy of this time). Children may fail to perceive their parents as valuing or loving them for their own sake and may instead recognize that their parents' love and attention are largely conditional on successful accomplishments. An introjection of this relationship would be expressed by the narcissistic belief that feelings of self-worth depend largely on the recognition by others of achievements, status, or success. The person might become preoccupied with the attention and accolades of an employer, as the boss could be a symbolic representation of the parents. They might react to constructive criticisms with feelings of rage, shame, or humiliation because this feedback is, symbolically, a devastating statement of the lack of their worth or value as a person. The narcissistic person may even seek relationships in which their worth and regard will be tested to recreate symbolically the pathogenic parent–child relationship (Gabbard, 2000). If one can overcome the issue within one's adult relationships, perhaps the lasting injury inflicted in childhood would be healed, at least symbolically.

BEHAVIORISTIC PERSPECTIVE

For the behaviorist, psychopathology is maladaptive behavior that has been acquired (learned) and maintained in the same way that adaptive normal behavior is learned; namely, through the processes of classical and operant conditioning (Plaud, 2001). The radical behaviorist might not even have a conceptualization of a pathology because speculations as to what might be occurring within the organism could be distracting, misleading, and largely irrelevant to a behavioristic focus on the environmental contingencies that are controlling the behavior (Follette & Houts, 1996). Designating a behavior as abnormal is said to be simply a social judgment that lacks any scientific credibility (Houts & Follette, 1998).

Watson, often referred to as the "father" of behaviorism, provided a dramatic demonstration of how a phobia could be developed through the process of classical conditioning. Watson and Rayner (1920) first demonstrated that Albert, an infant younger than one year old, lacked any apparent phobias and responded naturally with intense fear to the sound of a hammer striking a steel bar (i.e., an unconditioned response associated with an unconditioned stimulus). They then associated this unconditioned stimulus with the presence of a white rat by repeatedly clanging the steel bar when Albert approached the white rat. Eventually, Albert reacted with fright simply to the sight of the white rat, and there was even some generalization of the fear to a white rabbit, a seal fur coat, and white cotton.

This creation of a mental disorder within a psychologist's laboratory provided a dramatic demonstration of the potential explanatory power of behaviorism for the etiology of mental disorders (Harris, 1979). Mowrer (1939) subsequently indicated that such phobic reactions created originally through this classical conditioning could become further generalized and maintained through operant conditioning (i.e., positive reinforcement, negative reinforcement, and punishment). For example, as a person approaches a feared stimuli (e.g., a boss) anxiety levels increase (avoidant reaction is primed) and as the person walks away from or otherwise avoids the feared stimuli anxiety levels decrease (i.e., avoidant behavior is reinforced).

Lewinsohn (1974) proposed that depression is essentially the result of inadequate positive reinforcers, the presence of many punishing reinforcers, or both. Behavior is activated by positive reinforcers and is diminished by punishment. If a person's life becomes dominated by one particular positive reinforcer (e.g., a spouse with whom most to all pleasurable experiences become involved) then the loss of this reinforcer (e.g., death of a spouse) could be devastating to that person's ability to activate behavior and to obtain pleasurable experiences. The lethargy, passivity, withdrawal, despondency, pessimism, and other symptoms of depression are said by behaviorists to be direct and indirect results of the loss of positive reinforcers, many of which can in fact become a source of punishment, as they may serve to remind the person of the loss. A downward spiral could develop, as the decrease in behavior that results from the loss of positive reinforcers further decreases the likelihood of encountering original reinforcers and discovering new positive reinforcers.

Seligman (1975) suggested that abusive experiences in childhood could lead to adult mood (and other) mental disorders through a learned helplessness that he modeled in his laboratory with dogs. He exposed dogs to electric shocks from which they could not escape. The dogs eventually developed behavior that was comparable with human depression (e.g., sluggish behavior, decreased appetite, and the behavioral appearance of being dysphoric). Most important, they also developed a passive acceptance of future episodes of shock. When opportunities to avoid the shock became available, the dogs did not even try to escape even though they could have been easily successful. Seligman suggested that the dogs' learned helplessness is comparable with persons who accept victimization as an adult due to a history of being unable to escape victimization in childhood.

COGNITIVE PERSPECTIVE

Many clinicians refer to themselves as cognitive-behavioral clinicians rather than simply behavioral because they believe that attention must also be given to the cognitive schemas through which environmental stimuli are perceived and processed. A fundamental component of cognitive models is that the pathology underlying mental disorders are irrational, illogical, cognitive schemas that dominate a person's reasoning or processing of information. If neurobiological models of psychopathology deal with problems in the hardware of the brain (i.e., central nervous system), then cognitive models of psychopathology might be said to be dealing with problems in the software of the brain.

Seligman subsequently revised his behavioral model of depression to include a person's cognitive schema for interpreting failures or setbacks in life. Abramson, Seligman, and Teasdale (1978) suggested that persons at risk for mood disorders have a negative attributional style, characterized by the tendency to attribute blame for a failure to internal, global, and stable factors (e.g., "It is my fault because I am incompetent") rather than external, specific, and unstable factors (e.g., "This particular assignment was poorly articulated by my boss"). Cognitive therapists have since emphasized in particular a hopelessness cognitive schema in which a person views negative events as likely to occur and sees no prospects for change or improvement (Barlow et al., 2003).

Beck (1967) is the most influential cognitive theorist. He suggested that persons suffering from depression characteristically misperceive and misunderstand their past, themselves, and the future in an excessively negativistic manner. Beck and his colleagues identified several cognitive distortions common in persons suffering from depression, including arbitrary inferences, selective abstractions, overgeneralizations, magnifications and minimizations, personalizations, and absolutistic dichotomous perceptions. These irrational cognitive schemas may not seem at first to be so harmful as to cause a major depressive episode, but perhaps it should not be surprising that persons become depressed when they are continually, automatically, and repetitively pessimistic.

An implication of the cognitive model is that fully rational and logical persons are unlikely to develop psychopathology. It is logical and reasonable to be upset, troubled, or disappointed by negative events in life, but it may not be logical to feel devastated or ruined. For example, becoming a paraplegic is disabling, but many paraplegics do adjust and have lives that are more happy, meaningful, and fulfilling than persons who lack any significant disability. Life is a very limited period of time, and it is not particularly logical to use much of the time that remains after a significant loss by feeling sorry for oneself and by focusing on what one does not have or could have had. There may come a day in which one will look back and recognize how much potential for joy, pleasure, and satisfaction had in fact been available but was not obtained because of one's negativistic attitudes and assumptions.

Beck's (1967) cognitive models of pathology were confined initially to depression, but he subsequently expanded his model to include anxiety disorders (Beck & Emery, 1985) and personality disorders (Beck & Freeman, 1990). For example, a cognitive pathology of social phobia might be a hypervigilant cognitive schema that is excessively attuned to signs of threat (Heinrichs & Hofmann, 2001). Persons with a social phobia are often stricken with substantial anticipatory anxiety as they ruminate about potential failures and humiliations prior to a performance, and they impair themselves during their performance as they focus their attention on minor flaws and errors and scan for disinterest or rejection in the persons with whom they are interacting.

The irrational cognitive schemas identified by cognitive therapists bear a close resemblance to the defense mechanisms identified by psychodynamic clinicians (Westen, 1991). Both involve habitual distortions in the perceptions of oneself and of other persons. For example, the magnification and minimization emphasized in Beck's (1967) cognitive model of depression is similar in many respects to the defense mechanism of splitting (Gunderson, 2001), in which a person characteristically perceives events in a black-and-white manner. They are both cognitive pathologies in which the person fails to perceive himself or herself, other persons, and events in an accurate manner. A fundamental difference, however, is that psychodynamically oriented clinicians believe that a person has an unconscious motivation for developing and maintaining these irrational cognitive schemas. Clinicians think splitting is used by a person to avoid the anxiety and despair that would accompany an accurate perception of others (e.g., accurately perceiving that a parent was disinterested, denigrating, or abusive). For the cognitive theorist, the schemas would be simply the result of instruction, reinforcement, and modeling.

INTERPERSONAL AND SYSTEMS PERSPECTIVE

A fundamental principle of interpersonal and systems models of psychopathology is that human behavior should be understood in a wider context of social, interpersonal relationships (Reiss & Emde, 2003). The pathology that has resulted in a maladaptive behavior pattern might not reside within the person as an organismic mental disorder but may instead lie within the social system in which the person is functioning. A diagnosis of psychopathology within an individual acting within this social system might in fact be counterproductive, as it could identify incorrectly the individual as being the sole or primary source for the dysfunctional behaviors, feelings, and ideas, distracting attention away from the wider social network that is controlling the actions of the individual.

A substantial proportion of psychologists, psychiatrists, and social workers specialize in marital and family treatment, and they often find the APA (2000) diagnostic manual to be inadequate and misleading (First et al., 2002; Kaslow, 1996; Reiss & Emde, 2003). The *DSM-IV* is a manual for the diagnosis of mental (organismic) disorders. Disorders of pathologic relationships are included only within an appendix to the *DSM-IV-TR* for conditions that might be the focus of clinical attention (APA, 2000). Clinicians who believe that the pathology exists largely within the context of the relationship rather than within the cognitions, neurobiology, or unconscious conflicts of the individual often find that the *DSM-IV* impairs their efforts to address the wider interpersonal context.

One of the diagnoses proposed for the *DSM-III-R* (APA, 1987) was a self-defeating or masochistic personality disorder. The intention of the diagnosis was to identify persons who are characteristically pessimistic, self-blaming, and self-defeating. However, it was apparent that a proportion of these persons would be within physically abusive relationships and their self-defeating behaviors may say more about the constant threat of being physically harmed than about any organismic cognitive, neurobiological, or psychodynamic pathologies that might be present (Widiger, 1995). A diagnosis of masochistic or self-defeating personality disorder could in fact be used to blame the victim rather than the perpetrator. A historical example is provided by Snell, Rosenwald, and Robey (1964, p. 110), who explained the occurrence of twelve husbands charged with assault as "filling masochistic needs of the wife." Women who have been repeatedly physically, sexually, or psychologically abused during childhood do have an increased risk of developing cognitive, neurobiological, and psychodynamic pathologies that may increase the likelihood of being victimized again as adults. On the other hand, many current victims of abuse who seem unwilling or unable to extricate themselves from a relationship could be acting realistically in response to threats of physical harm and to the absence of a safe or meaningful alternative (Walker, 1989). It can be very difficult to leave a relationship in which one has invested a tremendous amount of emotional involvement, and it might seem better to suffer occasional assaults than to be harassed, stalked, and perhaps eventually killed.

Feelings of insecurity in women regarding their romantic and intimate relationships may say less about the women than about the persons with whom the women are involved. "Men and women may differ in what they seek from relationships, but they may also differ in what they provide to each other" (Coyne & Whiffen, 1995, p. 368). In other words, "Women might appear (and be) less dependent if they weren't involved with such undependable men" (Widiger & Anderson, 2003, p. 63). An implication for the treatment of depression in purportedly dependent women would be for the men (or any person) with whom they become involved to work on becoming more dependable rather than for the women to work on becoming less concerned about the dependability of their spouses.

One can extend this model even further to include the pathology of a community and even the wider society. It is perhaps no accident that many of the mental disorders diagnosed in the *DSM-IV* occur with a greater frequency in socially and economically deprived groups. Nevertheless, drug abuse, depression, and antisocial behaviors also can be due in part to impoverishment, deprivation, stress, and discrimination that are in turn due to the presence of a society that is exploitative, abusive, discriminatory, or negligent toward a particular subset of its members (Dohrenwend, 1998).

HUMANISTIC PERSPECTIVE

Fundamental to humanistic theory is the belief that persons have a free will (Rychlak, 1993). Persons have the ability to govern and direct their lives in a healthy, positive direction. However, exercising control of one's life includes considerable responsibility, burden, effort, and risk. Many of the choices that a person faces can be quite stressful, perhaps overwhelming and even horrific. Humanists suggest that persons avoid this responsibility by allowing their daily lives to be filled with and governed by relatively minor distractions. Abdicating the governance of life, however, allows it to be controlled instead by biological dispositions and external events. At some point one may find that much of life has slipped by, that many potential opportunities for growth and happiness have been missed, and perhaps even that life has gone in a direction that is ultimately disappointing, harmful, and disabling. Psychopathology would be one potential end result of a failure to exercise a willful control and mastery of life.

Hypochondriasis, for example, is at times associated with a recent life-threatening experience that has shattered a person's absorption in the pleasures, distractions, and minor demands of daily life. A person may spend little time, effort, or concern in contemplating major life issues, such as inevitable death (Becker, 1973). A life-threatening experience can undermine this blissful ignorance. Some persons respond to such events in a positive manner by affirming new goals and values, whereas others who are ill prepared for their own death can be overwhelmed. They may ruminate endlessly over their mortality and repeatedly seek from doctors a reassurance that they will not die (at least not in the immediate future).

For the humanist, PTSD is not a disease that is adequately reduced to a dysregulation along a neurochemical pathway. The phenomenology of being frightened by death or the appreciation of the horror of rape and warfare need to be understood in terms of their implications for one's personal meaning of oneself, one's neighbors, and life itself (Greenberg, Elliott, & Lietaer, 2003). Engaging in combat may not simply be an anxiety-provoking stimulus; it also may question a fundamental assumption that one is a good person living in a decent world. PTSD, from this perspective, is a struggle with the acceptance that life does include the potential for significant horror, disaster, and brutality yet also may still provide the potential for a pleasurable, meaningful, and benevolent social existence.

The emphasis on a volitional free will distinguishes the humanistic perspective from other models of psychopathology. There is no compelling neurobiological model for free will. Existing empirical research suggests that all thoughts, feelings, and behavior are the result of causal mechanisms beyond the expression of any volitional being (Bargh & Chartrand, 2000). For the behaviorist, choice is an illusory perception that is held despite the evidence to the contrary because it provides a feeling of comfort and self-confidence, whereas the alternative could be quite discouraging and even demoralizing (Skinner, 1987). The existence of a free will is a fundamental question of human existence that might be beyond the capacity of a science to refute or confirm (Howard & Conway, 1986; Wegner & Wheatley, 2000).

ANTHROPOLOGICAL PERSPECTIVE

The eighth and final paradigm of psychopathology is the anthropological or social-cultural. Social-cultural processes can bias the science of psychopathology by providing a misleading lens through which functioning is judged to be either adaptive or maladaptive (Fabrega, 1994). For example, a woman's housebound behavior might be diagnosed as agoraphobic within Western cultures but perhaps be considered normative or even virtuous within a Muslim culture; submissive behavior that is diagnosed as pathologic dependency within Western societies might be considered normative within an Asian culture (Kirmayer, Young, & Hayton, 1995). One should not presume that what is optimal, adaptive, healthy, or ideal in one's own culture is, or should be, optimal, adaptive, healthy, or ideal in any other particular culture (Mezzich, Kleinman, Fabrega, & Parron, 1996). On the contrary, optimal psychological functioning will vary, at least to some extent, across different environments and cultures.

Societies and cultures will disagree as to what constitutes optimal or pathological physical and psychological functioning (Lopez & Guarnaccia, 2000), and it is unclear how these differences should be understood (Widiger & Sankis, 2000). Universal acceptance of a diagnostic system is a desirable goal (Kessler, 1999), but respect for the belief systems of different cultures does not suggest that all systems of belief are equally correct. For example, the perceptual experiences of persons that would be diagnosed by the *DSM-IV* as the disorder of schizophrenia might be considered within a particular culture as an actual religious experience (Kirmayer, 1994). Those who share this belief system could be right. A person could in fact hear the voice of a god or might in fact be possessed by a demon. However, if this person also met the *DSM-IV* criteria for schizophrenia, including a six-month insidious deterioration in functioning (e.g., in self-care or work) and a one-month duration of disorganized speech, grossly disorganized behavior, and negative symptoms, along with hearing the voice of a god, one should be more confident in diagnosing this person with the mental disorder of schizophrenia no matter what his or her society believes than in concluding that he or she did in fact hear the voice of a god. This might not indicate the biases of a culture that does not value or believe in this god; it could just be consistent with the substantial amount of scientific research to support the validity of the diagnosis of schizophrenia (Nathan & Langenbucher, 2003) and the lack of comparable research to support the validity of the religious explanation.

It is unlikely to be the case that all societies are equally conducive toward optimal psychological functioning, if societies do in fact vary in the psychological functioning that they promote or discourage. Just as some families do a better job than other families of promoting physical or psychological health, so will some societies do a better job of promoting physical and psychological health within its members. For example, social mores vary across national boundaries and across time in their socialization of adequate, healthy, or optimal substance-use behavior and, likewise, in their failure to adequately address or minimize the development of the mental disorders of substance abuse and dependence.

CONCLUSIONS

The diagnosis of a mental disorder includes a value judgment that one should have healthy or at least adequate psychological functioning (Wakefield, 1992). Some persons adopting the anthropological or social-cultural perspective have argued that the existence of this value judgment indicates that the concept of psychopathology represents simply the preferences or biases of a particular culture (Kirmayer, 1994; Sadler, 2002). For the radical anthropologist, psychopathology as understood by the neurobiologist (Kandel, 1998), the analyst (Cooper, 1998), or the behaviorist (Plaud, 2001) are simply folklores of Western culture (Kirmayer, 1994).

The concept of a physical disorder, however, also includes this same value judgment (Widiger, 2002). In a world of persons who place no value on necessary, adequate, or optimal physical functioning or in a world in which there are virtually no impairments or threats to physical functioning, the concept of physical disorder would have no meaning or relevance. However, in the practical world, biological organisms do interact with and harm one another, and the construct of physical disorder does have substantial meaning and validity. Likewise, in the world as it currently exists, persons do relate to and interact with one another and do often wound and harm one another psychologically, and the construct of mental disorder has substantial meaning and validity. Meaningful and valid scientific research on the etiology, pathology, and treatment of physical disorders occurs because in the world as it currently exists there are impairments and threats to adequate physical functioning. It is provocative and intriguing to conceive of a world in which physical health and survival would or should not be valued or preferred over illness, suffering, and death, but this form of existence is unlikely to emerge anytime in the near future.

Valuing physical and psychological health may in fact be a natural result of evolution and compelled by a genetic disposition. It is difficult to imagine a species or a society that does not place any value on adequate, optimal, or healthy physical functioning surviving for long. Persons who value physical health will be more likely to survive and to have offspring than will persons who attempt to place themselves above nature by not putting any value on their physical health. Similarly, it is difficult to imagine a society developing or even maintaining its existence over time that did not place any value on adequate, optimal, or healthy psychological functioning.

There does appear to be many different ways in which things can go wrong psychologically. Psychopathology can result from dysregulation along neurochemical pathways, antiquated genetic dispositions, irrational cognitive schemas, or unconscious conflicts. Psychological health might be more difficult to achieve and maintain than physical health. The scientific study of each of the alternative models of psychopathology presented within this chapter will hopefully improve our chances of understanding and treating psychological dysfunctions.

References

Abramson, L. Y., Seligman, M. E. P., & Teasdale, J. D. (1978). Learned helplessness in humans: Critique and reformulation. *Journal of Abnormal Psychology, 87,* 49-74.

American Psychiatric Association. (2000). *Diagnostic and statistical manual of mental disorders* (4th ed., text revision). Washington, DC: Author.

American Psychiatric Association. (1987). *Diagnostic and statistical manual of mental disorders* (revised 3rd ed.) Washington, DC: Author.

Bargh, J. A., & Chartrand, T. L. (2000). The unbearable automaticity of being. *American Psychologist, 54,* 462-479.

Barlow, D. H., Pincus, D. B., Heinrichs, N., & Choate, M. L. (2003). Anxiety disorders. In G. Stricker, T. A. Widiger, & I. B. Weiner (Eds.), *Handbook of psychology. Volume 8. Clinical psychology* (pp. 119-172). New York: John Wiley.

Beck, A. T. (1967). *Depression: Clinical, experimental, and theoretical aspects.* New York: Harper and Row.

Beck, A. T., & Emery, G. (1985). *Anxiety disorders and phobias: A cognitive perspective.* New York: Basic Books.

Beck, A. T., & Freeman, A. (1990). *Cognitive therapy of personality disorders.* New York: Guilford.

Becker, E. (1973). *The denial of death.* New York: Free Press.

Buss, D. M., Haselton, M. G., Shackelford, T. K., Bleske, A. L., & Wakefield, J. C. (1998). Adaptations, exaptations, and spandrels. *American Psychologist, 53,* 533-548.

Cardena, E., Butler, L. D., & Spiegel, D. (2003). Stress disorders. In G. Stricker, T. A. Widiger, & I. B. Weiner (Eds.), *Handbook of psychology. Volume 8. Clinical psychology* (pp. 229-249). New York: John Wiley.

Cooper, S. H. (1998). Changing notions of defense within psychoanalytic theory. *Journal of Personality, 66,* 947-964.

Coyne, J. C., & Whiffen, V. E. (1995). Issues in personality as diathesis for depression: The case of sociotropy-dependency and autonomy-self-criticism. *Psychological Bulletin, 118,* 358-378.

Crews, F. (1996). The verdict on Freud. *Psychological Science, 7,* 63-67.

Dohrenwend, B. P. (Ed.). (1998). *Adversity, stress, and psychopathology.* New York: Oxford University Press.

Durrant, R., & Ellis, R. (2003). Evolutionary psychology. In M. Gallagher, R. J. Nelson, & I. J. Weiner (Eds.), *Handbook of psychology. Biological psychology* (Vol. 3, pp. 1-33). New York: John Wiley.

Fabrega, H. (1994). International systems of diagnosis in psychiatry. *Journal of Nervous and Mental Disease, 182,* 256-263.

First, M. B., Bell, C. B., Cuthbert, B., Krystal, J. H., Malison, R., Offord, D. R., Reiss, D., Shea, M. T., Widiger, T. A., & Wisner, K. L. (2002). Personality disorders and relational disorders: A research agenda for addressing crucial gaps in *DSM.* In D. J. Kupfer, M. B. First, & D. A. Regier (Eds.), *A research agenda for DSM-V* (pp. 123-199) Washington, DC: American Psychiatric Association.

Follette, W. C., & Houts, A. C. (1996). Models of scientific progress and the role of theory in taxonomy development: A case study of the *DSM. Journal of Consulting and Clinical Psychology, 64,* 1120-1132.

Frances, A. J., First, M. B., & Pincus, H. A. (1995). *DSM-IV guidebook.* Washington, DC: American Psychiatric Press.

Freud, S. (1933). Civilization and its discontents. In J. Strachey (Ed. and Trans.), *The standard edition of the complete psychological works of Sigmund Freud* (Vol. 21, pp. 64-74). London: Hogarth Press.

Gabbard, G. O. (2000). *Psychodynamic psychiatry in clinical practice* (3rd ed.). Washington, DC: American Psychiatric Press.

Greenberg, L. S., Elliott, R., & Lietaer, G. (2003). Humanistic-experiential psychotherapy. In G. Stricker, T. A. Widiger, & I. B. Weiner (Eds.), *Handbook of psychology. Volume 8. Clinical psychology* (pp. 301-325). New York: John Wiley.

Gunderson, J. G. (2001). *Borderline personality disorder: A clinical guide.* Washington, DC: American Psychiatric Press.

Harris, B. (1979). Whatever happened to Little Albert? *American Psychologist, 34,* 151-160.

Heinrichs, N., & Hofmann, S. G. (2001). Information processing in social phobia: A critical review. *Clinical Psychology Review, 21,* 751-770.

Houts, A. C., & Follette, W. C. (1998). Mentalism, mechanism, and medical analogues: Reply to Wakefield (1998). *Journal of Consulting and Clinical Psychology, 66,* 835-855.

Howard, G., & Conway, C. (1986). Can there be an empirical science of volitional action? *American Psychologist, 41,* 1241-1251.

Hyman, S. E. (1998). NIMH during the tenure of Director Steven E. Hyman, M.D. (1996-present): The now and future of NIMH. *American Journal of Psychiatry, 155*(Suppl.), 36-40.

Ilardi, S. S., & Feldman, D. (2001). The cognitive neuroscience paradigm: A unifying metatheoretical framework for the science and practice of clinical psychology. *Journal of Clinical Psychology, 57,* 1067-1088.

Judd, L. L. (1998). Historical highlights of the National Institute of Mental Health from 1946 to the present. *American Journal of Psychiatry, 155*(Suppl.), 3-8.

Kandel, E. R. (1998). A new intellectual framework for psychiatry. *American Journal of Psychiatry 155,* 457-469.

Kaslow, F. W. (Ed.). (1996). *Handbook of relational diagnosis and dysfunctional family patterns.* New York: John Wiley.

Kessler, R. C. (1999). The World Health Organization International Consortium in Psychiatric Epidemiology: Initial work and future directions—the NAPE lecture. *Acta Psychiatrica Scandinavica, 99,* 2-9.

Kirmayer, L. J. (1994). Is the concept of mental disorder culturally relative? In S. A. Kirk & S. D. Einbinder (Eds.), *Controversial issues in mental health* (pp. 2-9). Boston: Allyn & Bacon.

Kirmayer, L. J., Young, A., & Hayton, B. C. (1995). The cultural context of anxiety disorders. *Psychiatric Clinics of North America, 18,* 503-521.

Lewinsohn, P. M. (1974). A behavioral approach to depression. In R. J. Freidman & M. M. Katz (Eds.), *The psychology of depression: Contemporary theory and research* (pp. 157-170). Washington, DC: Winston-Wiley.

Loftus, E., & Ketcham, K. (1994). *The myth of repressed memory.* New York: St. Martin's Griffin.

Lopez, S. R., & Guarnaccia, P. (2000). Cultural psychopathology: Uncovering the social world of mental illness. *Annual Review of Psychology, 51,* 571-598.

Lummaa, V., Vuorisalo, T., Barr, R. G., & Lehtonen, L. (1998). Why cry? Adaptive significance of intensive crying in human infants. *Evolution and Human Behavior, 19,* 193-202.

Mezzich, J. E., Kleinman, A., Fabrega, H., & Parron, D. L. (Eds.). (1996). *Culture and psychiatric diagnosis. A DSM-IV perspective.* Washington, DC: American Psychiatric Press.

Mowrer, H. (1939). A stimulus-response analysis of anxiety and its role as a reinforcing agent. *Psychological Review, 46,* 553-565.

Nathan, P. E., & Langenbucher, J. (2003). Diagnosis and classification. In G. Stricker, T. A. Widiger, & I. B. Weiner (Eds.), *Handbook of psychology. Volume 8. Clinical psychology* (pp. 3-26). New York: John Wiley.

Nesse, R. M. (2000). Is depression an adaptation? *Archives of General Psychiatry, 57,* 14-20.

Ornduff, S. R. (2000). Childhood maltreatment and malevolence: Quantitative research findings. *Clinical Psychology Review, 20,* 991-1018.

Plaud, J. J. (2001). Clinical science and human behavior. *Journal of Clinical Psychology, 57,* 1089-1102.

Reiss, D., & Emde, R. N. (2003). Relationship disorders are psychiatric disorders: Five reasons they were not included in *DSM-IV.* In K. A. Phillips, M. B. First, & H. A. Pincus (Eds.), *Advancing DSM. Dilemmas in psychiatric diagnosis* (pp. 191-223). Washington, DC: American Psychiatric Association.

Rychlak, J. F. (1993). *Discovering free will and personal responsibility.* New York: Oxford University Press.

Sadler, J. Z. (2002). Values in developing psychiatric classifications: A proposal for *DSM-V.* In J. Z. Sadler (Ed.), *Descriptions and prescriptions. Values, mental disorders, and the DSMs* (pp. 301-322). Baltimore, MD: Johns Hopkins University Press.

Seligman, L. (1971). Phobias and preparedness. *Behavior Therapy, 2,* 307-430.

Seligman, L. (1975). *Helplessness: On depression, development, and death.* San Francisco: Freeman.

Skinner, B. F. (1987). Whatever happened to psychology as the science of behavior? *American Psychologist, 42,* 780-786.

Snell, J., Rosenwald, R., & Robey, A. (1964). The wifebeater's wife. A study of family interaction. *Archives of General Psychiatry, 11,* 107-112.

Stone, M. (1997). A brief history of psychiatry. In A. Tasman, J. Kay, & J. A. Lieberman (Eds.), *Psychiatry* (Vol. 2, pp. 1853-1875). Philadelphia: W. B. Saunders.

Tooby, J., & Cosmides, L. (1990). The past explains the present: Emotional adaptations and the structure of ancestral environments. *Ethology and Sociobiology, 11,* 375-424.

Wakefield, J. C. (1992). The concept of mental disorder: On the boundary between biological facts and social values. *American Psychologist, 47,* 373-388.

Walker, L. E. A. (1989). Psychology and violence against women. *American Psychologist, 44,* 695-702.

Watson, J. B., & Rayner, R. (1920). Conditioned emotional reactions. *Journal of Experimental Psychology, 3,* 1-14.

Wegner, D. M., & Wheatley, T. (2000). Apparent mental causation. Sources of the experience of will. *American Psychologist, 54,* 480-492.

Westen, D. (1991). Social cognition and object relations. *Psychological Bulletin, 109,* 429-455.

Westen, D. (1998). The scientific legacy of Sigmund Freud: Toward a psychodynamically informed psychological science. *Psychological Bulletin, 124,* 333-371.

Widiger, T. A. (1995). Deletion of the self-defeating and sadistic personality disorder diagnoses. In W. J. Livesley (Ed.), *The DSM-IV personality disorders* (pp. 359-373). New York: Guilford.

Widiger, T. A. (2002). Values, politics, and science in the construction of the *DSM*s. In J. Sadler (Ed.), *Descriptions and prescriptions: Values, mental disorders, and the DSMs* (pp. 25-41). Baltimore, MD: Johns Hopkins University Press.

Widiger, T. A., & Anderson, K. G. (2003). Personality and depression in women. *Journal of Affective Disorders, 74,* 59-66.

Widiger, T. A., & Sankis, L. M. (2000). Adult psychopathology: Issues and controversies. *Annual Review of Psychology, 51,* 377-404.

Williams, L. M., & Banyard, V. L. (1997). Perspectives on adult memories of childhood sexual abuse: A research review. In D. Spiegel (Ed.), *Repressed memories* (pp. 123-151). Washington, DC: American Psychiatric Press.

Yehuda, R. (1998). Psychoneuroendocrinology of post-traumatic stress disorder. *Psychiatric Clinics of North America, 21,* 359-379.

Yehuda, R., & McFarlane, A. C. (1995). Conflict between current knowledge about post-traumatic stress disorder and its original conceptual basis. *American Journal of Psychiatry, 152,* 1705-1713.

Yehuda, R., Resnick, H. S., Schmeidler, J., Yang, R.-K., and Pitman, R. K. (1998). Predictors of cortisol and 3-methoxy-4-hydroxy-phenylglycol responses in the acute aftermath of rape. *Biological Psychiatry, 43,* 855-859.

3

Stress, Working Conditions, and Work-Life Events

JAY C. THOMAS AND MANDY DAVIES
Pacific University

*A*t first glance, it appears easy to show how life events influence emotions, strain, and psychopathology. There are, after all, many novels and movies in which a single event radically changes a personality, usually in the direction of madness, but sometimes toward bitterness, angst, courage, empathy, or, in the case of Scrooge, philanthropy. Unfortunately, it is not so easy to show these changes in a scientifically rigorous manner. Kessler (1997), writing on the influence of life events on depression, identified two critical methodological problems that create this difficulty. First, Kessler describes how the effect of depression influences the way in which the presumed life events are reported. There may be some reciprocal causality in which events may contribute to depression and the depression places the person at increased risk of experiencing further depressogenic events. In addition, a person's mental or emotional state may influence how he or she recalls or interprets past events (Aiken & West, 1990), making some seem more significant than they may actually have been. Personality characteristics also may affect the recollection and reporting of events, as we describe later.

Kessler's second methodological problem in the study of life events lies in the logic of data analysis. Statisticians generally must assume that each event in a series of events is independent of all the others and is, also, a random occurrence in relation to other causes of a disorder such as depression. Yet, depression and other disorders influence the experiences a person has, so the assumptions are so incorrect as to make the results of the analyses very suspect.

The ideal method to avoid the problems Kessler (1997) identified is to study a large number of people in detail over a prolonged period of time, beginning at an early age, in the expectation that some will develop some form of psychopathology. This method has been used in few studies because it is difficult and expensive to carry out. In spite of there being few studies that adequately overcame these methodological difficulties, Kessler felt justified in proceeding with his review because taken as a whole there were sufficient studies to allow at least some conclusions to be drawn. Our topic is somewhat different than Kessler's in several ways. First, we are not solely concerned with one type of psychopathology as he was, but we can examine the full range as it relates to work. Second, our primary focus is on work or work-related conditions or events and their impact on the mental or emotional well-being of employees. Altogether there is a seemingly infinite variety of topics to cover, which allows us to select the areas that are well researched and most apt to be of interest to our readers. For much of what follows the methodological caveats identified by Kessler still hold, and our confidence in cause-and-effect relationships may have to be moderated in many cases.

The remainder of this chapter is organized into sections examining the effects of selected working conditions, conditions of work, and work-life events (mergers, acquisitions, downsizing, and unemployment) on the mental health of workers.

STRESS, WORK, AND LIFE

Stress is often blamed for many vicissitudes of daily life. Stress is a popular topic of features in the popular media. It is also a very popular topic in the professional literatures in psychology, medicine, biology, and other disciplines. The concept of stress was introduced to the scientific community in the 1920s by Walter Cannon and in the 1930s by Hans Seyle (Sapolsky 1998). Cannon proposed that an organism establishes an ideal set point for each of many factors, such as temperature, and when its condition deviates from that point the organism takes action to return to the ideal condition. This process is known as homeostasis. An example of homeostasis is body temperature. The normal body temperature for a human is 37C (98.6F). If body temperature gets too low, the person takes action, such as shivering or putting on a sweater. If body temperature gets too high, the person sweats, removes clothing, or perhaps, jumps in a pool of water. Today we recognize that there often is not a single optimal set point, but rather the ideal varies according to conditions such as time of day and the nature of activity. The concept of homeostasis has evolved into that of allostasis. Allostasis is similar in concept to homeostasis but it allows for changing set points, giving us the rather complicated notion that an organism is continually trying to maintain the status quo, but it is also actively reconsidering what the optimal status quo might be and accordingly making adjustments. Cannon also developed the idea of the fight-or-flight response, which we discuss shortly.

Seyle married biology and psychology in the arena of stress. As a young endocrinologist he was attempting to study the effects of an ovarian extract by injecting it into rats. Several rats sickened and died. Unfortunately, the same thing happened to control rats that he merely injected with saline solution. A series of studies indicated that his inept and clumsy handling of the rats was at fault, not the extract. He later misapplied the engineering concept of stress to the phenomena he was observing. Strictly speaking, *stress* is a force applied to an object and *strain* is the response of the object to the stressor. We should say that we are feeling strain, not stress, but the incorrect nomenclature has become so pervasive that it is difficult to escape it. Seyle eventually developed a theory of a general adaptation syndrome (GAS) to explain the biological effects of stress. Suppose a person is walking down the street and suddenly a hungry tiger pounces from behind some bushes. The individual has two choices if he or she wishes to survive this encounter. He or she can try to escape the tiger (flight) or fight the tiger and hope to win. Either way the body needs to make some adjustments from its normal condition. Muscles need to be energized and supplied with plenty of oxygen, which leads to changes in heart rate, blood pressure, metabolism, breathing, and other bodily functions. While resources are going into the immediate problem of flight or fight, other functions that are not useful for countering the immediate threat, for example, digestion and reproduction, are slowed down. Even mental functions change, as the attacked individual becomes hypervigilant and thinks only about the tiger, possible escape routes, and how to counter the tiger's attack. A whole host of nervous, hormonal, and other physiological changes take place in a very short time span. Others take place over a period of minutes, hours, or days. Detailing all of them is beyond our scope in this chapter.[1] Seyle's original GAS notion was that as the body was making these adaptations, it would eventually run out of stores such as glucose and hormones and these deficiencies would lead to propensity toward various diseases. Current stress researchers no longer accept the GAS theory because the actual situation is much more complicated. As Sapolsky (1998, p. 13) put it, "It's not so much the stress response runs out; rather with sufficient activation, *the stress response itself can become damaging.*" So, humans seem to have a pretty good system for dealing with immediate danger, but if that danger is repeated continually, day after day, that same system may make us sick.

As interesting as our response to tigers may be, this book is about psychopathology in the workplace. Most of us never run into a tiger, lion, wolf pack, or similar emergency at work. We do not even encounter that many potentially fatal experiences that might reasonably elicit a useful fight-or-flight response. We do encounter deadlines, angry customers, demanding bosses, and other conditions we speak of as being stressful. One problem we have as organisms is that we have replaced a life of occasional danger and mayhem with internal and external pressures, irritations, frustrations, problems and opportunities, and social and role conflicts. We have a body that treats the boss' deadline like a hungry tiger. The stress response continues, bringing high blood pressure, cardiovascular changes, suppressed immune system, and other possible ill-health effects.

Over the past few decades a number of theories of job and work stress have been developed to explain the relationship between working conditions and physical and mental health. Beehr (1998), in a revision of earlier work, presented perhaps the most comprehensive model of occupational stress. This model is shown in Figure 3.1. *Stresses in the workplace* comprise the factors we discuss below plus many others, which we cannot fully cover because of space limiations. They include the physical and social work environment and the nature of the work itself. *Situational*

---

[1] Readers interested in all the details should go to Sapolsky's (1998) book. It is an unusually readable and scientifically accurate resource.

characteristics are aspects of the environment that are not causes of stress but that may moderate the effects of stressors, much as rest pauses may delay onset of fatigue in physically demanding tasks. *Duration* of stressors experienced is important because fleeting exposure to stressors often has little impact. The exception may be experiencing or witnessing life-threatening trauma. In general, the longer a person is exposed to stressors the worse the outcome. *Personal characteristics* may include personality and abilities as well as job-specific factors such as level of training and experience. For example, we would expect a person with a medical background to experience much less stress than an ordinary citizen who is called to assist an injured person. In addition, a poor fit between a person and a job may result in stress and strain. *Strains* to the person come in three forms. The first of these forms is psychological strain, including anxiety and depression. The second form includes physical or physiological strains, involving such responses as hypertension and cortisol secretion. The third type of strain is behavioral. Behavioral strains are less researched, partly because of problems in defining exactly what they are. According to Beehr, behavioral strains must be a response to a stressor and be harmful to the person. Thus, increased tobacco usage would qualify, while quitting the job, being absent, or reducing job performance would not because the harm is to the organization, not to the person. These would be *organizational outcomes,* not personal outcomes.

Coping and adaptation are the final components to Beehr's (1998) model. These responses "consist of any actions taken to correct problems with the stressors, the strains, or the organizational outcomes" (Beehr, 1998, p. 9). These actions may be positive, such as using protective garb to prevent accidents, or negative, such as avoiding unpleasant or anxiety-provoking tasks or giving up sleep to balance demanding work and social obligations. Some coping and adaptive responses may have positive or negative short-term effects and the opposite long-term effects. Working extra hours to get a special project completed probably has mostly positive effects, but if this becomes a way of life we can bet that the effects will eventually turn negative. Many individual stress interventions emphasize developing more effective and positive coping strategies.

One form of coping comes very early in the process. Lazarus (1991) proposed that cognitive appraisal or evaluation of a stressor precedes any emotional response. According to his theory, a person has to recognize the tiger as a threat before responding. Similarly, a deadline loses much of its force as a stressor if it is not taken seriously. Cognitive-behavioral therapies for mental distress or disorders often concentrate on the cognitive appraisal process in the belief that at least some of the client's problems stem from seeing too much threat in a stimulus. Another cognitive aspect of coping and adaptation is the level of uncertainty the person has about obtaining outcomes. Beehr (1998) saw this as a key element in the process facet in his model of occupational stress. Based on the expectancy model of motivation, experienced stress is the product of perceived uncertainty about obtaining outcomes times the perceived importance of the outcomes times the duration of the uncertainties. An assistant professor who is certain she will be awarded tenure is not under much stress. The same professor is not stressed by the tenure decision if it is obvious that tenure is not forthcoming (although she may be under a good deal of stress in

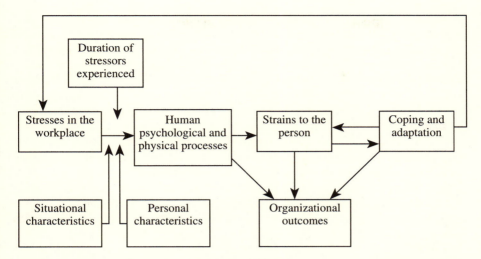

FIGURE 3.1 Beehr's Meta-Model of Occupational Stress. *Source*: "An Organizational Psychology Meta-Model of Occupational Stress," by T. A. Beehr, Theories of Organizational Stress (pp. 6-27), ed. C. L. Cooper, 1998, New York: Oxford University Press. Reproduced with permission.

other ways). The stress experienced by the assistant professor lies in not knowing what the tenure decision will be.

WORKING CONDITIONS AND CONDITIONS OF WORK

The term *working conditions* refers to the physical and social environment at work. *Conditions of work* are the arrangements under which work is conducted. They include methods, times, and amounts of compensation; hours of work; work shift; and organizational structure. Because these terms overlap and, for our purposes, create needless confusion, we simply use *working conditions* to cover both areas. The impact of working conditions on organizationally driven outcomes, such as efficiency and productivity, have been examined for over a century, beginning with the work of Frederick Taylor and extending to Frank and Lillian Galbraith's work, the Industrial Fatigue Board in Great Britain in the 1920s, and current research by industrial and organizational psychologists, engineering psychologists, industrial engineers, occupational medicine, and other ergonomics-related disciplines. A vast literature has been developed, and although physical health has received a good deal of attention (cf. Quick & Tetrick, 2002), little of this work is directly related to mental health issues.

Hours of Work and Shift Effects

It is an ironic fact of modern history that the effects of hours of work and different work shifts were not a medical or psychological concern until working hours were substantially reduced from their historical levels of 60 or more hours per week.

Between the 1890s and 1920s the workweek steadily decreased with the then surprising finding that with reduced working hours productivity actually increased and accidents decreased (Alluisi & Morgan, 1982). In spite of these findings we owe our current five-day, forty-hour workweek to economic factors in the Great Depression of the 1930s rather than to a scientific understanding of the effects of work schedules. This workweek did not become common in many other countries until the 1960s (Thierry & Jansen, 1998), and it is not yet the standard in some industrializing countries.

Once psychologists, sociologists, engineers, physicians, and members of other disciplines began to study the effects of work schedules, it did not take long to document several associated factors on health, mental health, and other aspects of life (Alluisi & Morgan, 1982; Costa, 1996). Workers on nonstandard shifts may be socially isolated. Even their families are usually on a different schedule. Their diets may be irregular, although nutritional differences are not shown in existing research (C. S. Smith, Folkard, & Fuller, 2003). Workers who are not working the standard day shift, and particularly those whose shift rotates, often have disrupted sleep patterns and may complain of headaches and fatigue. Sleep disruption is usually attributed to the worker's schedule conflicting with social demands and, more important, with conflicts with the worker's normal circadian rhythm. Many workers on a "swing" or "graveyard" shift often ingest caffeine or other stimulants to get through the night. This makes it even harder to obtain quality sleep once the shift is over. Overall, it stands to reason that these people should suffer impaired physical and psychological health.

Research has shown shift work to be related to several physical ailments, including gastrointestinal disorders, coronary heart disease, and several aspects of women's reproductive health (Costa, 1996; M. J. Smith, Karsh, Carayon, & Conway, 2003). This relationship is possibly exacerbated by difficulties in matching work and sleep schedules to medication schedules, such as those for diabetes and nervous disorders (Costa, 1996). Some small relationships between shift work and psychological disorders including depression have been reported. It is hypothesized that sleep disruption may be the primary culprit (C. S. Smith et al., 1999; M. J. Smith et al., 2003), although in our experience family disruptions may be blamed by individual workers for the emotional distress they encounter on shift work. Whatever the relationship between shift work and psychopathology may be, shift work certainly has an effect on work and family balance. Most of this effect is negative.

Compressed workweeks, known as COM in the literature, have been on the scene internationally for about thirty years. In COM arrangements workers may work three 12-hour days (3/12) or four 9- or 10-hour days (9/4 or 10/4) in a week. There is not much controversy surrounding COM. Most people like it (Thierry & Jansen, 1998). However, some workers complain about being fatigued by the end of the day and others complain about interference with home life (Thierry & Jansen, 1998). One author of this chapter (Jay Thomas) has some personal experience with the 3/12 arrangement. Some years ago, when our children ranged in age from infancy to about seven years, my wife worked three 12-hour day shifts, while I worked a regular five-day shift. Having four nonwork days a week allowed my wife to concentrate on the children and home environment more than she would have been able to do with a five-day workweek. She also was able to get as much rest and to pursue as many hobbies as is possible with small children in the house. However, workdays were fatiguing. She basically arose, commuted to work, worked, and commuted home to go to sleep, then off to work again early in the morning. Sometimes the two youngest children did not see her at all, and the oldest may have spent just a few minutes a day with her mother. Infants and very young children do not take kindly to seemingly being "ignored" by their mother. This work arrangement did have the unexpected advantage of forcing me, the father, to spend more quality time with the children than may have otherwise been the case given my work schedule. While the 3/12 arrangement seemed ideal, it had sufficient drawbacks that after shifting to another job my wife never looked back. Today, her employer offers a limited number of 3/12 positions but even with the children grown and gone she feels that the rigors of a twelve-hour nursing shift would be too taxing to be enjoyable and could result in an injury that would shorten her career. In addition, she would miss keeping up with her patients after the third day and she would miss being a part of the daily hospital milieu. One family's experience is not enough on which to base conclusions, but it is obvious that there are other factors beyond those examined in the research literature that should be explored. An innovation in work scheduling can result in a need to change personal and family dynamics in unanticipated ways that could have positive and negative unexpected effects on mental health.

The Physical Work Environment

Several physical conditions of the work environment have been correlated with psychosocial stress and, possibly as a consequence of this stress, medical conditions such as cardiovascular disease, low back disorders, and musculoskeletal disorders of the upper extremity (M. J. Smith et al., 2003). These conditions include noise and organizational and job or task demands.

In addition, exposure to certain chemicals may have a neurotoxic effect and may result in cognitive deficits in attention, reasoning, judgment, and memory (M. J. Smith et al., 2003). Such exposure also may cause psychotic or aberrant behavior, personality changes, and other problems related to psychopathology (M. J. Smith et al., 2003). Fortunately, most countries have strict laws regulating exposure to these chemicals and these reactions are more rare today than in years past. However well-regulated and controlled chemical work is, there is still the possibility that some workers will be exposed to dangerous levels of chemicals. Chemical exposure should be suspected when previously reliable employees begin acting in an unusual manner. This is particularly true if more than one person in a work environment shows behavioral change. These effects are not confined to the worker. M. J. Smith et al. (2003) pointed out that a priority area for research by the National Institute for Occupational Safety and Health is the effect of prenatal exposure to workplace chemicals, which could lead to developmental disabilities in employees' children.

The Social Work Environment

It should not come as a surprise that the social environment at work can affect stress and the resulting strain. Everyone might agree that working with grouchy, whiney, incompetent, petulant, angry, impatient, or passive-aggressive people can be unpleasant. Truax and McDonald (2002) reviewed the relationship between the social environment at work and depression and found that poor work relationships, particularly poor relations with co-workers, were a risk factor for depression.

There are several components of social support. Frese (1999, p. 179) listed affective support ("love, liking, and respect"), confirmation ("confirming moral and factual 'rightness' of actions and statements"), and direct help (assistance). Frese noted that these components are normally interrelated. On the contrary side of the construct, Spielberger, Vagg, and Wasala (2003) saw lack of support as one of two critical factors leading to the perceived severity of stressors (the other factor is job pressures). Exactly how social support buffers the effects of stress has been the subject of some controversy. One possibility is it acts a moderator so that high support would be protective and low support would have either no effect or a negative one. An alternative, the match hypothesis, originated by Cohen and Wills (1985), predicts that the moderating effect will vary depending on the circumstances influencing its relevance for optimal coping strategies. It should be more relevant for social dysfunctions, such as social anxiety, than for nonsocial dysfunctions, such as psychosomatic illness.

Perhaps the most rigorous test of the effects of social support was a two-year longitudinal study of 206 German autoworkers between 1979 and 1981 that was conducted by Frese (1999). He found that, as expected, stressors measured at Time 1 positively correlated with psychological dysfunction at Time 2 and social support measured at Time 1 negatively correlated with psychological dysfunction. However, when types of psychological dysfunction were separated into social and nonsocial per the match hypothesis, there was some evidence of social support serving as a moderator (i.e., significant change in R^2 after main effects of stressors and social support were removed), but the moderation effect accounted for only about 3 to 4 percent of the variance. Interestingly, the expected buffer effects were observed for the "social dysfunctions" of irritation or strain, anxiety, and unexpectedly, to a lesser extent, psychosomatic complaints. Strangely, the effect of physical stressors on the development of depressive symptoms was slightly enhanced by social support. This latter finding had been observed in other studies and is worthy of further attention.

One special type of social relationship at work is that between a mentor and a younger, less-experienced person. Work socialization is vitally important for a successful career. It is a process that begins at a very young age in a person's family of origin and that continues throughout life (Feij, 1998). The mentor is the organizational continuation of that socialization process. Mentors are more experienced, usually older, fellow employees or members of the same profession. They help orient the person to the workings of the organization, job, or profession; introduce a new person to important contacts and help with networking; help solve problems; and, in general, "teach them the ropes." Mentors have been found to be beneficial for a variety of career outcomes (Ragins & Cotton, 1999).

A very interesting longitudinal study found that having a mentor relates to mental health in men many years after the mentoring (Westermeyer, 1998). Undergraduate and graduate students at a private college in 1958-59 completed extensive question-naires for a study on mental health. Most students went into careers in physical education, the YMCA, or related fields. They were recontacted thirty-two years later and either interviewed or completed questionnaires about their careers, family life, standing and service in the community, health, and mental health symptoms and therapy experience. Of the 87 men in the final sample, a "large minority reported moderate or serious symptoms at some point in their lives" (Westermeyer, 1998, p. 269). This majority included 17 percent who reported two or more alcohol-abuse symptoms and 21 percent with three or more depressive symptoms. Overall, 20 percent showed moderate or severe symptoms or functioning problems, as indicated by the Global Assessment Scale (GA) (Endicott, Spitzer, Fleiss, & Cohen, 1976). Having had a mentor while a young adult predicted overall mental health thirty-two years later, with a correlation of .30 (95 percent confidence interval of .10 to .48). This is a reasonably high relationship over that long of a time period. It is possible that those with the best mental health while young attracted mentors, while those with poor adjustment were not found acceptable by mentors, especially because anger control and social adjustment also predicted GA at follow-up. But, regardless of the underlying cause, failure to develop this sort of social support as a young adult is a reason for concern.

WORK-LIFE EVENTS

Mergers and Downsizing

Mergers, acquisitions, and downsizing have become a fact of life in the past several years (Panchal & Cartwright, 2001). This is not a startling fact. However, when this fact is taken in conjunction with the other stressors that are faced in the work environment and when the impact of these changes is examined, the reason for concern is readily apparent. High turnover, low morale, low satisfaction and com-mitment, unproductive behavior, sabotage, and absenteeism are negative employee attitudes and behaviors that accompany many acquisitions according to Morrison and Robinson (1997; cited in Nikandrou, Papalexandris, & Bourantas, 2000).

Downsizing obviously has a negative impact on some employees as they are laid off or demoted. Perhaps more subtle, but still stressful, is the effect that such changes can have on the employees who still have their jobs after the transition. In fact, research indicates that anxiety is stimulated by the announcement that people are leaving an organization (Astrachan, 1995). Remaining employees are faced with fewer resources, more workload demands, and uncertainty regarding their future employment (Sverke & Hellgren, 2002). Further stressors associated with remaining employees or those employees whose companies have been acquired through a merger include violation of expectations, fear of the unknown, loss of autonomy, the need to cope with previous antagonism toward the acquiring organization, and the fear of streamlining (Blake & Mouton, 1983). When downsizing is larger, the impact is more severe; research has shown that the greater the downsizing, the higher employees rate their job insecurity and the lower they rate their feeling of job control (Kivimaki et al., 2001).

Employees of the acquiring company also face new stressors associated with the merger. These changes include pride of ownership, a presumption of understanding of the organization that is being acquired, and the expectation of spontaneous cooperation (Blake & Mouton, 1983). Although these factors alone may not have the face validity of being distressing, these assumptions are often quickly shattered. Once their expectations are failed it is difficult for members of the acquiring organization to foster appropriate expectations and to successfully merge with the new corporation and its employees.

Despite the negative impacts that corporate changes can have on employees (both those who lose their job and those who remain after a corporate action), companies continue to participate in mergers, acquisitions, and downsizing. It is not realistic (or desirable) to expect business to stop or for companies to remain stagnant and to resist any change. There are, however, certain factors (both intracompany and intrapersonal) that mediate the effects that mergers, downsizing, and acquisitions have on employees. When companies merge, the corporate identity of the organization and therefore the individuals associated with a particular organization changes.

To decrease the negative impact of mergers, the various stakeholders should nurture the new corporate identity to help foster a sense of belonging (Balmer & Dinnie, 1999). To help clarify identity and role changes within the organization, companies should address leadership (Balmer & Dinnie, 1999). Through the process of this merger, new leaders may emerge and people who formerly were at the top of a company may find themselves feeling somewhere in the middle. Corporate leadership should also address cultural issues within the company (Balmer & Dinnie, 1999). For example, some organizations, by their nature, are more devoted to serving underserved populations at a low fee for the consumer whereas others are characterized by the desire to increase the profit margin by a larger percentage each year. While it is unlikely that organizations such as Americorps and Sony will merge, there are more subtle differences that must be resolved before a successful merger can occur. While some responsibility of forming a new corporate identity does belong to the entering company, successful acculturation is mostly contingent on how the buying company manages the integration (Larsson & Lubatkin, 2001).

Although culture is one aspect of mergers that should be considered, it would be grossly negligent for an acquiring corporation to focus on nurturing culture and corporate identity only to facilitate a successful merger. Postacquisition management should try to minimize employees' economic uncertainty by making clear its economic policy (Nikandrou et al., 2000). Employees need both useful information regarding coming changes and frequent communication to develop positive attitudes and trust for the new management (Nikandrou et al. 2000). It also is necessary to focus on external factors, such as new technology, changes in the marketplace, changing customer demands, competitor activities, legislation, prevailing political views, and the economy (Kitchen & Daly, 2002).

While the merger, downsizing, or acquisition affects everyone associated with an organization, the severity of the impact is variable. (In actuality, some individuals are positively affected by these changes.) Although there is variance across situations, people tend to be rather stable in their reaction styles to stressful events (Kasch, Klein, & Lara, 2001). Although various events are not always attributed to the same cause, ways of responding to similar events have been shown to remain stable. People may maintain a characteristic explanatory style for bad events across situations throughout their life (Burns & Seligman, 1989). The stability of explanatory style compares favorably with the stability of other personality variables across longer and more directly comparable time spans.

Unemployment

Unemployment has been consistently associated with mental disturbance in studies conducted around the world (Feather, 1989; Lai, Chan, & Luk, 1997; Warr, 1987). Losing a job brings a threat of loss of identity, uncertainty, loss of self-esteem, and financial hardship, and it may result in family conflict (Cartwright & Cooper, 1997; Committee on Prevention of Mental Disorders, 1994). Not surprisingly, the most common psychopathologies observed to follow job loss are depression and anxiety (Kessler, House, & Turner, 1987; Kessler, Turner, & House, 1988). Both of these disorders can have serious consequences, including suicide attempts, which make them potentially fatal conditions. The Committee on Prevention of Mental Disorders (1994) of the Institute of Medicine, National Academy of Science, cited unpublished research by Gordus (1984) that indicates there is some epidemiological evidence that unemployment rates also may be associated with such mental health problems as alcohol abuse, child abuse, and marital conflict. Although the nature of these studies does not allow a cause-and-effect interpretation of these associations, it seems reasonable to conclude that losing a job probably puts a person at greater risk of several psychological problems.

Fortunately, there is evidence that reemployment will help reverse some of the negative effects of job loss. Feather (1989) found that depression waned after laid-off workers found new jobs. The JOBS Program is a model intervention for the unemployed that emphasizes enhancement of self-efficacy and development of job search skills. Two large-scale randomized studies showed the program's efficacy in helping people obtain reemployment and reduce depressive symptoms (Caplan, Vinokur, Price, & van Ryn, 1989; Vinokur, Price, & Schul, 1995). Recent long-term follow-up data indicate that the JOBS Program reduced the odds of a major depressive episode by nearly one-half, possibly partly through its effect on reemployment (Vinokur, Schul, Vuori, & Price, 2000). A program in Finland that was based on the JOBS Program recently showed similar effects (Vuori, Silvonen, Vinokur, & Price, 2002). The Finnish study also showed that those who were at greatest risk for depression prior to the intervention benefited the most. A study by Wanberg (1997) highlighted the importance of having interventions such as the JOBS program for the unemployed. She studied more than five hundred unemployment insurance applicants over three months. Her data indicated that people who employed negative coping strategies (emotional distancing) were less likely to be reemployed than those who used positive coping strategies (e.g., proactive job search behaviors). Proactive job search was associated with negative mental health outcomes only for those who thought they were unlikely to find a job even if they looked for one. This suggests that counselors should take care to ensure that unemployed clients develop useful attitudes and coping strategies as well as practical job search skills.

CASE EXAMPLE: A WOMAN WITH DEPRESSION AND ANXIETY DUE TO WORKING CONDITIONS[1]

Adele Costa was diagnosed with depression and anxiety (post-traumatic stress disorder). She believed that her condition was engendered by the working conditions she had endured for approximately the past two years.

Brief Chronology

Ms. Costa is in her mid-50s. She is the former Pullman branch manager for Palouse Savings and Loan (PSL) and, later, Longitude Bank and Trust (LBT) after the latter took over PSL. She is the daughter of a controlling mother and alcoholic father who beat her. She has been married for more than thirty years and has four children. She describes her marriage and family life as being good; her husband has provided strong support during her emotional problems. She has not been an alcoholic or a drug abuser. After graduating from college she taught school briefly, and then settled into a role as housewife and mother. In 1991, she returned to the labor force by going to work with PSL. Later in 1991, she moved to Pullman as branch manager for PSL. In 1994, she moved to East Spokane branch as branch manager. In 1995, she moved back to the Pullman branch, again as branch manager. In 1997, LBT merged with PSL in an unfriendly takeover. On August 14, 1997, major changes were made at her branch, including introduction of a new computer system, new security procedures and policies, and new methods of doing business (e.g., internal forms, types of accounts offered). In April 1998, LBT introduced a special loan promotion that continued for many months. By July 1998, Ms. Costa was suffering a major depressive episode with comorbid anxiety, including panic attacks and thoughts of suicide, and was advised by her physician to take some time off from work. To this date she has been unable to work effectively. Prior to this time Ms. Costa's performance as branch manager was viewed favorably and was, perhaps, outstanding in many respects. Records indicate that her branch won company awards for high performance several times.

Were the Conditions under Which Ms. Costa Worked Known to Contribute to Occupational Stress?

Ms. Costa encountered many conditions that are known to contribute to heightened stress in employees. For purposes of this report, we deal with each one separately.

---

[1] This case is based on an actual case for which Dr. Jay Thomas served as an expert witness regarding stress and working conditions. The names of all persons and organizations as well as dates and some other details have been changed to protect confidentiality. Dr. Thomas originally prepared this summary for Ms. Costa's attorney about a year after Ms. Costa ceased her employment with LBT.

However, it is important to recognize that although any single condition may have caused her problems, the various conditions worked together so that the simultaneous existence of several stressors became a source of stress.

Computer Problems

Perhaps the most outstanding form of stress Ms. Costa encountered was with the computer problems after the new computer system was installed. When working with computers, people often distinguish between hardware, the actual electrical components constituting a computer and its associated devices such as printers, and software, the written programs that instruct the computer how to perform its tasks.

LBT changed both the hardware and the software. The hardware was the latest design, but the software was primitive compared with the system it replaced. The tellers entered some transactions (e.g., a deposit by a customer) into the computer system. However, other types of transactions, known as general ledger items (including cashier's checks, traveler's checks, and money orders) were not processed by the computer system and had to be completed manually. The new system was unable to calculate all of the entries for a day's business, so at the end of the day the branch manager, and possibly one or more tellers, had to spend about two hours (when things went well) completing paperwork that was formerly done by the computers. In addition, every day the branch manager was required to check the entries for each of the preceding four days. Thus, without consideration of any other factors, the branch manager had considerably more work to do each day after the conversion than before.

Simply adding to a person's workload would not ordinarily lead to debilitating stress. However, in this case the increased workload had characteristics that set it apart from what could be considered typical changes in job requirements: LBT management practices and incorrectly installed hardware that made it impossible to perform these tasks adequately.

The computer system at the Pullman branch communicated with the computer at the head office (in Atlanta) through a modem. During installation of the computer systems in August 1997, the modem was installed incorrectly so that much of what it transmitted was garbled. This meant that roughly 30 to 50 percent of the transactions entered by a teller (out of two hundred to three hundred a day) would be transmitted incorrectly to the head office computer. The teller had no way of knowing whether a given transaction was correctly transmitted until the end of the day.

Existence of the fault in the computer system made it impossible for the Pullman branch to balance its records of transactions with those of the head office at the end of each day. Because banks and savings and loans require accuracy in accounting for transactions, the branch employees, and particularly the branch manager, were forced to stay after hours to reconcile the books. This resulted in Ms. Costa working, on average, more than sixty hours per week. Although there was an indication in the computer at the East Spokane branch that there was a malfunction in the Pullman branch's modem during this entire period, Ms. Costa was ridiculed by her supervisor as being incapable of performing her duties and as being a complainer. Finally, in

February 1998, a technician was assigned to check out the system and to correct the modem problem.

Being responsible for results over which one has no control is known to result in feelings of stress. Also, working on balancing the books due to the garbled data entries took time and energy away from other important duties (described later), resulting in feelings of role conflict, which also are related to feelings of increased stress. It is also possible that having to spend a great deal of time and effort on a task that previously had been much less complex could have contributed to feelings of stress. The contribution of the supervisor is examined in more detail later.

Customer Relations

Ms. Costa reported that management of PSL considered good customer relations of paramount importance and that her attitude of placing a priority on good customer service was encouraged. Conversion to LBT introduced a number of customer relations problems that, since they continued for many months (and Ms. Costa believes they are still continuing), can be described only as mismanagement in the extreme. These problems included printing incorrect statements, reporting incorrect interest rates on statements (e.g., several months of earning 0 percent interest), and confusing customers' funds because of systemwide errors (e.g., the statement errors).[1] LBT did not make any attempt to inform the branches. Branch personnel first learned of the problem from the customers.

During the months between April 1998 and September 1998, the bank advertised a special loan promotion campaign in which customers were offered quick service that the company had no means of accomplishing because of a lack of processing staff. As branch manager, Ms. Costa had to deal with increasing numbers of irate customers every day and was powerless to assist them in any meaningful way. In addition, if she asked for assistance or for clarification from her superior or the operations manager, she was punished for bothering them.

Dealing with irate customers is stressful. It is more stressful when the company's actions are what makes them irate and when the company makes no effort to mitigate the problems that are irritating the customers. This situation produces feelings of despair and helplessness in the employee that then can lead to depression. There is also the problem of "role conflict," or having to perform incompatible actions: keep satisfied customers and remain loyal to the company. Another stressful aspect of the customer relations problems was the loss of business engendered by the poor service combined with increasing performance demands by the bank. The company was driving away business and demanding the branch managers to produce more business. Ms. Costa was caught in the middle.

---

[1] Each type of account had its own series of account numbers. An account number would indicate the branch and the serial position of the account, so the first person to open an account of a given type was assigned a number representing 1, the second person was given a number representing 2, and so on. When there was not an indication of the type of account, it was common for several customers of a branch to have the same account number. This resulted in frequent mix-ups in which customer's funds were deposited or withdrawn from someone else's account.

Staffing

Throughout her tenure as branch manager at the Pullman branch, Ms. Costa's staff was short handed. In spite of numerous requests for additional staff, she was denied. Having to get by with "float" personnel would normally be stressful, although usually not so much that we would expect a manager to become overly stressed. However, because Ms. Costa was spending the bulk of her time trying to unravel the bookkeeping problems caused by the short in the modem and dealing with customer complaints, any additional unnecessary stress was detrimental to her well-being.

Conversion to LBT from PSL

Mergers, even friendly ones, are stressful to employees. This is especially true when one firm is taken over by another. However, there are a few steps that can be taken to alleviate the stress experienced by employees. These steps basically involve helping people work through their emotional reaction to the takeover (people go through a grieving period similar to that experienced when a loved one dies, although perhaps not so severe), exchanging valid and useful information (including providing training on new systems, policies, procedures, etc.), sharing cultural information and practices between the companies, and maintaining communication between the two companies. The latter was not possible because Mr. Daniel Mallard, district manager, would not permit his subordinates to communicate with anyone above him in the organization.

Ms. Costa reports that in the beginning she and the other branch managers were hopeful that becoming part of LBT would solve a number of problems that PSL had been unable to solve because of its small size. However, when the conversion was made there were a number of changes in policies and procedures, product lines, internal record keeping, and security measures. LBT made no attempt to train anyone on how to implement these changes. As stated earlier, when Ms. Costa called the operations manager for assistance or advice on implementing these changes, she was reported to her supervisor and punished at the next weekly meeting through public social censure by her supervisor. Thus, Ms. Costa was faced with responsibility for results without being given the means or the authority to influence those results.

Supervisor

Ms. Costa's supervisor was a source of stress, as well as a contributor to the other sources described previously. It has been demonstrated that a supportive supervisor can reduce the effects of stressful conditions at work. In other words, if the supervisor acts in a considerate manner, takes complaints seriously, and acts to relieve an exhausting workload, then the sorts of stressors encountered by Ms. Costa are less likely to result in feelings of stress. Because Ms. Costa's supervisor, Mr. Mallard, was demonstrably unsupportive, he contributed to her experience of stress. In addition, he was a source of stress. Statements from other managers and employees indicated that Ms. Costa and possibly one other branch manager were singled out for especially harsh treatment. Examples of Mr. Mallard's conduct include continually belittling

Ms. Costa, publicly accusing her of being nothing more than a complainer (with no basis), attempting to subvert her authority by encouraging her employees to spy on her, attempting to embarrass her in front of the other branch managers, failing to investigate her reports of equipment malfunction, ignoring her pleas for help, and pestering her to improve her performance in the balancing of the branch's books during the time when the malfunctioning modem made that impossible. Branch managers were not permitted to make routine inquires about policies and procedures or even to ask for information about the status of their own pension plan.

Research has shown that "boss stress" of this sort can create additional stress because a person is distracted from using his or her intelligence and experience to solve the problems that brought on the attention from the boss. In other words, Mr. Mallard's behavior was precisely the sort that would be most effective in preventing Ms. Costa from dealing with the problems at the Pullman branch. In addition, he made a practice of pointing out Ms. Costa's "failures" at the weekly managers meeting. Because these failures were not under Ms. Costa's control, the meetings became a significant source of stress. Public social censure for matters beyond the person's control has been recognized as a major cause of worker stress reactions, including the development of "combat neurosis" and other anxiety-related disorders. In our opinion, the behavior of Ms. Costa's supervisor was the leading cause of her job stress in that he could have solved the computer problems, could have mitigated the customer relations problems, could have allowed for normal communications with the operations manager and other support personnel, and possibly could have arranged for more training in the LBT methods. Without his inattention the problems of role conflict, role overload, role insufficiency, responsibility for outcomes beyond Ms. Costa's control, and social censure would not have escalated to the point where she could no longer function.

Role of Personal Characteristics

A final issue is whether a characteristic within Ms. Costa or one caused by her personal history could have been responsible for her feelings of stress. The record indicates that she suffered physical (but not sexual) abuse at the hand of her alcoholic father. Psychiatrist Allen J. Peterson, M.D., concluded that this abuse was the sole causal factor in the development of Ms. Costa's psychopathology. However, psychiatrist Howard Lee, M.D., disagreed and maintained that childhood trauma had little to do with Ms. Costa's current problems. Although research in psychology suggests such childhood trauma as being a relevant factor, there is no reason to expect that it played a central role. Childhood trauma of this sort is best seen as a risk factor. Thus, Ms. Costa's childhood abuse possibly increased Ms. Costa's susceptibility to depression and anxiety given prolonged exposure to the conditions she worked under. These different theories are illustrated in Figure 3.2.

Ms. Costa was ultimately awarded a settlement that allowed her to retire. She continued in psychotherapy with a counselor and achieved some improvement in her depression and anxiety. Her supervisor, Mr. Mallard, was fired by LBT after his actions toward Ms. Costa and several other women employees were publicized. LBT went out of business about a year after this report was prepared. The branches

Dr. Peterson's Model:

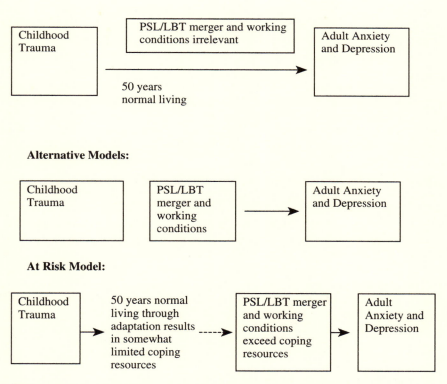

FIGURE 3.2 Alternative Models Explaining Ms. Costa's Stress Reaction.
Note. PSL = Palouse Savings and Loan; LBT = Longitude Bank and Trust.

formally associated with PSL were bought by a local bank and have been successful since then.

Learning Point from This Case

The disagreement between psychiatrists Dr. Peterson and Dr. Lee created a fair amount of confusion about LBT's responsibility in causing Ms. Costa's condition. A sketch of Figure 3.2 was discovered by LBT's attorney and introduced into evidence at a hearing. This was a mistake, as it allowed another view to be entered into the record, which tipped the balance in Ms. Costa's favor. Normally, I (Jay Thomas), an industrial and organizational psychologist, would not presume to testify about the origins of a case of psychopathology, and the rules of evidence would not allow it. In this case LBT's attorney introduced my sketch into evidence and asked me about it, thus allowing me to present a different view of the case. One moral of the story is to graphically portray causal theories in a way that heightens the understanding of professionals and nonprofessionals. A second moral is to keep an open mind and keep reasonably up-to-date with all of psychology, not just a narrow specialty. A third moral, should any of our readers become attorneys, is never ask a witness a question for which you do not know the answer.

References

Aiken, L. S., & West, S. G. (1990). Invalidity of true experiments: Self report pretest biases. *Evaluation Review, 14,* 374-390.

Alluisi, E. A., & Morgan, B. B. (1982). Temporal factors in human performance and productivity. In E. A. Alluisi & E. A. Fleishman (Eds.), *Human performance and productivity: Stress and performance effectiveness* (Vol. 3, pp. 165-248). Hillsdale, NJ: Lawrence Erlbaum.

Astrachan, J. (1995). Organization departures: The impact of separation anxiety as studied in mergers and acquisitions simulation. *Journal of Applied Behavioral Sciences, 31,* 31-50.

Balmer, J., & Dinnie, K. (1999). Corporate identity and communication: The antidote to merger madness. *Corporate Communications, 4,* 182-192.

Beehr, T. A. (1998). An organizational psychology meta-model of occupational stress. In C. L. Cooper (Ed.), *Theories of organizational stress* (pp. 6-27). New York: Oxford University Press.

Blake, R., & Mouton, J. (1983). The urge to merge: Tying the knot successfully. *Training and Development Journal, 37,* 41-46.

Burns, M., & Seligman, M. (1989). Explanatory style across the life span: Evidence for stability over 52 years. *Journal of Personality and Social Psychology, 56,* 471-477.

Caplan, R. D., Vinokur, A. D., Price, R. H., & van Ryn, M. (1989). Job seeking, reemployment, and mental health: A randomized field experiment in coping with job loss. *Journal of Applied Psychology, 74,* 759-769.

Cartwright, S., & Cooper, C. L. (1997). *Managing workplace stress.* Thousand Oaks, CA: Sage.

Cohen, S., & Wills, T. A. (1985). Stress, social support, and the buffering hypothesis. *Psychological Bulletin, 98,* 310-357.

Committee on Prevention of Mental Disorders. (1994). *Reducing risks for mental disorders: Frontiers for preventative intervention research.* Washington, DC: National Academy Press.

Costa, G. (1996). The impact of shift and night work on health. *Applied Ergonomics, 27,* 9-16.

Endicott, J., Spitzer, R. L., Fleiss, J. L., & Cohen, J. (1976). The Global Assessment Scale: A procedure for measuring overall severity of psychiatric disturbance. *Archives of General Psychiatry, 33,* 766-771.

Feather, N. T. (1989). Reported changes in behaviour after job loss in a sample of older, unemployed men. *Australian Journal of Psychology, 41,* 175-185.

Feij, J. A. (1998). Work socialization of young people. In P. J. D. Drenth, H. Thierry, & C. J. deWolf (Eds.), *Handbook of work and organizational psychology (2nd ed.). Volume 3: Personnel psychology* (pp. 207-255). East Sussex, UK: Psychology Press.

Frese, M. (1999). Social support as a moderator of the relationship between work stressors and psychological dysfunctioning: A longitudinal study with objective measures. *Journal of Occupational Health Psychology, 4,* 179-192.

Kasch, K., Klein, D., & Lara, M. (2001). A construct validation study of the response styles questionnaire rumination scale in participants with a recent-onset major depressive episode. *Psychological Assessment, 13,* 375-383.

Kessler, R. C. (1997). The effects of stressful life events on depression. *Annual Review of Psychology, 48,* 191-214.

Kessler, R. C., House, J. S., & Turner, J. B. (1987). Unemployment and health in a community sample. *Journal of Health and Social Behavior, 28,* 51-59.

Kessler, R. C., Turner, J. B., & House, J. S. (1988). Effects of unemployment on health in a community survey: Main, modifying, and mediating effects. *Journal of Social Issues, 44,* 69-85.

Kitchen, P., & Daly, F. (2002). Internal communication during change management. *Corporate Communications, 7,* 46-53.

Kivimaki, M., Vahtera, J., Pentti, J., Thompson, L., Griffiths, A., & Cox, T. (2001). Downsizing, changes in work, and self-rated health of employees: A 7-year 3-wave panel study. *Anxiety, Stress, and Coping, 14,* 59-73.

Lai, J., Chan, R. K. H., & Luk, C.-L. (1997). Unemployment and psychological health among Hong Kong Chinese women. *Psychological Reports, 81,* 499-505.

Larsson, R., & Lubatkin, M. (2001). Achieving acculturation in mergers and acquisitions: An international case survey. *Human Relations, 54,* 1573-1607.

Lazarus, R. (1991). *Coping and adaptation.* New York: Oxford University Press.

Nikandrou, I., Papalexandris, N., & Bourantas, D. (2000). Gaining employee trust after acquisition: Implications for managerial action. *Employee Relations, 24,* 334-355.

Panchal, S., & Cartwright, S. (2001). Group differences in post-merger stress. *Journal of Managerial Psychology, 16,* 424-433.

Quick, J. C., & Tetrick, L. (Eds.). (2002). *Handbook of occupational health psychology.* Washington, DC: American Psychological Association.

Ragins, B. R., & Cotton, J. L. (1999). Mentor functions and outcomes: A comparison of men and women in formal and informal mentoring relationships. *Journal of Applied Psychology, 84,* 529-550.

Sapolsky, R. M. (1998). *Why zebras don't get ulcers: An updated guide to stress, stress-related diseases, and coping* (2nd ed.). New York: W. H. Freeman.

Smith, C. S., Folkard, S., & Fuller, J. A. (2003). In J. C. Quick & L. E. Tetrick (Eds.), *Handbook of occupational health psychology* (pp. 163-184). Washington, DC: American Psychological Association.

Smith, C. S., Robie, C., Folkard, S., Barton, J., Macdonald, I., Smith, L., et al. (1999). A process model of shiftwork and stress. *Journal of Occupational Health Psychology, 4,* 207-218.

Smith, M. J., Karsh, B.-T., Carayon, P., & Conway, F. T. (2003). Controlling occupational safety and health hazards. In J. C. Quick & L. E. Tetrick (Eds.), *Handbook of occupational health psychology* (pp. 35-68). Washington, DC: American Psychological Association.

Spielberger, C. D., Vagg, P. R., & Wasala, C. F. (2003). Occupational stress: Job pressures and lack of support. In J. C. Quick & L. E. Tetrick (Eds.), *Handbook of occupational health psychology* (pp. 185-200). Washington, DC: American Psychological Association.

Sverke, M., & Hellgren, J. (2002). The nature of job insecurity: understanding employment uncertainty on the brink of a new millennium. *Applied Psychology: An International Review, 51,* 23-42.

Thierry, H., & Jansen, B. (1998). Work time and behaviour at work. In P. J. D. Drenth, H.Thierry, & C. J. de Wolff (Eds.), *Handbook of work and organizational psychology (2nd ed.). Volume 2: Work psychology.* (pp. 89-119). East Sussex, UK: Psychology Press.

Truax, P., & McDonald, T. (2002). Depression in the workplace. In J. C. Thomas & M. Hersen (Eds.), *Handbook of mental health in the workplace* (pp. 123-154). Thousand Oaks, CA: Sage.

Vinokur, A. D., Price, R. H., & Schul, Y. (1995). Impact of the JOBS intervention on unemployed workers varying in risk for depression. *American Journal of Community Psychology, 23,* 39-74.

Vinokur, A. D., Schul, Y., Vuori, J., & Price, R. H. (2000). Two years after a job loss: Long-term impact of the JOBS program on reemployment and mental health. *Journal of Occupational Health Psychology, 5,* 32-47.

Vuori, J., Silvonen, J., Vinokur, A. D., & Price, R. H. (2002). The Työhön job search program in Finland: Benefits for the unemployed with risk of depression or discouragement. *Journal of Occupational Health Psychology, 7,* 5-19.

Wanberg, C. R. (1997). Antecedents and outcomes of coping behaviors among unemployed and reemployed individuals. *Journal of Applied Psychology, 82,* 731-744.

Warr, P. (1987). *Work, unemployment, and mental health.* Oxford, UK: Oxford University Press.

Westermeyer, J. F. (1998). Predictors and characteristics of mental health among men at midlife: A 32 year longitudinal study. *American Journal of Orthopsychiatry, 68,* 265-273.

Assessment of Psychopathology

NADIA E. STELLRECHT, THOMAS E. JOINER, JR.,
ANDREA B. BURNS, AND
NATALIE SACHS-ERICSSON
Florida State University

JEREMY W. PETTIT
University of Houston

*M*any people spend almost as much time at their place of employment as they do at their home. As a consequence, the personalities and problems that employees bring to their work environment have a great chance of influencing the tone of that environment in positive and negative directions. It is likely that mental health issues will be prominent among the problems workers experience. Mental illness is not uncommon in today's society, whether it is depression, anxiety, or a substance-use disorder. Such illnesses, when they occur, influence the sufferer in many ways, including his or her attitudes, efficiency, and ability to get along with others. In the workplace, the distress that the person experiences may translate into a negative work environment and thus lower productivity of the business in general. Therefore, business organizations must be alert to people who are dealing with psychological distress and mental disorders.

There are many important aspects involved in hiring employees and evaluating job performance and satisfaction. One primary concern for employers is to assess a worker's ability to thoughtfully and efficiently carry out his or her job. Maintaining a certain level of functioning is necessary to carry out day-to-day tasks and to keep a company running smoothly; consequently, the negative impacts that mental illness can have (i.e., absenteeism, accidents, interpersonal conflict, poor job performance, and poor job satisfaction) on employees and their co-workers makes this area critical to workplace performance (Kahn & Langlieb, 2003). For example, in a longitudinal, prospective, epidemiological study of disability and its relationship to days lost from work, Broadhead, Blazer, George, and Tse (1990) found that individuals with major depression and minor forms of depression were all at greater risk of having days lost from work than were those individuals without depression.

Another study conducted by Wittchen, Carter, Pfister, Montgomery, and Kessler (2000) found that having either generalized anxiety disorder or major depression was associated with high impairment, including at least three days of limited or impaired functioning. Furthermore, when mental illnesses and medical illnesses occur simultaneously, rates of impairment at work are even higher (Kessler, Greenberg, Mickelson, Meneades, & Want, 2001).

In addition, Ciarlo, Shern, Tweed, and Kilpatrick (1992) administered a statewide survey (the Colorado Social Health Survey) of 4,754 adults from the Colorado general population. This study included self-report measures of functioning on tasks of everyday living. Briefly, the researchers found that, among participants who were employed full-time (35 hours or more per week), 20.4 percent of those participants with a *Diagnostic and Statistical Manual of Mental Disorders–Fourth Edition* (*DSM-IV*) (American Psychiatric Association, 1994) current diagnosis scored higher on a measure of problems with productivity at work, compared with only 9.9 percent of the participants who did not carry a *DSM-IV* diagnosis.

Ethical Issues Related to Assessment in the Workplace

Clearly, there are many negative consequences to unrecognized mental health problems in employees. This makes the need to identify such problems even more pressing. However, several factors may adversely affect the ability of the employer to gather such information. Evaluation in the workplace, on any level, is frequently viewed with suspicion by many employees, and when questions about mental health are thrown into the mix, the likelihood of a defensive response increases substantially. This response may be due to several factors; most notably, fear of stigmatization, negative employment effects (e.g., being fired or passed over for a promotion), and a general desire to appear self-reliant and able to cope with external stressors (Kahn & Langlieb, 2003). With factors such as these in play, it is incumbent on the employer or management team to make discussions of mental health commonplace and acceptable in the work environment. Employers should make it known that psychological assessment and treatment for employees is encouraged and the beneficial results recognized (Kahn & Langlieb, 2003).

In addition to specific employee concerns, the need for competent mental health professionals and where to find them also should be evaluated. It is important that management recognize when mental health issues should be handled within the business organization and when such issues should be addressed by outside help. Many companies employ psychological consultants or counselors or contract with a psychological care organization to provide help for employees who may have emotional difficulties. Whatever a company decides to do, it must be aware of the ethical considerations involved in dealing with mental health issues in a business environment.

Perhaps the most important ethical considerations revolve around issues of confidentiality. It is imperative that both employer and employee understand to whom and under what conditions a mental health professional can disclose information to the business organization or to others, such as the police. There are standard limits to confidentiality, as in the case of child abuse or risk of harm to self or others, of which those entering assessment or treatment must be aware. Notification of the limits of confidentiality (either general or company specific) should be given to the employee, or potential employee, prior to any initial consultation in which sensitive personal information may be disclosed. Furthermore, it is wise to consider to what extent the evaluation or treatment agent is involved with the organization. If the mental health professional is directly employed by the organization or has a financial interest in the organization, the employee under evaluation may perceive a conflict of interest that may hinder his or her desire to disclose information (Kahn & Langlieb, 2003).

There also are ethical issues particularly relevant to assessment in the workplace; most notably, the problem of making decisions to hire, fire, or promote in context of mental health diagnosis or other personal information irrelevant to the specific job. For example, in 1989 a class-action invasion-of-privacy and employment discrimination lawsuit was filed on behalf of security guard applicants at Target's 113 California stores. Saroka, the plaintiff, applied for a security guard position with Target and was required, as part of the application process, to take the California Psychological Inventory (CPI), and the Minnesota Multiphasic Personality Inventory (MMPI). The plaintiff argued that the test questions probed into his private thoughts and deepest feelings and were irrelevant for evaluating his suitability for the position of security guard (Cohen & Swerdlik, 2002). The court agreed that some of the test questions did indeed invade the applicants' privacy because these questions asked about religious beliefs and sexual preferences (*Saroka v. Target,* 1989). The Supreme Court acknowledged that Target had an interest in employing emotionally stable people as security guards but also stated that Target did not show how some information contained in the CPI and MMPI would have any bearing on emotional stability and would thereby provide a compelling reason for the invasion of privacy constituted by the test questions.

It is unlikely that some of the questions on the MMPI (e.g., "I am very attracted to members of my own sex"; "I go to church almost every week") would ever be asked in a job interview. Furthermore, companies often make the mistake of assuming that mental health professionals, as part of a screening evaluation, can ask questions that would be illegal for the company to ask. It is important to remember that the mental health professional is acting on behalf of the company.

In a society that is increasingly litigious, a business organization's recognition of its responsibility for the fair treatment of its employees is extremely important. Given the need to identify mental health problems, and the sensitive nature of such issues (both personally and legally), confidentiality and professional competence, as well as fairness and relevance in testing, must be primary concerns. Given such considerations, the process of choosing an assessment instrument may not be easy and identifying psychopathology, perhaps even less so. For the remainder of this chapter, we present several standard ways of assessing the presence of psychopathology. In addition and given the relationship between psychopathology and impaired functioning, we provide an alternative to these standard methods of assessment in the form of "functional assessment."

TYPES OF ASSESSMENT INSTRUMENTS

A test or evaluation instrument, as defined by Kaplan and Saccuzzo (1997, p. 7), is a "measurement device or technique used to quantify behavior or aid in the understanding and prediction of behavior." Clinical assessment and diagnosis involve application of one or more tests toward the evaluation of behaviors and mental activities that are considered relevant to human functioning and mental health. While testing is generally a straightforward process, there are inherent problems with this process to bear in mind. First, the nature of the clinical phenomena or constructs being measured is often not well understood by those who construct or give tests. Second, threats to the measurement process may bias the assessment in some manner, thereby producing inaccurate or equivocal results, though such threats can sometimes be minimized. Even when this is the case, the problem of adequate knowledge of clinical constructs will likely plague assessment and diagnosis until the discovery of an alternative approach to understanding psychopathology. Having said this, let us now survey some assessment and diagnostic techniques commonly used to identify psychopathology: structured clinical interviews, symptom scales, and projective tests.

Structured Clinical Interviews

A clinical interview, in its broadest sense, can be thought of as a conversation with a purpose or goal (Nietzel, Bernstein, & Milich, 1998). Such conversations can provide the interviewer not only with answers to particular questions but also with valuable samples of verbal and nonverbal behavior. When an interview is structured, the interviewer asks specific questions phrased in a standardized fashion and presented in a preestablished order. This type of interview also provides consistent rules for scoring answers and additional probes if more information is needed from the client. There are several advantages, as outlined by Nietzel, Bernstein, and Milich (1998), to using structured clinical interviews. First, the structured format imparts improved reliability of assessment. Interviewers may bring many biases and expectations to the interview setting, which are likely to influence their interpretations of client behavior or symptom reporting. This, in turn, may affect the interviewer's ability to make accurate diagnoses. By delineating clear and explicit criteria for category inclusion and exclusion, structured interviews reduce the level of error inherent in unstructured approaches, which rely to a greater extent on clinical judgment (Joiner & Pettit, 2003). See also Nisbett and Ross (1980) for an argument about how clinician's evaluations of covariation, cause, and prediction are often colored by biases.

Second, a structured format allows interviews to be conducted systematically by people other than professional clinicians, such as trained nonprofessionals and even computers. Furthermore, the efficiency and ease with which structured clinical interviews are scored makes this approach appropriate for those wishing to use economical resources efficiently. Third, there is some assurance that the interview will be long enough and comprehensive enough to reach assessment goals.

Some disadvantages that may arise from the routine nature of a structured format are that it may be more difficult to establish rapport with the client. The impersonal nature of asking question after question and the fact that interviewers may not need as much information as the client could, or may want to provide, can preclude the forming of a working relationship between interviewer and client. Furthermore, interviewers who become too reliant on test protocol as the only way to gather relevant information may miss critical factors that would be important to include in the results of the interview. One final point is that the results of structured interviews often depend heavily on the client variables such as memory, candor, and descriptive abilities. If clients are poor at any of these tasks, the results of the assessment may be significantly influenced (i.e., inaccurate) (Nietzel, Bernstein, & Milich, 1998).

The Structured Clinical Interview for the *DSM-IV* (SCID-I) (First, Spitzer, Gibbon, & Williams, 1995) is perhaps the most commonly used in that format. The SCID is a comprehensive interview used to make Axis I diagnoses for the *DSM-IV* (e.g., major depressive episode), and as such, it closely conforms to the *DSM-IV* diagnostic decision trees. A companion interview, the SCID-II (First, Spitzer, Gibbon, Williams, & Benjamin, 1994), is available to derive Axis II personality disorder diagnoses. In addition, the SCID-I (Mini-SCID) (First, Gibbon, Williams, & Spitzer, 1995) and SCID-II (AutoSCID-II) (First, Gibbons, Williams, & Spitzer, 1996) also are available in computerized versions.

The SCID is designed for use by a trained professional. Its format includes a number of open-ended queries and item skip structures, thereby requiring a moderate degree of clinical judgment. Because of the SCID's comprehensive nature, length of administration time may be of concern. However, selection of appropriate modules (e.g., based on an initial screen) may be used instead of administering the entire schedule.

Symptom Scales

One of the most commonly used assessment tools is the symptom scale. This type is also the most economical. First, while some symptom scales are rather lengthy, many are short and take only minutes for the client to fill out. Also, scoring and interpreting a symptom scale often can be done rapidly given the availability of standardized norms and cutoff scores. One problem with symptom scales is that, while they may alert the clinician to the level of emotional distress and general psychological functioning, attempting to make diagnoses based on the information provided can be problematic. First, many symptoms included on a scale may actually be criteria for more than one disorder. Therefore, it can be difficult to distinguish which disorder a pattern of symptoms is most indicative of. Second, as with clinical interviews, the ability to obtain accurate information rests largely on the client. Those clients, or those applying for a job, may seek to distort their responses in a more favorable light with an eye to what responses might be most socially desirable. Furthermore, memory and self-insight may also hinder a client's ability to endorse items that provide an accurate picture of him or her.

One type of symptom scale that is common in assessing job applicants is the personality inventory. The personality inventory is particularly useful because it can be seen as an indicator of overall emotional distress and general psychological functioning. There is no need to make a specific diagnosis to decide if further interviews or evaluations are required to assess the applicant's capabilities. Furthermore, personality inventories (such as the MMPI-2 and CPI) have validity scales built into the inventory that tap general test-taking attitudes and whether the applicant is trying to present himself or herself in an overly favorable or overly negative light (Groth-Marnat, 1999).

The MMPI-2 is a 567-item, empirically derived standardized self-report inventory that typically requires one to two hours to complete. Test takers are asked to respond "true" or "false" to a series of self-descriptive statements that, when scored together, yield a quantitative measure of an individual's emotional adjustment and attitude toward test taking (Groth-Marnat, 1999). *T* scores greater than sixty-five on any MMPI-2 scale are considered in the clinical range. The MMPI-2 is often used to screen personnel for sensitive jobs (e.g., police officer). Some criticisms of the MMPI-2 are that it is too lengthy and does not provide enough information for normal populations, as it was normed on individuals with psychological disorders.

The CPI (developed by Gough, 1948) is a paper-and-pencil questionnaire that can be administered in an individual or group setting. It contains more than one-third of the items from the MMPI-2. Items consist of true–false statements that ask about a person's typical behavior, feelings, opinions, and attitudes about social, ethical, and family matters. The constructs tapped by the CPI are referred to as "folk concepts" because they are based on concepts of human behavior held by most people within most cultures (i.e., the test is not theoretically derived). Unlike the MMPI-2, the CPI was normed on populations without psychopathology. Test–retest reliability ranges from .53 to .80 and overall reliability is .70. High scores are considered to be good but are not standard across ages (i.e., a certain score may mean different things depending on the test taker's age). Like the MMPI-2, the CPI has several scales that assess test takers' tendencies to present themselves in an overly favorable or overly negative light. Assets of the CPI, as outlined by Groth-Marnat (1999), are as follows. Because the CPI targets normal populations, it is available for use with many people, not just those with psychopathology, as is the case with the MMPI-2. The CPI uses folk concepts that are found in most societies and are easily understood by many people, as descriptions are straightforward and easy to interpret. The CPI may be useful in personnel selection and vocational guidance to the extent that it can predict performance.

One limitation of the CPI is that it has not been sufficiently validated in a clinical context. Therefore, while we can make statements about the results obtained by normal test takers, there is less certainty regarding the results obtained by those with mental health concerns. Furthermore, using the CPI to predict performance needs to be carefully validated, as correlations of test scores and future success have been somewhat weak. Last, most test takers' scores tend to fall in a narrow range, and not at either extreme, which makes interpretation (i.e., recognition of problems) difficult.

Projectives

Perhaps the most controversial of the assessment tools are the projective techniques, such as the Rorschach Inkblot Test (Rorschach, 1921/1942). The main assumption of such tests is that, when presented with ambiguous stimuli, people will interpret the stimuli in a manner that is indicative or representative of their thought processes, feelings, needs, and previous experiences (Frank, 1939). While advocates of these tests maintain that there is valuable clinical information to be gleaned from the results of projective tests, detractors voice concern over the often poor psychometric properties of projectives and argue for the discontinuation of their application as diagnostic tools.

While one advantage of projective techniques is that they are relatively easy and quick to administer, the drawback is that they often have complicated and time-consuming scoring and interpretation procedures. Another advantage of projectives is that they do not rely on the respondent to provide accurate, self-evaluation reports. As such, they are not as susceptible to the "faking" or "denial" problems that hinder structured interviews and symptoms scales.

A critical drawback of projective techniques is that empirical research has found little evidence for their validity. Many authors (e.g., Chapman & Chapman, 1967; Garb, Wood, & Nezworski, 2000; Groth-Marnat & Roberts, 1998; Halperin & McKay, 1998; Petot, 2001; Wood, Lilienfeld, Garb, & Nezworski, 2000) have raised concerns about what projective tests are actually measuring and if such information is truly useful above and beyond that which is provided by techniques with established, research-supported reliability and validity. Furthermore, extensive training is required for those who wish to score responses to projective techniques, and, in most cases, no clear system of scoring has been developed, making scoring across raters unreliable. In light of these considerations, projective techniques may not be well suited for the workplace environment.

FUNCTIONAL ASSESSMENT

As noted earlier in this chapter, the relationship between mental health problems and poor workplace functioning is quite significant. Specifically, we see higher rates of absenteeism, accidents, interpersonal conflict, and poor job performance in those who suffer from psychiatric illnesses. Since psychopathology is likely to impact one's functioning, difficulties in functioning also may indicate mental health problems that need to be addressed. Assessing functioning may be a reasonable way to assess whether further mental health or medical evaluations need to be conducted.

As we mentioned previously, one efficient way to gauge whether an employee is able to carry out duties in the workplace is to assess general functioning, particularly psychological functioning. The degree to which an individual can navigate through day-to-day activities will certainly play a role in whether he or she is able to function in a work environment. Techniques to evaluate this ability are called functional assessments. Specifically, functional assessment is the systematic evaluation of an individual's ability to perform tasks of everyday living. Such tasks may include the ability to meet one's basic needs, the ability to get along with others, the ability to be productive at a job, or even the ability to get from one place to another (e.g., taking the bus).

The World Health Organization, in the International Classification of Impairment, Disability, and Handicap (ICIDH-2) (World Health Organization, 1999), proposed the study of functioning and disability at three levels, each of which may be affected after the onset of a disabling condition. These levels are body, activity, and participation. For the level of the body, evaluators consider functioning in terms of the integrity of bodily functions. For the level of activity, evaluators consider the performance of whole-person activities, such as communication, eating, or ambulation. For the participation level, evaluators consider the person's involvement in normative life situations (e.g., education, employment, or parenting). Other factors, such as a person's social environment or personality attributes, may hinder functioning at one or all of these levels.

The relevant question, then, becomes "How can one measure day-to-day functional abilities?" There are a variety of functional assessment scales that are available for use in many settings. The scales vary greatly in depth and scope, and there is currently no common consensus as to which scale is the best scale. Most of these scales are face valid (i.e., how well a test measures what it purports to measure, based solely on "appearances" such as the content of the test's items) (Cohen & Swerdlik, 2002). However, research in this area of assessment is limited (Sachs-Ericsson & Ciarlo, 1992). Furthermore, there is not an established gold standard to define or to assess functioning. That is, we cannot take a scale and measure its validity against some known "truth" of functional assessment. In addition, functioning encompasses a broad range of activities, all of which cannot be covered by a single scale. Therefore, while the areas one wishes to assess may depend on a given client's identified difficulties and goals, there is no guarantee that a scale to measure these specific areas exists.

Given the relationship established between mental health and functioning, it is useful to look at commonly used functional assessment tools, despite the concerns outlined earlier. The most familiar of these scales is the Global Assessment of Functioning Scale (GAF) (Endicott, Spitzer, Fleis, & Cohen, 1976). This scale is included in the *DSM-IV* (American Psychiatric Association, 1994). The GAF is a system used by clinicians to evaluate a client's overall level of functioning with scores ranging from 100 (*superior*) to 1 (*inability to self-care*). The strengths of the scale are that its reliability and validity are adequate and that it is relatively simple to administer (Endicott et al., 1976). However, the assessment of functioning provided by this scale is global and therefore encompasses a wide variety of activities relevant to functioning. Thus, if the individual is rated as having significant problems in functioning, it is unclear where the specific difficulties lie.

Another scale to consider is Colorado Client Assessment Record (CCAR) (Ellis, Wilson, & Foster, 1984). Administering the CCAR at intake and termination is required for all clients receiving treatment in any Colorado facility that uses public health funds. The scale consists of 78 items that are organized hierarchically into nine domains of functioning, including mood, thinking, medical and physical problems, substance use, family living, interpersonal functioning, role performance, social and legal problems, and self-care and basic needs. Generally, the scale's items identify the presence or absence of a problem in one or more areas and also provide an indicator of severity. There is an additional section of the CCAR that allows for the assessment of client resources and strengths.

The reliability and the validity of the CCAR have been shown to be adequate, and scales derived from the checklist items have been shown to have good internal consistency and a coherent factor structure (Barrett, Bartsch, Zahniser, & Belanger, 1998; Ellis, Wackwitz, & Foster, 1991). The state of Colorado maintains a Web site (www.colorado.gov) at which the CCAR materials can be found through the Colorado Department of Human Services. This Web site allows access to the CCAR instrument, manual, and instructions for rating. The CCAR is considered public domain. As with the GAF, the CCAR assesses a wide range of abilities and therefore a more in-depth clinical assessment would be needed to identify specific problem areas.

The last scale we briefly consider is a self-report measure called the Behavior and Symptom Identification Scale (BASIS-32) (Uttaro & Gonzalez, 2002). This scale consists of 32 items designed to assess difficulty in the functioning domains of self-understanding, daily living skills, interpersonal relations, role functioning, impulsivity, and substance abuse. The psychometric properties of the BASIS-32 have been adequately validated by several studies (see Doerfler, Addis, & Moran, 2002, and Uttaro & Gonzalez, 2002). This scale may be helpful in identifying symptoms of mood disturbance, anxiety, suicidality, and psychosis.

Although the information provided by functional assessments is typically broad and nonspecific, the fact that they provide information about global functioning can be a starting point from which to identify impairing mental health concerns. Once general problems are identified, steps can be taken to help the impaired person regain an appropriate level of functioning and return to productivity.

SUMMARY

In this chapter, we have discussed the need for identification of psychopathology in business settings, particularly as it relates to decreases in productivity among employees. We outlined important legal and ethical considerations for testing and assessment of employees. Key considerations included confidentiality and relevance of test content to job performance. We also reviewed three major approaches to assessment and diagnosis. We commented briefly on their basic features, assets, and limitations, and we provided relevant examples of these approaches. Structured clinical interviews, often considered the gold standard of assessment, offer a systematized approach, which increases reliability by reducing room for human error and clinical judgment. Symptom scales offer a more economical approach than do structured interviews and at times even outperform them. Nevertheless, symptom scales are subject to the denial bias and depend heavily on client characteristics, such as memory and insight. Projectives provide a means of avoiding the denial bias yet are plagued by poor psychometric properties. Decisions as to which instruments to use in assessments and what outside professional aid to enlist for such tasks will depend in large part on the resources of a particular company or work environment. Although evaluation may be time-consuming and costly, identifying and treating mental health problems is likely to be helpful in keeping a company running smoothly.

References

American Psychiatric Association. (1994). *Diagnostic and statistical manual of mental disorders* (4th ed.). Washington, DC: Author.

Barrett T. J., Bartsch D. A., Zahniser J. H., & Belanger S. (1998). Implementing and evaluating outcome indicators of performance for mental health agencies. *Journal of Healthcare Quality, 20*(3), 6-13.

Broadhead, W. E., Blazer, D. G., George, L. K., & Tse, C. K. (1990). Depression, disability days, and days lost from work in a prospective epidemiologic survey. *Journal of the American Medical Association, 19,* 2524-2528.

Chapman, L. J., & Chapman, J. P. (1967). Genesis of popular but erroneous psychodiagnostic observations. *Journal of Abnormal Psychology, 72*(3), 193-204.

Ciarlo, J. A., Shern, D. L., Tweed, D. L., & Kilpatrick, L. A. (1992). II: The Colorado social health survey of mental health service needs: Sampling, instrumentation, and major findings. *Evaluation and Program Planning, 15*(2), 133-147.

Cohen, R. J., & Swerdlik, M. E. (2002). *Psychological testing and assessment: An introduction to tests and measurement* (5th ed.). New York: McGraw-Hill Higher Education.

Doerfler, L. A., Addis, M. E., & Moran, P. W. (2002). Evaluating mental health outcomes in an inpatient setting: Convergent and divergent validity of the OQ-45 and BASIS-32. *Journal of Behavioral Health Services and Research, 29,* 394-403.

Ellis, R. H., Wackwitz, J. H., & Foster, M. (1991). Uses of an empirically derived client typology based on level of functioning: Twelve years of the CCAR. *Journal of Mental Health Administration, 18,* 88-100.

Ellis, R. H., Wilson, N. Z., & Foster, F. M. (1984). Statewide treatment outcome assessment in Colorado: The Colorado Client Assessment Record. *Community Mental Health Journal, 20*(1), 72-89.

Endicott, J., Spitzer, R. L., Fleis, J. L., & Cohen, J. (1976). The Global Assessment Scale. A procedure for assessing the overall severity of psychiatric disturbance. *Archives of General Psychiatry, 33,* 766-771.

First, M. B., Gibbon, M., Williams, J. B., & Spitzer, R. L. (1995). *Users manual for the Mini-SCID (for DSM-IV-version 2).* North Tonewanda, NY: Multi-Health Systems/American Psychiatric Association.

First, M. B., Gibbon, M., Williams, J. B., & Spitzer, R. L. (1996). *Users manual for the AutoSCID-II (for DSM-IV).* North Tonewanda, NY: Multi-Health Systems/American Psychiatric Association.

First, M. B., Spitzer, R. L., Gibbon, M., & Williams, J. B. (1995). *Structured Clinical Interview for DSM-IV Axis 1 disorders—Patient edition. (SCID-I/P, Version 2.0).* New York: Biometrics Research Department, New York State Psychiatric Institute.

First, M. B., Spitzer, R. L., Gibbon, M., Williams, J. B. W., & Benjamin, L. (1994). *Structured Clinical Interview for DSM-IV Axis II personality disorders. (SCID-II, Version 2.0).* New York: Biometrics Research Department, New York State Psychiatric Institute.

Frank, L. K. (1939). Projective methods for the study of personality. *Journal of Psychology, 8,* 343-389.

Garb, H. N., Wood, J. M., & Nezworski, M. T. (2000). Projective techniques and the detection of child sexual abuse. *Child Maltreatment: Journal of the American Professional Society on the Abuse of Children, 5*(2), 161-168.

Gough, H. G. (1948). A new dimension of status: I. Development of a personality scale. *American Sociological Review, 13,* 401-409.

Groth-Marnat, G. (1999). *Handbook of psychological assessment* (3rd ed.). New York: Wiley.

Groth-Marnat, G., & Roberts, L. (1998). Human Figure Drawings and House Tree Person drawings as indicators of self-esteem: A quantitative approach. *Journal of Clinical Psychology, 54*(2), 219-222.

Halperin, J. M., & McKay, K. E. (1998). Psychological testing for child and adolescent psychiatrists: A review of the past 10 years. *Journal of the American Academy of Child and Adolescent Psychiatry, 37*(6), 575-584.

Joiner, T., & Pettit, J. (2003). Clinical assessment and diagnosis: Current status and future directions. In M. Roberts & S. Ilardi (Eds.), *Handbook of research methods in clinical psychology* (pp. 284-304). New York: Blackwell.

Kahn, J. P., & Langlieb, A. M. (Eds.) (2003). *Mental health and productivity in the workplace: A handbook for organizations and clinicians.* San Francisco: Jossey-Bass.

Kaplan, R. M., & Saccuzzo, D. P. (1997). *Psychological testing: Principles, applications, and issues* (4th ed.). Pacific Grove, CA: Brooks/Cole.

Kessler, R. C., Greenberg, P. E., Mickelson, K. D., Meneades, L. M., & Want, P. S. (2001). The effects of chronic medical conditions on work loss and work cutback. *Journal of Environmental Medicine, 43,* 218-225.

Nietzel, M. T., Bernstein, D. A., & Milich, R. (1998). *Introduction to clinical psychology* (5th ed.). Englewood Cliffs, NJ: Prentice Hall.

Nisbett, R., & Ross, L. (1980). *Human inference: Strategies and shortcomings of social judgment.* Englewood Cliffs, NJ: Prentice Hall.

Petot, J. (2001). Interest and limitations of projective techniques in the assessment of personality disorders. *European Psychiatry, 15*(Suppl. 1), 11-14.

Rorschach, H. (1942). *Psychodiagnostik* (Hans Huber Verlag, Trans.). Bern: Bircher. (Original work published 1921)

Sachs-Ericsson, N., & Ciarlo, J. (1992). III. Determining "cases" of mental health-related dysfunction from continuous scales of everyday functioning. *Evaluation and Program Planning, 15*(2), 149-164.

Uttaro T., & Gonzales A. (2002). Psychometric properties of the Behavior and Symptom Identification Scale administered in a crisis residential mental health treatment setting. *Psychological Reports, 91,* 439-443.

Wittchen, H., Carter, R. M., Pfister, H., Montgomery, S. A., & Kessler, R. C. (2000). Disabilities and quality of life in pure and comorbid generalized anxiety disorder and major depression in a national survey. *International Clinical Psychopharmacology 15*(6), 319-328.

Wood, J. M., Lilienfeld, S. O., Garb, H. N., & Nezworski, M. T. (2000). The Rorschach test in clinical diagnosis: A critical review, with a backward look at Garfield (1947). *Journal of Clinical Psychology, 56*(3), 395-430.

World Health Organization. (1999). *ICIDH-2: International classification of functioning, disability and health* (beta-2 draft, full version). Geneva, Switzerland: Author.

Part II

Categories of Dysfunction

5

Dual Diagnosis

SETH A. BROWN
University of Northern Iowa

MELANIE E. BENNETT
University of Maryland School of Medicine

INTRODUCTION

S ubstance-use disorders and mental illnesses cause serious and pernicious social, health, economic, and psychiatric consequences for individuals, families, and society. Both sets of disorders often involve debilitating symptoms and negative consequences that profoundly impact life, social, and employment functioning. Over the past two decades, it has become increasingly apparent that many people are affected by both mental illness and substance-use disorders. While individually these disorders convey a range of problems, they generate an even more negative impact on the lives and functioning of individuals when combined.

In this chapter, we describe the unique issues that are relevant to individuals with dual diagnosis for both entrance into and maintenance of employment. First, we discuss challenges in defining and measuring dual diagnosis and review the rates of dual psychiatric and substance-use disorders in community and workplace samples. Second, we discuss the impact of dual diagnosis on workplace functioning. Finally, we review a range of issues related to dual diagnosis in the workplace and provide suggestions for recognizing, treating, and referring these individuals within the context of the employment environment.

ISSUES IN ASSESSING DUAL DIAGNOSIS

The term *dual diagnosis* has been used to describe individuals who meet diagnostic criteria for some Axis I or Axis II mental disorder (or disorders), along with one or more substance-use disorders. The term is somewhat misleading in that many so-called dual diagnosis patients meet diagnostic criteria for more than two disorders (Kessler et al., 1994). That is, individuals with dual diagnosis often experience multiple psychiatric disorders as well as one or more substance-use disorders. Some of the more common diagnostic combinations of dual diagnosis include depression and alcohol dependence, schizophrenia or bipolar disorder with polysubstance abuse or dependence, and major depression and an anxiety disorder along with some substance-use disorder. Because of the many diagnostic combinations, dual diagnosis encompasses a heterogeneous population that has a range of complex and diverse functional limitations and treatment needs.

There are several methodological issues that make it difficult to precisely measure prevalence rates of dual diagnosis in the general population. First, rates of dual diagnosis are affected by the population that is assessed, as well as the setting in which the assessment occurs. Large-scale epidemiological studies provide representative information on rates of dual diagnosis in the general population. Studies of clinical populations, although not representative, provide valuable and detailed information on individuals seeking treatment in clinical settings. Clinical studies generally yield higher rates of dual diagnosis. Second, making comparisons across studies is difficult, as studies use different diagnostic criteria and measures, as well as focus on different substances in their assessments of dual diagnosis. For example, studies typically assess drinking, along with use of a range of illicit drugs including cocaine, heroin, hallucinogens, and stimulants. However, there are other substances that are less frequently assessed, either because they are rarely (e.g., inhalants) or commonly (e.g., nicotine) used in the general population. This is particularly problematic given that these substances can have an important relationship to mental health and functioning. For instance, nicotine use is typically not assessed, even though a growing literature suggests that nicotine dependence has links, perhaps biological in nature, to both major depression and schizophrenia. Third, those people with dual diagnosis often have patterns of symptoms and substance use that change over time. For example, people can cycle through periods of depression or anxiety, as well as change over time in the quantity and frequency of their substance use. As a result, mental health and substance-abuse problems are not static; rather they change over time and can yield different diagnoses. Taken together, factors such as the setting in which the assessment occurs, the types of substances and mental health issues that are assessed, and the changing nature of symptoms and substance-use status confound studies of prevalence rates of dual diagnosis, as well as contribute to the heterogeneity of this population.

These issues also are relevant in estimating rates of dual diagnosis in the workplace. Rates will differ depending on the type of workplace setting in which the assessment takes place and the types of mental health and substance-use issues that are relevant to the particular workforce. For example, estimates that come from a general survey of workers are likely to differ substantially from those taken from workers referred to employee assistance programs (EAPs). In addition, research suggests that there are differences in the prevalence of psychiatric disorders across occupations and that the impact of mental illness may be more or less severe in terms of workdays lost and workplace costs depending on the type of disorder assessed (Kouzis & Eaton, 1994). It is likely that such fluctuations apply to those with dual diagnoses as well. Workers may be uncomfortable disclosing information regarding mental health and substance use, which will affect the validity of the assessments. Finally, the specific disorders and substances assessed are relevant here as well, and more narrowly focused assessments are likely to miss underrepresented or uncommon combinations of dual disorders.

PREVALENCE OF DUAL DIAGNOSIS IN THE GENERAL POPULATION AND WORKPLACE

Despite these methodological challenges, several studies offer good estimates of dual diagnosis prevalence. Two major epidemiological studies have examined rates of dual diagnosis in the general population. The Epidemiologic Catchment Area Study (ECA) (Regier et al., 1990) surveyed more than 20,000 adults in five cities across the United States, both in the community and in institutions. The findings documented high rates of dual diagnosis. For example, respondents with mental illness were more than twice as likely to be diagnosed with an alcohol-use disorder and more than three times as likely to be diagnosed with a drug-use disorder as were those respondents without a mental illness. Substantial rates of dual diagnosis also were found in primary substance abusers, with more than one-third of individuals with an alcohol disorder and more than half of those with a drug-use disorder having a comorbid mental illness. The second major epidemiological study of comorbidity is the National Comorbidity Survey (NCS) (Kessler et al., 1994), which assessed 12-month and lifetime prevalence rates for psychiatric disorders in more than 8,000 noninstitutionalized individuals. Findings of dual diagnosis were similarly striking. Respondents with mental illness had at least twice the risk of lifetime alcohol- or drug-use disorder, with even greater risk for individuals with certain types of mental illnesses. In addition, the majority of respondents with an alcohol- or drug-use disorder had a history of some psychiatric disorder that was not related to substance abuse.

While we have good information on rates of dual diagnosis in the general population, it is unclear if general population rates are directly applicable to the workplace. There are few studies that assess rates of dual diagnosis specifically among people who are employed. Given the extent of difficulties often suffered by those with dual diagnosis (particularly those with more severe mental illnesses), many do not work. However, it appears that the number of individuals with less severe forms of mental illness (e.g., major depression, anxiety disorders) that are comorbid with substance-use disorders are common and therefore well represented in workplace settings. Kessler and Frank (1997) examined the relationship between psychiatric disorders and work impairment in 4,091 employed respondents in the NCS. Overall, 18.2 percent of the employed NCS participants reported one or more psychiatric disorders in the past 30 days, with 3.7 percent meeting diagnostic criteria in two or more of the domains assessed. Specifically, 0.9 percent of the sample met criteria for a combination of anxiety and substance-use disorders, 0.2 percent met for both affective and substance-use disorders, and 0.5 percent met diagnostic criteria for all three types of disorders (anxiety-affective-substance use). These percentages show that a significant group of workers is affected by dual diagnoses and that depression, anxiety, and substance-use disorders are all represented in this population. Importantly, even small percentages translate into large numbers of affected individuals nationwide, as well as millions of work-loss days and cutback days (days in which the respondent felt unable to perform his or her normal activities while on the job). Overall, Kessler and Frank estimate that comorbid anxiety, affective, and substance use disorders (involving at least one disorder from each category) translates into many millions of days or lost work and decreased productivity per year nationally.

Bromet and colleagues (1990) examined prevalence rates of comorbid depression and alcohol-use disorders in a sample of 1,870 managers and professional staff working at a large U.S. corporation. Overall, men showed a 22.9 percent lifetime rate of depression and a 10.5 percent lifetime rate of alcohol-use disorders. Women showed a 36.0 percent lifetime rate of depression and a 5.1 percent lifetime rate of alcohol-use disorders. Rates of comorbidity of the two disorders were substantial, as evidenced by the fact that 17.7 percent of men and 7.1 percent of women who met criteria for major depression also met criteria for an alcohol-use disorder. Conversely, 38.4 percent of men and 50.0 percent of women who met criteria for an alcohol-use disorder also met criteria for major depression. Moreover, among men, the risk of having an alcohol-use disorder was twice as great if depression also was present (Bromet et al., 1990). Such findings show not only that comorbid mental and substance-use disorders are present in the workplace but also that one disorder may serve as an important risk factor for the occurrence of the other disorder.

IMPACT OF DUAL DIAGNOSIS ON WORKPLACE FUNCTIONING

Individuals with dual diagnosis experience a range of serious and negative consequences in most if not all areas of life functioning. Studies from many countries show that patients with dual diagnosis exhibit greater symptoms of mental illness, more frequent hospitalizations, more frequent relapses, and a poorer course of illness than patients with a single diagnosis. In addition to psychiatric symptoms, dual diagnosis patients exhibit poorer life functioning, higher rates of violence and suicide, less social stability, more use of welfare resources, lower life satisfaction, more legal involvement, greater rates of homelessness, and higher health care costs (Bennett & Barnett, in press).

Not surprisingly, there also are consequences of dual diagnosis on employment. Substance abuse on its own creates a range of negative consequences that affect work performance, including greater sickness absences from work, impaired performance, and greater safety risk and hazards due to both drug intoxication and withdrawal. In addition, work problems stem from the immediate and long-term effects of alcohol and drugs, such as deficits in perceptual and motor skills, attention, learning and memory, decision making, and abstract reasoning (Laitinen-Krispijn & Bijl, 2000). Even after a period of abstinence, vocational problems continue among those recovering from alcohol-use disorders (Brown & Saura, 1996). Similarly, mental illness has detrimental effects on workplace performance. Depressed individuals have been found to be absent from work because of health problems twice as often as those who are not depressed, and when these employees do present for work, their performance often is poor (Druss, Schlesinger, & Harris, 2001; Laitinen-Krispijn & Bijl, 2000). Those with mental illness report a greater number of days of work performance as difficult and below expectations when compared with those without mental health problems (Dewa & Lin, 2000).

Although the literature on dual diagnosis in the workplace is small, it is clear that the difficulties encountered with either substance-use or mental health disorders alone are compounded when both problems exist within the same individual. Overall, such studies find that individuals with dual diagnosis suffer in terms of work functioning. For example, substance abusers who report significant depression also report a greater percentage of workdays missed than do those people with only substance-abuse disorders (Donohue, Acierno, & Kogan, 1996). Newman and colleagues (1996) examined the impact of different types of dual disorders (including but not limited to dual substance-abuse–psychiatric disorder combinations) on life functioning in a large sample of young adults. Multiple disorder cases showed poorer functioning than single disordered cases in many domains relevant to work functioning, including greater employment problems, more months disabled because of psychiatric illness, less social stability, more residence changes, and greater use of welfare for support. Similarly, in their longitudinal analysis of the occurrence and impact of psychiatric and substance-use disorders in young adults, Wittchen, Nelson, and Lachner (1998) found that dual disorders were related to greater reductions in work productivity, including both self-reported disability in work or school activities and missed days of work. Dewa and Lin (2000) examined data from more than 4,000 employed adults in Canada who represented a range of job types. Results showed that those with recent (30-day) comorbid psychiatric disorders (including but not limited to substance-abuse–psychiatric disorder combinations) showed greater days of "partial disability," defined as days in which an individual came to work but was unable to function in a fully normal capacity while on the job, as well as "extra effort" days, defined as being able to function normally only with "extreme effort." Such studies illustrate the extent and type of work difficulties experienced by those with dual disorders.

The negative impact of dual diagnosis on the workplace also is supported by epidemiological research. In their analysis of NCS data, Kessler and Frank (1997) examined information about work-loss days and work cutback days. Individuals with a single diagnosis had more than five times more work-loss days and six times more diminished performance days than did those without a disorder. Those with dual diagnosis fared even worse, with twenty-five times more lost workdays and more than 30 times more poor performance days than those without a disorder. Kessler and Frank (1997) estimated that these percentages translate into more than 15 million work-loss days and 110 million work cutback days for people with two or more psychiatric disorders. Clearly, comorbidity in general, and dual diagnosis of psychiatric and substance-use disorders in particular, yields greater work consequences than does one disorder alone. Moreover, such numbers reflect the fact that a small percentage of those who are employed (3.7 percent in the NCS data) represent a significant number of workdays lost and the resulting costs of missed days of work. This trend is consistent with findings on the treatment costs of dual diagnosis: individuals with dual diagnosis show greater rates of service use and cost of health care than do those with either mental illness or substance-use disorders alone.

Finally, Spak, Hensing, and Allebeck (1998) examined ten years of sick leave insurance records from female Swedish workers in the general population and compared the annual number of sick days and the duration of sick leave episodes among those without a disorder, those with alcohol dependence only, those with mental illness only, and those with mental illness and alcohol dependence. Using the no-disorder group as a reference, the single diagnosis groups used approximately two times more sick days, while the dual diagnosis group used more than three times more sick days. Moreover, dual diagnosis workers had a significantly higher incidence of sick leave episodes as well as a longer duration of sick leave episodes than all of the other groups. That is, women with dual diagnosis have more occasions of sick leave and are out of work for longer periods of time during each occasion than are those without a disorder or with a single disorder (Spak et al., 1998).

ISSUES RELATED TO DUAL DIAGNOSIS IN THE WORKPLACE

Prevalence of dual diagnosis, and the negative consequences that result from it, have clear implications for employers and workers. There are a number of issues related to dual diagnosis in the workplace that must be considered for employers, vocational counselors, employee assistance professionals, counselors, and others to be able to effectively identify, treat, and refer dual diagnosis individuals. There has been limited research in this area, with the majority conducted with patients with severe mental illness and substance-use disorders, a population that is typically less widely employed. However, the issues identified with this population are more broadly applicable to those with other forms of dual diagnosis, and they have implications for those who are represented in the workforce.

Benefits of Employment for Individuals with Dual Diagnosis

Employment has numerous benefits for individuals with dual diagnosis. Work helps to improve personal finances, as well as reduce taxpayer burden (e.g., reduced welfare benefits, increased tax base). Importantly, work has benefits beyond the economic ones for those with dual disorders. Studies have shown that employment is related to reductions in psychiatric hospitalization and symptomatology in patients with severe mental illness and substance-abuse disorders, as well as improvements in quality of life and increased feelings of self-esteem in these individuals (Blankertz, McKay, & Robinson, 1998; Drake, McHugo, Becker, Anthony, & Clark, 1996). In their review of work as a rehabilitative tool for individuals with dual diagnosis, Blankertz and colleagues (1998) outlined several benefits of work for this population. These benefits include providing structure and a venue for meeting and socializing with peers who are not substance-using and getting the patient involved in alternate activities that prevent the boredom that often is associated with substance use, as well as providing distraction from activities that are involved in attaining drugs. The social component of work is an important one. Individuals with dual disorders, especially those with severe mental illness, often have difficulty meeting new people who do not use substances and socializing in a substance-free environment. In addition, work can provide a valuable contingency for use in treatment and rehabilitation and serve as a reinforcer for an individual's continued participation in treatment for or abstinence from substance use. Similarly, in a review of the vocational rehabilitation needs of those with severe mental illness and substance-use disorders, Brown and Saura (1996) suggested that a structured workplace provides a healthy environment in which to practice newly learned skills that support abstinence and that work can serve as a setting that is conducive to continued progress and, as such, limits relapse. Overall, there are real and important economic, social, and therapeutic benefits from work for those with dual disorders.

Risks of Employment for Individuals with Dual Diagnosis

Despite notable benefits, potential hazards of employment exist for individuals with dual diagnosis. These include the potential for contact with substance-using co-workers, money as a cue to purchasing alcohol and drugs, and drops in self-esteem because of work loss (Blankertz et al., 1998). On-the-job issues, such as getting to and from work on time, performing the daily tasks associated with one's job, and interacting with co-workers and bosses can be an additional source of stress for those with dual disorders. Another stressor is the struggle to cope with the disruptive symptoms of mental illness and substance-use disorders while on the job, such as getting to work when feeling depressed, performing job responsibilities while suffering from symptoms of mental illness, having a craving while at work, and interacting appropriately with others in the workplace. Moreover, the iatrogenic effects of treatment (e.g., medication side effects, missed work time because of treatment) can make work adjustment even more difficult and contribute to greater stress.

Employer Challenges

From an administrative perspective, individuals with dual diagnosis can be challenging. The many and complex problems that these individuals face can impact their commitment to and performance on the job and often are too much for supervisors or workplace resources to handle. Importantly, the impact of dual disorders on an individual's work performance may in some cases be subtle. In their examination of the impact of mental health problems on work performance, Dewa and Lin (2000) found that the workers with comorbid conditions often made it to work, but once there they either were less able to fully perform their job duties or were able to function only with extreme effort. Such a pattern may make it much more difficult for employers to identify employees who are struggling because of mental illness and substance abuse. Once identified, it is unclear how work goals will fit with short-term treatment goals. That is, will an individual with dual diagnosis require a period of time off from work to pursue treatment? Or should an employer hold a job for an individual who might need a prolonged period of treatment?

RECOMMENDATIONS FOR ASSESSMENT, INTERVENTION, AND REFERRAL

Intervening with dually diagnosed individuals and addressing the impact of these problems in the workplace present challenges to a system that has been designed to consider these issues separately. In the United States, substance abuse and mental illness historically have been viewed as separate problems, and the service systems designed to address these disorders developed relatively independently (see Grella, 1996, for a review). The mental health system has traditionally focused on the use of medications and treatment delivered by medical professionals, an approach that has excluded some issues deemed important by the substance-abuse treatment community, including addressing spiritual factors in treatment, using self-help groups in recovery, and using medication-free approaches to treatment. Moreover, employment has, until recently, largely been considered an issue to be addressed once formal treatment has ended or as a part of discharge planning. As a result, many counselors specialize in either substance abuse or mental illness, often receive no formal training outside their specific area of expertise, and frequently know very little about employment-related issues for this population. For example, one survey of mental health and vocational rehabilitation counselors working with mentally ill patients found that there were significant training needs in the areas of vocational assessment, job development strategies, and employment-retention strategies (Shafer, Pardee, & Stewart, 1999). Thus, many settings are poorly equipped to treat, or they refuse to treat, the sizeable number of patients with both mental health and substance-use disorders. Overall, our lack of knowledge and training about dual diagnosis means that employment settings often are left with little to guide them when faced with the complex problems that these individuals often bring to the workplace.

Given the challenges outlined, it is necessary for workplace administrators and health care professionals to have some background in recognizing individuals with dual diagnosis in employment settings and in assessing and intervening with these individuals. In addition, professionals need to understand when a referral is necessary and what types of referrals yield timely and effective benefit.

Identification and Assessment of Dual Disorders

Identification of dual disorders in the workplace presents a number of employee- and employer-related challenges. Many employees will not voluntarily seek out screening for mental health and substance-use disorders, because of the negative repercussions surrounding the positive identification of either, especially the loss of employment. Such concerns are particularly relevant to occupations where public safety issues are paramount (e.g., air traffic controller), as well as to agencies with "zero tolerance" policies. The stigma of substance-abuse disorders and mental health problems is also an issue. Employees may fear that others in the workplace will learn of their problems, which could lead to their embarrassment and to ridicule from their co-workers. In addition, supervisors may assign less responsibility to those with dual diagnosis, as well as pass them over for promotion. Employers may be concerned about violent or bizarre behaviors, recurrence of illness, and inability to deal with work pressures among workers with psychiatric disorders, issues that would be compounded for workers with multiple problems. Importantly, mandatory identification of substance-abuse and mental health disorders can be viewed as intrusive and lead to lower morale among the entire workforce.

Despite these issues, identification of dual disorders in the workplace is important. The workplace may be one of the first places where individuals with dual diagnoses experience difficulties, and as such may be a point of early identification of problems. That is, some of the first signs of trouble for an individual may be decreased work performance, unreliability at work, or absence from work, and such signs can be used in the early recognition and treatment of comorbid substance-abuse disorders and mental illness. Importantly, safety—for the employee, others in the workplace, and others in the community—is a crucial reason for involvement of employers in identification of these problems. Employees who are suffering from substance-abuse disorders and mental health problems may not be up to performing their job tasks reliably and safely (e.g., issues that are central to highly skilled occupations as well as those that involve provision of health or other social services).

Given the impact of dual diagnosis in the workplace, employment settings should be proactive yet supportive when identifying those persons with dual diagnoses. First, an agency must strive to minimize the negative consequences of the identification of dual disorders on employees' job security and stability. This would not only encourage employees to voluntarily seek out treatment for dual diagnosis but also contribute to better recovery from both sets of problems. Second, personnel who deal with employee problems and concerns should have some basic knowledge of the symptoms of substance-abuse disorders and mental illness, as well as some background in talking to employees about these issues. Employees will feel more comfortable talking to someone who is trained to understand mental health and substance-use problems and to communicate empathically about them. This includes providing an atmosphere that is nonjudgmental in which an employee can talk freely about his or her symptoms without fear of job-related repercussions. Third, for safety-relevant occupations, an agency can consider a system of proactive identification. Substance-abuse screening can be conducted through routine random testing of all employees. Additional methods, including psychological testing, screening interviews, and informant interviews (e.g., family members, co-workers), can be used to identify both substance-abuse disorders and mental health problems. Identification of individuals must be performed with skill and must minimize the costs associated with being identified as having dual disorders.

There are a number of brief questions and measures that can be used to identify substance-abuse disorders and mental health problems. For both, probably the quickest and easiest way to get information about dual disorders is to simply and without judgment ask individuals about them. Such questioning can take the form of inquiring more generally about a person's health; revealing that some in the workplace have noticed the individual to be looking stressed, unwell, or both; and conveying an attitude of caring and concern when asking what is troubling them. More objectively, brief screening instruments such as the Michigan Alcoholism Screening Test, the Drug Abuse Screening Test, and the Symptom Checklist assess a range of symptoms of substance abuse or mental illness in a short amount of time (see Allen & Columbus, 1995, for a review). Whether using interview or questionnaire methods, keeping employee information confidential and assuring employees of this confidentiality is important in securing accurate information from employees on these sensitive issues.

Employer-Provided Intervention

Appropriate treatment must be obtained following identification of those with dual diagnosis. Despite the complexities of this population, there is much that can be done. In recent years, knowledge about the biological and psychosocial factors involved in mental illness and substance-use disorders has emerged. As a result, effective psychosocial and pharmacological treatments, which go beyond symptom management, have been developed. That is, there are now treatment options for many of the common disorders seen in the workplace, including depression, anxiety disorders, and substance-use disorders. Treatment can involve medication, cognitive and behavioral interventions, group treatments, self-help groups, and combinations of these to yield comprehensive programs that are tailored to the needs, preferences, and lifestyles of individuals. Having a range of treatment options, and involving individuals in the selection of interventions, can be beneficial in motivating and helping people achieve social and vocational goals.

While there is good reason to be optimistic about treating those with dual diagnoses, there are many challenges. The first concerns determining which treatment setting is most appropriate. Treatment may use an agency's internal resources or involve referral to an external provider. Many companies have EAPs or other counseling services that are designed to help employees with substance-abuse disorders, mental health problems, or both in order to contain the impact that these problems have on work performance. Typically EAPs and internal counseling departments are equipped to deal with employees whose problems are not severe, especially those employees who are just beginning to show signs of difficulty. The benefit of such in-house facilities is that they can quickly respond to the first signs of trouble, and participation and follow-through on recommendations can be linked to continued employment.

In-house departments often are small and as such are limited in the services they can provide, with individual counseling as the primary mode of treatment. However, there are many strategies that can be used to great effect in such a setting, especially when used with individuals who show less severe problems or problems that are short in duration. Importantly, there is much that is known about effective treatments for alcohol problems and mental health problems that can be used with individuals with dual diagnosis in workplace counseling settings. For example, research documents the effectiveness of motivational interviewing (MI), an intervention that incorporates collaboration with clients and attention to client motivation (Miller & Rollnick, 1991). MI is nonconfrontational and directive, and it involves providing clear feedback and advice along with negotiating goals and problem solving to overcome barriers to treatment. MI combines the therapeutic elements that have been found to be successful components of brief interventions for substance abuse, including giving clear advice and feedback, using an empathic counseling style, and addressing barriers to treatment. Cognitive-behavioral interventions, including cognitive-behavioral therapy for depression, relapse prevention for substance abuse, behavioral treatment for panic and other anxiety disorders, and different forms of skills training for depression and substance abuse have all shown effectiveness with some of the most common comorbid disorders (see Nathan & Gorman, 2002, for a review). These strategies can be used on an individual basis and are important tools for those in EAPs or counseling department settings with counselors who have received appropriate training.

Importantly, there are ethical issues that arise in regard to the provision of dual diagnosis treatment in the workplace. The most pressing issue is confidentiality. EAPs and counseling departments must be clear in terms of what information is kept strictly confidential from supervisors and what, if any, is to be shared with others in the workplace. For example, documenting and reporting current levels of substance use or psychiatric symptoms not only may be stigmatizing but may affect job status as well.

Referral to Treatment in the Community

General Treatment Issues

While EAPs and other counseling departments have distinct benefits, most are not equipped to treat employees with severe or long-standing dual disorders, and often the professionals involved in such programs lack training in both substance abuse and mental illness. Given the complexities inherent to dual diagnosis, referral to other treatment providers often is necessary. Many variables affect the type of referral that is made, including the severity of the problems and the types of disorders the individual is experiencing, the types of services available in the community, who is paying for treatment, and the individual's readiness to change.

First, problem severity and type of disorder are relevant considerations when making a referral for an employee with dual disorders. Issues in problem severity include the length of time the individual has been experiencing symptoms, the nature of the symptoms, the degree to which substance abuse has affected the person's functioning across life domains, and the personal resources the individual has at his or her disposal to aid in treatment. For example, referral to inpatient treatment or more intensive outpatient treatment may be warranted for a person who has been highly symptomatic for weeks or months, has been drinking or using drugs frequently or daily and has tried unsuccessfully to cut down or stop, has suicidal or violent behavior, or has been experiencing a deterioration in functioning not only at work but also in many other domains of functioning. Type of disorder also is relevant here. Those with more severe forms of mental illness including schizophrenia and bipolar disorder may require hospitalization to begin or to readjust medications; those who are suicidal may need hospitalization to protect themselves from harm; those with more moderate forms of depression or anxiety may benefit from regular outpatient contact; others requiring detoxification from alcohol or drugs may need medical hospitalization. An employee's personal resources also make a difference. Those with spouses, concerned significant others, or other strong social supports can benefit from the involvement of these people in the treatment process, either directly with family or marital therapy or indirectly with the provision of so-called tangible supports such as financial help, transportation to treatment, and assistance with any other difficulties.

Second, availability of services that address both substance abuse and mental illness can be scarce in many communities, especially for those with limited funds or without insurance. Commonly, one will be able to find specialists in either mental health disorders or substance-use disorders, and these services are typically found in medical hospitals, substance-abuse treatment centers, or community mental health centers. In addition, vocational rehabilitation agencies, designed to address employment among those with substance-abuse disorders and severe mental illness who have not been in the workforce, are increasingly entering the mix of service providers in an attempt to get these patients trained for and involved in different forms of employment. While all of these types of services are relevant and have benefits to offer those with dual disorders, each was designed to address its own area and typically have staff who are specialized to treat one domain but not all three. It is more difficult, but necessary for those with dual diagnosis, to find treatment that addresses both sets of problems and integrates treatment for both disorders into a comprehensive program. Moreover, program requirements can be too difficult for many people with dual diagnosis to meet, presenting an added barrier to intervention. For example, many mental health and substance-abuse treatment programs require a period of abstinence or symptom remission before providing service, as well as requiring continued abstinence or remission as a condition for remaining in the program—a criterion that may be too difficult for some people with dual diagnosis to meet. Grella and Hser (1997) surveyed 45 drug treatment programs in Los Angeles County and found that most restricted admissions of dual disorder patients. Moreover, almost half believed that such patients were not well served within the county drug treatment system. The paradox of this problem is that it denies treatment to a large percentage of patients who may be those most in need of treatment.

Given the links between substance abuse and mental illness, integrated treatment that addresses both sets of problems in the same facility is recommended, especially for those with more severe forms of mental illness. There is evidence that, when appropriately structured, comprehensive programs can benefit workers and employers alike. Meisler, Blankertz, Santos, and McKay (1997) described an intensive interdisciplinary program designed for individuals with dual diagnosis (substance-use disorders and severe mental illness) that involves monitoring medication closely, acquiring basic living needs, training and reinforcing skills, providing support in coping, and minimizing stress levels. Outcomes showed that those with dual diagnoses exhibited similar levels of employment as those with only one diagnosis. Such findings illustrate that when an intervention is tailored to the needs of this population, those with dual diagnoses can achieve important vocational goals.

Comprehensive treatment for dual disorders is also highly relevant to those with less severe forms of mental illness. For example, a person needing treatment for both alcohol dependence and depression may be less likely to get adequate treatment if he or she has to go to different places and work with different professionals to address both issues. Rather, people may be more likely to get treatment for both disorders if their treatment is integrated—if it occurs in one setting, with treatment professionals who know about both sets of problems and work together to treat them, and who regularly work together and communicate about the individual's treatment and progress. For example, the ability to go to one treatment center to receive medication and behavioral treatment for depression, along with treatment for substance abuse, would simplify the structure of treatment and facilitate communication among the different treatment providers involved in the individual's care.

Third, source of payment for treatment is an issue that affects the availability of services and the confidentiality of that treatment from the employer. Treatment for dual diagnosis can be costly, depending on the types of services needed, and issues related to employer payment or use of health insurance or public funds must be worked out. It is important to remember that although treatment may be costly, an employee who is successfully treated will likely show increases in work attendance and performance that will more than make up for treatment costs. Importantly, the extent of information (if any) to be communicated back to the employer must be clearly delineated prior to the start of treatment. In the circumstances where the employer is more involved in paying for treatment, confidentiality becomes more complicated. The converse is a situation in which the employee independently seeks and pays for treatment, which results in fewer attachments to the work setting.

Fourth, it is important to determine where the individual is in terms of unhappiness with his or her current situation, desire for treatment, and motivation to change. People do not come to the process of treatment in the same place. A useful model for thinking about motivation for change is the Stages of Change model of Prochaska and DiClemente (1992). The idea guiding the model is that people come to treatment at different stages of motivation for change, with many being opposed to or ambivalent about change. Precontemplators are not considering change and often come to treatment because of coercion (by work, the legal system, or a relative). Contemplators are considering change but remain ambivalent. Those in the action stage are ready to engage in attempts to change, and individuals in the maintenance stage are focused on sustaining change. During this process, many clients will relapse to an earlier stage. It is important to determine where a particular individual is in his or her motivation to change, and those with dual disorders may be at different levels of readiness to change depending on the disorder, or not be ready to change either problem area. For example, the employee suffering from both depression and alcohol dependence may be able to acknowledge the depression but not consider the drinking an important treatment issue. Others may be more comfortable recognizing and addressing substance abuse than mental illness. In contrast, precontemplators may not recognize either area as a problem and need interventions to get them motivated to change. The employer can be useful in this regard, in that problems in workplace performance can be used to persuade someone into treatment. Once there, the therapist must work to create doubt and concern, to help the precontemplator learn how substance abuse and mental illness are affecting him or her, and to show what might happen if he or she continues as is. It is important to consider the individual's assessment of the situation and to start where the person is in terms of motivation for treatment. If an employee wants to start by getting treatment for depression, then a referral and subsequent treatment can begin by addressing the depression and using the mental illness as an entryway to comprehensive treatment for both substance abuse and mental illness. If an employee believes that he or she is not in need of treatment, exploring the work situation and problems in other areas of life in an empathic and nonjudgmental way may allow for an acknowledgment of some current difficulties.

Recommendations for Those with Dual Substance Abuse and Severe Mental Illness

People with dual substance-abuse problems and severe mental illness experience unique difficulties in their attempts to seek and maintain employment, including severe symptoms, cognitive impairment, social difficulties, and often a lack of experience in the workplace. As discussed earlier, comprehensive and integrated treatment is recommended for patients with substance-abuse disorders and severe mental illness. In addition to comprehensive programs, Blankertz and colleagues (1998) offered several recommendations that modify treatment for this group of individuals with dual diagnosis. Given the difficulties in establishing rapport and trust, the individual should receive some type of immediate benefit, such as quick resolution of a small problem, in order to get the patient engaged in and trusting of intervention. Treatment should be specifically tailored to address the severity of substance use and the amount of substance use in the work environment. The negative effects of substances in individuals with severe mental illness may be present even at use levels that may not be problematic in the general population, illustrating the need to carefully assess the nature of substance use and abuse for each individual. In addition, case management may be needed. Individuals with dual substance-abuse problems and severe mental illness bring to treatment a range of problems that require both short- and long-term intervention. Importantly, treatment must also accommodate the cognitive deficits that are often seen in people with dual substance-abuse problems and severe mental illness (Blankertz et al., 1998). Individuals must be taught about their psychiatric disorder, medications, and how substance abuse interacts with both. Adequate understanding of these issues may help in developing realistic treatment goals. Advantages of working and disadvantages of not working should be frequently reviewed to help individuals keep sight of their progress. Importantly, those who are new to the workforce must be taught about money management, pay schedules, and strategies for holding onto one's money. Some who have never received a paycheck may spend all of the money at once, resulting in negative feelings that can impact their work performance or feelings toward employment.

SUMMARY

Professionals in the workplace need some knowledge of how to address substance-use and mental health disorders in the workplace. Currently we can say with certainty that dual diagnosis is common in the general population, which means that there are a fair number of individuals with dual disorders in the workplace. We also know that dual diagnosis impacts the workplace in many ways, most notably in work absences and substandard work performance by affected individuals. More indirectly, workers suffering from dual disorders experience many and varied negative consequences that impact their overall functioning, which must be of great concern to employers as well. Importantly, working provides clear benefits for these individuals, and employers have an interest in keeping trained and experienced employees and assisting them with their difficulties. The workplace can also be helpful in terms of the identification of individuals experiencing problems from dual disorders, and continued employment can serve as an important motivator and reward for engaging in treatment.

There are several steps for research and practice in this area. First, research must study the workplace to improve prevalence estimates of dual diagnosis, and studies must also examine what happens to these employees as their symptoms become increasingly severe. Outcome studies of in-house versus community treatment are needed to determine what the best treatment options are for which types of dual disorders. In addition, clinicians both within the workplace and out in the community require better training in issues related to dual disorders, as well as in placing work and vocational functioning as high among treatment priorities. Improving the links among substance abuse, mental health, and vocational interventions will help in treating these complex and recurring problems.

References

Allen, J. P., & Columbus, M. (Eds.). (1995). *Assessing alcohol problems: A guide for clinicians and researchers* (National Institute on Alcohol Abuse and Alcoholism Treatment Handbook Series 4, NIH Publication No. 95-3745).Bethesda, MD: National Institute of Health.

Bennett, M. E., & Barnett, B. (in press). Adult psychopathology and diagnosis: Dual-diagnosis. In M. Hersen & S. M. Turner (Eds.), *Adult psychopathology and diagnosis* (4th ed.). New York: John Wiley.

Blankertz, L., McKay, C., & Robinson, S. (1998). Work as a rehabilitative tool for individuals with dual diagnoses. *Journal of Vocational Rehabilitation, 11,* 113-123.

Bromet, E. J., Parkinson, D. K., Curtis, E. C., Schulberg, H. C., Blane, H., Dunn, L. O., Phelan, J., Dew, M. A., & Schwartz, J. E. (1990). Epidemiology of depression and alcohol abuse/dependence in a managerial and professional work force. *Journal of Occupational Medicine, 32,* 989-995.

Brown, A. L., & Saura, K. M. (1996). Vocational rehabilitation needs of individuals with dually diagnosed with with substance abuse and chronic mental illness. *Journal of Applied Rehabilitation Counseling, 27,* 3-10.

Dewa, C. S., & Lin, E. (2000). Chronic physical illness, psychiatric disorder, and disability in the workplace. *Social Science and Medicine, 51,* 41-50.

Donohue, B., Acierno, R., & Kogan, E. (1996). Relationship of depression with measures of social functioning in adult drug abusers. *Addictive Behaviors, 21*(2), 211-216.

Drake, R. E., McHugo, G. J., Becker, D. R., Anthony, W. A., & Clark, R. E. (1996). The New Hampshire study of supported employment for people with severe mental illness. *Journal of Consulting and Clinical Psychology, 64,* 391-399.

Druss, B. G., Schlesinger, M., & Harris, A. M. (2001). Depressive symptoms, satisfaction with health care, and 2-year work outcomes in an employed population. *American Journal of Psychiatry, 158,* 731-734.

Grella, C. E. (1996). Background and overview of mental health and substance abuse treatment systems: Meeting the needs of women who are pregnant or parenting. *Journal of Psychoactive Drugs, 28*(4), 319-343.

Grella, C. E., & Hser, Y. (1997). A county survey of mental health services in drug treatment programs. *Psychiatric Services, 48*(7), 950-952.

Kessler, R. C., & Frank, R. G. (1997). The impact of psychiatric disorders on work loss days. *Psychological Medicine, 27,* 861-873.

Kessler, R. C., McGonagle, K. A., Zhao, S., Nelson, C. B., Hughes, M., Eshleman, S., Wittchen, H., & Kendler, K. S. (1994). Lifetime and 12-month prevalence of *DSM-III-R* psychiatric disorders in the United States. *Archives of General Psychiatry, 51,* 8-19.

Kouzis, A. C., & Eaton, W. W. (1994). Emotional disability days: Prevalence and predictors. *American Journal of Public Health, 84,* 1304-1307.

Laitinen-Krispijn, S., & Bijl, R. V. (2000). Mental disorders and employee sickness absence: The NEMESIS study. *Social Psychiatry and Psychiatric Epidemiology, 35,* 71-77.

Meisler, N., Blankertz, L., Santos, A. B., & McKay, C. (1997). Impact of assertive community treatment on homeless persons with co-occuring severe psychiatric and substance use disorders. *Community Mental Health Journal, 33,* 113-122.

Miller, W. R., & Rollnick, S. (1991). *Motivational interviewing: Preparing people to change addictive behaviors.* New York: Guilford.

Nathan, P. E., & Gorman, J. M. (2002). *A guide to treatments that work* (2nd ed.). New York: Oxford University Press.

Newman, D. L., Moffitt, T. E., Caspi, A., Magdol, L., Silva, P. A., & Stanton, W. R. (1996). Psychiatric disorder in a birth cohort of young adults: Prevalence, comorbidity, clinical significance, and new case incidence from ages 11 to 21. *Journal of Consulting and Clinical Psychology, 64,* 552-562.

Prochaska, J. O., & DiClemente, C. C. (1992). Stages of change in the modification of problem behaviors. In M. Hersen, R. M. Eisler, & P. M. Miller (Eds.), *Progress in behavior modification* (Vol. 28). Sycamore, IL: Sycamore Publishing.

Regier, D. A., Farmer, M. E., Rae, D. S., Locke, B. Z., Keither, S. J., Judd, L. L., & Goodwin, F. K. (1990). Comorbidity of mental disorders with alcohol and other drug abuse. *Journal of the American Medical Association, 264,* 2511-2518.

Shafer, M. S., Pardee, R., & Stewart, M. (1999). An assessment of the training needs of rehabilitation and community mental health workers in a six-state region. *Psychiatric Rehabilitation Journal, 23*(2), 161-169.

Spak, F., Hensing, G., & Allebeck, P. (1998). Sick-leave in women with alcohol dependence or abuse: Effects of additional psychiatric disorders. *Social Psychiatry and Psychiatric Epidemiology, 33,* 613-619.

Wittchen, H. U., Nelson, C. B., & Lachner, G. (1998). Prevalence of mental disorders and psychosocial impairments in adolescents and young adults. *Psychological Medicine, 28,* 109-126.

6

Substance Abuse

MARILYN J. STRADA
BRAD C. DONOHUE
University of Nevada, Las Vegas

DESCRIPTION OF THE DISORDER AND WORKPLACE MANIFESTATIONS

*A*ffecting nearly 125 million individuals (Substance Abuse and Mental Health Services Administration, [SAMHSA, 2002]), substance abuse is associated with increased mortality rates, detriments to physical and mental health, social conflicts, and legal and economic problems (Ames, 1993). Health care expenses, accidents, crime, and decreased productivity resulting from alcohol and illicit drug abuse are estimated to exceed $245 billion annually (Harwood, Fountain, Livermore, & the Lewin Group, 1998). Given that most individuals abusing substances are employed, a large portion of this cost is attributed to workplace-related losses (Ames, 1993). Consequently, awareness and concern about the presence of substance abuse in the workplace has increased substantially during the past few decades. This chapter presents an overview of substance disorders within the workplace context, including their clinical presentation, identification, methods of referral, and intervention approaches.

Workplace manifestations of substance abuse involve use of mind-altering substances within two hours prior to beginning work, or during the course of work-related activities (Ames, 1993). In contrast, the *Diagnostic and Statistical Manual of Mental Disorders IV-TR (DSM-IV-TR)* (American Psychiatric Association [APA], 2000) distinguishes between substance abuse and dependence according to the severity of the condition. Substance abuse requires the presence of significant problems associated with repeated use of the substance, legal problems due to substance use, continued use despite adverse consequences related to its use (e.g., frequent absenteeism at work), or substance use in dangerous situations (e.g., intoxicated while working with heavy machinery) within a 12-month period. Substance dependence, on the other hand, implies psychological or physical addiction, or both, to a substance.

A diagnosis of substance dependence is made when three or more of the following criteria are met within the same 12-month period: (1) tolerance (i.e., dosage must be increased with continued use to achieve the same effects that were obtained initially); (2) withdrawal (i.e., substance-specific reactions resulting from the abrupt cessation of the substance, such as trembling, headaches, nausea, perspiration, irritability); (3) failure to cut down or control substance use despite efforts or desire to do so; (4) desire and/or unsuccessful efforts to reduce substance use; (5) significant amounts of time devoted to obtaining and/or using the substances and/or recovering from substance use; (6) substance use leads to absence of or decrease in social, occupational, or recreational activities; and (7) continued use despite awareness of how substance use contributes to physical or psychological problems (APA, 2000).

The signs of intoxication vary depending on the type of substance. For instance, depressants (e.g., alcohol, Valium, Xanax, phenobarbital) reduce activity in the central nervous system (CNS), causing body functions to slow down. Individuals who demonstrate intoxication due to CNS depressants often slur their speech, stagger, demonstrate poor coordination, and experience difficulties with attention, memory, and judgment. Other symptoms specific to alcohol, the most widely abused substance in the workplace, include glassy eyes, alcohol odor in breath, and unexplained accidents.

Marijuana, a cannabinol, is among the drugs abused most commonly in the United States (Tapert, Tate, & Brown, 2001). Intoxication is characterized by impaired motor coordination and judgment, increased appetite, dry mouth, euphoria, and sometimes anxiety in high dosages. Opiates, such as opium, morphine, and heroin, act on the brain to create feelings of euphoria and analgesia (APA, 2000). To a much lesser degree, medicine preparations, such as codeine and oxycodone, which are consumed for the relief of pain and cough suppression, have similar effects on the body (Tapert et al., 2001). Signs of opioid intoxication include apathy preceded by euphoria, dysphoria, impaired judgment and memory or attention, pupillary constriction, drowsiness, slurred speech, and psychomotor agitation or retardation (APA, 2000).

As opposed to the CNS depressants, stimulants (e.g., amphetamine, cocaine) increase CNS activity, creating perceptions of alertness and increasing energy levels. Symptoms of intoxication for these substances include pupillary dilation, euphoria, hypervigilance, and increases in blood pressure, pulse rate, and respiration (APA, 2000). Other physical signs include nosebleeds or other nasal problems, raspy voice, heavy coughing, and bruises on arms and legs. In addition, signs of cocaine intoxication include psychomotor agitation, evidence of weight loss, and muscular weakness.

A third category, hallucinogens, includes lysergic acid diethylamide (LSD) and designer drugs, such as methylenedioxymethamphetamine (i.e., "ecstasy"). Intoxication signs of hallucinogens include impaired motor coordination and judgment, anxiety, depression, paranoid ideation, pupillary dilation, palpitations, sweating, and tremors (APA, 2000).

Partly because the use of some substances is more prevalent in the workplace than in other settings, researchers have focused on the examination of manifestations and consequences of those substances that are considered to most negatively influence labor environments. For instance, Schneider, Casey, and Kohn's (2000) review of the literature suggested that alcohol abuse has a greater economic impact on society than the abuse of all other drugs combined. Losses resulting from alcohol abuse are estimated to be $165 billion annually (Harwood et al., 1998). Thus, consequences of alcohol abuse in the workplace have been examined extensively. One approach has been to group consequences of alcohol abuse into four categories (Ames, 1993). The category "economic consequences" refers to all the factors related to alcohol consumption that contribute to economic losses. Among these factors are increases in absenteeism rates as a result of alcohol-related conditions, such as hangovers and illnesses (Holder & Cunningham, 1992). Along those lines, Blum, Roman, and Martin (1993) found that employed heavy drinkers made greater efforts to minimize absenteeism and tardiness than their light- and moderate-drinking co-workers, with the intention of concealing a potential drinking problem, and self-reported problem drinkers appear to be almost three times more likely to miss work because of injuries than were nonproblem drinkers (Ames, Grube, & Moore, 1997). Other factors in the economic consequences category include losses due to reduced productivity, employee wages, company earnings, health care cost increases due to higher insurance premiums, and damage to company property (Holder & Cunningham, 1992).

The category "social and health consequences" includes issues related to how employees' drinking habits impact those who share their environments. Examples in this category include decreases in employee morale and job satisfaction and conflicts with co-workers and family members. This category also includes consequences related to health issues, such as injuries or accidents caused by the drinking employee, which also account for significant portions of losses. Stallones and Krause (1993) estimated that approximately 4 percent of work-related injuries during a 12-month period involved alcohol, and Matano, Wanat, Westrup, Koopman, and Whitsell (2002) reported that at least 3 percent of a workforce admitted to being responsible for injuring a co-worker because of alcohol use. Furthermore, Bennett and Lehman's (1998) survey of two samples of municipal employees ($N = 909$ and $N = 1,068$) revealed that approximately 40 percent of employees reported one or more negative consequences as a result of the substance abuse of a co-worker.

Losses due to premature deaths from alcohol-related diseases and accidents are comprised within the "mortality consequences" category (Ames, 1993). Major losses can be attributed to the category of "legal responses to alcohol use and misuse." Consequences in this category are associated with employers' liability for accidents caused by the drinking employee during working hours or after drinking at employer-sponsored events in which alcohol is provided.

Another approach to understanding the manifestations of alcohol abuse in the workplace is to classify their impact into three domains specifically related to productivity (Garcia, 1996). Poor job performance is characterized by changes in performance, particularly an increase in inconsistent patterns of functioning that result in lower productivity from less output, mistakes (e.g., inability to recall instructions, missed deadlines), disciplinary issues, impairment, and robbery (Browne Miller, 1991). There is ample evidence in the literature to support the link between work performance and alcohol abuse. Mangione and colleagues (1999), for example, found a positive relationship between work performance problems and employee drinking level. Other researchers have reported similar findings. For instance, Blum and colleagues' (1993) analyses of collateral and self-reports found the scores of heavier drinkers to be lower than lighter drinkers on job performance scales measuring self-direction, conflict management, and interpersonal relations. Ames and colleagues (1997) examined the relationship between employee's drinking patterns, before and during work, hangovers, and job performance. They found modest support that indicated that heavy drinking and going to work with hangovers are predictive variables for overall number of workplace problems related to performance (e.g., falling asleep on the job, arguments with supervisors).

Browne Miller's (1991) classification of alcohol abuse manifestation in the workplace also included increased absenteeism (i.e., unanticipated or excessive absences, tardiness, and leaving the work site unexpectedly) and poor interpersonal relationships on the job (e.g., regular conflicts with co-workers, unusual or inappropriate behavior, and decreased ability to provide customer service).

EPIDEMIOLOGY

Alcohol and marijuana are the most commonly abused substances, with alcohol's estimated overall dependence rate at 5 percent and marijuana's estimated lifetime abuse or dependence rate at almost 5 percent (APA, 2000). Estimates for other substances are relatively lower, ranging from lifetime abuse and dependence rates of 0.6 percent for hallucinogens to 2 percent for cocaine. Findings from SAMHSA's National Household Survey on Drug Abuse (2002) suggested that alcohol use varies as a function of age. Sixty-four percent of adults ages 21 to 25 years use alcohol, whereas 60 percent of those between 26 and 34 years use alcohol. Lower rates are reported for past month use as age increases, with the lowest rate of 33 percent for individuals older than 65 years. Similar rate patterns are reported for binge drinking and heavy alcohol use.

Of the illicit drugs, marijuana is reported to be the drug of choice for 76 percent of individuals abusing drugs. The number of individuals using pain relievers is estimated to be 3.5 million, and 1.4 million individuals report using tranquilizers. This and other surveys (e.g., Matano et al., 2002) indicate a greater likelihood of drug use reports from males than females, with minimal gender differences in reports of psychotherapeutics (i.e., females reporting higher consumption of antidepressants). However, as applied to the workplace, findings from this survey must be interpreted with caution given that in most cases responses from individuals 12 years old and older are included (i.e., youth do not enter the workplace until they are 15 years old).

Of particular relevance to the workplace, both alcohol and drug use consumption rates are higher among those unemployed, particularly among binge and heavy drinkers. Nevertheless, the majority of alcohol and drug users, at least 18 years old, are employed full- or part-time (SAMHSA, 1999). Although it has been suggested that substance abuse rates vary as a function of demographic and environmental variables (e.g., place of residence, income), Matano and colleagues (2002) found evidence to support the contrary. Their survey of 504 highly educated employees at a major Silicon Valley corporation found alcohol consumption prevalence rates similar to those found in the general population. They also reported a lifetime alcohol dependence rate of 12 percent and a current drinking problem rate of 5 percent. Other findings reflect variances in comparison to the general population. For instance, 42 percent reported the use of mood-altering prescription drugs, mostly antidepressants, during the past 12-month period, 13 percent admitted to the weekly use of drugs, and 11 percent reported using illicit drugs during the past year.

Current rates of consumption for illicit drug and heavy alcohol use (i.e., binge drinking) also have been found to vary according to occupational category. These rates are presented in Table 6.1.

CASE ILLUSTRATION

Tom was a 25-year-old Caucasian man with a chronic history of alcohol abuse. The onset of his alcohol use occurred when he was 12 years old at a get-together with three of his closest friends. During this time, he reportedly drank more than a half dozen shots of whiskey and a few beers within a couple of hours. Throughout high school he became intoxicated from beer nearly every weekend, and increasingly became intoxicated on weekdays. He continued to use alcohol despite awareness that his grades were dropping because of frequent absenteeism from school and lack of motivation to perform school assignments. He also became easily agitated with

TABLE 7.1
Rates of Current Heavy Alcohol and Illicit Drug Consumption by Occupational Category

Occupation Category	Illicit Drugs Use (%)	Heavy Alcohol Use or Binge Drinking (%)
Administrative support	3.2	5.1
Construction	14.1	12.4
Executive, administrative, and managerial	7.0	7.5
Extractive and precision production	4.4	5.5
Food preparation, waiters, waitresses, and bartenders	18.7	15.0
Other service	12.5	11.4
Precision production and repair	4.4	11.6
Professional specialty	5.1	4.4
Protective service	3.0	7.8
Sales	9.1	4.1
Technicians and related support	7.0	5.1

Note: From *Results from the 2001 National Household Survey on Drug Abuse: Summary of National Findings,* by Substance Abuse and Mental Health Services Administration, Office of Applied Studies (NHSDA Series H-17, DHHS Publication No. SMA 02-3758), 2002, Rockville, MD: Author.

others, particularly his parents. He was eventually expelled from school for beating up a classmate during lunch.

Upon his expulsion from high school, Tom was hired by a large construction company to work as a security monitor. During his first year of employment he never consumed alcohol while working, although he was frequently intoxicated at home after work. About this time, his girlfriend of six months left him because she "couldn't take his drinking anymore." The separation resulted in his daily use of hard liquor (e.g., whiskey, bourbon) during working hours. To cover up his alcohol use during business hours, Tom chewed gum and carefully restricted his use to nonintoxicating levels. However, his disheveled appearance (e.g., messy hair, failure to tuck in his shirt), decrease in job productivity (e.g., arriving late for work, unauthorized breaks), and unsteady gait led his boss to conclude Tom needed help.

Consistent with company policy, Tom was consequently administered a breath-alyzer test by his boss to validate that he had, indeed, used alcohol while working on-site. The testing report indicated alcohol use, and he was consequently mandated to participate in substance-abuse counseling. Although reluctant to participate in counseling, he attended his first scheduled session on time. When asked why he was seeking treatment, Tom responded, "Because if I didn't my boss said he'd be forced to fire me, otherwise I wouldn't be here."

RECOGNIZING AND EVALUATING PSYCHOPATHOLOGY

Having recognized the seriousness of substance abuse as a costly corporate problem, companies in the United States are taking proactive steps to promote drug-free work environments. However, this initiative has been met with controversy, particularly in relation to legal issues. Although efforts to establish and maintain drug prevention programs, including drug testing, are supported by President Reagan's 1986 Executive Order No. 12564, known as Drug-Free Federal Workplace, the U.S. Department of Health and Human Services (Galvin, 2000), the General Duty Clause of the OSH Act of 1970, and the 1991 Title VII of the Civil Rights Act, only the latter two apply to the private sector. The former two are specific to federal employment settings and private corporations doing business with the government. Furthermore, opponents of drug testing call attention to the Fourth, Fifth, and Fourteenth Constitutional Amendments to challenge this practice. Some consider drug testing to be a form of unreasonable search and self-incrimination, and, especially when done randomly, it is thought to increase the likelihood of racial discrimination (Bryan, 1998).

Although federal laws do not require the instituting of drug testing in private companies, corporations often view drug testing as a preventive measure that fosters a safe and productive work environment. Consequently, its application is widespread, with more than 80 percent of large companies adopting drug testing as a standard practice (Sovereign, 1999). As a result, various methods of drug testing have become available for use in the workplace setting, including biological markers (i.e., urinalysis, hair tests) and standardized self-report measures. Of these methods, biological markers are considered highly objective (Goldberger & Jenkins, 1999), although no one method has been found to be absolutely accurate (Osterloh & Becker, 1990).

Enhanced sensitivity of urinalysis testing is dependent on the drug being assessed, as well as several other factors, including chronic substance use, obesity, and low levels of physical activity of the individual being tested. For instance, marijuana can usually be detected in urine up to one week after its ingestion in most thin individuals without a chronic history of use, but in chronic obese users, the detection period may extend up to three or four weeks. For amphetamines, tranquilizers, and most other hard drugs, the detection period is usually a few days (Goldberger & Jenkins, 1999). Most hallucinogens and alcohol may be detected for only a few hours. An exception to the preceding is PCP (i.e., "angel dust"), which may be detected for up to one week.

A limitation of urinalysis is that sophisticated drug users are able to bring about false-negative results (i.e., no detection of use when use has occurred) by commercially available drinking solutions, such as those found in eye drops, vinegar, and goldenseal health products. Other strategies include diluting the urine sample with toilet water, ingesting diuretics, and substituting with drug-free specimens (Osterloh & Becker, 1990). Limitations of this test also include the possibility of obtaining a false-positive result (i.e., urinalysis indicates use when no use has occurred). However, false-positive results are rare when testing facilities follow guidelines that have been established by the National Institute on Drug Abuse (NIDA); (Brookler, 1992). NIDA's mandatory guidelines for drug testing of federal employees require an initial immunoassay for major illicit drugs (i.e., marijuana, cocaine, amphetamines, PCP, and opiates). Positive test results are then required to undergo confirmatory assays, such as gas chromatography–mass spectrometry. While hair tests are less likely to result in inaccurate results, they, nevertheless, present some disadvantages. For instance, it has been suggested that hair tests can detect past, but not current or recent, frequency and quantity of drug use (Harris & Heft, 1992).

Drug testing in the workplace is commonly practiced for the purpose of screening applicants and identifying substance abuse among employees when performance issues arise. Thus, drug testing is usually implemented as a pre-employment condition, and random testing, although less common, often occurs throughout the course of employment. Pre-employment testing is the most common type, possibly because of its cost-effectiveness and minimal liability to the employer (Osterloh & Becker, 1990). The average cost of pre-employment testing in a 12-month period, $16,000, is much lower than the annual average cost for random testing, $33,159 (Sovereign, 1999). In addition, testing of applicants is thought to be effective in reducing drug use in the workplace. In contrast, random testing has several weaknesses. For instance, it can produce inaccurate false positives, false negatives, or both. Moreover, not anticipating a random drug test, employees may consume medications and foods that may be mistaken for illicit substances in drug tests (Osterloh & Becker, 1990).

Also common is the practice of testing an employee for alcohol and drug use when there is probable cause, such as when accidents and on-the-job injuries occur, when signs of intoxication are apparent, and when decreases in performance and productivity are observed (Osterloh & Becker, 1990). Random and probable-cause drug testing also may serve to identify the presence of a disorder, ideally at an early stage. From early detection, a referral for treatment may follow (Schottenfeld, 1989).

Standardized self-report assessment measures designed to predict consumption of substances have been used primarily as part of the screening process. Although they are cost-effective, easy to administer, and less intrusive than biological markers, their psychometric properties within workplace settings have not been properly evaluated (Harris & Heft, 1992). Conversely, measures of this type are increasingly being used in primary prevention programs, such as employee wellness programs (EWPs). Identification of substance abuse occurs usually when EWPs bring educational presentations on lifestyle issues to the workplace and help identify factors that pose health threats to employees, including substance abuse (Lapham, Chang, & Gregory, 2000).

Within the clinical setting, some of the common measures include self-administered inventories and structured interviews. The Cut Down, Annoyed, Guilty, Eye Opener (CAGE; Ewing, 1984) is a self-administered inventory designed to identify individuals who are diagnosed with alcohol abuse and dependence. The CAGE consists of four brief questions using a "yes" or "no" forced-choice response format. Another self-administered inventory is the Michigan Alcohol Screening Test (MAST; Selzer, 1971). The MAST consists of 25 items with a "true" or "false" response format intended to screen for lifetime alcohol-related problems and alcoholism. Among the structured interviews, the Addiction Severity Index (ASI; McLellan et al., 1992) assesses overall drug-use severity as manifested along the following seven dimensions: Drug Use, Alcohol Use, Medical Status, Employment/Support Status, Legal Status, Family/Social Relationship, and Psychiatric Status. The ASI is useful in providing measures of consumption and in predicting treatment outcome. Another instrument of this type, the Structured Clinical Interview for *DSM* (SCID; Spitzer, Williams, Gibbon, & First, 1990), is a highly comprehensive structured interview that requires professional training and takes about an hour to administer. The SCID contains a module designed specifically for psychoactive substance-use disorders (Groth-Marnat, 1999).

REFERRAL STRATEGIES

Getting substance-abusing employees into appropriate treatment is a major challenge for employers. Nevertheless, after the substance-abuse problem is identified, the next step is referral for treatment. Referral can be medical or by a supervisor or self. Although self-referral appears to be the most common, it has been questioned whether it is indeed self-initiated, as the decision to enter treatment may be influenced by family members or minor conflicts at work (Scanlon, 1986). In fact, Roman and Blum (2002) found that less than a third of self-referrals are actually self-initiated. Some factors influencing employees' decisions to seek help include subsidized services and assurance of confidentiality. However, even when confidential, employees may be hesitant to self-refer because of denial, shame, and fear related to job loss. Although there are no empirical studies that have evaluated employees' reluctance to seek help, some (Browne Miller, 1991) speculated the obstacles are found within the workplace (i.e., employees' perceptions that supervisors and co-workers lack understanding of their substance-abuse problem, lack of support, and social and workplace stigma).

Supervisory referral typically follows after a series of events have occurred. After recognition and documentation of poor performance, supervisors may issue informal verbal warnings, hold corrective interviews, provide written warnings, or discipline by paid or unpaid work suspension. Upon lack of performance improvement, supervisors may decide to refer employees for treatment. Under these circumstances, treatment outcome is linked with job security, as recovery may be a condition for returning to work (Scanlon, 1986).

Helping employees maintain their jobs while in treatment (Roman & Blum, 2002), employee assistance programs (EAPs) have been widely used in the workplace for more than two decades to address mental health–related issues that affect both employees and their families (Schneider et al., 2000). EAP services include some form of assessment and case management, although employees with substance–abuse problems are usually referred to outside providers (Scanlon, 1986). Often, EAP services include posttreatment follow-up. However, findings specific to EAPs have not found this practice to influence treatment outcome. The examination of the effectiveness of EAPs has been limited, despite their wide use (Schneider et al., 2000). Nonetheless, Roman and Blum's (2002) survey of 6,400 employees from 84 different work sites who used EAPs suggested all reports at initial intake, 18, and 24 months were favorable.

To a lesser extent, medical referrals are often indicated in the workplace because of substance abuse. Indeed, it has been estimated that almost 50 percent of all patients seen by medical practitioners have a diagnosable substance disorder (Miller & Gold, 1998). Assessment, medications, and referrals for psychological intervention are available to employees through their physicians.

WORKPLACE OR HOME STRESSORS WITH PARTICULAR RELEVANCE TO THIS DISORDER

Given the consequences to corporations and individuals as a result of substance abuse in the workplace, an examination of stressors that influence this disorder is warranted. Roman and Blum's (2002) review of the literature suggested the association between workplace stressors and increased alcohol consumption rates, though small, are consistent across studies. Job dissatisfaction is related to increased alcohol consumption, and substance use is higher among individuals with simple jobs. Moreover, individuals with cognitive abilities lower than that required for their jobs have greater consumption rates of alcohol, cigarettes, and marijuana than do individuals with high cognitive abilities whose jobs are more complex (Oldham & Gordon, 1999).

Other stressors that have been found to be associated with psychological distress and increased substance abuse in the workplace include sexual harassment and generalized abuse (Richman, Shinsako, Rospenda, Flaherty, & Freels, 2002). Sexual harassment refers specifically to unwanted sexual advances, requests for sexual favors, and any related sexual behavior that prevents the employees from performing their jobs (Sovereign, 1999). Generalized abuse involves, but is not limited to, acts of humiliation committed against employees, such as threats, verbal abuse, and denial of resources (Richman et al., 2002).

Presence of other mental disorders has been found to exacerbate substance-abuse disorders (Richman et al., 2002). Substance abuse is comorbid with a number of other disorders and conditions. For instance, alcohol is often consumed to relieve symptoms caused by consumption of other substances or by other disorders, such as depression and anxiety. In some cases, symptoms of depression result from acute alcohol intoxication. Similarly, depression and anxiety often are comorbid with regular use of marijuana and cocaine. Other disorders that may be associated with substance-related disorders are mood disorders, schizophrenia, and antisocial personality disorders (APA, 2000).

Workplace stress has been found to influence substance abuse as a function of gender. In occupations with high psychological demand, men have been found to be twenty-seven times more prone to develop a substance disorder than men in jobs with low psychological demands. However, women in high and low psychological demand job positions have demonstrated similar risks involving the development of substance disorders (Crum, Muntaner, & Eaton, 1995).

EMPIRICALLY BASED TREATMENTS

Although research examining development and implementation of substance-abuse treatments in workplace settings is limited, empirically based interventions have been designed to generalize to a broad range of individuals. Therapeutic methods employed in individual therapy, such as brief interventions, have been found to be successful in the treatment of substance disorders. As reviewed by Maisto, Wolfe, and Jordan (1999), motivational interviewing is a type of brief intervention that combines Miller's (1995) set of six motivational factors (i.e., feedback, responsibility, advice, menu, empathy, self-efficacy) to promote behavior change. In motivational interviewing, therapists are instructed to follow certain principles, including the avoidance of confrontation and the expression of empathy, to increase awareness of the discrepancy between individuals' current behavior and their personal goals (Maisto et al., 1999). Furthermore, in their review of the empirical literature, Maisto and colleagues' (1999) reported that most studies support the effectiveness of motivational interviewing in the reduction of substance use.

Social skills training is another approach used in individual therapy, although it can be extended to facilitate family therapy. Social skills deficits have been found to influence substance-abusing individuals' ability to cope with addiction (Tapert et al., 2001). Therefore, coping and social skills training emphasize the acquisition of interpersonal skills, the management of emotions and stress, and the regulation of responses to the accessibility of substances. Social skills training involves conducting a comprehensive assessment of the individual's skills level and role-playing scenarios related to drink refusal, communication, conflict resolution, establishment of support networks, and assertiveness (Monti, Rohsenow, Colby, & Abrams, 1995).

Another method employed to help individuals develop skills essential for obtaining decreases in substance use is the community reinforcement approach. The community reinforcement approach is similar to social skills training in its emphasis on the acquisition of skills to improve communication, obtain or keep a job, and control reactivity to substance use cues. In the community reinforcement approach, these skills are learned within the context of the environmental variables that tend to influence substance use, such as social, recreational, familial, and occupational supports. One of the goals in the community reinforcement approach is to identify and increase the individual's awareness regarding high-risk substance-use-related situations and pleasurable experiences that are not related to substance abuse. Functional analysis is instrumental in the accomplishment of this goal. Both the therapist and client examine the antecedents and consequences of the substance-abusing behaviors to identify skills in need of development. Pleasurable experiences are examined in the same manner to help individuals recognize the possibility of feeling enjoyment without the use of substances (Smith & Meyers, 1995; Tapert et al., 2001).

Also widely used are behavioral interventions, such as Azrin and colleagues' (1994) behavior therapy for drug abuse. Several components are comprised within this form of therapy. Some of these components include (1) stimulus control, which is designed to remove environmental factors that trigger or exacerbate the use of substances and to increase participation in activities that promote sobriety; (2) urge control, which employs *in vitro* imagery to develop ways of managing internal factors (e.g., thoughts) found to precede prior episodes of substance use; and (3) social control, in which the support of family members and friends is enlisted to assist with the recovery process. In addition to improving relationships and decreasing depression and alcohol and drug use, behavior therapy has led to significant improvements in work attendance among substance-abusing individuals throughout 12 months of therapy (Azrin et al., 1994) and up to nine-months of follow-up (Azrin et al., 1996).

Some treatment modalities view marital and family conflicts as contributing factors in the development and maintenance of substance disorders. Therefore, treatment approaches, such as family therapy, elicit the commitment of all family members involved to identify problems and generate and implement solutions. This form of therapy also emphasizes the development of communication and negotiating skills for all family members, thus reducing the number of stressors that may trigger substance use. Some strategies implemented within family therapy include behavioral contracting, participation in family recreational activities, and acquisition of problem-solving skills. Family therapy also can be implemented to supplement individual therapy (O'Farrell, 1995; Walitzer, 1999).

Self-help groups based on the twelve-step tradition are widely used to complement individual or family therapy. Twelve-step programs, such as Alcoholic Anonymous, promote regular attendance to meetings where individuals share negative experiences related to substance use. In addition, participants are encouraged to become familiar with the twelve-step principles (e.g., recognition of powerlessness over addiction and need for the help from a higher power) and obtain sponsorship from individuals who have been successful at overcoming addiction. Despite widespread practice of traditional twelve-step programs, research to evaluate its effectiveness has been limited (McGrady & Delaney, 1995).

Aside from therapeutic interventions, some pharmacological approaches have demonstrated efficacy in the reduction of symptoms associated with substance disorders. For instance, disulfiram produces adverse physical effects with alcohol ingestion. Other medications have their effects directly on the brain (e.g., benzodiazepines) and are sometimes prescribed during the detoxification and withdrawal stages of alcohol dependence to allay anxiety, irritability, and sleeplessness (Rone, Miller, & Frances, 1995). The opiate, naloxone, has assisted in the reduction of relapse rates of alcohol-abusing individuals by reducing cravings. Similar pharmacological treatments are available for other illicit substances of abuse (Anton, Brady, & Moak, 1999).

RELAPSE PREVENTION

Relapse is a major concern in the recovery process of individuals with substance disorders. Indeed, the majority of individuals who attain abstinence from drug and alcohol abuse tend to experience lapses and relapses throughout the recovery process (Daley & Salloum, 1999; Dimeff & Marlatt, 1995). Therefore, relapse may be viewed as a stage in the recovery process rather than as treatment failure.

Relapse prevention uses a combination of behavioral skills training and cognitive techniques to help individuals initiate and maintain behavior changes conducive to sober living (Dimeff & Marlatt, 1995). Some of these skills include the identification of high-risk situations, lapse and relapse signs (e.g., rapid heart rate or physiological craving when in the presence of the substance), negative affect (e.g., anxiety, irritability), and environmental factors (e.g., peer pressure). Other areas of emphasis are management of interpersonal conflict and development of support networks (Daley & Salloum, 1999).

Relapse prevention has been widely employed and evaluated with substance-abusing populations. For instance, Carroll's (1996) review of 24 randomized controlled trials found that although relapse prevention has been examined across substances, there is insufficient evidence supporting higher effectiveness with any particular substance. However, an examination of relapse prevention in comparison with no, or minimal, treatment for individual substances suggests that relapse prevention effectiveness is superior in these cases. In addition, relapse prevention effects are comparable with those effects of other therapeutic treatments (i.e., interpersonal process, counseling, interactional therapy, supportive therapy, interpersonal therapy), and are more effective when relapse prevention components are incorporated into the treatment program. Furthermore, relapse prevention has been found to be more effective in reducing the number of relapse episodes, extending the period between relapses, and treating the more severe cases of substance abuse than other therapeutic methods.

Companies can support the recovery process by communicating to the employee the ways in which he or she is valuable to the organization. In some cases, the employer and aftercare therapist maintain contact regarding the employee's progress and potential for relapse. Thus, employers should be provided with information about the role of relapse in the recovery process (McGrady, Dean, Dubreuil, & Swanson, 1985).

THERAPEUTIC BENEFITS OF WORK

Platt, Widman, Lidz, Rubenstein, and Thompson's (1998) review of the literature on substance abuse indicated that employment is crucial to the recovery process. Other findings also suggested that individuals' abilities to sustain employment contribute to the maintenance of improvements gained in treatment by providing a legal source of income, helping to increase self-esteem (Renwick & Krywonis, 1992), and creating an environment where individuals can associate with others who are not substance abusers and can develop support networks. Therefore, employment is sometimes applied in outcome studies as a reinforcement of abstinence, as well as an indicator of treatment outcome (Silverman, Svikis, Robles, Stitzer, & Bigelow, 2001). For instance, Silverman and colleagues (2001) implemented use of employment salary as a reinforcer of drug abstinence with a population of 40 unemployed pregnant and postpartum women who were predominately addicted to opioids and cocaine. Participants were required to test negative for drugs in urinalyses (three times per week) and were given salary increases with sustained abstinence and regular work attendance. Drug test results during the six-month treatment showed higher abstinence rates for individuals randomly assigned to this therapeutic workplace intervention (59 percent) than for those in the controlled condition (33 percent). Past studies, reviewed by Silverman and Robles (1999), indicated that this approach is also effective with a variety of other substances (e.g., benzodiazepines, polydrug use).

In addition to functioning as a reinforcer to abstinence, the workplace provides individuals with opportunities to remain occupied with legitimate activities (Renwick & Krywonis, 1992), develop and increase their sense of responsibility, and promote personal growth. These factors are widely applied in therapeutic community programs in which substance-abusing individuals are entrusted with the management of treatment facilities. In these programs, recovering individuals perform activities such as cleaning, coordinating schedules and meetings, preparing food, and completing all other tasks needed to run the facilities (De Leon, 1999). Reviews indicate there is a positive relationship between drug use and time availability (e.g., Silverman & Robles, 1999).

SUMMARY

Substance abuse in the workplace setting is an epidemic problem that has led to widespread cost to society. Having recognized the seriousness of substance abuse as a corporate problem, businesses are taking proactive steps to promote drug-free work environments. However, this development has been controversial. For instance, although federal laws do not require the instituting of drug testing in private companies, corporations often view drug testing as a preventive measure that fosters a safe and productive work environment. Indeed, most large companies have adopted drug testing as a standard practice. Standardized self-report assessment measures designed to predict consumption of substances have been used primarily as part of the screening process. Although self-report measures are cost-effective, easy to administer, and less intrusive than biological markers, the psychometric properties of these scales within workplace settings have yet to be empirically determined.

There is a wide variety of intervention programs that have been used in the treatment of substance abuse. Some of the more popular empirically supported substance abuse intervention approaches for adults that address job performance include motivational interviewing, social skills training, the community reinforcement approach, family behavior therapy, and some pharmacological approaches (e.g., disulfiram, naloxone). However, research examining the effectiveness of these interventions in workplace settings is limited.

Because the majority of individuals who attain abstinence tend to experience lapses and relapses throughout the recovery process, relapse prevention programs appear particularly promising in workplace settings. These programs often include the identification of high-risk situations and practice in improving skills that may assist in the avoidance of alcohol- or drug-use behavior. Of great importance, evidence supporting the utility of relapse prevention in the treatment of substance abuse is strongly supported in the outcome literature. However, like the aforementioned intervention programs, controlled evaluation of relapse prevention is limited in workplace settings.

In conclusion, steps have been taken in corporate America to prevent, identify, and treat substance abuse in the workplace. However, much work needs to be done in this area. Interestingly, one of the promising approaches to abstinence of illicit drugs and alcohol in workplace settings is effective employment. The workplace provides individuals with opportunities to remain occupied with legitimate activities, develop and increase their sense of responsibility, and promote personal growth. Along these lines, therapeutic community programs have been created in which substance-abusing individuals are entrusted with the management of treatment facilities. In these programs, recovering individuals perform activities such as cleaning, coordinating schedules and meetings, and preparing food. These programs have been shown to be effective in controlled trials of substance-abusing adults. However, the development of the therapeutic community is only in the nascent stages at this time.

References

American Psychiatric Association. (2000). *Diagnostic and statistical manual of mental disorders* (4th ed. text revision). Washington, DC: Author.

Ames, G. (1993). Research and strategies for the primary prevention of workplace alcohol problems. *Alcohol Health and Research World, 17*(1), 19-28.

Ames, G. M., Grube, J. W., & Moore, R. S. (1997). The relationship between drinking and hangovers to workplace problems: An empirical study. *Journal of Studies on Alcohol, 58,* 37-47.

Anton, R. F., Brady, K. T., & Moak, D. H. (1999). Pharmacotherapy. In P. J. Ott, R. E. Tarter, & R. T. Ammerman (Eds.), *Sourcebook on substance abuse* (pp. 303-314). Boston: Allyn & Bacon.

Azrin, N. H., Acierno, R., Kogan, E. S., Donohue, B., Besalel, V. A., & McMahon, P. T. (1996). Follow-up results of supportive versus behavioral therapy for illicit drug use. *Behavior, Research, and Therapy, 34*(1), 41-46.

Azrin, N. H., McMahon, P. T., Donohue, B., Besalel, V. A., Lapinski, K. J., Kogan, E. S., Acierno, R. E., & Galloway, E. (1994). Behavior therapy for drug abuse: A controlled treatment outcome study. *Behavior, Research, and Therapy, 32*(8), 857-866.

Bennett, J. B., & Lehman, W. E. K. (1998). Workplace drinking climate, stress, and problem indicators: Assessing the influence of teamwork. *Journal of Studies on Alcohol, 59*(5), 608-618.

Blum, T. C., Roman, P. M., & Martin, J. K. (1993). Alcohol consumption and work performance. *Journal of Studies on Alcohol, 54,* 61-70.

Brookler, R. (1992). Industry standards in workplace drug testing. *Personnel Journal, 71*(4), 128-131.

Browne Miller, A. (1991). *Working dazed: Why drugs pervade in the workplace and what can be done about it.* New York: Plenum Press.

Bryan, L. A. (1998). Drug testing in the workplace. *Professional Safety, 43*(10), 28-32.

Carroll, K. M. (1996). Relapse prevention as a psychosocial treatment: A review of controlled clinical trials. *Experimental and Clinical Psychopharmacology, 4*(1), 46-54.

Crum, R. M., Muntaner, C., & Eaton, W. W. (1995). Occupational stress and the risk of alcohol abuse and dependence. *Alcoholism: Clinical and Experimental Research, 19*(3), 647-655.

Daley, D. C., & Salloum, I. (1999). Relapse prevention In P. J. Ott, R. E. Tarter, & R. T. Ammerman (Eds.), *Sourcebook on substance abuse* (pp. 255-263). Boston: Allyn & Bacon.

De Leon, G. (1999). Therapeutic communities. In P. J. Ott, R. E. Tarter, & R. T. Ammerman (Eds.), *Sourcebook on substance abuse* (pp. 321-336). Boston: Allyn & Bacon.

Dimeff, L. A., & Marlatt, G. A. (1995). Relapse prevention. In R. K. Hester & W. R. Miller (Eds.), *Handbook of alcoholism treatment approaches: Effective alternatives* (pp. 176-194). Boston: Allyn & Bacon.

Ewing, J. A. (1984). Detecting alcoholism: The CAGE questionnaire. *Journal of the American Medical Association, 252,* 1905-1907.

Galvin, D. M. (2000). Workplace managed care: Collaboration for substance abuse prevention. *Journal of Behavioral Health Services and Research, 27*(2), 125-130.

Garcia, F. E. (1996). The determinants of substance abuse in the workplace. *Social Science Journal, 33*(1), 55-68.

Goldberger, B. A., & Jenkins, A. J. (1999). Drug toxicology. In P. J. Ott, R. E. Tarter, & R. T. Ammerman (Eds.), *Sourcebook on substance abuse* (pp. 185-196). Boston: Allyn & Bacon.

Groth-Marnat, G. (1999). *Handbook of psychological assessment.* New York: John Wiley.

Harris, M. M., & Heft, L. L. (1992). Alcohol and drug use in the workplace: Issues, controversies, and directions for future research. *Journal of Management, 18*(2), 239-277.

Harwood, H., Fountain, D., Livermore, G., & the Lewin Group. (1998). *The economic costs of alcohol and drug abuse in the United States, 1992.* Rockville, MD: National Institute on Drug Abuse.

Holder, H. D., & Cunningham, D. W. (1992). Alcoholism treatment for employees and family members: Its effect on health care costs. *Alcohol Health and Research World, 16*(2), 149-153.

Lapham, S. C., Chang, I., & Gregory, C. (2000). Substance abuse intervention for health care workers: A preliminary report. *Journal of Behavioral Health Services and Research, 27*(2), 131-143.

Maisto, S. A., Wolfe, W., & Jordan, J. (1999). Short-term motivational therapy. In P. J. Ott, R. E. Tarter, & R. T. Ammerman (Eds.), *Sourcebook on substance abuse* (pp. 284-292). Boston: Allyn & Bacon.

Mangione, T. W., Howland, J., Amick, B., Cote, J., Lee, M., Bell, N., & Levine, S. (1999). Employee drinking practices and work performance. *Journal of Studies on Alcohol, 60*(2), 261.

Matano, R. A., Wanat, S. F., Westrup, D., Koopman, C., & Whitsell, S. D. (2002). Prevalence of alcohol and drug use in a highly educated workforce. *Journal of Behavioral Health Services and Research, 29*(1), 30-44.

McGrady, B. S., Dean, L., Dubreuil, E., & Swanson, S. (1985). The problem drinkers' project: A programmatic application of social-learning based treatment. In G. A. Marlatt & J. R. Gordon (Eds.), *Relapse prevention* (p. 455). New York: Guilford.

McGrady, B. S., & Delaney, S. I. (1995). Self-help groups. In R. K. Hester & W. R. Miller (Eds.), *Handbook of alcoholism treatment approaches: Effective alternatives* (pp. 160-175). Boston: Allyn & Bacon.

McLellan, A., Kushner, H., Metzger, M., Peters, R., Smith, I., Grissom, G., Pettinati, H., & Argeriou, M. (1992). The fifth edition of the Addiction Severity Index. *Journal of Substance Abuse Treatment, 9,* 199-213.

Miller, W. R. (1995). Increasing motivation for change. In R. K. Hester & W. R. Miller (Eds.), *Handbook of alcoholism treatment approaches: Effective alternatives* (pp. 89-104). Boston: Allyn and Bacon.

Miller, N. S., & Gold, M. S. (1998). Management of withdrawal syndromes and relapse prevention in drug and alcohol dependence. *American Family Physician, 58*(1), 139-147.

Monti, P. M., Rohsenow, D. J., Colby, Z. M., & Abrams, D. B. (1995). Coping and social skills training. In R. K. Hester & W. R. Miller (Eds.), *Handbook of alcoholism treatment approaches: Effective alternatives* (pp. 221-241). Boston: Allyn & Bacon.

O'Farrell, T. J. (1995). Marital and family therapy. In R. K. Hester & W. R. Miller (Eds.), *Handbook of alcoholism treatment approaches: effective alternatives* (pp. 195-220). Boston: Allyn & Bacon.

Oldham, G. R., & Gordon, B. I. (1999). Job complexity and employee substance use: The moderating effects of cognitive ability. *Journal of Health and Social Behavior, 40,* 290-306.

Osterloh, J. D., & Becker, C. E. (1990) Chemical dependency and drug testing in the workplace. *Western Journal of Medicine, 152*(5), 506-513.

Platt, J. J., Widman, M., Lidz, V., Rubenstein, D., & Thompson, R. (1998). The case for support services in substance abuse treatment. *American Behavioral Scientist, 41*(8), 1050-1062.

Renwick, R. M., & Krywonis, M. (1992). Personal and environmental factors related to employment: Implications for substance abuse intervention. *Journal of Rehabilitation, 58*(1), 23-28.

Richman, J. A., Shinsako, S. A., Rospenda, K. M., Flaherty, J. A., & Freels, S. (2002). Workplace harassment/abuse and alcohol-related outcomes: The mediating role of psychological distress. *Journal of Studies on Alcohol, 63,* 412-419.

Roman, P. M., & Blum, T. C. (2002). The workplace and alcohol problem prevention. *Alcohol Research and Health, 26*(1), 49-57.

Rone, L. A., Miller, S. I., & Frances, R. J. (1995). Psychotropic medications. In R. K. Hester & W. R. Miller (Eds.), *Handbook of alcoholism treatment approaches: Effective alternatives* (pp. 267-277). Boston: Allyn & Bacon.

Scanlon, W.F. (1986). *Alcoholism and drug abuse in the workplace: Employee assistance programs.* NY: Praeger.

Schneider, R. J., Casey, J., & Kohn, R. (2000). Motivational versus confrontational interviewing: A comparison of substance abuse assessment practices at employee assistance programs. *Journal of Behavioral Health Services and Research, 27*(1), 60-74.

Schottenfeld, R.S. (1989). Drug and alcohol testing in the workplace — objectives, pitfalls, and guidelines. *American Journal of Drug and Alcohol Abuse, 15*(4), 413-428.

Selzer, M. L. (1971). The Michigan Alcoholism Screening Test: The quest for a new diagnostic instrument. *American Journal of Psychiatry, 127,* 1653-1658.

Silverman, K., & Robles, E. (1999). Employment as a drug abuse treatment intervention: A behavioral economic analysis. In F. J. Chaloupka, M. Grossman, W. K. Bickel, & H. Saffer (Eds.), *The economic analysis of substance use and abuse* (pp. 279-310). Chicago: University of Chicago Press.

Silverman, K., Svikis, D., Robles, E., Stitzer, M. L., & Bigelow, G. E. (2001). A reinforcement-based therapeutic workplace for the treatment of drug abuse: Six-month abstinence outcomes. *Experimental and Clinical Psychopharmacology, 9*(1), 14-23.

Smith, J. E., & Meyers, R. J. (1995). The community reinforcement approach. In R. K. Hester & W. R. Miller (Eds.), *Handbook of alcoholism treatment approaches: Effective alternatives* (pp. 221-241). Boston: Allyn & Bacon.

Sovereign, K. L. (1999). *Personnel law.* Upper Saddle River, NJ: Prentice Hall.

Spitzer, R., Williams, B., Gibbon, M., & First, M. (1990). *User's guide for the Structured Clinical Interview for DSM-III-R.* Washington, DC: American Psychiatry Press.

Stallones, L., & J. F. Kraus. (1993) The occurrence and epidemiologic features of alcohol-related occupational injuries. *Addiction, 88*(7), 945-951.

Substance Abuse and Mental Health Services Administration. (2002). *Results from the 2001 National Household Survey on Drug Abuse: Summary of national findings* (Office of Applied Studies, NHSDA Series H-17, DHHS Publication No. SMA 02-3758). Rockville, MD: Author.

Substance Abuse and Mental Health Services Administration, Office of Applied Studies. *Worker drug use and workplace policies and programs: Results from the 1994 and 1997 National Household Survey on Drug Abuse—Main findings.* Rocksville, MD: Author.

Tapert, S. F., Tate, S. R., & Brown, S. A. (2001). Substance abuse: An overview. In P. B. Sutker & H. E. Adams (Eds.), *Comprehensive handbook of psychopathology* (pp. 559-594). New York: Kluwer Academic/Plenum Publishers.

Walitzer, K. S. (1999). Family therapy. In P. J. Ott, R. E. Tarter, & R. T. Ammerman (Eds.), *Sourcebook on substance abuse* (pp. 337-349). Boston: Allyn & Bacon.

7

Anxiety

JOHN P. FORSYTH, MEGAN M. KELLY,
TIFFANY K. FUSÉ, AND MARIA KAREKLA
University at Albany, State University of New York

Anxiety disorders are the most common group of mental health problems, affecting approximately 19.1 million adults (ages 18 to 54 years) each year in the United States. Yet, less than one-third of such persons receive proper treatment or are otherwise misdiagnosed, resulting in estimated costs to the U.S. economy in excess of $42.3 billion every year, or $1,542 per sufferer (cf. Greenberg et al., 1999). Approximately 10 percent of the known costs of anxiety disorders are attributable to diminished workplace productivity and absenteeism, whereas 85 percent of the economic burden results from costs associated with medical (54 percent) and psychiatric (31 percent) treatment. Given estimates that approximately 16 percent of the U.S. workforce suffers from an anxiety disorder, and that such disorders cost employers approximately $256 per employee (Greenberg et al., 1999), a moderately sized organization with 200 employees would likely lose more than $8000 per year because of lost productivity and absenteeism resulting from anxiety-related problems. Such estimates do not include additional costs associated with increased use of all forms of health care services by persons suffering from anxiety disorders (Siegel, Jones, & Wilson, 1990; Swinson, Cox, & Woszcyzna, 1992), and thus the costs to employers are likely much greater than those noted earlier. Collectively, these data attest to the economic costs associated with untreated anxiety disorders in the workplace and only begin to provide a window on the enormous personal and interpersonal suffering that often accompanies such problems, particularly in terms of reduced overall quality of life. Fortunately, many of these costs are avoidable with appropriate diagnosis and treatment. Our purpose here, therefore, is to provide an overview of the anxiety disorders and their relation to the workplace, with an eye on describing available psychosocial and pharmacologic treatments with known evidence of efficacy. We hope that such information may be of use to professionals, co-workers, and employers who can expect to make contact with someone in their organization who suffers from an anxiety-related disorder.

Before proceeding, we wish to alert the reader to the obvious, namely, that anxiety, fear, and stress are not uniformly pathogenic negative emotional states. It has been known for some time that moderate levels of anxiety, fear, and even stress are necessary for people to meet deadlines and to complete moderately difficult tasks efficiently and effectively (Yerkes & Dodson, 1908). Such emotional responses also serve important adaptive functions in that they mobilize humans to respond appropriately to real or impending threat or danger.

Although both anxiety and fear are similar in that they often are accompanied by wide-ranging unpleasant autonomic symptoms, thoughts (i.e., worry or dread), and the behavioral tendency to escape or avoid, they also differ with respect to immediacy and intensity. For instance, anxiety is generally regarded as a future-oriented mood state, involving anxious apprehension, worry, heightened and sustained activity of the sympathetic nervous system, and wide-ranging autonomic symptoms (e.g., increased muscle tension, chest tightness). Fear, by contrast, is often characterized by an abrupt and acute surge of the sympathetic branch of the autonomic nervous system, accompanied by wide-ranging and more intense physiological symptoms (e.g., increased perspiration, rapid heart beat, breathlessness, dizziness), and a powerful action tendency to fight or flee from perceived or real environmental and bodily signs of threat or danger (see Barlow, 2001; Forsyth & Eifert, 1996, 1998). Anxiety, therefore, would be a more typical response to the thought of the possibility of seeing a bear during a forthcoming hiking trip in the woods, whereas fear would be more typical of the response that might occur when confronting an actual bear on the trail while hiking in the woods. Persons suffering from anxiety-related disorders experience such anxious and fearful responses in situations or contexts wherein such responses are disproportionate to the actual threat or danger. Such responses, in turn, are quite disruptive and can quite literally impact most domains of life experience that are of importance to the individual (e.g., education, work, social functions, recreational activities, sleep, family, sexual behavior, health). The disorders we describe later all share in common the experience of inappropriate and excessive anxiety and fear that is disproportionate to the risk of threat or danger or the task at hand. Such problems, in turn, often are accompanied by unpleasant physical symptoms, excessive worry, distressing thoughts, behavioral compulsions, and powerful tendencies to escape and avoid cues and situations that are associated with anxious and fearful responding. Indeed, it is when excessive anxiety and fear get in the way of meaningful and valued life domains, and result in significant distress and impairment, that we speak of a shift from normal anxiety and fear to disordered experiences of anxiety and fear. It is to a discussion of such problems and their workplace manifestations that we now turn.

OVERVIEW OF ANXIETY DISORDERS AND WORKPLACE MANIFESTATIONS

The most common clinical presentations of anxiety disorders, as characterized in the *Diagnostic and Statistical Manual for Mental Disorders–Fourth Edition* (American Psychiatric Association [APA], 1994) include the following: panic disorder with and without agoraphobia, social phobia, generalized anxiety disorder (GAD), specific phobia, post-traumatic stress disorder (PTSD), and obsessive-compulsive disorder (OCD). Acute stress disorder, a form of PTSD of lesser duration, anxiety disorders due to a general medical condition or induced by a substance, pure cases of agoraphobia without a history of panic disorder, and anxiety disorders "not otherwise specified" are less common than those just mentioned and are not discussed here, as knowledge of such conditions remains somewhat limited.

Panic Disorder with and without Agoraphobia

Panic disorder is defined, in large part, by an individual experiencing unexpected or "out of the blue" panic attacks (i.e., a sudden intense onset of fear or discomfort that is accompanied by rapid heart rate, chest pain, sweating, trembling, difficulty breathing or a shortness of breath, dizziness, fear of dying, or feelings of going crazy or losing control) (APA, 1994), worrying about having additional attacks, being concerned about the consequences of the attacks, and changing behavior so as to avoid subsequent attacks. Although panic attacks can and often do occur in other anxiety disorders, persons with panic disorder are fearful of panic itself—a short-lived and extremely unpleasant experience—and its consequences. Panic disorder sufferers often go to great lengths to avoid activities that may be associated with the probability of having a panic attack (e.g., small enclosed spaces, driving, physical exercise or exertion, sex, and most activities that could increase arousal). Avoidance is often most apparent in situations where escape might be difficult or embarrassing should one panic (e.g., taking public transportation, being in a crowded area, shopping, being alone, traveling, and being in confined spaces). Such agoraphobic avoidance, in turn, is a frequent consequence of a history of severe and untreated panic attacks, and panic disorder with agoraphobia is often more debilitating than panic disorder alone.

The workplace is a challenging environment for persons suffering from panic disorder. Such challenges include difficulties getting to work (e.g., being unable to drive) and difficulties negotiating the workplace environment (e.g., walking stairs, riding elevators, working in small spaces). Deadlines, interpersonal conflicts, and workplace stress may all set the occasion for panic attacks. Such attacks, in turn, may present initially as angina and look similar to someone in the midst of having a heart attack. The overwhelming nature of panic attacks may result in an employee feeling an urgent need to escape the workplace for a more safe and secure location (e.g., outside, home). Such employees also may dread the possibility of humiliation and embarrassment resulting from having a panic attack in front of supervisors, co-workers, or customers, and quite often they fear that they are dying or going crazy. In severe cases, agoraphobic avoidance may generalize to the workplace, particularly if the work environment is associated with a past history of panic attacks. As a result, the employee may increasingly delegate responsibilities to others, particularly if such responsibilities are associated with panic and its negative consequences. This pattern, in turn, sets up a vicious cycle in which the employee is unable to engage in normal workplace activities for fear of panic, resulting in further avoidance, restricted range of functioning, difficulties completing workplace tasks and activities, and so on. Employees with panic disorder show high rates of unemployment, absenteeism, health care use, financial strain, and poor quality of life as a consequence of the disorder (Barlow, 2001).

Specific Phobia

Specific phobia is defined, in large part, by a marked and unreasonable fear of an object or event. Although any object or event could be a focus of a specific phobia, the most common clinical presentations include excessive and unreasonable fears of spiders, bugs, mice, snakes, and heights (Barlow, 2001; Bourdon et al., 1988). Individuals with specific phobias often experience panic attacks upon exposure to the feared object or situation (Craske, 1991; Forsyth & Eifert, 1996), or to verbal and nonverbal cues that are related to the phobic stimulus (e.g., the word *spider*). The one exception is blood-injury-injection phobia, where the response involves a sudden drop in blood pressure (i.e., vasovagal reaction) to the sight of needles, blood, or injection, and ultimately fainting as a consequence. We should add that persons with specific phobias recognize that their fear is extreme and unreasonable. Yet, such persons often avoid the feared object or endure being in its presence with great distress. Indeed, it is because most phobic objects can be readily avoided and minimally interfere with life functioning that few seek treatment for such fears (Barlow, 2001). The feared object or event must, therefore, cause clinically significant distress and impairment in social or occupational functioning to warrant a diagnosis of specific phobia.

Specific phobias can interfere with workplace functioning if the job requires exposure to the feared stimulus or is set in a context where exposure to the feared stimulus is likely. For instance, persons with a specific phobia of heights may have difficulty working in an office on the upper floors of an office building, particularly near large windows. Similarly, persons with a claustrophobic fear may experience significant distress riding an elevator, working in a small office, or being in a crowded room. Medical settings, and medical evaluations required for employment, may pose challenges for persons suffering from blood-injury-injection phobias. For the most part, however, persons with specific phobias are quite adept at managing to work around confronting the object of their fear and self-select occupations that minimize the probability of exposure to phobic stimuli. Unexpected encounters with the phobic stimulus or event (e.g., seeing a spider in an office) can result in acute distress similar to a panic attack and some disruption of ongoing workplace activities. Yet, relative to panic disorder, such phobic reactions are typically less severe and can be managed by simply avoiding the feared stimulus from the workplace, or by restructuring the workplace environment. When compared with other anxiety disorders, therefore, specific phobias result in the less overall occupational impairment and disruption of life functioning (Greenberg et al., 1999).

Social Phobia

Social phobia (or social anxiety disorder) is a marked and persistent fear of one or more social or performance situations involving exposure to unfamiliar people or the possible scrutiny of others. For instance, individuals with social phobia commonly fear and avoid attending parties or meetings, eating in front of others, writing in front of others, meeting new people, speaking in public, using public restrooms, and engaging in related situations that entail interactions with people (even speaking on the telephone). Such fears may be specific (e.g., speaking in public) or may be more pervasive in that the phobic response is generalized to most social encounters. In such social contexts, persons with social phobia believe that they will act in a way (or show anxiety symptoms) that will be humiliating or embarrassing (APA, 1994). Not surprisingly, exposure to the feared social situation almost invariably provokes anxiety, which may take the form of a situationally bound or situationally predisposed panic attack. As a result, feared social or performance situations are avoided or are endured with intense anxiety and distress, despite the individual recognizing that the fear is excessive or unreasonable. As with the other anxiety disorders, one would need to rule out medical (e.g., Parkinson's disease) and psychiatric conditions (e.g., panic disorder, eating disorders), including substance abuse, as these and other conditions could involve significant social anxiety as a secondary problem. In social phobia, therefore, the social anxiety must be a central problem in that it causes significant distress, interference with normal routines, impairment in social activities and relationships, or occupational (and academic) functioning.

With few exceptions, the workplace is a setting that involves significant social interactions, whether among employees or employers or between workers and the general public (i.e., consumers). Hiring and firing decisions, including merit increases and promotions, often entail a significant evaluative component. These and other features of the workplace make it an extremely difficult and challenging setting for those suffering from social phobia. The social and evaluative dimensions of the workplace, in turn, may evoke characteristic styles of thinking (e.g., a belief that others are watching, staring, or judging them negatively) or the tendency to misinterpret benign social cues negatively as indicators of disapproval or threat. Such modes of thinking, coupled with workplace stress, may contribute to episodes of excessive anxiety or panic attacks and subsequent efforts to avoid social interactions. Difficulties initiating conversations, maintaining eye contact, and being appropriately assertive are common workplace manifestations of social anxiety. Often individuals with social anxiety are so excessively and self-consciously afraid of being humiliated or criticized that their performance at work suffers.

Generalized Anxiety Disorder

GAD is characterized by excessive, chronic, and uncontrollable worry about several life domains or activities (e.g., work, finances, school, health, family, relationships) (APA, 1994). The central problem here is not simply worry but uncontrollable worry that is generalized across numerous life domains (Borkovec, Shadick, & Hopkins, 1991). The chronic nature of generalized anxiety, in turn, may include restlessness, fatigue, impaired concentration, irritability, muscle tension, and problems with the quality and quantity of sleep. For an individual's symptoms to be diagnosed as GAD, the symptoms must be severe enough to cause significant distress and interference with social and occupational functioning.

By definition, the problems associated with GAD are generalized, meaning that the problems manifest across several life domains, including work. Persons suffering from GAD often find it difficult to relax and think clearly, and they more often than not appear as though they are "on edge" or "keyed up." Common work-related worries include concerns about being perceived as competent, finishing a project on time, being accepted by a supervisor, handling an important account, or making a major (or even minor) mistake at work. We should note that such worry-related content is normative (and even adaptive) to some degree in the workplace. Yet, persons with GAD find it difficult to control such worries, and they can spend hours each day consumed by worry, instead of getting things done. Productivity, in turn, may suffer, and procrastination related to excessive worry is common. This problem can be quite disabling, rendering the person unable to work to his or her full potential, or even being able to hold a job at all. We provide a case illustration a bit later that illustrates the nature of this problem and its workplace manifestations.

Post-Traumatic Stress Disorder[1]

Persons suffering from PTSD have either experienced or witnessed a traumatic life-threatening event involving actual or threatened death or serious injury, coupled with the feeling of intense fear, helplessness, or horror (APA, 1994). PTSD can develop following several types of traumatic events, including terrorist attacks, military combat, rape, torture, crime, natural disasters, serious accidents, or the sudden death of a loved one.

Persons suffering from PTSD typically experience three clusters of symptoms: (1) reexperiencing the event (e.g., intrusive memories of the trauma, flashbacks, daytime fantasies, or distressing nightmares), (2) avoidance and emotional numbing (e.g., avoidance of reminder cues, memories, blunted emotional responsiveness), and (3) symptoms of elevated arousal (e.g., sleeplessness, hypervigilance for threat, enhanced startle). Avoidance of cues that trigger memories of the traumatic event may include people, places, or objects that may bear only a loose resemblance to aspects of the original trauma. Symptoms must be present for at least one month posttrauma and cause significant distress and functional impairment to meet diagnostic criteria for PTSD.

The acute and long-term effects of trauma, as the events of 9/11 attest, are often extremely disruptive and negatively impact interpersonal relationships, health, quality of life, and occupational functioning. On- and off-the-job stress, including other negative life events, can serve as triggers for reexperiencing the original trauma, and such reexperiencing can severely disrupt an individual's ability to function in the workplace. Such reexperiencing may, in turn, manifest as a panic attack and may include flashbacks, dissociation, and efforts to escape the situation. Trauma associated with acts committed by others (e.g., rape, assault, combat) may result in difficulties forming close and emotionally rich relationships with others, including fellow co-workers. Many PTSD sufferers also experience considerable anger and guilt about the trauma, and such anger may manifest as workplace conflict,

---

[1] *Editor's note:* PTSD is covered in more detail in Chapter 8.

particularly with more senior-level employers but also with potential customers and other employees. Difficulties managing anger, both in and outside the workplace, can have deleterious effects on interpersonal relationships, resulting in social isolation, unemployment, and financial strain. Moreover, the emotional numbing and avoidance symptoms of PTSD also can manifest as a tendency for the individual to isolate him- or herself from others, thus undermining the development of a positive social support network at work and elsewhere. Hypervigilance for signs of threat, including sleep disturbance, can disrupt performance at a job and can contribute to fatigue, absenteeism, poor concentration, and susceptibility to injury and illness. Such problems will likely be exacerbated when the original trauma occurs on the job or in the workplace, resulting in the individual avoiding the job altogether or otherwise showing a tendency to experience intrusive recollections at work due to the presence of extensive reminder cues.

Obsessive-Compulsive Disorder

OCD can be a particularly distressing and impairing anxiety disorder. OCD is characterized by the presence of obsessions (i.e., recurrent and intrusive thoughts, ideas, images, or impulses that are considered inappropriate and cause marked anxiety) and compulsions (i.e., repetitive, ritualistic behaviors or mental acts that are performed to reduce anxiety generated by the obsessions) (see APA, 1994). For instance, persons with an obsession about contacting germs may have intrusive thoughts about the dangers of carrying germs (e.g., becoming seriously ill), especially on their hands, and may fear or avoid touching any objects that may harbor them (e.g., a door handle, a restroom stall, computer keyboard, other people). Such obsessions, in turn, generate severe anxiety and distress and often involve a fear of disastrous consequences, such as a fear that oneself or others will be harmed. To alleviate such anxiety, individuals with obsessions of germs and contamination may wash their hands 40 times or more after simply touching a doorknob, and this cycle may be repeated numerous times each day. Persons suffering from OCD frequently recognize that their obsessions are irrational and yet remain unable to manage the accompanying anxiety and prevent themselves from engaging in compulsive behaviors. Although there is no limit to the kinds of obsessions and compulsions that may be experienced by persons suffering from OCD (Foa & Wilson, 2001), the most common forms include concern about contamination (e.g., fears of germs, dirtiness, chemicals, AIDS, cancer), doubt (e.g., whether appliances are turned off, doors are locked, written work is accurate), disturbing sexual or religious thoughts (e.g., sexual thoughts about a holy person; satanic thoughts; distressing thoughts regarding morality), checking (e.g., locks; appliances; paperwork; driving routes), the need to create order (e.g., arranging objects to achieve exactness or symmetry), repeated actions (e.g., turning lights on and off; getting up and down in chairs; rereading; rewriting), hoarding (e.g., magazines, flyers, clothing, information), and thinking rituals (e.g., repeatedly praying or counting to oneself). Such obsessions and compulsions must be sufficiently distressing and time-consuming to warrant a diagnosis of OCD.

The workplace context can be a particularly challenging environment for persons suffering from OCD. For instance, orderliness, attention to detail, and a certain degree of compulsiveness are valued employee behaviors in many employment settings, so long as they translate into meeting deadlines, accomplishing tasks, and being productive. Persons with OCD, however, can spend hours each day preoccupied by their obsessions (e.g., with order, perfection, and the like), including compensatory compulsive behaviors (e.g., cleaning, checking, creating order). Such preoccupations, in turn, interfere with working efficiently, concentrating, and accomplishing tasks. Moreover, obsessions and compulsions occurring outside the workplace environment can result in missing appointments, arriving late to work, using excessive sick days, or, in severe cases, having prolonged absenteeism due to hospitalization. co-workers and supervisors may believe that a person with this disorder is irresponsible, lazy, or strange, thus inhibiting the development of good work relationships. The result is often lower productivity, and those suffering from OCD may quit or lose their jobs because of compromised workplace performance (Miranda & Rollins, 1997). Such negative outcomes are not an invariable consequence of OCD. As we later describe more fully in a case illustration, persons with OCD can have successful careers, provided that they receive adequate treatment and are given minor workplace accommodations.

EPIDEMIOLOGY

Anxiety disorders are among the most prevalent psychological disorders, affecting as many as 25 percent of the general population at some point in time (Bourdon et al., 1988; Eaton, Dryman, & Weissman, 1991; Kessler et al., 1994, 1996). Although there is variation across the anxiety disorders with respect to age of onset (e.g., specific phobias), most typically start in the late teens or mid-20s (Burke, Burke, Regier, & Rae, 1990; Flint, 1994; Mannuzza, Fyer, Liebowitz, & Klein, 1990; Noyes et al., 1992; Rasmussen & Eisen, 1991) and run a chronic course if left untreated. Females are, with few exceptions (e.g., OCD, some forms of specific phobia), at greater risk for presenting with an anxiety disorder than males (Clum & Knowles, 1991; Kessler et al., 1994; Kessler, Sonnega, Bromet, Hughes, & Nelson, 1995; Robins et al., 1984). Moreover, several epidemiological studies have shown that of all the anxiety disorders specific phobias are most common, affecting as many as 11.2 percent of the general population (Eaton et al., 1991). As indicated, however, the remaining anxiety disorders often cause comparatively more occupational and functional impairment than do specific phobias. For instance, epidemiological studies suggest that between 3.6 percent and 7.8 percent of the general population will suffer from PTSD at some point in time (Kessler et al., 1995), whereas 4 percent will suffer from GAD (Blazer, Hughes, George, Schwartz, & Boyer, 1991). From such studies we also know that approximately 3.5 percent of the population will suffer from panic disorder, followed closely by social phobia (2.7 percent) and OCD (2.4 percent) (see Bourdon et al., 1988; Eaton et al., 1991; Kessler et al., 1994, 1995, 1996). Finally, it is important to note that it is common for persons with anxiety disorders to suffer from a second or third co-occurring psychological problem (e.g., substance abuse, depression), most often another anxiety disorder (Brown, Campbell, Lehman, Grisham, & Mancill, 2001; Sanderson, DiNardo, Rapee, & Barlow, 1990).

Such patterns of comorbidity suggest the need for a comprehensive approach in evaluating and treating anxiety disorders in the workplace.

Despite the high prevalence rates of anxiety disorders in the general population, many individuals suffering from an anxiety disorder do so privately and do not seek professional help, and many others go undiagnosed. Indeed, when anxiety sufferers seek help, they tend to visit their primary care physician, not a mental health professional (Pollard, Henderson, Frank, & Margolis, 1989; Swinson et al., 1992). Statistics compiled from primary care offices suggest that anxiety is among the most common type of presenting complaint by patients seeking outpatient medical services, followed only by hypertension, cuts and bruises, and sore throats (Marsland, Wood, & Mayo, 1976). In addition, persons suffering from anxiety disorders show the highest rates of use of emergency and nonemergency medical services for problems with an emotional basis (Rees, Richards, & Smith, 1998). For instance, persons suffering from panic disorder use psychiatric and nonpsychiatric services seven times more often than the general population (Siegel et al., 1990) while also missing twice as many days of work as the general population. Not surprisingly, such patterns of use are associated with significant costs to the individual suffering from the disorder, to the health care system, and to the community at large. Examples of direct costs include poor health, hospitalization, and financial strain, whereas indirect costs include lost work productivity, social isolation, restricted lifestyle, and reduced quality of life (Barsky, Delamater, & Orav, 1999; Klerman, Weissman, Ouellette, Johnson, & Greenwald, 1991; Leon, Portera, & Weissman, 1995; Markowitz, Weissman, Ouellette, Lish, & Klerman, 1989; Salvador-Carulla, Segui, Fernadez-Cano, & Canet, 1995; Siegel et al., 1990). Individuals suffering from panic disorder, GAD, PTSD, and social phobia appear more likely to experience adverse workplace outcomes (e.g., work loss due to absenteeism or work cutback days) than persons with other anxiety disorders. Some anxiety disorders (i.e., panic disorder, OCD, and phobias) also tend to covary with elevated rates of financial dependence and unemployment, increased rates of disability payments, welfare, unemployment compensation, and alcohol and drug misuse (DuPont et al., 1996; Markowitz et al., 1989). Overall, all anxiety disorders (with the exception of specific phobia) are associated with substantial impairment in the workplace. We briefly describe in the following section two cases that illustrate workplace difficulties associated with OCD and GAD, respectively.

CASE ILLUSTRATIONS

OCD: The Case of Bob

Bob (a pseudonym), a 32-year-old production manager, presented with problems associated with OCD. Although Bob only recently sought professional mental health treatment at our clinic, he noted struggling with patterns of obsessive-compulsive behavior for as long as he could remember. Specifically, Bob described numerous obsessive thoughts related to faith, religiosity, and fears of mortality. Furthermore, Bob noted difficulties with multiple compulsions, which included hoarding behavior, counting, and the compulsion for order and pattern symmetry. Bob attributed his effectiveness at work, including numerous promotions, to his attention to detail and ability to form and maintain patterns. Yet, some of his other obsessive-compulsive behaviors appeared to have impaired his ability to function at work, resulting in on-the-job problems. For example, Bob could not throw anything away, and as a result would collect and retain numerous objects that he came in contact with, such as pieces of trash paper, old candy wrappers, and office supplies. Such difficulties were especially evident at his workplace where, as part of his job as production manager, he often had to complete and submit numerous documents in a timely fashion. According to Bob, his office was cluttered with piles of miscellaneous papers and other random items, making it extremely difficult to locate needed documents and related paperwork. This pattern of hoarding, in turn, resulted in significant and quite humiliating confrontations with his employers. In one such incident, Bob was one week late to turn in his monthly report and had trouble retrieving it from the plethora of objects in his office. As a consequence, Bob's supervisor became very upset, entered Bob's office, and overturned everything in the office so as to locate the report. This incident, in turn, resulted in an explosive argument between Bob and his supervisor, and a warning that Bob would be fired if his behavior did not change. After this event, Bob concluded that it was time to seek professional help.

GAD: The Case of James

James (a pseudonym), a 35-year-old successful accountant for a moderately sized company, presented with symptoms of GAD. James indicated good relationships with his co-workers and described himself as being very productive in the workplace. Yet, he complained of chronic feelings of stress and anxiety during the workday. James indicated that he would wake up in the morning feeling "on edge," and this feeling was coupled with numerous intrusive worries about tasks that he needed to complete at work. Though James's co-workers described him as a perfectionist and a hard worker, James nonetheless constantly worried about losing his job, particularly if he made a minor mistake at work. James attempted to solve such problems by not taking vacations. Avoiding vacations, however, appeared to be driven by James's worry that others would not follow his instructions and mistakes would be made in his absence. Moreover, despite being in perfect health, James chronically worried about illness and health-related matters and feared that he would be unable to work if he happened to become ill. James discussed these and other concerns with his immediate supervisor, and such discussions were often met openly, with calm and reassurance. Yet, reassurance from James's supervisor only resulted in brief reductions (i.e., less than one hour at most) in his worry and anxiety, only to be followed by a resurgence of the same worries and anxious feelings shortly thereafter. When the vice president of the company took over one of James's tasks and made a mistake adding up the numbers of a transaction, James became very distraught about the additional work he would have to do to correct the mistake, and he confronted the vice president about it. James told his superior that he was not only worried about losing his job if he or other members of his office made mistakes (including the vice president) but also worried over the anxiety he experienced related to the extraordinary pressures he put on himself (i.e., getting the task done as fast as possible).

A heated confrontation with the vice president ensued over James's inability to handle mistakes at work. This confrontation, in turn, resulted in James avoiding interactions with the vice president of the company. James reported that he was feeling very tense and fatigued, having difficulty sleeping, and having a hard time concentrating on tasks at work because of his constant worrying. Such problems, in turn, led James to seek treatment that would help him learn ways to manage his worry and anxiety related to his performance in the workplace.

RECOGNIZING AND EVALUATING ANXIETY DISORDERS

It is because anxiety is a ubiquitous emotional facet of human experience, and also quite adaptive under many circumstances, that it can be difficult to recognize when anxiety has exceeded normal limits and has moved into the pathological range. Problematic or disordered experiences of anxiety and fear are often indexed by extent of distress and functional impairment related to anxious and fearful symptoms and by the degree to which associated cognitive, physiological, and behavioral symptoms interfere with, or otherwise restrict, life functioning. Extent of impairment and distress may wax and wane depending on the circumstances. Moreover, symptoms associated with anxiety disorders often mimic various physical illnesses (e.g., endocrine problems such as hyperthyroidism, vestibular dysfunctions, seizure disorders, and cardiac conditions) and the effects of controlled substances. For example, heart palpitations and chest pain are among the most commonly reported symptoms of panic attacks but also frequently accompany some heart conditions (e.g., coronary heart disease). Such symptoms also may occur as side effects of various over-the-counter medications (e.g., antihistamines) and substances of use and abuse (e.g., caffeine, nicotine, and stimulants such as amphetamines, cocaine). Indeed, anxiety-related disorders are often difficult to distinguish from medical conditions and may even develop as a consequence of having a physical condition. Thus, it is important that medical and substance-related causes of anxiety-related symptoms be ruled out with a thorough physical evaluation before considering a psychiatric diagnosis of an anxiety disorder. If the symptoms cannot be attributed to a medical condition or effects of a known substance, then a mental health professional should be consulted to further assess and investigate the psychosocial nature of any anxiety-related difficulties.

A comprehensive psychosocial evaluation for anxiety-related problems is conducted by a trained mental health professional. Such assessments can aid not only in providing a differential diagnosis but also in better understanding psychological and experiential factors that contribute to the development and maintenance of an anxiety disorder (Antony, 2001). Information gleaned from assessment is often useful in determining the nature and scope of anxiety-related difficulties and the presence of comorbid psychological problems that may warrant clinical attention. Such information, in turn, is used to develop a case formulation, and ultimately to make decisions regarding the most effective form of intervention for an individual case. Assessment, therefore, facilitates understanding the course of the problem, including associated patterns of thinking, avoidance, symptoms, skills deficits, extent of impairment, treatment goals, and response to treatment. Several empirically supported methods exist to achieve such aims (see Antony, Orsillo, & Roemer, 2001), with the most commonly used approaches, including structured (e.g., the Anxiety Disorders Interview Schedule-IV) (Brown, Di Nardo, & Barlow, 1994) and semistructured clinical interviews, paper-and-pencil self-report measures (e.g., Anxiety Sensitivity Index, Beck Anxiety Inventory, Penn State Worry Questionnaire, the State and Trait Anxiety Inventory), behavioral observation (e.g., behavioral approach tests, self-monitoring diaries), and methods designed to assess psychophysiological arousal and reactivity to feared cues and contexts. Typically, a mental health professional will use more than one of these methods so as to develop an accurate (i.e., reliable and valid) differential diagnosis and a clear understanding of the extent and nature of an individual's problems (e.g., see Barlow, 2001; Heimberg, Liebowitz, Hope, & Shneier, 1995). As we later describe more fully in the context of empirically supported treatments, assessment and evaluation are critical when considering the problem of comorbidity and selection of the most appropriate forms of intervention.

REFERRAL STRATEGIES

Several referral strategies exist for employers and co-workers who suspect that a fellow employee is suffering from an anxiety-related disorder. Before offering a referral for either an evaluation or a treatment, it is important to be mindful that employees suffering from anxiety disorders are often extremely bothered, distressed, and even ashamed and embarrassed about their problems. Moreover, by the time workplace manifestations of an anxiety-related disorder become clear to others, the employee often has been actively struggling with his or her problems in an effort to manage and control them, often with only limited success. It should not be assumed that the employee is aware of the relation between difficulties at work and elsewhere and the presence of an anxiety disorder, nor should it be assumed that this person is aware that anxiety-related problems are amenable to treatment. Such issues, including the considerable stigma attached to having a mental illness and obtaining mental health care, require an open, supportive, and educative approach when discussing work-related problems and when making a referral. Discussion of anxiety-related problems in the workplace (and elsewhere) should, therefore, be done privately. Set in a context of openness and genuine concern for the individual, the commonsense and straightforward referral strategies described later stand the greatest likelihood of making a difference.

Referral strategies obviously depend on having referral sources, thus employers should compile a list of outpatient psychological services in the community. Depending on the nature and severity of the presenting problems, as well as on personal preference, persons suffering from anxiety disorders may be evaluated and treated by either doctoral-level or master's-level mental health practitioners (e.g., clinical psychologists, counselors, psychiatrists, master's-level therapists). In most geographical areas, listings of private therapists, some of whom may specialize in the treatment of anxiety disorders, are available in the telephone directory. In addition, state-funded mental hospitals commonly provide outpatient services, and some larger universities have faculty and staff with expertise in evaluating and treating anxiety disorders. Provider resources also are available from most state departments of mental health, including employee assistance programs that are part of many larger businesses and corporations. Although anxiety disorders are typically treated on an outpatient basis, severe cases may require inpatient treatment (e.g., OCD), including cases in which anxiety is associated with other comorbid psychological problems (e.g., major depression, substance abuse, eating disorders, suicidal ideation or intent). If unaware of the nature and type of mental health services available locally, an employer or co-worker may simply suggest that the individual contact his or her primary care physician. The primary care physician, in turn, will perform a thorough physical examination to rule out possible organic causes of the employee's psychological difficulties. Thereafter, an employee may be referred to a trained mental health professional for further evaluation and treatment. We suggest, however, that employers offer employees with anxiety-related difficulties a minimum of two referrals to mental health professionals in addition to the suggestion to consult with a primary care physician. We also suggest that employers and co-workers show a willingness to make accommodations (e.g., flexible hours) in the workplace so as to encourage employees to set and keep appointments with their medical and mental health providers. Employers should not assume, however, that referrals will lead to the most appropriate care or that other referring sources are knowledgeable about best practices with regard to evaluation and treatment of anxiety disorders. In fact, several studies have shown that persons suffering from anxiety-related disorders often do not receive the most appropriate form of treatment (Pollard et al., 1989; Swinson et al., 1992); namely, one of several empirically supported cognitive-behavioral interventions that we describe in more detail shortly.

WORKPLACE OR HOME STRESSORS WITH PARTICULAR RELEVANCE TO ANXIETY DISORDERS

The effects of stress, both at home and work, are synergistic and function to exacerbate problems associated with anxiety-related disorders. In vulnerable individuals, stress also contributes to the development of such disorders (Barlow, 2001). For instance, risk factors for the development of panic disorder with and without agoraphobia include the occurrence of stressful life events such as illness, loss (e.g., death of a loved one, loss of home, job), and marital conflict (Favarelli & Pallanti, 1989); individual perceptions about the consequences of negative life events (e.g., losing a job, financial strain); and the belief that a negative life event is likely in the future (Pollard, Pollard, & Corn, 1989). Moreover, stress associated with attempts to quit using substances (e.g., alcohol, nicotine, caffeine, cocaine, marijuana), and managing the resulting withdrawal symptoms, can create an occasion for panic attacks and can exacerbate symptoms associated with all anxiety disorders. Exposure to unpredictable and uncontrollable negative life events, such as pain or trauma, can function similarly to exacerbate anxiety symptoms and even can contribute to the development of PTSD and phobias. Unfortunately, knowledge of the relation between stress and risk for the development and exacerbation of anxiety disorders remains somewhat underdeveloped, and our knowledge of protective factors (e.g., experience with mastery and control, social support) for anxiety disorders is equally limited. Nonetheless, excessive stress does appear to exert deleterious effects on quality of life, physical and mental health, and workplace performance, and it often precedes the development of anxiety disorders (Barlow, 2001; Marcaurelle, Bélanger, & Marchand, 2003). As a general rule, any stimulus or event that is the focus of clinical attention or functions as a trigger for anxiety (e.g., in the case of social phobia, speaking in front of a group), including important work and life activities that are disrupted because of anxiety-related symptoms (e.g., having intimacy with a partner for fear of panic attacks, being able to drive to work, shopping for groceries, being on time), will likely function as a stressor and negatively impact life functioning at home and work. A supportive and accommodating workplace environment may help to mitigate the psychosocial impact of stressors and the exacerbation of symptoms in individuals suffering from anxiety disorders. A more durable solution, however, is to assist anxiety suffers in making contact with treatment providers who can apply psychosocial, and in some cases pharmacological, treatments with known evidence of efficacy. It is to a discussion of such empirically supported treatment options that we now turn.

EMPIRICALLY BASED TREATMENTS FOR ANXIETY DISORDERS

Although several treatment options exist for persons suffering from anxiety-related disorders, those with the most empirical support include (1) cognitive-behavior therapy (CBT) (i.e., psychotherapy) alone, (2) pharmacologic interventions (i.e., drug therapy) alone, or (3) a combined approach that includes CBT and medications (Ballenger, 1999). Next we provide an overview of each approach, beginning with CBT.

Psychosocial Treatments: CBT

CBT is a structured, time-limited (i.e., 8 to 15 weeks), problem-focused intervention approach, with a strong evidentiary base showing that it is the psychosocial treatment of choice for the anxiety disorders (Barlow, 2001; Chambless et al., 1996; Task Force, 1995). Most empirically derived CBTs begin with the premise that anxiety-related problems are learned, in much the same way as more adaptive forms of behavior are learned. The therapeutic context, therefore, is viewed as a means to teach clients new and more adaptive ways of behaving with respect to their thoughts, feelings, and environment more generally. In the process, symptoms are targeted directly, and clients are taught strategies to gain control over their symptoms while also learning ways to more fully engage in valued life activities such as being productive in the workplace or school or being able to move about the environment freely with minimal anxiety and fear (e.g., Barlow, Rapee, & Brown, 1992). Often this is achieved, or at least initiated, by getting clients to confront feared objects or aversive bodily events in a safe therapeutic context (i.e., exposure), which is believed to facilitate corrective emotional learning and fear reduction. For instance, an individual with a spider phobia may have learned that spiders are dangerous by having been bitten by a spider, watching someone react fearfully to a spider, or simply hearing that spiders are bad or harmful. As a consequence, this person may avoid spiders and contexts where exposure to spiders is likely. Such avoidance, in turn, prevents opportunities to learn that spiders are not necessarily harmful, and thus serves to maintain phobic responding. Structured and systematic exposure to the feared object or situation allows for attenuation of excessive anxiety and fear and alters the powerful action tendency to escape or avoid. Indeed, repeated, systematic, and controlled exposure is at the core of virtually all empirically supported treatments for anxiety disorders. Such treatments also address problematic modes of thinking (e.g., negative thoughts, danger appraisals, worry, obsessions, coping statements) that precede or maintain an individual's problems.

The overarching goal of the cognitive components of CBT is to challenge and modify unrealistic thoughts, and thereafter assist the client in learning to use more realistic, less anxiety-inducing appraisals (see Beck & Emery, 1985). For example, a person with panic disorder might have the thought that a slight increase in heart rate is the sign of an impending heart attack. A clinician might help the client to evaluate the accuracy of this cognition and lead them to replace the thought with a more realistic appraisal of their bodily sensations (e.g., "An increase in heart rate has happened before and I have never had a heart attack," or "Increases in heart rate are perfectly normal when physically active," or "Such increases may be due to recently drinking a cup of coffee or walking up a flight of stairs").

Several cognitive and behavioral techniques are available to facilitate the process of corrective emotional learning and behavior change in persons suffering from anxiety disorders, including *in vivo* and imaginal exposure, thought stopping, response prevention, flooding and implosive therapy (i.e., an intense form of exposure therapy for PTSD), systematic desensitization, worry control and decatastrophizing, cognitive restructuring, guided imagery, breathing retraining, and applied muscle relaxation, to name a few. To facilitate new learning and to reinforce skills learned during treatment, therapists will frequently assign homework exercises. Such homework, in turn, may include activities that are to be completed at work (e.g., a person with social phobia is instructed to approach his or her supervisor about a work-related matter). Other techniques also may be used in conjunction with cognitive-behavioral interventions, including stress management, assertiveness training, participant modeling, and psychoeducation. Many of these and other related techniques have been shown to be efficacious in producing symptom reduction and relief from excessive and inappropriate anxiety and fear for most clients most of the time. Not surprisingly, such techniques are now included as components of comprehensive treatment manuals developed specifically for each of the anxiety disorders: panic disorder (i.e., interoceptive and exteroceptive exposure, applied relaxation, cognitive restructuring) (e.g., Barlow, 2001; Craske & Barlow, 2000), specific phobias (i.e., exposure and systematic desensitization) (e.g., Craske, Antony, & Barlow, 1997; Öst, Salkovskis, & Hellstrom, 1991), social phobia (i.e., exposure in a group treatment context, systematic desensitization, cognitive restructuring) (e.g., Feske & Chambless, 1995; Heimberg et al., 1995; Hope, Heimberg, & Bruch, 1995; Hope, Heimberg, Juster, & Turk, 2000), OCD (i.e., exposure and response prevention) (Kozak & Foa, 1997), GAD (i.e., worry control and exposure, applied relaxation)

(Borkovec & Whisman, in press; Zinbarg, Craske, & Barlow, 1993), and PTSD (i.e., systematic guided exposure and trauma reprocessing) (Brom, Kleber, & Defares, 1989; Foa & Kozak, 1986; Foy, 1992; Solomon, Gerrity, & Muff, 1992), to name a few. Finally, we should add that length of treatment and positive treatment response depends on a number of factors (e.g., severity of the disorder, co-occurring conditions, level of motivation for treatment, number and frequency of treatment sessions, and the quality of the working relationship between the client and therapist). Therapeutic gains, in turn, can be somewhat delayed and are often preceded by a worsening of symptoms (including associated problems at work) as clients begin to expose themselves to previously avoided cues and situations.

Pharmacological Interventions

Several classes of medications have been shown to be more effective than placebo in the treatment of most anxiety disorders (the exception being specific phobias). Medications also tend to offer more immediate symptom relief relative to psychosocial interventions. Several studies, for example, suggest that benzodiazepines (e.g., alprazolam, clonazepam, adinazolam, lorazepam) are efficacious in the treatment of symptoms associated with panic disorder with and without agoraphobia (Bennett, Moioffer, Stanton, Dwight, & Keck, 2000) and most other anxiety disorders with the exception of OCD (Mavissakalian & Ryan, 1997). Benzodiazapines, and their close cousin buspirone, are relatively fast acting and usually are taken to manage acute episodes of anxiety or panic. Yet, benzodiazapines often are accompanied by several unpleasant side effects (e.g., sedation, memory impairment, and increased anger and dysphoria), and the potential for dependence and addiction is high (Hoehn-Saric, 2000; Mavissakalian & Ryan, 1997; Moller, 1999). Moreover, benzodiazepines (e.g., alprazolam) tend to be associated with earlier improvements (Cross National Collaborative Panic Study, Second Phase Investigators, 1992) and greater rates of relapse following discontinuation (Rickels, Schweizer, Weiss, & Zavodnick, 1993) relative to antidepressants (e.g., imipramine) in the treatment of panic disorder. This has led investigators to develop additional cognitive-behavioral treatment programs to assist patients in discontinuing use of this class of medication (Otto et al., 1993). For these and other reasons, routine use of benzodiazapines as a first-line treatment for anxiety disorders has declined somewhat in recent years.

Unlike the benzodiazepines, selective serotonin reuptake inhibitors (SSRIs) (e.g., clomipramine), monoamine oxidase inhibitors (MAOIs) (e.g., phenelzine, tranylcypromine), and tricyclic antidepressants (e.g., imipramine) are not associated with dependence or addiction and are widely used in the treatment of several anxiety-related disorders. Specifically, the SSRIs and MAOIs appear equally efficacious when compared with benzodiazapines and more effective relative to placebo in the treatment of panic disorder and social phobia (Bennett et al., 2000; van Ameringen, Mancini, Oakman, & Farvolden, 2000). The SSRIs (i.e., clomipramine, fluoxetine, fluvoxamine) also appear effective in treating OCD (see Clomipramine Collaborative Study Group, 1991; Greist et al., 1990; Hoehn-Saric, McLeod, Zimmerli, & Hipsley, 1993; Park, Jefferson, & Greist, 2000) and GAD (Hoehn-Saric, 2000) and are increasingly being used as a first-line medication in the treatment of those suffering from PTSD (Fichtner, Poddig, & deVito, 2000). Likewise, evidence supports the efficacy of tricyclic antidepressants in the treatment of panic disorder (Bennett et al., 2000), OCD (Park et al., 2000), and social phobia (van Ameringen et al., 2000). Yet, tricyclics work less well in the treatment of PTSD (Fichtner et al., 2000) and do not appear efficacious as a treatment for GAD (Hoehn-Saric, 2000). Although the SSRIs, MAOIs, and tricyclic antidepressants are usually well tolerated, they are nonetheless associated with mild-to-severe side effects such as nausea, dry mouth, increased heart rate, diarrhea, sexual dysfunction, sedation and weight gain, stomach upset, and headache (Bennett et al., 2000; Hoehn-Saric, 2000; Mavissakalian & Ryan, 1997). Use of MAOIs also require that patients adhere to specific dietary restrictions; avoid all foods containing tyramine (e.g., most cheeses, sour cream, homemade yogurts, aged meats and fish, overripe bananas, and most alcoholic beverages); and over-the-counter cold medicines (including nose drops or sprays), amphetamines, diet pills, tricyclic antidepressants, and certain antihistamines so as to prevent a lethal reaction (Bennett et al., 2000). Many patients find such restrictions prohibitive and opt for SSRIs or tricyclic antidepressants as a first option. Moreover, unlike the benzodiazalines, SSRIs, MAOIs, and tricyclics often require three to six weeks before any therapeutic effects may become evident (Bennett et al., 2000; Mavissakalian & Ryan, 1997). On the whole, antidepressants are useful in helping anxiety sufferers manage acute anxiety symptoms, but they are not regarded as a long-term therapeutic solution.

Combined Pharmacological and Psychosocial Interventions

Although evidence supports the efficacy of CBT alone and medications alone in the treatment of anxiety disorders, there remains considerable disagreement about the relative merits of combining treatments. The studies that have been done showed that it appears that combining CBT with medications (CBT vs. imipramine or CBT vs. benzodiazapines) results in equivalent, and in some cases better, long-term outcomes for cases of panic disorder with and without agoraphobic relative to either treatment modality alone (Clark et al., 1994; Klein, Ross, & Cohen, 1987; Marks et al., 1983, 1993). Yet, CBT by itself generally outperforms medications (i.e., imipramine) in the long term but not in the short term (Barlow, Gorman, Shear, & Woods, 2000; see also Boyer, 1995; Clum, Clum, & Surls, 1993 ; Cox, Endler, Lee, & Swinson, 1992). Similar patterns have been observed with social phobia (Heimberg et al., 1994; Turner, Beidel, & Jacob, 1994), although with OCD and GAD, the tendency is for combined treatments to result in better long-term treatment gains relative to CBT or SSRIs alone (Cottraux et al., 1995; Kasvikis & Marks, 1988; Power, Simpson, Swanson, & Wallace, 1990a, 1990b). Data regarding the efficacy of combined treatments for PTSD are still too limited to draw any meaningful conclusions. Poorer long-term outcomes with combined treatments relative to CBT alone has been attributed to several factors, chief among them being that patients tend to attribute improvement to the medications and not their own efforts to change how they think, feel, and behave with respect to their anxiety. Poorer treatment outcome in general, whether with combined or singular treatment approaches, is associated with poor initial social and work adjustment, greater pretreatment severity, use of medications, longer duration of the disorder, more pervasive avoidance, poor compliance with treatment or homework, and comorbidity with other forms of psychopathology.

RELAPSE PREVENTION

Evidence supporting the efficacy of medications and CBT, either alone or in combination, is well established for most anxiety disorders. Yet, at present, there is no treatment available that can offer a cure. As described earlier, anxiety disorders tend to be chronic conditions that wax and wane over time and are associated with high-rates of comorbidity, poor quality of life, and impairments in both psychosocial and occupational functioning. Given the current state of treatment development, most agree that full functional recovery is an achievable and reasonable treatment goal. This should not be taken to mean that one should expect complete resolution of symptoms and invulnerability to relapse. Rates of relapse, or a return of symptoms and functional difficulties after a period of apparent recovery, are quite high following medication discontinuation relative to CBT alone (Barlow, 2001). Indeed, individuals who believe that their improvements are due to the medications are at a greater risk for relapse than individuals who attribute their improvement to psychosocial interventions (Basoglu et al., 1994). Lingering symptoms, vulnerability to "normal" anxiety, and stress-related intensification of symptoms and anxiety also may contribute to ongoing risk of relapse following treatment. Experiencing a relapse back to maladaptive behavior patterns after the termination of successful treatment may be very disheartening for the client and may negatively impact performance at work. An employee may experience emotions such as shame, disappointment, sadness, frustration, or confusion following a relapse. Most treatment approaches, therefore, incorporate some form of relapse prevention.

Several strategies have been integrated successfully into medication therapy and CBT to minimize relapse, while reinforcing treatment gains. For instance, in some cases individuals may be instructed to continue with their medication regimen for a period of six months or more beyond the acute treatment phase so as to prevent a return of anxiety-related symptoms. Such continuation treatment may be supplemented with maintenance treatment consisting of long-term use of medications, with the goal being to prevent a recurrence of anxiety episodes. Maintenance treatment is normally reserved for individuals who show recurrent and severe episodes of anxiety or significant impairments and disability associated with past episodes. As indicated, medications are not viewed as a cure or long-term solution for anxiety-related problems. Moreover, medications alone do nothing to teach clients new ways of managing and coping with their anxious responses, including their social and nonsocial environment. Thus, long-term comprehensive relapse prevention must include some form of psychosocial intervention. For instance, unlike medication therapies, CBTs teach clients skills and strategies to anticipate and manage recurrent episodes of anxiety and fear outside of the therapy context, where it counts. Such skills, in turn, are often difficult for clients to develop readily, and thus psychosocial interventions may include additional booster sessions following the acute treatment phase, while also stressing the importance of continued practice with therapeutic exercises post-therapy (e.g., exposure, relaxation) so as to reinforce skills development and to promote maintenance and generalization of treatment gains. These and other components of CBT have been shown to minimize relapse while contributing to maintenance of treatment gains (Hiss, Foa, & Kozak, 1994).

Employers should, therefore, expect some minor, and in some cases major, setbacks after an employee completes treatment for an anxiety disorder. Although successful work performance is an expected outcome of successful treatment, the employee may have difficulty adapting to increased work responsibilities and job stress after a period of time in which expectations may have been relaxed. A gradual return to work-related responsibilities may, therefore, be helpful as a method to minimize the probability of relapse. Similarly, efforts should be made to promote normal workplace functioning by gradually removing of any workplace accommodations that may have been put in place prior to treatment. Employees with past histories of anxiety-related problems should be encouraged to attend follow-up appointments with their therapist, join support groups in their local community, or both. Employer support and flexibility may be necessary for the client to engage in follow-up activities in cases where support groups or individual follow-up session are held during normal work hours.

THERAPEUTIC BENEFITS OF WORK

Employment may confer several important primary and secondary benefits to employees who suffer from anxiety disorders. Work provides individuals with financial resources, a sense of identity and purpose, self-esteem, structure, opportunities to create and innovate, and social interaction and support. The financial and social consequences of work, in turn, often facilitate access to other valued life domains, such as education, quality health care, child care, recreation, leisure time, and tangible items such as food, clothing, and shelter. The primary and secondary benefits of work may play a crucial role in the alleviation or prevention of anxiety disorders, whereas the loss of such benefits can have serious negative consequences. Indeed, performing well at one's job and remaining employed represent two domains that often serve to motivate individuals to seek out and adhere to treatment. Insufficient financial resources, whether because of low wages, unemployment, limited benefits, or poor health care, can impede access to quality treatment for anxiety-related problems. Unemployment simply compounds anxiety-related problems and associated conditions (e.g., depression).

As indicated, most psychosocial interventions include homework and other structured exercises that are to be completed outside of therapy. Exercises are frequently integrated into normal workplace routines, and thus it is useful to think of employment as functioning as an important therapeutic context. For instance, an individual suffering from debilitating worry regarding employment and workplace situations may be encouraged to design and conduct experiments in the workplace setting so as to learn to disconfirm distorted cognitions (e.g., "If I take the full time allotted for my lunch break, then I will be fired"). Such an experiment may simply involve the individual taking a full lunch break in order to teach him or her that worry-related negative consequences do not follow. Similarly, an employee with panic disorder who fears sensations of breathlessness may be instructed by his or her therapist to use the stairs whenever possible instead of taking the elevator. Because the employment setting is away from home, it may function to counteract the tendency toward agoraphobic avoidance. Together with the employee, the employer may assist in treatment by providing an employee suffering from social phobia with opportunities to interact with others. The same is true in cases of specific phobias, though the focus shifts to practiced exposure to fear cues or situations (e.g., elevators, modes of transportation, insects, heights). The practice of engaging in exposure exercises in the workplace may have somewhat less relevance for PTSD. Yet, if an employee's PTSD was precipitated by work-related trauma (e.g., accident, assault), completing exposure exercises in the workplace may be an important and valuable component of treatment. Anxiety sufferers also may derive vicarious therapeutic benefits by having opportunities to observe co-workers modeling appropriate behaviors in the workplace. These are just a few examples of a range of possible therapeutic benefits of work, and they illustrate the therapeutic importance of the workplace in the promotion of treatment and recovery.

SUMMARY

Five of the most common anxiety disorders were reviewed, including clinical and workplace manifestations, epidemiology, and available pharmacological and psychosocial treatments with known evidence of efficacy. All of the anxiety disorders reviewed are associated with high rates of comorbidity with other psychological problems, significant distress, and varied degrees of impairment in social, interpersonal, and occupational functioning. Both pharmacological and cognitive-behavioral treatments are efficacious in the treatment of anxiety disorders. Evidence is mixed regarding the efficacy of combining medication and CBT, particularly with regard to long-term outcomes. Data regarding other cost-effective modes of intervention involving minimal therapist contact (e.g., self-help books and self-administered treatments) appear promising with panic disorder, but the jury is still out about their usefulness with other anxiety-related problems. Direct and indirect costs associated with anxiety-related problems are enormous, and yet the costs of anxiety disorders in the workplace are only recently becoming clear. Employment confers numerous benefits and challenges for anxiety disorder sufferers, and we hope that this brief overview will be of use in minimizing the disruption that can result from such problems in and outside the workplace.

References

American Psychiatric Association. (1994). *Diagnostic and statistical manual of mental disorders* (4th ed.). Washington, DC: Author.

Antony, M. M. (2001). Specific phobia: A brief overview and guide to assessment. In M. M. Antony, S. M. Orsillo, & L. Roemer (Eds.), *Practitioner's guide to empirically based measures of anxiety* (pp. 127-132). New York: Kluwer.

Antony, M. M., Orsillo, S. M., & Roemer, L. (Eds.). (2001). *Practitioner's guide to empirically based measures of anxiety.* New York: Kluwer.

Ballenger, J. C. (1999). Current treatments of the anxiety disorders in adults. *Biological Psychiatry, 46,* 1579-1594.

Barlow, D. H. (2001). *Anxiety and its disorders: The nature and treatment of anxiety and panic* (2nd ed.). New York: Guilford.

Barlow, D. H., Gorman, J. M., Shear, M. K., & Woods, S. W. (2000). Cognitive-behavioral therapy, imipramine, or their combination for panic disorder: A randomized controlled trial. *Journal of the American Medical Association, 283,* 2529-2536.

Barlow, D. H., Rapee, R. M., & Brown, T. A. (1992). Behavioral treatment of generalized anxiety disorder. *Behavior Therapy, 23,* 551-570.

Barsky, A. J., Delamater, B. A., & Orav, J. E. (1999). Panic disorder patients and their medical care. *Psychosomatics, 40,* 50-56.

Basoglu, M., Marks, I. M., Swinson, R. P., Noshirvani, H., O'Sullivan, G., & Kuch, K. (1994). Pre-treatment predictors of treatment outcome in panic disorder and agoraphobia treated with alprazolam and exposure. *Journal of Affective Disorders, 30,* 123-132.

Beck, A. T., & Emery, G. (1985). *Anxiety disorders and phobias: A cognitive perspective.* New York: Basic Books.

Bennett, J. A., Moioffer, M., Stanton, S. P., Dwight, M., & Keck, P. E., Jr. (2000). A risk-benefit assessment of pharmacological treatments for panic disorder. In K. J. Palmer (Ed.), *Pharmacotherapy of anxiety disorders* (pp. 31-42). Hong Kong: Adis International.

Blazer, D. G., Hughes, D., George, L. K., Schwartz, M., & Boyer, R. (1991). Generalized anxiety disorder. In L. N. Robins & D. A. Regier (Eds.), *Psychiatric disorders in America: The Epidemiologic Catchment Area study* (pp. 180-203). New York: Free Press.

Borkovec, T. D., Shadick, R., & Hopkins, M. (1991). The nature of normal and pathological worry. In R. M. Rapee & D. H. Barlow (Eds.), *Chronic anxiety, generalized anxiety disorder, and mixed anxiety depression* (pp. 29-51). New York: Guilford.

Borkovec, T. D., & Whisman, M. A. (in press). Psychosocial treatment for generalized anxiety disorder. In M. Mavissakalian & R. Prien (Eds.), *Anxiety disorders: Psychological and pharmacological treatments.* Washington, DC: American Psychiatric Press.

Bourdon, K. H., Boyd, J. H., Rae, D. S., Burns, B. J., Thompson, J. W., & Locke, B. Z. (1988). Gender differences in phobias: Results of the ECA Community Study. *Journal of Anxiety Disorders, 2,* 227-241.

Boyer, W. (1995). Serotonin uptake inhibitors are superior to imipramine and alprazolam in alleviating panic attacks: A meta-analysis. *International Journal of Clinical Psychopharmacology, 10,* 45-49.

Brom, D., Kleber, R. J., & Defares, P. B. (1989). Brief psychotherapy for posttraumatic stress disorders. *Journal of Consulting and Clinical Psychology, 57,* 607-612.

Brown, T. A., Campbell, L. A., Lehman, C. L., Grisham, J. R., & Mancill, R. B. (2001). Current and lifetime comorbidity of the *DSM-IV* anxiety and mood disorders in a large clinical sample. *Journal of Abnormal Psychology, 110,* 585-599.

Brown, T. A., Di Nardo, P., & Barlow, D. H. (1994). *Anxiety Disorders Interview Schedule for DSM-IV.* San Antonio, TX: Psychological Corporation.

Burke, K. C., Burke, J. D., Regier, D. A., & Rae, D. S. (1990). Age of onset of selected mental disorders in five community populations. *Archives of General Psychiatry, 47,* 511-518.

Chambless, D. L., Sanderson, W. C., Shoham, V., Bennett Johnson, S., Pope, K. S., Crits-Christoph, P., Baker, M., Johnson, B., Woody, S. R., Sue, S., Beutler, L., Williams, D. A., & McCurry, S. (1996). An update on empirically validated therapies. *The Clinical Psychologist, 49,* 5-18.

Clark, D. M., Salkovskis, P. M., Hackmann, A., Middleton, H., Anastasiades, P., & Gelder, M. (1994). A comparison of cognitive therapy, applied relaxation and imipramine in the treatment of panic disorder. *British Journal of Psychiatry, 164,* 759-769.

Clomipramine Collaborative Study Group. (1991). Clomipramine in the treatment of patients with obsessive-compulsive disorder. *Archives of General Psychiatry, 48,* 730-738.

Clum, G. A., Clum, G. A., & Surls, R. (1993). A meta-analysis of treatments for panic disorder. *Journal of Consulting and Clinical Psychology, 61,* 317-326.

Clum, G. A., & Knowles, S. L. (1991). Why do some people with panic disorders become agoraphobic? A review. *Clinical Psychology Review, 11,* 295-313.

Cottraux, J., Note, I., Cungi, C., Legeron, P., Heim, F., Chneiweiss, L., Bernard, G., & Bouvard, M. (1995). A controlled study of cognitive behaviour therapy with buspirone or placebo in panic disorder with agoraphobia. *British Journal of Psychiatry, 167,* 635-641 .

Cox, B. J., Endler, N. S., Lee, P. S., & Swinson, R. P. (1992). A meta-analysis of treatments for panic disorder with agoraphobia: Imipramine, alprazolam, and in vivo exposure. *Journal of Behaviour Therapy and Experimental Psychiatry, 23,* 175-182.

Craske, M. G. (1991). Phobic fear and panic attacks: The same emotional states triggered by different cues? *Clinical Psychology Review, 11,* 599-620.

Craske, M. G., Antony, M. M., & Barlow, D. H. (1997). *Mastery of your specific phobia.* Boulder, CO: Graywind.

Craske, M. G., & Barlow, D. H. (2000). *Mastery of your anxiety and panic—Third edition (MAP III).* Boulder, CO: Graywind.

Cross National Collaborative Panic Study, Second Phase Investigators. (1992). Drug treatment of panic disorder. *British Journal of Psychiatry, 160,* 191-202.

DuPont, R. L., Rice, D. P., Miller, L. S., Shiraki, S. S., Rowland, C. R., & Harwood, H. J. (1996). Economic costs of anxiety disorders. *Anxiety, 2,* 167-172.

Eaton, W. W., Dryman, A., & Weissman, M. M. (1991). Panic and phobia. In L. N. Robins & D. A. Regier (Eds.), *Psychiatric disorders in America: The Epidemiological Catchment Area study* (pp. 155-203). New York: Free Press.

Favarelli, C., & Pallanti, S. (1989). Recent life events and panic disorder. *American Journal of Psychiatry, 146,* 622-626.

Feske, U., & Chambless, D. L. (1995). Cognitive behavioral versus exposure only treatment for social phobia: A meta-analysis. *Behavior Therapy, 26,* 695-720.

Fichtner, C. G., Poddig, B. E., & deVito, R. A. (2000). Post-traumatic stress disorder: Pathophysiological aspects and pharmacological approaches to treatment. In K. J. Palmer (Ed.), *Pharmacotherapy of anxiety disorders* (pp. 61-92). Hong Kong: Adis International.

Flint, A. J. (1994). Epidemiology and comorbidity of anxiety disorders in the elderly. *American Journal of Psychiatry, 151,* 640-649 .

Foa, E. B., & Kozak, M. J. (1986). Emotional processing of fear: Exposure to corrective information. *Psychological Bulletin, 99,* 20-35.

Foa, E. B., & Wilson, R. (2001). *Stop obsessing! How to overcome your obsessions and compulsions* (Rev. ed.). New York: Bantam Books.

Forsyth, J. P., & Eifert, G. H. (1996). Systemic alarms and fear conditioning I: A reappraisal of what is being conditioned. *Behavior Therapy, 27,* 441-462.

Forsyth, J. P., & Eifert, G. H. (1998). Phobic anxiety and panic: An integrative behavioral account of their origin and treatment. In J. J. Plaud & G. H. Eifert (Eds.), *From behavior theory to behavior therapy* (pp. 38-67). Needham, MA: Allyn & Bacon.

Foy, D. W. (1992). *Treating PTSD: Cognitive-behavioral strategies.* New York: Guilford.

Greenberg, P. E., Sisitsky, T., Kessler, R. C., Finkelstein, S. N., Berndt, E. R., Davidson, J. R. T., Ballenger, J. C., & Fyer, A. J. (1999). The economic burden of anxiety disorders in the 1990s. *Journal of Clinical Psychiatry, 60,* 427-435.

Greist, J. H., Jefferson, J. W., Rosenfeld, R., Gutzmann, L. D., March, J. S., & Barklage, N. E. (1990). Clomipramine and obsessive-compulsive disorder: Placebo-controlled double-blind study of 32 patients. *Journal of Clinical Psychiatry, 51,* 292-297.

Heimberg, R. G., Juster, H. R., Brown, E. J., Holle, C., Schneier, F. R., & Gitow, A. (1994, November). *Cognitive-behavioral versus pharmacological treatment of social phobia: Posttreatment and follow-up effects.* Paper presented at the Annual Meeting of the Association for Advancement of Behaviour Therapy, San Diego, CA.

Heimberg, R. G., Liebowitz, M. R., Hope, D. A., & Shneier, F. R. (Eds.). (1995). *Social phobia: Diagnosis, assessment, and treatment.* New York: Guilford.

Hiss, H., Foa, E. B., & Kozak, M. J. (1994). Relapse prevention program for treatment of obsessive-compulsive disorder. *Journal of Consulting and Clinical Psychology, 62,* 801-808.

Hoehn-Saric, R. (2000). Generalized anxiety disorder: Guidelines for diagnosis and treatment. In K. J. Palmer (Ed.), *Pharmacotherapy of anxiety disorders* (pp. 1-15). Hong Kong: Adis International.

Hoehn-Saric, R., McLeod, D. R., Zimmerli, W. D., & Hipsley, P. A. (1993). Symptoms and physiological manifestations in obsessive-compulsive patient before and after treatment with clomipramine. *Journal of Clinical Psychiatry, 54,* 272-276.

Hope, D. A., Heimberg, R. G., & Bruch, M. A. (1995). Dismantling cognitive-behavioral group therapy for social phobia. *Behaviour Research and Therapy, 33,* 637-650.

Hope, D. A., Heimberg, R. G., Juster, H. R., & Turk, C. L. (2000). *Managing social anxiety: A cognitive-behavioral therapy approach.* Boulder, CO: Graywind.

Kasvikis, Y., & Marks, I. (1988). Clomipramine, self-exposure, and therapist-accompanied exposure in obsessive-compulsive ritualizers: Two-year follow-up. *Journal of Anxiety Disorders, 2,* 291-298.

Kessler, R. C., McGonagle, K. A., Zhao, S., Nelson, C. B., Hughes, M., Eshleman, S., Wittchen, H. U., & Kendler, K. S. (1994). Lifetime and 12-month prevalence of *DSM-III-R* psychiatric disorders in the United States: Results from the National Comorbidity Survey. *Archives of General Psychiatry, 51,* 8-19.

Kessler, R. C., Nelson, C. B., McGonagle, J., Liu, M., Swart, M., & Blazer, D. G. (1996). Co-morbidity of *DSM-III-R* major depressive disorder in the general population: Results of the U.S. National Comorbidity Survey. *British Journal of Psychiatry, 168,* 17-30.

Kessler, R. C., Sonnega, P. E., Bromet, E., Hughes, M., & Nelson, C. B. (1995). Posttraumatic stress disorder in the National Comorbidity Survey. *Archives of General Psychiatry, 52,* 1048-1060.

Klein, D. F., Ross, D. C., & Cohen, P. (1987). Panic and avoidance in agoraphobia: Application of path analysis to treatment studies. *Archives of General Psychiatry, 44,* 377-385.

Klerman, G. L., Weissman, M., Ouellette, R., Johnson, J., & Greenwald, S. (1991). Panic attacks in the community: Social morbidity and health care utilization. *Journal of the American Medical Association, 265,* 742-746.

Kozak, M. J., & Foa, E. B. (1997). *Mastery of obsessive-compulsive disorder: A cognitive-behavioral approach*. Boulder, CO: Graywind.

Leon, A. C., Portera, L., & Weissman, M. M. (1995). The social costs of anxiety disorders. *British Journal of Psychiatry, 166*, 19-22.

Mannuzza, S., Fyer, A. J., Liebowitz, M. R., & Klein, D. F. (1990). Delineating the boundaries of social phobia: Its relationship to panic disorder and agoraphobia. *Journal of Anxiety Disorders, 4*, 41-59.

Marcaurelle, R., Bélanger, C., & Marchand, A. (2003). Marital relationship and the treatment of panic disorder with agoraphobia: A critical review. *Clinical Psychology Review, 23*, 247-276.

Markowitz, J. S., Weissman, M. M., Ouellette, R., Lish, J. D., & Klerman, G. L. (1989). Quality of life in panic disorder. *Archives of General Psychiatry, 46*, 984-992.

Marks, I. M., Gray, S., Cohen, D., Hill, R., Mawson, D., Ramm, E., & Stern, R. S. (1983). Imipramine and brief therapist-aided exposure in agoraphobics having self-exposure homework. *Archives of General Psychiatry, 40*, 153-162.

Marks, I. M., Swinson, R. P., Basoglu, M., Kuch, K., Noshirvani, H., O'Sullivan, G., Lelliott, P. T., Kirby, M., McNamee, G., Sengun, S., & Wickwire, K. (1993). Alprazolam and exposure alone and combined in panic disorder with agoraphobia: A controlled study in London and Toronto. *British Journal of Psychiatry, 162*, 776-787.

Marsland, D. W., Wood, M., & Mayo, F. (1976). Content of family practice: A data bank for patient care, curriculum, and research in family practice. *Journal of Family Practice, 3*, 25-68.

Mavissakalian, M. R., & Ryan, M. T. (1997). The role of medication. In W. T. Roth (Ed.), *Treating anxiety disorders* (pp. 175-203). San Francisco: Jossey-Bass.

Miranda, R., Jr., & Rollins, C. W. (1997). Obsessive compulsive disorder: A vocational perspective. *Journal of Applied Rehabilitation Counseling, 28*, 28-30.

Moller, H. J. (1999). Effectiveness and safety of benzodiazepines. *Journal of Clinical Psychopharmacology, 19*(6, Suppl 2), 2S-11S.

Noyes, R., Woodman, C., Garvey, M. J., Cook, B. L., Suelzer, M., Clancy, J., & Anderson, D. J. (1992). Generalized anxiety disorder vs. panic disorder: Distinguishing characteristics and patterns of comorbidity. *Journal of Nervous and Mental Disease, 180*, 369-379.

Öst, L., Salkovskis, P. M., & Hellstrom, K. (1991). One-session therapist-directed exposure vs. self-exposure in the treatment of spider phobia. *Behavior Therapy, 22*, 407-422.

Otto, M. W., Pollack, M. H., Sachs, G. S., Reiter, S. R., Meltzer-Brody, S., & Rosenbaum, J. F. (1993). Discontinuation of benzodiazepine treatment: Efficacy of cognitive-behavioral therapy for patients with panic disorder. *American Journal of Psychiatry, 150*, 1485-1490.

Park, L. T., Jefferson, J. W., & Greist, J. H. (2000). Obsessive-compulsive disorder: Treatment options. In K. J. Palmer (Ed.), *Pharmacotherapy of anxiety disorders* (pp. 43-59). Hong Kong: Adis International.

Pollard, C. A., Henderson, J. G., Frank, M., & Margolis, R. B. (1989). Help-seeking patterns of anxiety-disordered individuals in the general population. *Journal of Anxiety Disorders, 3*, 131-138.

Pollard, C. A., Pollard, H. J., & Corn, K. J. (1989). Panic onset and major events in the lives of agoraphobics: A test of contiguity. *Journal of Abnormal Psychology, 98*, 318-321.

Power, K. G., Simpson, R. J., Swanson, V., & Wallace, L. A. (1990a). A controlled comparison of cognitive-behaviour therapy, diazepam, and placebo, alone and in combination, for the treatment of generalized anxiety disorder. *Journal of Anxiety Disorders, 4*, 267-292.

Power, K. G., Simpson, R. J., Swanson, V., & Wallace, L. A. (1990b). Controlled comparison of pharmacological and psychological treatment of generalized anxiety disorder in primary care. *British Journal of General Practice, 40,* 289-294.

Rasmussen, S., & Eisen, J. L. (1991). Phenomenology of OCD: Clinical subtypes, heterogeneity, and coexistence. In J. Zohar, T. Insel, & S. Rasmussen (Eds.), *The psychobiology of obsessive-compulsive disorder* (pp. 13-43). New York: Guilford.

Rees, C. S., Richards, J. C., & Smith, L. M. (1998). Medical utilization and costs in panic disorder: A comparison with social phobia. *Journal of Anxiety Disorders, 12,* 421-435.

Rickels, K., Schweizer, E., Weiss, S., & Zavodnick, S. (1993). Maintenance drug treatment for panic disorder: Short- and long-term outcome after drug taper. *Archives of General Psychiatry, 50,* 61-68.

Robins, L. N., Helzer, J. E., Weissman, M. M., Orvaschel, H., Gruenberg, E., Burke, J. D., & Regier, D. A. (1984). Lifetime prevalence of specific psychiatric disorders in three sites. *Archives of General Psychiatry, 41,* 949-958.

Salvador-Carulla, L., Segui, J., Fernadez-Cano, P., & Canet, J. (1995). Costs and offset effects in panic disorders. *British Journal of Psychiatry, 166,* 23-28.

Sanderson, W. C., DiNardo, P. A., Rapee, R. M., & Barlow, D. H. (1990). Syndrome comorbidity in patients diagnosed with a *DSM-III-R* anxiety disorder. *Journal of Abnormal Psychology, 99,* 308-312.

Siegel, L., Jones, W. C., & Wilson, J. O. (1990). Economic and life consequences experienced by a group of individuals with panic disorder. *Journal of Anxiety Disorders, 4,* 201-211.

Solomon, S. D., Gerrity, E. T., & Muff, A. M. (1992). Efficacy of treatments for posttraumatic stress disorder: An empirical review. *Journal of the American Medical Association, 268,* 633-638.

Swinson, R. P., Cox, B. J., & Woszcyzna, C. B. (1992). Use of medical services and treatment for panic disorder with agoraphobia and for social phobia. *Canadian Medical Association Journal, 147,* 878-883.

Task Force on Promotion and Dissemination of Psychological Procedures. (1995). Training in and dissemination of empirically-validated psychological treatments: Report and recommendations. *The Clinical Psychologist, 48,* 3-23.

Turner, S. M., Beidel, D. C., & Jacob, R. G. (1994). Social phobia: A comparison of behaviour therapy and atenolol. *Journal of Clinical and Consulting Psychology, 62,* 350-358.

van Ameringen, M., Mancini, C., Oakman, J. M., & Farvolden, P. (2000). In K. J. Palmer (Ed.), *Pharmacotherapy of anxiety disorders* (pp. 17-30). Hong Kong: Adis International.

Yerkes, R. M., & Dodson, J. D. (1908). The relation of strength of stimuli to rapidity of habit-formation. *Journal of Comparative Neurology and Psychology, 18,* 459-482.

Zinbarg, R. E., Craske, M. G., & Barlow, D. H. (1993). *Mastery of your anxiety and worry.* Boulder, CO: Graywind.

8

Acute and Post-Traumatic Stress Disorder

ELISA BOLTON
New Hampshire–Dartmouth Psychiatric Research Center

DANA R. HOLOHAN
Salem VA Medical Center

LYNDA A. KING AND DANIEL W. KING
VA Boston Healthcare System and Boston University School of Medicine

DESCRIPTION OF THE DISORDER AND WORKPLACE MANIFESTATIONS

Post-traumatic stress disorder (PTSD) is a chronic and potentially debilitating mental condition that develops in response to an extreme stressor. It is defined by its hallmark symptoms, which can be categorized by three symptom clusters. The first symptom cluster includes reliving the event through recurring nightmares or other intrusive images that may appear as if they pop into one's head. People who suffer from PTSD may have extreme emotional or physical reactions, such as uncontrollable shaking, heart palpitations, or panic, to reminders of the event as well. The second symptom cluster is characterized by feelings of emotional numbness and behaviors in which an individual attempts to avoid reminders of the event, including places, people, thoughts, or other activities associated with the trauma. People with PTSD often report feeling emotionally empty, they may withdraw from friends and family, and they may lose interest in everyday activities. The third symptom cluster is characterized by feelings of being on guard, hyperaroused, or both. This may include feelings of irritability or sudden anger, difficulty sleeping, lack of concentration, and feeling overly alert or easily startled. However, PTSD cannot be diagnosed until these symptoms have been present for at least one month.

There are several other problems that are frequently associated with the diagnosis of PTSD. These include acute stress disorder (ASD), feelings of depression and guilt, and other anxiety reactions, such as panic attacks. The essential features of ASD are similar to those of PTSD. ASD can be diagnosed if a person has been exposed to a traumatic event in which the person experiences feelings of dissociation, reexperiences symptoms, shows marked avoidance of reminders of the traumatic event, and experiences hyperarousal. For the diagnosis of ASD to be given, the distress must be present for a minimum of two days and a maximum of four weeks and must occur within four weeks of the traumatic event. Other common reactions to extreme stressors include physical complaints, such as chronic pain, fatigue, stomach pains, breathing problems, and headaches, and self-destructive or impulsive behavior, such as alcohol or drug abuse, high-risk sexual behavior, suicidal impulses, and fast or reckless driving.

The symptoms of PTSD/ASD are often manifest in the workplace and can significantly impact one's occupational functioning. The frequency and intensity of symptom presentation within the workplace, as well as the extent of impairment, likely depend to some extent on the nature of the traumatic event, as well as on the proximity of the trauma to the work environment. PTSD/ASD associated with a work-related trauma (defined as a trauma that is associated with one's work duties or one that occurs in close proximity to one's work environment) is likely to result in more prominent symptoms at work. However, PTSD/ASD following the experience of any traumatic event can profoundly affect one's work functioning, regardless of whether the traumatic event itself was work related.

Workplace manifestations of PTSD/ASD encompass the full range of symptoms of these disorders. The reexperiencing symptoms of the disorders are likely to be particularly notable in the work environment for the employee who has experienced a work-related trauma, as the work environment will likely serve as a reminder or trigger of the traumatic event for the employee. Therefore, the employee may understandably become quite uncomfortable in the work setting and may experience intense feelings, such as anxiety, fear, and sadness.

In addition, some individuals may experience dissociative symptoms. The employee may appear to zone out, lose track of where he or she is or what he or she is doing, and may be experienced by others as "flighty." Reminders of the traumatic event that may or may not be obvious to others may trigger these symptoms. Smells, sights, noises, and people all can serve as triggers to PTSD/ASD symptoms. For example, the bank teller who was robbed at gunpoint may become distressed entering the bank or counting money at the time of day of the robbery or whenever a man approaches her in the bank. Alternatively, the scent of a co-worker's cologne could trigger reexperiencing symptoms of a woman who was raped by a man wearing the same cologne. Similarly, a loud screeching sound outside the office building could trigger symptoms for a motor vehicle accident victim.

Avoidance symptoms associated with these disorders may also be manifest in the work environment. Employees may isolate themselves as a means of avoiding talking or thinking about the trauma. Employees may, for example, excuse themselves from lunch engagements and other social activities. In addition, individuals with PTSD/ASD may avoid specific places and things associated with the traumatic event. If the traumatic event took place in the context of the work environment, it is clear that performing at work may be quite challenging. For example, a nurse who was assaulted by a delirious male patient may have trouble administering care to all male patients. Similarly, a woman who was raped in the parking lot after leaving work may avoid the parking lot and also begin to avoid all spaces in which she feels vulnerable, which may include the elevator, the stairwell, and the hallway in the back of the office. In more severe cases, avoidance of trauma-related cues, if unaddressed, may lead to termination of one's employment.

Significant arousal symptoms associated with the disorders may also impact work functioning. For example, the difficulties with sleep associated with the disorders may result in tardiness and absenteeism from work, decreased concentration, and irritability with co-workers. An employee also may exhibit physiological responses, such as shaking, a rapid heart rate, and sweating. The employee may appear to have a short fuse, appear uncomfortable in a group setting, or seem jumpy or easily startled.

Clearly, the presence of such symptoms can significantly affect work performance. An employee with PTSD/ASD may appear unmotivated, lazy, and even irresponsible to an employer, especially if the reason for the employee's behavior is unknown or not discussed. Overall, if unaddressed, PTSD/ASD symptoms may result in frequent work difficulties, likely highlighted by tardiness, absenteeism, social isolation, problems with co-workers, and impaired cognitive functioning in the work environment. Individuals with PTSD/ASD also may exhibit difficulty returning to the work environment itself.

EPIDEMIOLOGY

Research suggests that a large proportion of the population (approximately 60 percent) will experience at least one traumatic event in their lifetime and approximately 8 percent develop PTSD (Kessler, Sonnega, Bromet, Hughes, & Nelson, 1995). Although research on ASD is in its early stages, studies have reported prevalence rates for ASD among motor vehicle accident victims as 21 percent (e.g., Holeva, Tarrier, & Wells, 2001) and approximately 19 percent in a study of victims of violent crime (e.g., Brewin, Andrews, Rose, & Kirk, 1999). These numbers suggest that across occupational groups, a significant number of individuals in the workforce will have had a diagnosis of PTSD/ASD. Within specific at-risk occupational groups, such as police officers and rescue workers, the prevalence of PTSD/ASD is likely even more pronounced (Rick, Perryman, Young, Guppy, & Hillage, 1998).

CASE ILLUSTRATIONS

Case 1: ASD Arising from an Event at Work

A week after being held hostage for three hours at knifepoint by a patient seeking narcotics, Dr. Smith, a 37-year-old emergency room physician, was referred for treatment. She noted that she had been having difficulty making it to work on time, in part because her anxiety level would rise dramatically as she approached the hospital. She described feeling exhausted yet unable to sleep at night. Although many of her co-workers had attempted to be supportive of her, she stated that she preferred to stay busy with work and to avoid talking with others, especially about the hostage situation. She remarked that some of the details of the event were crystal clear to her but that other aspects of the three hours seem hazy to her.

Dr. Smith also stated that she had been having a hard time concentrating. She noticed that she had made a few minor mistakes. Whereas she had previously been able to juggle numerous demands at one time, she now felt as if she could take care of only one task at a time while at home or at work. Finally, she described herself as having overwhelming waves of anxiety that felt like they came "out of the blue" and that this feeling was often accompanied by stomach upset or a tension headache.

Case 2: Workplace Demands Exacerbating the Symptoms of PTSD

Mr. Sullivan, a 55-year-old man, presented for treatment approximately a year after his son had been killed in a head-on collision. In the weeks after the accident, Mr. Sullivan noted that he would often appear for work exhausted and grief-stricken. Over the course of the year he noted that he had continued to experience nightmares, feelings of extreme sadness, and irritability. He felt as if he had been struggling to come to terms with his son's death. More recently, however, he had begun to feel worse, despite the fact that he had been given a promotion to area sales representative. He noted that he had begun to have more nightmares about his son's car accident and to have even greater trouble falling and staying asleep. As a result, he was extremely tired.

In addition, he indicated that he had been feeling very jumpy, that he would frequently "fly off the handle," and that he had been spending an inordinate amount of time contemplating suing the city over the dangerous design of the intersection at which his son was killed. Although he had previously thought of himself as a solid team player, he stated that he had been feeling very critical of just about everybody with whom he was working. He described going to the doctor not too long ago because he had been having a great deal of trouble with stomach upset, back pain, and shortness of breath. However, his doctor had not been able to identify a cause for his physical discomforts. He said that he had been feeling miserable and was expecting to be feeling better and not worse at this point.

At first he was unable to identify any changes in his life that might be contributing to the increase in his distress. After some discussion, he revealed that he and his wife had been having a difficult time getting along ever since his son died and that had led him to wonder if she might leave him. Furthermore, he had been feeling a great deal of pressure at work as a result of his promotion, a decline in the economy, and an increase in his sales requirements, which had previously been lowered out of respect for his loss and his need to grieve. Finally, he noted that his new route required him to drive through the intersection where his son's accident had occurred, which he had previously managed mostly to avoid.

RECOGNIZING AND EVALUATING PSYCHOPATHOLOGY

Usually the purpose of the assessment and the training of the technician or clinician conducting the evaluation will guide whether an individual is evaluated for PTSD/ASD formally or informally. Typically, professionals trained in assessment and standardized interview techniques are the ones who conduct formal evaluations. Often these assessments are based on psychometrically sound measures, such as the Clinician Administered PTSD Scale (CAPS) (Blake et al., 1995), the Structured Clinical Interview (SCID-IV) (First, Spitzer, Gibbon, & Williams, 1996), and the Anxiety Disorders Interview Schedule (ADIS-IV) (Brown, Di Nardo, & Barlow, 1994). These are well-established measures that assess the presence of each of the 17 symptoms of PTSD, as well as the severity of the distress in the case of the CAPS.

A broader range of individuals with less assessment experience usually conducts informal evaluations. These individuals may be assessing for PTSD/ASD as part of a triage system within an institution or as part of a research study. For individuals conducting informal or screening assessments for PTSD/ASD, standardized, psychometrically sound self-report measures such as the PTSD Checklist (PCL) (Weathers, Litz, Herman, Huska, & Keane, 1993), the Posttraumatic Diagnostic Scale (PDS) (Foa, Cashman, Jaycox, & Perry, 1997), or the Mississippi Scale for PTSD (Keane, Caddell, & Taylor, 1988) often are employed. Measures such as these are brief and easy to administer to screen for distress following exposure to traumatic life events. They use a self-report format and assess each of the 17 symptoms of PTSD.

Alternatively, there are many common emotions, physical responses, and behaviors that can be gauged by observation following an individual's exposure to traumatic events. Specifically, it is common for people to express anxiety and fear about the future, sadness, distrust, anger or desire for revenge, feelings of helplessness, guilt for surviving the event or for being involved in the event, or strong feelings of blame because the event was not prevented. Frequently, individuals who have experienced a traumatic event also will report or exhibit signs of fatigue or exhaustion, problems with sleep (trouble falling or staying asleep), headaches, decreased or increased appetite, stomach upset, and increased frequency of illness. Other signs include preoccupation with the event, difficulty focusing on other things, avoidance of public places, a desire to be alone more often than usual or not wanting to be alone at all, crying more easily than usual, being overly protective of loved ones, moodiness or irritability toward others, and distractibility or inability to stay focused.

The strength and duration of these reactions vary across individuals. Although highly stressful and traumatic events may cause considerable distress, these reactions generally do not become long-lasting problems. Even among people who have experienced a traumatic event directly, most recover within several weeks to several months.

REFERRAL STRATEGIES

If there is reason to believe that a co-worker or employee is suffering from PTSD, there are several potential questions to ask that could help you lead them to appropriate help. Consider asking the following questions:

- Are there things happening that are making it difficult to focus on your work?
- How are things at home?
- How is your relationship with your boyfriend/girlfriend or husband/wife?

Alternatively, it might be helpful to offer an impression. For example, you might say, "I've noticed that your attention in meetings and to your work has dropped recently. Has something happened that you would like to talk about," or "I've noticed that recently you have been spending a great deal of time alone." If the co-worker or employee chooses to confide in you, it is important to be sensitive in your response and to respect the person's reaction if he or she becomes upset. In addition, if the person is not able or interested to talk in the moment you approach him or her, you can offer an "open door" so that if there is ever anything the person would like to discuss in the future he or she will know that you are interested in hearing from that person. Furthermore, it is important to ask questions in private, not in front of others, and in a place where the person is likely to feel comfortable responding to you.

If you are a supervisor of the person, if the person is a reserved individual, or if your workplace is small and intimate, the individual might not feel comfortable discussing his or her experiences with you. You can encourage the person to seek or continue treatment and provide emotional support by listening. It is critical that you be patient and have realistic expectations for recovery. However, in a workplace environment it is most appropriate to encourage the person to seek support from family or friends or to look into professional assistance. It would be appropriate to refer the individual to an employee assistance program if your place of work has one. Alternatively, the person might find a referral through his or her primary care physician, an insurance company, or through organizations such as the Anxiety Disorders Association of America, the Association for Advancement of Behavior Therapy, or the American Psychological Association, each of which can be accessed through Web sites.

WORKPLACE OR HOME STRESSORS WITH PARTICULAR RELEVANCE TO THIS DISORDER

Clearly, there are a number of stressors that have particular relevance to PTSD/ASD. First and foremost are traumatic events that contribute to the development of either disorder. A traumatic event, as defined in the American Psychiatric Association's (1994) *Diagnostic and Statistical Manual of Mental Disorders–Fourth Edition* (*DSM-IV*), is one "experienced, witnessed, or confronted" by an individual that "involved actual or threatened death or serious injury, or a threat to the physical integrity of self or others." In addition, to be considered a traumatic event, the person's response must involve "intense fear, helplessness, or horror" (pp. 427-428).

Traumatic stressors that can occur within the work environment are numerous, particularly for certain occupations. The following occupational groups have specifically been identified as at high risk for trauma exposure: military personnel, transportation workers (e.g., railways, maritime, aviation, road transport), emergency service workers (e.g., fire, police, ambulance), workers in the commercial or financial sector (e.g., bank employees, retail employees), health care workers (e.g., nurses, doctors), and industry workers (e.g., offshore oil and gas, nuclear industries) (Rick et al., 1998). For each occupational group identified, there are specific duties associated with traumatic exposure risk. For military personnel, for example, exposure to combat, exposure to hostages or POWs, and participation in humanitarian and rescue operations have been identified as duties associated with trauma exposure (Rick et al., 1998). In the transport industries, witnessing crashes, capsized boats, and suicides, as well as experiencing hostage or hijack incidents are some examples of work-related traumatic events. In addition, the transportation industry is particularly affected by the frequency of motor vehicle accidents, although this risk is clearly present across occupational groups. For emergency workers, involvement in recovery and rescue can result in multiple trauma exposure. Common traumatic events for public health and safety departments include exposure to the death of children or co-workers and the threat of death or injury to self and co-workers. Within the retail sector, bank tellers and store clerks have faced robberies, burglaries, and assaults, as well as hostage taking, while working. Finally, in the industrial occupational groups, there is a potential for a rig disaster, mining accident, explosion, or nuclear accidents.

Although certain occupational groups have an increased risk of trauma exposure, it is not limited to these groups. Any employee may experience a motor vehicle accident, witness others being severely injured or killed, or be mugged or raped. These incidents may or may not be work related. Other traumatic events with relevance to the disorders include witnessing or experiencing the sudden death of a loved one, a disaster or hazardous exposure, or a life-threatening illness.

In addition to the traumatic stressors, there are a number of work-related and home stressors that may exacerbate PTSD/ASD symptomatology. Stressors that result in significant changes in one's level of functioning or in one's social support system may exacerbate trauma-related symptoms. In addition, stressors that trigger feelings of helplessness, loss of control, and vulnerability also may be particularly challenging. Some experiences that may precipitate a reactivation of PTSD symptoms include trauma anniversaries, the loss of a loved one (e.g., divorce, separation, death), a life-threatening illness, and retirement or loss of employment (e.g., Christenson, Walker, Ross, & Maltbie, 1981). Stress added either at work (e.g., increased workload) or at home (spouse returns to work, marital discord, new child) also can reduce the resources one has available and thereby negatively impact one's level of functioning at work.

EMPIRICALLY BASED TREATMENTS

Current treatments for PTSD include pharmacology, individual psychotherapy, and group psychotherapy (see Foa, Keane, & Friedman, 2000, for a more extensive review). Medications are generally recognized as an efficient way to treat individuals with PTSD, and they have been found to have a wide range of benefits. Specifically, they have been shown to reduce core symptoms of PTSD, such as reexperiencing, avoidance, arousal, and associated symptoms, such as depression, sleep disturbance, physical health problems, and anger. However, with the range of social, interpersonal, occupational, and health problems frequently associated with chronic PTSD and the side effects of and the noncompliance with medications, psychosocial interventions often provide critical benefits not provided from medication alone.

Numerous psychotherapeutic treatments for PTSD have been developed. In general, these treatments focus on eliminating the conditioned fear response thought to underlie PTSD, correcting maladaptive beliefs, developing anxiety management skills, and/or increasing an individual's understanding of how current relationship patterns have been impacted by past trauma and PTSD. These treatments include variations of exposure therapy, cognitive therapy, anxiety management, and interpersonal psychotherapy. The following is a description of these therapeutic approaches and a brief review of the empirical evidence for their effectiveness.

Exposure therapy consists of repeated presentations of anxiety-provoking stimuli without the use of anxiety-reducing techniques in order to provide an opportunity for extinction of the individual's conditioned emotional reactions and integration of new, potentially corrective, thoughts and feelings. Although exposure methods vary, they share the common feature of confronting the frightening stimuli until the anxiety diminishes. Typically, exposure is achieved by having the client confront the traumatic event by describing it aloud, repeatedly, in the present tense for approximately 45 to 60 minutes or until the individual experiences a significant decrease in anxiety. The number of sessions required for exposure therapy to be effective generally range from one to sixteen sessions.

The efficacy of exposure therapy for PTSD has been established through several well-controlled studies with veterans, victims of sexual assault, and survivors of various other types of traumatic events. These studies indicate that this treatment approach has been particularly successful in reducing reexperiencing symptoms, such as nightmares and intrusive recollections, and hyperarousal. However, some researchers have suggested exposure therapy appears to be less effective at reducing avoidance and social withdrawal. There is also some research to indicate that exposure therapy may be less effective for patients in which guilt or anger is the primary emotion.

In cognitive therapy, treatment focuses on altering maladaptive thinking patterns. This treatment is based on theories that propose that certain maladaptive beliefs create feelings of anxiety, depression, anger, guilt, or shame. Individuals are taught to identify these dysfunctional patterns, challenge them, and replace them with functional beliefs. Cognitive therapy with trauma survivors focuses particular attention on beliefs about safety, trust, and self-worth. Similar to the course of exposure therapy, cognitive therapy for PTSD generally ranges from 12 to 16 sessions. Although the evidence suggests that cognitive therapy is an effective treatment for PTSD, many clinicians and researchers believe that including an exposure component with cognitive therapy is critical.

Anxiety management is another approach that has been used to treat individuals with PTSD. This eclectic method evolved from the theory that traumatized individuals would benefit from skills developed to manage their anxiety that would, as a result, reduce their avoidance as well. These approaches include stress inoculation training (SIT), assertiveness training, and biofeedback and relaxation training.

Although SIT has shown some promise as a treatment for survivors of sexual assault, its efficacy at reducing symptoms of PTSD produced by exposure to other types of trauma has not been established. In addition, the evidence for assertiveness training and biofeedback and relaxation is limited, which suggests that they should not be considered as sole and primary approaches to treating individuals with PTSD.

In addition, other treatment approaches, such as short-term psychodynamic therapy, offer much promise but have less empirical support to date. These treatments focus on the effects of trauma on relationship functioning, the exploration of the meaning of traumatic events, as well as an examination of themes of fear, alienation, and shame. Psychodynamic treatments generally include an emphasis on building a strong therapeutic alliance as well as the examination of this relationship over the course of treatment.

In general, there are no known long-term side effects of psychotherapy. However, one of the core symptoms of PTSD is avoidance of reminders of the traumatic event, including avoidance of people, places, things, and feelings associated with the incident. In addition, treatment for PTSD typically involves some discussion of the event. Thus, it is not unusual for individuals with PTSD to experience an initial increase in distress during the onset of treatment. Although this initial increase in symptoms can be alarming if the individual is not prepared for this experience, it is most often manageable for the individual and not significantly more upsetting than the experience of the symptoms of PTSD.

RELAPSE PREVENTION

Research suggests that the course of PTSD is quite chronic, lasting on average three to five years, with many patients reporting experiencing PTSD for more than ten years (Kessler et al., 1995). Despite its chronicity, the course of PTSD symptoms is somewhat unknown. Some research indicates that the frequency and intensity of symptoms may fluctuate over time and across individuals (e.g., McFarlane, 1988). Factors that would result in remission of symptoms or relapse have yet to be clearly identified.

There are some basic guidelines related to mental health in general that may be useful in discussing prevention of PTSD relapse. For example, relapse is more likely if one's social support system is limited, one's stressors increase, and/or one's coping resources are reduced or limited. Much of the trauma literature has focused on the protective nature of social support in particular (e.g., King, King, Fairbank, Keane, & Adams, 1998). Building a strong social network in which one feels comfortable and supported may be an important step in relapse prevention. This may be established informally, through one's connections at work, in religious organizations, and through community organizations and activities. In addition, one may benefit from the more formal support of psychotherapy groups or support groups offered in the community. For example, a firefighter with a history of PTSD who is going through a divorce may benefit from attending a support group for fathers without partners or one focused on divorce and separation. Alternatively, a rape victim recently experiencing increased PTSD symptoms may choose to attend a therapy group for rape survivors or a community support group for women.

Another important consideration for relapse prevention is minimization of risk and stress management. Trauma victims with a past history of trauma exposure are more likely to develop PTSD following a subsequent trauma (Resnick, Yehuda, Pitman, & Foy, 1995). Although risk for experiencing a traumatic event cannot be eliminated completely, minimizing risk in one's environment can reduce the prevalence of PTSD/ASD. If one is working in an at-risk occupational group, minimizing this exposure may be particularly challenging and could contribute to increased avoidance behaviors. However, being aware of the risks associated with one's environment and feeling prepared to handle these risks increases one's sense of self-efficacy and control.

Other suggestions for relapse prevention include the normalization of symptoms and reactions and the early identification of symptom exacerbation. As discussed earlier, PTSD symptoms may be triggered by a number of experiences. It is helpful to understand and accept that one's symptoms may wax and wane and are likely to be exacerbated by certain triggers, such as the anniversary date of the traumatic experience. Recognizing also when symptoms warrant intervention can prevent a serious deterioration in functioning. If reexperiencing symptoms are worsening, avoidance behavior is increasing, and/or arousal symptoms are escalating, an employee may benefit from a referral for appropriate evaluation. Recognizing these symptoms may enable an employee to get appropriate treatment before his or her work functioning has resulted in significant impairment or loss of employment. If the problem goes unnoticed and unaddressed, it has the potential to become much more destructive (e.g., frequent absences from work, decreased productivity levels).

PTSD symptoms also may be triggered by an unrelated or additional stressor(s) in the employee's current life. Practicing relaxation techniques and focusing on one's stress management will enable an employee to decrease anxiety levels, increase available resources, and practice healthy coping behaviors on a regular basis. Some relaxation techniques include deep breathing, progressive muscle relaxation, and guided imagery.

THERAPEUTIC BENEFITS OF WORK

As with other disorders, the therapeutic benefits of work for an individual with PTSD/ASD can be quite significant. Although not causative, unemployment is associated with increased psychiatric distress (Feehan, Nada-Raja, Martin, & Langley, 2001), anger, and hostility (Frueh, Henning, Pellegrin, & Chobot, 1997). Of course, the more distressed individuals may have a more difficult time keeping or returning to employment. However, it is also likely that returning to work reduces distress for individuals suffering from PTSD/ASD.

One important therapeutic benefit of work, especially for those who have experienced a work-related trauma, is the reduction of avoidance behaviors associated with the disorders. A significant component of PTSD is avoidance. Unfortunately, when an individual avoids certain situations and things that are not inherently dangerous as a result of the association with the traumatic experience, he or she does not gather any contradictory evidence to challenge trauma-related beliefs (e.g.,

"The world is a dangerous place and I cannot trust anyone"). By reengaging at work and progressively experiencing previously avoided situations, an individual may be able to decrease his or her anxiety level in these situations and challenge beliefs of perceived danger. This may be done with the help of a professional therapist trained in the treatment of these disorders.

In addition to tackling avoidance that may be associated with increased distress, work offers individuals with a history of PTSD/ASD an opportunity to feel competent again. Self-esteem is often shattered following a traumatic event, and increasing one's feelings of self-efficacy and competence in some areas is particularly essential for recovery after a traumatic event. One may begin to question his or her abilities and judgment following a trauma. Having positive work experiences and getting positive feedback from others allows an individual to challenge his or her beliefs regarding incompetence and inability and regain a sense of self-worth.

Often a loss of a sense of meaning in one's life also can occur following the experience of a traumatic event; functioning at work, and feeling important and necessary in a work environment, can aid one's recovery from trauma. As a result, many individuals who have survived a traumatic event choose professional careers in which they can help others. This can lead to a fulfilling career and a reestablishment of a sense of meaning. Of course, this can also be problematic if individuals choose a career to help themselves cope with their own difficulties but do not have sufficient resources to handle the work and to work effectively to help others.

Work also offers an opportunity for regular social contact. Following a traumatic event, individuals tend to isolate themselves. Going to work allows an individual to have a safe, structured environment with frequent interactions with others. In addition, work offers an opportunity for engagement with peers that can provide a significant amount of social support. Other co-workers may have gone through similar experiences and can validate the employee's feelings and thoughts. Others can offer an emotional outlet and a source of information of how they coped with their distress.

Finally, having a regular routine at work and an area that is safe and predictable offers a trauma victim an opportunity to challenge his or her all-or-nothing thinking that the world is always a dangerous place and that no one can be trusted. The more an individual isolates and avoids everyday, positive contact, the less likely he or she will have evidence to contradict trauma-related cognitions. Work offers an individual the opportunity to return to everyday functioning and to have continual experiences with others in which one is not harmed or violated. In addition, as with other disorders, work allows the individual with PTSD/ASD to have some structure and predictability to his or her day that may be beneficial to recovery. Work also enables an individual to increase or resume his or her activity level, which likely will decrease comorbid symptoms of depression.

SUMMARY

Most individuals are exposed to at least one potentially traumatic event over the course of their lifetime. In response, some individuals will develop symptoms of

ASD, PTSD, or both, such as reexperiencing of the traumatic event(s), avoidance of trauma-related cues, and heightened arousal. These symptoms can significantly impact one's occupational functioning and can result in decreased productivity, increased absenteeism, tardiness, poor concentration, social isolation, and even termination of employment. The symptoms expressed at work will likely depend on whether the trauma was work-related as well as the severity of the disorder. If an employee presents with symptoms suggestive of PTSD/ASD, he or she may benefit from a referral to a trained mental health professional. There are a number of effective treatments for PTSD; obtaining treatment may enable an individual to improve his or her mental health and occupational functioning.

References

American Psychiatric Association. (1994). *Diagnostic and statistical manual of mental disorders* (4th ed.). Washington, DC: Author.

Blake, D. D., Weathers, F. W., Nagy, L. M., Kaloupek, D. G., Gusman, F. D., Charney, D. S., et al. (1995). The development of a clinician-administered PTSD scale. *Journal of Traumatic Stress, 8,* 75-90.

Brewin, C. R., Andrews, B., Rose, S., & Kirk, M. (1999). Acute stress disorder and posttraumatic stress disorder in victims of violent crime. *American Journal of Psychiatry, 156,* 360-366.

Brown, T. A., Di Nardo, P., & Barlow, D. H. (1994). *Anxiety Disorders Interview Schedule for DSM-IV.* San Antonio, TX: Psychological Corporation.

Christenson, R. M., Walker, J. I., Ross, D. R., & Maltbie, A. A. (1981). Reactivation of traumatic conflicts. *American Journal of Psychiatry, 138,* 984-985.

Feehan, M., Nada-Raja, S., Martin J. A., & Langley, J. D. (2001). The prevalence and correlates of psychological distress following physical and sexual assault in a young adult cohort. *Violence and Victims, 16,* 49-63.

First, M. B., Spitzer, R. L., Gibbon, M., & Williams, J. B. W. (1996). *Structured Clinical Interview for DSM-IV Axis I disorders—Patient edition (SCID-I/P, Version 2.0).* New York: Biometrics Research Department, New York State Psychiatric Institute.

Foa, E. B., Cashman, L. A., Jaycox, L., & Perry, K. (1997). The validation of a self-report measure of posttraumatic stress disorder: The Posttraumatic Diagnostic Scale. *Psychological Assessment, 4,* 445-451.

Foa, E. B., Keane, T. M., & Friedman, M. J. (2000). *Effective treatments for PTSD.* New York: Guilford.

Frueh, B. C., Henning, K. R., Pellegrin, K. L., & Chobot, K. (1997). Relationship between scores on anger measures and PTSD symptomatology, employment, and compensation-seeking status in combat veterans. *Journal of Clinical Psychology, 53,* 871-878.

Holeva, V., Tarrier, N., & Wells, A. (2001). Prevalence and predictors of acute stress disorder and PTSD following road traffic accidents: Thought control strategies and social support. *Behavior Therapy, 32,* 65-83.

Keane, T. M., Caddell, J. M., & Taylor, K. L. (1988). Mississippi Scale for Combat-Related Posttraumatic Stress Disorder: Three studies in reliability and validity. *Journal of Consulting and Clinical Psychology, 56,* 85-90.

Kessler, R. C., Sonnega, A., Bromet, E., Hughes, M., & Nelson, C. B. (1995). Posttraumatic stress disorder in the National Comorbidy Survey. *Archives of General Psychiatry, 52,* 1048-1060.

King, L. A., King, D. W., Fairbank, J. A., Keane, T. M., & Adams, G. A. (1998). Resilience/recovery factors in posttraumatic among female and male Vietnam veterans: Hardiness, postwar social support, and additional stressful life events. *Journal of Personality and Social Psychology, 74,* 420-434.

McFarlane, A. C. (1988). The longitudinal course of posttraumatic morbidity: The range of outcomes and their predictors. *Journal of Nervous and Mental Disease, 176,* 30-39.

Resnick, H. S., Yehuda, R., Pitman, R. K., & Foy, D. W. (1995). Effect of previous trauma on acute plasma cortisol level following rape. *American Journal of Psychiatry, 152,* 1675-1677.

Rick, J., Perryman, S., Young, K., Guppy, A., & Hillage, J. (1998). Workplace trauma and its management: Review of the literature. Retrieved January 3, 2003, from http://www.hse.gov.uk/research/crr_pdf/1998/crr98170.pdf.

Weathers, F. W., Litz, B. T., Herman, D. S., Huska, J. A., & Keane, T. M. (1993, November). *The PTSD checklist: Reliability, validity and diagnostic utility.* Paper presented at the Annual Meeting of the International Society for Traumatic Stress Studies, San Antonio, TX.

Depression

TERRY MICHAEL MCCLANAHAN
The Permanente Medical Goup

DAVID O. ANTONUCCIO
University of Nevada School of Medicine

INTRODUCTION

*T*he World Health Organization (2000) estimates that unipolar depression is currently the most prevalent psychiatric condition and predicts it to become the second most significant cause of global disease burden by 2020. These global statistics hold true for the U.S. society as well. For instance, the seminal epidemiological study on psychiatric disorders conducted by Kessler et al. (1994) found that unipolar depression affects between 3 percent and 13 percent of Americans annually. Thus, depression affects approximately eleven million Americans annually. Of those affected by unipolar depression, it is estimated that as many as 20 percent of American adults will experience some depressive symptoms at any given point in time, and the lifetime incidence of depression is estimated to affect between 20 percent and 55 percent of American adults.

Various researchers have determined that depression affects women twice as often as males (Antonuccio, Danton, & DeNelsky, 1995; Kessler et al., 1994; World Health Organization, 2000), which may contribute to intergenerational learned depression because women continue to provide the majority of parental care to offspring.

The manifestations of depression are estimated to burden the U.S. economy as much as $44 billion per year (Greenberg, Stiglin, Finkelstein, & Berndt, 1993). Indirect costs to the economy include increased accident rates, increased substance abuse, increased medical hospitalization, and increased somatic illnesses and out-patient medical use (Greenberg et al., 1993). The most significant indirect cost is decreased productivity, which is a result of increased absenteeism.

The American Psychiatric Association (APA) stipulates that depression is manifested by a depressed mood most of the day (emotional impairment), markedly diminished interest or pleasure in all or almost all activities of the day (behavioral withdrawal), a significant weight loss or gain (physical symptoms), insomnia or hyposomnia, psychomotor agitation or retardation, fatigue or loss of energy, diminished ability to concentrate or indecisiveness, or recurrent thoughts of death (APA, 1994).

For the patient's symptoms to be diagnosed as a major depressive episode, five or more of the previously mentioned symptoms must be present for the majority of the day nearly every day for a two-week period (APA, 1994). The symptoms will be diagnosed as Major Depressive Disorder if the patient has experienced at least one major depressive episode. If the patient has experienced two or more major depressive episodes, then the appropriate diagnosis would be Major Depressive Disorder, Recurrent.

Depression in the workplace can be manifested as primarily in one domain (cognitive, behavioral, emotional, or physical) or in combination. As Table 9.1 depicts, the employee who used to take pride in the company and in his or her contribution may suddenly become the disgruntled employee. The person who was previously decisive may become indecisive. The person who previously would volunteer for projects may seem uninterested and withdrawn. The employee who previously was gregarious and was the team player suddenly becomes isolated and nonparticipatory. The employee who previously was laid back now has become agitated and argues with co-workers, or one who once was prompt and dependable is now frequently absent or late to work. Projects that were once completed may now be left undone. The employee may not be able to concentrate or often daydreams. An employee also may become prone to making errors. Projects that previously would have been completed in a timely fashion and to perfect standards may now become tedious for the depressed employee and they may be partially or totally incomplete.

TABLE 10.1
Depressive Symptoms in an outpatient Populatin and Workplace Manifestations

Typical Clinical Symptoms (*DSM-IV*)	Symptoms in the Workplace
Cognitive	
Concentration difficulties	Unfinished projects
Indecisiveness	Indecisiveness
Thoughts of suicide	May go unnoticed
Emotional	
Tearful	Irritable
Feelings of sadness or emptiness	Substandard work performance
Worthlessness	Loss of interest in work
Behavioral	
Loss of interest in pleasurable activities	Disinterested in activities
Physical	
Weight loss or gain	Skips lunch or overeats
Insomnia or hypersomnia	Fatigued, tired
Psychomotor agitation or retardation	Hyperactive or sluggishness
Fatigue or loss of energy	Fatigue or loss of energy

CASE ILLUSTRATION

Dennis is a 34-year-old, Caucasian male professional. Previously he enjoyed his day-to-day duties at work and often "looked forward to going to work." He has been employed by his current employer for six years and was recently promoted to a managerial level position. His new responsibility requires him to travel to another branch office two days each week. The one-way distance from his home to the branch office is 90 miles, most of which is in heavy traffic. He reports that a one-way commute often requires a two-hour drive. On the days that he has to visit the branch office, he will leave his home at 5:30 a.m. and he typically returns around 8 p.m. that same day.

He reports that over the past six months he also has been having difficulty at home. He feels that his wife and two small children are very demanding and he feels guilty that he cannot spend more time with them. He also feels that his wife has more time and should be contributing more than he does at home.

His supervisor has noticed that Dennis has accumulated hundreds of hours in vacation and sick leave. In fact, he has not taken a vacation in the past two years. Dennis feels that "things would fall apart" if he were absent for two or three weeks from his job. Dennis also tends to be perfectionistic, and he likes things to be done "his way." His co-workers often tease him that he is "Mr. Perfectionistic" in that everything has to be done to exacting standards.

RECOGNIZING AND EVALUATING PSYCHOPATHOLOGY

Recognizing psychopathology can be difficult; however, several standards of care in this regard have been clearly established. Patterson and McClanahan (1999) suggested two instruments for the clinician who wants to perform a formalized assessment—the Beck Depression Inventory, Second Edition (BDI-II) (Beck, Steer, & Brown, 1996) and the Structured Clinical Interview for *DSM-IV* (SCID) (Spitzer, Williams, Gibbon, & First, 1990). Other formal instruments include the Symptom CheckList (SCL-90-R) (Derogatis, 1983). Ultimately, assessing the severity and acuity of depression is best derived from the clinical interview conducted by a competently trained professional. The overriding criterion in the assessment process has to do with social impairment, "Is the person able to perform his or her daily roles?" If the answer to this question is no, then the person has an acute and debilitating disorder.

A multitude of psychosocial events can exacerbate a person's ability to cope with daily stress. For instance, marital discord can create secondary anger that can be displaced onto co-workers. An argument with a child can contribute to workplace tension. If the employee is experiencing financial shortfall, he or she may experience depressive symptoms. Likewise, if there is a child at home who is having behavioral difficulties, the employee may experience an increase in stress.

The scenario of the depressed employee often presents a dilemma for the employee's manager. On one hand, production must continue, yet the compassionate manager should also be concerned for the well-being of the employee. The manager must present the issue at hand to the employee in a nonthreatening manner.

The National Institute of Mental Health (1995) suggests that the first step for a supervisor is to gather information. For instance, the supervisor can learn about depression—symptoms, treatment options, community resources. Thus, the manager is better able to assist the employee. One way for the manager to broach the issue is to approach the situation from a position of concern for the employee's welfare. For instance, the manager might begin with a statement such as "I've noticed that you don't seem to be yourself lately. I don't know if things in your personal life are affecting you, but if they are we have a confidential employee assistance plan that might be able to help." Some supervisors are fearful that this may open the floodgate. While this might be true in some instances, it might also suggest to the employee that outside psychosocial stressors are affecting his or her productivity. If the manager approaches the situation with this strategy, it also is advisable for the manager to maintain appropriate boundaries. For instance, if the employee mentions marital discord, problems with a child, financial problems, and so forth, the manager should be empathic but should limit the conversation. At this point the manager can offer the employee the telephone number for the employee assistance program or suggest that it would serve the employee well to consider outside professional counseling through health care benefits, a community clinic, an employee assistance plan, or even through pastoral counseling.

EMPIRICALLY BASED TREATMENT

There are several approaches to treating depression. One of the earliest empirically validated approaches was developed by Lewinsohn, Youngren, and Grosscup (1979). These researchers proposed that depression results when a psychosocial stressor disrupts behavioral patterns and this disruption causes a reduction in the rate of response contingent positive reinforcement. This reduction of positive reinforcement is assumed to be related to the availability of reinforcing events in the person's environment, personal skills to act on the environment, or in the patient's ability to interact, adjust, and cope with the stressor. When the individual fails to reverse the negative balance of reinforcement, an increased self-awareness follows, which can lead to a negative self-evaluation and subsequent depressive state (Lewinsohn, Hoberman, Teri, & Hautzinger, 1985). According to this model, familial environment and social networks may inadvertently reinforce depressive behavior by providing increased attention to negative behaviors such as suicidality or substance abuse.

The literature indicates that depressed patients have low rates of pleasant activities and obtained pleasure and tend to lack social skills, especially during the depressive period, which contributes to the depressive episode. The Coping With Depression (CWD) course was developed to correct these deficiencies (Lewinsohn, Antonuccio, Steinmetz-Breckenridge, & Teri, 1984).

Structure of Treatment

The CWD course was originally designed as a psychoeducational seminar that could be administered to individuals or small groups. The course focuses on teaching patients new ways to cope with their depression. Specifically, the CWD course is designed to help patients increase the frequency and quality of their engagement in pleasant activities and reduce the frequency of aversive events. A broad approach is used to instill in patients skills most directly related to their depression—learning relaxation, increasing pleasant activities, changing depressogenic cognitions, and increasing social skills.

When some individuals begin to experience psychosocial stressors, they tend to withdraw from activities. Figure 9.1 depicts a patient pretreatment with the CWD course. This individual was engaging in only a few pleasurable activities each day and the BDI-II score indicated significant depressive symptoms. Withdrawal from pleasurable activities tends to increase the depressive feelings and cognitions. For instance, an individual may experience an unpleasant event in his or her environment. This event can trigger automatic thoughts that are self-critical, judgmental, and self-deprecating. These thoughts make the person feel less likely to venture into the environment. This can become an escalating depressive cycle with high depressive scores and low levels of activity.

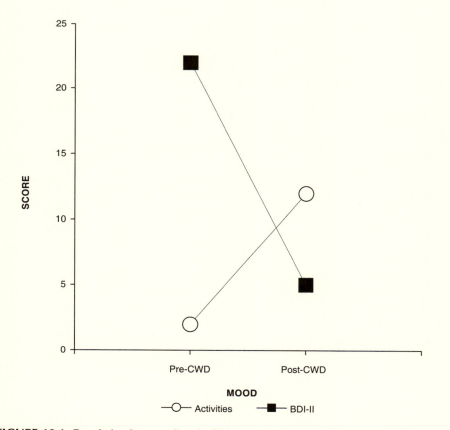

FIGURE 10.1 Correlation between Level of Pleasurable Activities and Mood (Note: CWD = Coping with Depression course; BDI-II = Beck Depression Inventory, Second Edition.)

Part of the treatment for this scenario is to increase activities, thus increasing the likelihood of receiving positive feedback and enforcement from the environment. As Figure 9.1 indicates, the likelihood of having a high score on the BDI-II is very high when there are few activities. However, when the level of activities is increased the likelihood of having a high score on the BDI-II is greatly reduced. Thus, Figure 9.1 depicts the depressed patient (pre-CWD course treatment) who has few pleasurable activities as compared with the patient who has numerous activities (post-CWD course treatment), which helps to reduce the depressive score.

Table 9.2 lists common cognitive distortions, which include all-or-nothing thinking, overgeneralization, mental filtering, discounting the positive, jumping to conclusions, magnification or minimization, emotional reasoning, should statements, labeling, and blaming (Burns, 2002). Cognitive distortions are common whenever emotions are involved. Cognitive-behavioral treatment first attempts to help the individual to identify maladaptive patterns of which cognitive distortions are a significant impediment. Then treatment attempts to present ways for the patient to challenge these thoughts with more reasonable, rational, and accurate thoughts. For instance, as Table 9.2 lists, an overgeneralization would be when an individual thinks "My boss doesn't like me because he criticized my work today" instead of "Although he criticized my work today, he frequently gives me compliments on my work and last month he nominated me for the employee of the month—that suggests he likes at least some of my work." Challenging the automatic thoughts tend to help the individual learn to be less judgmental and self-critical of themselves, which ultimately helps ameliorate depressogenic thoughts and symptoms of depression.

Treatment sessions within the CWD course are highly structured and use the text *Control Your Depression* (Lewinsohn, Muñoz, Youngren, & Zeiss, 1992). The text was designed as a self-help manual, and it provides the theoretical tenets of this treatment approach. Research has established that patients do well with manuals (i.e., bibliotherapy), but some need the social facilitation and structure provided by a program such as the CWD course (Ackerson, Scogin, McKendree-Smith, & Lyman, 1998; Robinson et al., 1995; Scogin, Jamison, & Davis, 1990; Scogin, Jamison, Floyd, & Chaplin, in press). Thus the need for treatment provided by a competently trained professional. It is obviously inappropriate for a professional who is not behaviorally oriented to initiate this type of treatment without first acquiring competence through graduate-level coursework in behaviorism, supervision from a competent behaviorist, or significant consultation from a behaviorally trained professional (McClanahan, in press).

A therapist manual provides session scripts, homework exercises, and guidelines for the treatment (Lewinsohn et al., 1984). The participants are given the workbook *Participant Workbook for the Coping with Depression Course* (Brown & Lewinsohn, 1984a), which provides the patient with the session syllabi and the forms necessary to track and implement various aspects of treatment. The CWD course is conducted over 12 sessions during an eight-week period. The sessions are initially held twice weekly for the first four weeks and once per week thereafter. The groups are designed to consist of six to ten individuals, with one competently trained professional conducting each of the sessions. One- and six-month booster sessions are held to share treatment gains and prevent relapse. Because relapse is common in depression,

TABLE 10.2
Typical Cognitive Distortions of Someone Who Is Depressed and Challenges to the Cognitive Distortion

Typical Distortion	Challenge to Distortion
Overgeneralization	
"I always mess up"	"I mess up sometime, but not always"
Polarized thinking	
"I'm not good enough"	"I am a good person"
Mental filtering	
"Focus on the negative"	"This could be better, but it'll pass"
Mind reading	
"They don't like me"	"Some people won't like me, and that's OK"
Control fallacies	
"All the good ones are gone"	"There's one out there somewhere"
Self-blame	
"Apologize for everything"	"I'm not responsible for everything"
Personalization	
"If only I were good enough"	"I do a good enough job"
Emotional reasoning	
"Feel bad, so am bad"	"I feel bad, and it'll pass"
Global labeling	
"All men are angry"	"Some people are angry people"
Catastrophizing	
"It's all over"	"Things will work out, somehow"
Fortune-telling	
"I'll be depressed forever"	"This too shall pass"
Shoulds	
"I should be able to handle this"	"Shoulds don't help me feel better"

booster sessions are integral to long-term treatment and are incorporated into the patient's initial treatment plan.

Clinical Efficacy of the CWD Course

As one of the first manualized treatments that relied heavily on participant workbooks and homework assignments, the CWD course has been widely evaluated over the past twenty years. The CWD course was designed to treat depression with adults (Brown & Lewinsohn, 1984b; Hoberman, Lewinsohn, & Tilson, 1988; Steinmetz, Lewinsohn, & Antonuccio, 1983; Teri & Lewinsohn, 1986), and has been adapted to treat adolescents (Clarke et al., 1995; Clarke, Rohde, Lewinsohn, Hops, & Seeley, 1999; Lewinsohn, Clarke, Hops, & Andrews, 1990; Lewinsohn, Clarke, Rohde, Hops, & Seeley, 1996; Rohde, Lewinsohn, & Seeley, 1994; Rohde, Lewinsohn, Clarke, & Seeley, in press), geriatric patients (Haringsma, Engels, Spinhoven, & Cuijpers, 2001; Teri, Logsdon, Uomoto, & McCurry, 1997; Thompson, Gallager, Nies, & Epstein, 1983), and in prevention efforts (Cuijpers, 1998a; Kuhner, Angermeyer, & Veiel, 1996; Muñoz, 2001; Muñoz & Ying, 1993; Muñoz, Ying, Armas, Chan, & Gurza, 1987).

In one of the largest meta-analyses of the CWD course, Cuijpers (1998b) evaluated 20 studies (727 participants) conducted between 1984 and 1996 wherein the CWD course was compared with other approaches to treating depression. Of ten experimental studies that included a control group, the mean effect size ($M_1 - M_2/SD_{pooled}$) of the CWD condition was 0.65, which constituted a relatively large effect size (Cohen, 1988). In the other ten studies where a control group was not used, the effect size (pretest to posttest) was calculated and resulted in a mean effect size of 1.21, which according to Cohen (1988) is extremely large. In these 20 studies, Cuijpers reported that the large effect sizes were maintained at one-month, six-month, one-year, and two-year follow-up.

Gelhart and King (2001) conducted a controlled study using the CWD course in the treatment of 92 adults with unipolar depression. Multimodal assessment was conducted at pre- and posttreatment, and results were statistically significant at the .0001 level. These effects were maintained at one-, six-, twelve-, eighteen-, and twenty-four-month follow-up. These researchers concluded that the CWD course significantly increased mood, decreased hopelessness, increased social adjustment, and reduced anxiety—all of which often accompany depression. This study is of particular interest—the participants were diagnosed with "double depression," a condition that has historically been less responsive to treatment (Keller, Lavori, Endicott, Coryel, & Klerman, 1983; Marin, Kocsis, Frances, & Parides, 1994; Prudic, Sackeim, Devanand, & Kiersky, 1993).

Haringsma et al. (2001) compared the CWD course with a wait-list control group in a multisite study involving fifteen prevention departments of community mental health institutions. This study included 143 participants of whom 43 percent were diagnosed with current Major Depressive Disorder and 80 percent had a lifetime diagnosis of Major Depressive Disorder. The posttest results indicated that the CWD group's depression scores were 50 percent less than those of the control group.

The CWD course also has been compared to pharmacologic intervention and was shown to be more efficacious over the long term. For instance, Hautzinger and de Jong-Meyer (1996) conducted two multisite studies comparing the CWD course and amitriptyline, a tricyclic antidepressant, alone or in combination. The first study included 191 participants of whom 80 percent had a diagnosis of major depressive disorder and the remaining 20 percent had a diagnosis of dysthymic disorder. The participants included 116 participants (71 females) who were treated as outpatients and 75 participants (49 females) who were treated as psychiatric inpatients. Hautzinger and de Jong-Meyer (1996) reported that the CWD treatment, when applied singularly, was as effective as the tricyclic antidepressant applied singularly. However, at one-year follow-up the CWD was statistically as effective as the CWD plus the amitriptyline, which were both statistically more effective than the amitriptyline alone.

Using Manualized Treatment in Prevention Efforts

The efficacy of using the CWD course in the treatment of depression has been unequivocally established. It is therefore logical to apply the principles of CWD in the area of preventing depression. Milgrom, Martin, and Negri (2000) adapted the CWD course to treat postpartum depression in women who had recently given birth.

Brown and Lewinsohn (1984b) had previously established brief telephonic counseling as a modality of treatment. Thus, the brief telephonic counseling format may be applicable to patients who are too busy to seek out mental health services, such as those who have recently given birth. Muñoz (2001) suggested that courses dealing with depression should be incorporated into curricula in primary and secondary schools to teach children coping skills that help retard future depressive episodes.

Kuhner et al. (1996), using a matched-pair design, evaluated the effectiveness of using the CWD course to prevent depression or relapse in a general outpatient population. These researchers reported that patients who received the CWD course were three times less likely to become depressed during the six-month pre- to posttreatment period. CWD patients also were less likely to become depressed even when compared with patients who had received antidepressant medication. The final conclusion was that using the CWD course could be instrumental in the clinical aftercare of depressed patients within the psychiatric outpatient setting.

CONCLUSIONS

The seminal National Comorbidity Survey (Kessler et al., 1994) found that as many as 17 percent of American adults will suffer from at least one major depressive episode at some point during their lives. Americans are not the only ones to experience depression. In fact, the World Health Organization predicts that depression will be the leading cause of disability in the world by 2010 (Murray & Lopez, 1990). Thus, it is imperative to develop and employ empirically valid approaches to treating this disorder.

The CWD course is a manualized treatment approach that has demonstrated that it is effective in treating depression in adults, adolescents, and geriatric patients. It has been extensively evaluated not only in the United States but also in Europe (Hautzinger & de Jong-Meyer, 1996; Kuhner et al., 1996). It has proved effective in preventing depression (Clarke et al., 1995; Kuhner et al., 1996; Muñoz, 2001; Muñoz & Ying, 1993; Muñoz et al., 1987), and it is an effective intervention with people of color (Muñoz, 2001; Organista, Muñoz, & Gonzalez, 1994). It also has shown to be equally as effective as antidepressants in the short term and more efficacious in the long term (Hautzinger & de Jong-Meyer, 1996; Kuhner et al., 1996). For these reasons, the CWD course should be considered a first-line treatment for unipolar depression.

The key components of the CWD course involve behavioral activation (i.e., increasing pleasurable activities and social skills training), relaxation, and correction of maladaptive cognitions. The potential benefit of each of these skill areas can be applicable for employees who experience depression. Americans often identify with their occupation and may suffer more by being out of the workforce than by enduring and overcoming the stress on the job. Sometimes the employee may not be aware that a life stressor may be negatively affecting his or her job performance. It is therefore incumbent on the supervisor to be aware of symptoms of depression and to be knowledgeable of company and community resources for appropriate referral. Returning to work may be of significance for the employee. Employment has been anecdotally linked to personal fulfillment and gratification. Thus, aspects of the job can be essential to recovery from depression.

A final word of caution is imperative in this discussion of depression in the workplace. First, the manager should not become the employee's therapist. To some this may seem obvious, but the rationale for this boundary is because of the potential role confusion between the manager and the employee. The manager can most appropriately deal with the situation by referring the employee to a competently trained professional. In most instances, the manager's referral of choice is to the employee assistance plan. Whenever a professional assumes the treatment of an individual who is experiencing depressive symptoms, it is incumbent on that professional to employ empirically validated treatment and to ensure that he or she has demonstrated competence in the use of that treatment approach. Thus, it is obviously inappropriate for a professional who is not behaviorally oriented to initiate this type of treatment without first acquiring competence through graduate-level coursework (e.g., principles of behaviorism, behavioral assessment, behavior modification), obtaining supervision from a competent behaviorist, or seeking significant consultation from another professional who has demonstrated competence in behavioral treatment (McClanahan, in press).

References

Ackerson, J., Scogin, F., McKendree-Smith, N., & Lyman, R. D. (1998). Cognitive bibliotherapy for mild and moderate adolescent depressive symptomatology. *Journal of Consulting and Clinical Psychology, 66,* 685-690.

American Psychiatric Association. (1994). *Diagnostic and statistical manual of mental disorders* (4th ed.). Washington, DC: Author.

Antonuccio, D. O., Danton, W. G., & DeNelsky, G. Y. (1995). Psychotherapy versus medication for depression: Challenging the conventional wisdom with data. *Professional Psychotherapy: Research and Practice, 26*(6), 574-585.

Beck, A. T., Steer, R. A., & Brown, G. K. (1996). *Beck Depression Inventory—Second edition manual.* San Antonio, TX: Psychological Corporation.

Brown, R. A., & Lewinsohn, P. M. (1984a). *Participant workbook for the Coping with Depression course.* Eugene, OR: Castalia Publishing.

Brown, R. A., & Lewinsohn, P. M. (1984b). A psychoeducational approach to the treatment of depression: Comparison of group, individual, and minimal contact procedures. *Journal of Consulting and Clinical Psychology, 52,* 774-783.

Burns, D. D. (2002). *Feeling good.* Alexandria, VA: Time Life.

Clarke, G. N., Hawkins, W., Murphy, M., Sheeber, L. B., Lewinsohn, P. M., & Seeley, J. R. (1995). Targeted prevention of unipolar depressive disorder in an at-risk sample of high school adolescents: A randomized trial of a group cognitive intervention. *Journal of the American Academy of Child and Adolescent Psychiatry, 34,* 312-321.

Clarke, G. N., Rohde, P., Lewinsohn, P. M., Hops, H., & Seeley, J. R. (1999). Cognitive-behavioral treatment of adolescent depression: Efficacy of acute group treatment and booster sessions. *Journal of the American Academy of Child and Adolescent Psychiatry, 38*(3), 272-279.

Cohen, J. (1988). *Statistical power analysis for the behavioral sciences.* Hillsdale, NJ: Lawrence Erlbaum.

Cuijpers, P. (1998a). Prevention of depression in chronic general medical disorders: A pilot study. *Psychological Reports, 82,* 735-738.

Cuijpers, P. (1998b). A psychoeducational approach to the treatment of depression: A meta-analysis of Lewinsohn's "Coping with Depression" course. *Behavior Therapy, 29,* 521-533.

Derogatis, L. R. (1983). *Administration, scoring, and procedures manual, II.* Baltimore, MD: Clinical Psychometric Research.

Gelhart, R. P., & King, H. L. (2001). The influence of comorbid risk factors on the effectiveness of cognitive-behavioral treatment of depression. *Cognitive and Behavioral Practice, 8,* 18-28.

Greenberg, P. E., Stiglin, L. E., Finkelstein, S. N., & Berndt, E. R. (1993). The economic burden of depression in 1990. *Journal of Clinical Psychiatry, 54,* 405-418.

Haringsma, R., Engels, G. I., Spinhoven, P., & Cuijpers, P. (2001, October). *Efficacy of coping with depression for elderly: Preliminary results.* Symposium conducted at the World Congress of Behavioral and Cognitive-Behavioral Therapies, Vancouver, British Columbia.

Hautzinger, M., & de Jong-Meyer, R. (1996). Cognitive-behavioral therapy versus pharmacotherapy in depression. In C. Mundt, M. J. Goldstein, K. Hahlweg, & H. Fielder (Eds.), *Interpersonal factors in the origin and course of affective disorders* (pp. 329-340). Dorset, England: Dorset Press.

Hoberman, H. M., Lewinsohn, P. M., & Tilson, M. (1988). Group treatment of depression: Individual predictors of outcome. *Journal of Consulting and Clinical Psychology, 56,* 393-398.

Keller, M. B., Lavori, P. W., Endicott, J., Coryel, W., & Klerman, G. L. (1983). "Double depression": Two-year follow-up. *American Journal of Psychiatry, 140,* 689-694.

Kessler, R. C., McGonagle, K. A., Shanyang, Z., Nelson, C. B., Hughes, M., Eshleman, S., Wittchen, H. U., & Kendler, K. S. (1994). Lifetime and 12-month prevalence of *DSM-II-R* psychiatric disorders in the United States: Results from the National Comorbidity Survey. *Archives of General Psychiatry, 51*(1), 8-19.

Kuhner, C., Angermeyer, M. C., & Veiel, H. O. F. (1996). Cognitive-behavioral group intervention as a means of tertiary prevention in depressed patients: Acceptance and short-term efficacy. *Cognitive Therapy and Research, 20*(4), 391-409.

Lewinsohn, P. M., Antonuccio, D. O., Steinmetz-Breckenridge, J. L., & Teri, L. (1984). *The Coping with Depression course: A psychoeducational intervention for unipolar depression.* Eugene, OR: Castalia Publishing.

Lewinsohn, P. M., Clarke, G. N., Hops, H., & Andrews, J. (1990). Cognitive-behavioral treatment for depressed adolescents. *Behavior Therapy, 21,* 385-401.

Lewinsohn, P. M., Clarke, G. N., Rohde, P., Hops, H., & Seeley, J. R. (1996). A course in coping: A cognitive-behavioral approach to the treatment of adolescent depression. In E. D. Hibbs & P. S. Jensen (Eds.), *Psychosocial treatments for child and adolescent disorders: Empirically based strategies for clinical practice.* Washington, DC: American Psychological Association.

Lewinsohn, P. M., Hoberman, H. M., Teri, L., & Hautzinger, M. (1985). An integrated theory of depression. In S. Reiss & R. Bootzin (Eds.), *Theoretical issues in behavior therapy* (pp. 331-359). New York: Academic Press.

Lewinsohn, P. M., Muñoz, R. F., Youngren, M. A., & Zeiss, A. M. (1992). *Control your depression* (2nd ed.). Englewood Cliffs, NJ: Prentice Hall.

Lewinsohn, P. M., Youngren, M. A., & Grosscup, S. J. (1979). Reinforcement and depression. In R. A. Dupue (Ed.), *The psychobiology of depressive disorders: Implications for the effect of stress* (pp. 291-316). New York: Academic Press.

Marin, D. B., Kocsis, J. H., Frances, A. J., & Parides, M. (1994). Desipramine for the treatment of "pure dysthymia" versus "double" depression. *American Journal of Psychiatry, 151,* 1079-1080.

McClanahan, T. M. (2004). *Ethical and legal aspects of professional psychology: Establishing standards of care for the 21st century.* Manuscript submitted for publication.

Milgrom, J., Martin, P. R., & Negri, L. M. (2000). *Treating postnasal depression: A psychological approach for health care practitioners.* Chichester, NY: Wiley.

Muñoz, R. F. (2001). On the road to a world without depression. *Journal of Primary Prevention, 21*(3), 325-337.

Muñoz, R. F., & Ying, Y. W. (Eds.). (1993). *The prevention of depression: Research and practice.* Baltimore, MD: Johns Hopkins University Press.

Muñoz, R. F., Ying, Y. W., Armas, R., Chan, F., & Gurza, R. (1987). The San Francisco Depression Prevention Project: A randomized trial with medical outpatients. In R. F. Muñoz (Ed.), *Depression prevention: Research directions* (pp. 199-215). Washington, DC: Hemisphere Press.

Murray, C. J. L., & Lopez, A. D. (1990). *The global burden of disease: Summary.* Boston: Harvard University Press.

National Institute of Mental Health. (1995). *What to do when an employee is depressed: A guide for supervisors* (NIH 97-3919). Washington, DC: Author.

Organista, K. C., Muñoz, R. F., & Gonzalez, G. (1994). Cognitive-behavioral therapy for depression in low-income and minority medical outpatients: Description of a program and exploratory analyses. *Cognitive Therapy and Research, 18,* 241-259.

Patterson, T. E., & McClanahan, T. M. (1999). *The couple and family clinical documentation sourcebook: A comprehensive collection of mental health practice forms, handouts, and records.* New York: Wiley.

Prudic, J., Sackeim, H. A., Devanand, D. P., & Kiersky, J. E. (1993). The efficacy of ECT in double depression. *Depression, 1*(1), 38-44.

Rohde, P., Lewinsohn, P. M., Clarke, G., & Seeley, J. R. (in press). The adolescent coping with depression course: A cognitive-behavioral approach to the treatment of adolescent depression. In E. D. Hibbs & P. S. Jensen (Eds.), *Psychosocial treatments for child and adolescent disorders: Empirically based approaches.* Washington, DC: American Psychological Association.

Rohde, P., Lewinsohn, P. M., & Seeley, J. R. (1994). Response of depressed adolescents to cognitive-behavioral treatment: Do differences in initial severity clarify the comparison of treatments? *Journal of Consulting and Clinical Psychology, 62*(4), 851-854.

Robinson, P., Bush, T., Von Korff, M., Katon, W., Lin, E., Simon, G. E., & Walker, E. (1995). Primary care physician use of cognitive behavioral techniques with depressed patients. *Journal of Family Practice, 40,* 386-400.

Scogin, F., Jamison, C., & Davis, N. (1990). Two-year follow-up of bibliotherapy for depression in older adults. *Journal of Consulting and Clinical Psychology, 58,* 665-667.

Scogin, F., Jamison, C., Floyd, M., & Chaplin, W. (in press). Measuring learning in depression treatment: A cognitive bibliotherapy test. *Cognitive Therapy and Research.*

Spitzer, R. L., Williams, J. B. W., Gibbon, M., & First, M. B. (1990). *User's guide for the Structured Clinical Interview for DSM-III-R.* Washington, DC: American Psychiatric Press.

Steinmetz, J. L., Lewinsohn, P. M., & Antonuccio, D. O. (1983). Prediction of individual outcome in a group intervention for depression. *Journal of Consulting and Clinical Psychology, 51,* 331-337.

Teri, L., & Lewinsohn, P. M. (1986). Individual treatment of unipolar depression: Comparison of treatment outcome and identification of predictors of successful treatment outcome. *Behavior Therapy, 17,* 215-228.

Teri, L., Logsdon, R. G., Uomoto, J., & McCurry, S. M. (1997). Behavioral treatment of depression in dementia patients: A controlled clinical trial. *Journal of Gerontology: Psychological Sciences, 52B,* 159-166.

Thompson, L. W., Gallager, D., Nies, G., & Epstein, D. (1983, November). *Cognitive-behavioral vs. other treatments of depressed alcoholics and inpatients.* Paper presented at the 17th Annual Convention of the Association for the Advancement of Behavior Therapy, Washington, DC.

World Health Organization. (2000). *Women's mental health: An evidence based review.* Geneva: Author.

10

Personality Disorders

THOMAS R. LYNCH AND LESLIE E. HORTON
Duke University Medical Center

*A*n important component of individual well-being is satisfaction derived from interactions with others. Because the average American adult spends around half of his or her waking life at the workplace, it comes as no surprise that this environment is a key element of one's social life. Positive interactions with co-workers can boost one's mood; can increase the quality, efficiency, and productivity of both individual and group tasks; and can help co-workers maintain manageable levels of stress in their life. Because both individuals and the workplace as a whole benefit greatly from strong working relationships, it is vitally important to understand the factors that contribute to or detract from these relationships. One key factor is the personalities of those in the working environment.

Personality is an important variable in the interpersonal dynamics of the workplace because it guides a great deal of one's actions, remains remarkably consistent over time, and provides an important source of identity. Difficulties in working relationships often can be linked to personality, which is illustrated by the fact that people often term disagreements "personality conflicts" or "personality clashes." Some of the most serious conflicts in an employment setting may involve those with a pathology known as a personality disorder. Personality disorders are defined by the *Diagnostic and Statistical Manual of Mental Disorders—Fourth Edition–Text Revision* (*DSM-IV-TR*) (American Psychiatric Association, 2000) as long-lasting patterns of inner experiences and behaviors that differ significantly from an individual's culture in the areas of cognition, emotion, interpersonal functioning, or impulse control. This pattern must be consistent and inflexible across a broad range of situations, must be traced back to adolescence or early adulthood, and must be a negative influence on one's social or occupational functioning. Overall, personality disorders can be conceptualized within a framework of two fundamental developmental issues: coping interpersonally (e.g., getting along with others) and regulating private experience (e.g., controlling thoughts, emotions, or impulses).

The personality disorders are grouped by the *DSM-IV-TR* into three clusters based on related characteristics. Cluster A includes paranoid, schizoid, and schizotypal personality disorders. Those diagnosed with a disorder in this cluster often appear odd or eccentric to those around them. Individuals with paranoid personality disorder are constantly distrustful and falsely interpret the behavior of others as malevolent and menacing. Those with schizoid personality disorder have no desire to interact with others because they do not enjoy close interpersonal relationships. Those with schizotypal personality disorder have a pattern of eccentric behavior, discomfort with social interaction, and unusual ways of thinking or behaving.

Cluster B personality disorders are antisocial, borderline, histrionic, and narcissistic. Individuals with a diagnosis in this cluster behave in unusually erratic, emotional, or dramatic ways. Antisocial personality disorder is a pattern of consistently violating and ignoring the rights of others with no remorse or feelings of empathy. Individuals with borderline personality disorder have impulsive behavior patterns, a fear of abandonment, and unstable moods and relationships with others. A diagnosis of histrionic personality disorder indicates one has a constant need to be the center of attention, which one attempts by behaving in overly dramatic and emotional ways. Narcissistic personality disorder is characterized by a persistent need for other's admiration, extreme arrogance, and a lack of empathy for the wants and needs of others.

The final group of diagnoses, Cluster C, includes avoidant, dependent, and obsessive-compulsive personality disorders. The *DSM-IV-TR* groups these diagnoses together because those with disorders in this cluster often seem excessively afraid or anxious. Those with an avoidant personality disorder diagnosis have very low self-esteem and are hypersensitive to criticism or rejection, which causes them to feel socially inhibited. An individual with dependent personality disorder has an overwhelming need to be taken care of, fears separation, and behaves in excessively clingy and submissive ways. Obsessive-compulsive personality disorder is a pattern of being highly perfectionistic and controlling at the expense of efficiency and flexibility.

Because an essential feature of personality disorders is extreme difficulty functioning in social or occupational realms, or both, an individual with one of these diagnoses can greatly impact the stress level and job performance of his or her co-workers. Although few empirical studies address this issue explicitly, a study by Cavaiola and Lavender (1999) showed that more than 80 percent of people interviewed cited a negative relationship with a co-worker as one of the most significant sources of stress in their life. These same individuals described behaviors common in personality disorders as the most distressing. Conflicts between employees may be exacerbated by the fact that one individual may not realize that a personality-disordered co-worker has a diagnosable condition.

Personality disorders also come at a great cost to the affected individual, as these disorders can negatively influence the most essential areas of life. Research by Reich, Yates, and Nduaguba (1989) indicated that those with personality disorders have more problems acquiring and maintaining employment and more difficulties within the workplace than those without these clusters of maladaptive traits. Personality disorders are notoriously difficult to treat and often accompany other psychiatric conditions, like depression and alcohol abuse. In addition, because of frequent interpersonal difficulties, lack of treatment or poor treatment may function to maintain suffering for the individual and those around him or her in the workplace.

EPIDEMIOLOGY OF PERSONALITY DISORDERS

While it seems clear that personality disorders are relatively common in the general population, reports of prevalence vary. Diagnostic and methodological problems in existing personality disorder research may account for this variability and should limit or caution definitive conclusions that can be drawn from this research. One reason is that personality disorders can be difficult to diagnose, even by trained clinicians, so the accuracy of the diagnoses in research settings is uncertain. In addition, different research studies use varied methods of diagnosis, and some of these methods may be less accurate or reliable than others. Finally, researchers also may use differing methods of participant recruitment, which could result in different rates of individual disorders (Rosowsky & Gurian, 1991).

Despite these difficulties interpreting epidemiological statistics, researchers generally agree that 10 percent to 13.5 percent of adults have at least one personality disorder (Torgerson, Kringlen, & Cramer, 2001; Weissman, 1993). These results suggest that personality disorders are twice as prevalent as clinical depression and are comparable in prevalence to alcoholism. Reports of the rates of specific personality disorders vary from study to study depending on the type of assessments used but range from less than 1 percent to nearly 7 percent for each diagnosis.

Personality disorders are universally more common in clinical settings. One study (Casey & Tyrer, 1990) estimated that 28 percent of those treated for any psychiatric disorder in outpatient medical clinics also have a personality disorder. Overall, several studies looking at prevalence of personality disorders among clinical populations, including one study by Mellman, Leverich, Hauser, & Kramlinger (1992), indicated that 30 percent to 40 percent of those with anxiety or depressive disorders, or both, also carry a personality disorder diagnosis. Affected individuals frequently have more than one kind of personality disorder. One study (Torgerson et al., 2001) estimated that the average number of personality disorders possessed by one individual in the general population is 1.48. Because individuals with personality disorders are likely to have more than one type or another psychiatric disorder, it often is difficult for mental health providers to diagnose and treat these disorders effectively.

In addition to examining overall rates of prevalence in community and clinical samples, researchers have examined the relationship of demographic factors to personality disorder diagnoses. Gender is one demographic variable examined in research, and studies differ regarding whether personality disorders are more common overall in men or women. Some researchers believe that the rates may be roughly the same overall, although certain personality disorders are higher in one gender. For example, antisocial personality disorder is reported by the American Psychiatric Association (2000) to be more common in men, and borderline personality disorder is more common in women.

Marital status is another important demographic variable. One study (Zimmerman & Coryell, 1989) suggested that those with personality disorders are more likely to be single, divorced, or separated than those without these diagnoses. These data strengthen the argument that deficits in interpersonal interactions are characteristic features of a personality disorder diagnosis and may have deleterious effects for establishing and maintaining intimate relationships.

Age may be related to personality disorder diagnoses as well. Despite earlier misconceptions that personality disorders might "burn out" in late life, a meta-analysis by Abrams and Horowitz (1996) suggested that the overall prevalence rate of older adult personality disorders are essentially equivalent to younger populations. However, the *DSM-IV-TR* (American Psychiatric Association, 2000) stated, "Some types of personality disorders (Cluster B) tend to become less evident or to remit with age, whereas this appears to be less true for some other types (Clusters A and C)." To date, explanations of these apparent age-related changes have remained essentially atheoretical (p. 688).

It is probable that reinforcement (i.e., feedback) from the environment shape the expression of personality pathology. Supporting this is strong experimental evidence suggesting that individuals are particularly likely to seek verification of self-views over other reinforcers, particularly if their self-views are extreme and firmly held. Repeated studies also have confirmed that people with negative self-views seek unfavorable feedback and partners, become anxious when they cannot readily dismiss self-discrepant feedback, nullify disconfirming feedback, and withdraw from relationships in which they receive disconfirming feedback. Thus, individuals seek out confirmation of their beliefs and avoid feedback that might suggest otherwise (Pelham & Swann, 1994; Swann, 1997).

However, emotional growth probably requires at least occasional disconfirmation. An environmental feedback hypothesis suggests that a person controls mental and social interactions to avoid aversive feedback, but unfortunately for the individual, avoidance may function to reinforce pathology. For example, by repeatedly staying away from stressful interpersonal situations individuals with the avoidant personality disorder never learn that they can cope in new situations. Paranoid individuals are suspicious and avoid confiding in others and therefore never learn that others are not exploiting or deceiving them. The obsessive-compulsive individuals never discover that being flexible can have beneficial consequences. We consider it probable that decades of reinforcement without disconfirming feedback function to maintain and exaggerate personality pathology.

In contrast, Cluster B disorders are thought to decline with age. These disorders not only are characterized by interpersonal problems but also typically are associated with inappropriate emotion expression and problems with impulse control. Because older adults tend to have less intense emotions, they may exhibit fewer of the impulsive behaviors characterized by Cluster B disorders. Alternatively, disconfirming environmental feedback may function to punish or extinguish maladaptive behaviors. For example, self-injury (i.e., a symptom of borderline personality disorder) not only is difficult to hide but likely will elicit negative social feedback from family members and health care providers. Indeed, impulsive, dramatic behaviors in general are likely to elicit little social confirmation. Over time, this may slowly shape these behaviors out of a person's repertoire.

CASE ILLUSTRATION

In this transcript, the patient is a 32-year-old Caucasian woman presenting for psychotherapy with borderline personality disorder, social phobia, and problems with anger at work. This patient had a history of childhood invalidation and alcohol dependence. In this prototypical example, we present elements from a treatment that is designed specifically for personality disorders: dialectical behavior therapy. During this session, the therapist conducts a behavioral analysis of a recent upsetting work experience, identifies possible skills, connects in-session behavior to the behavioral analysis, and obtains a commitment to a skills-based solution.

T: So, let's think back to last week when you yelled and ran out of the office party slamming a door. What we're going to do is a behavioral analysis of that incident, because we really need to understand how that happened and how we can prevent that from happening again. Now, before we begin, I want to check in with you about whether you remain committed to working on anger at work as an important problem.

P: Um. Yeah.

T: Because I think making changes in how you respond to your co-workers is going to be very difficult. And although you convinced me last week that you are committed to change, I think changing anger for you will be particularly hard.

P: I don't know why I get so angry, but I am committed to trying not to.

T: Great. But remember, it's not so much that we want to get rid of the anger altogether, but instead learn how to modulate it and change our actions when mad. So, let's work together to figure out what happened when you ran out of work last week. Think back to Wednesday.

P: I don't remember much about Wednesday. I think I hid out in my office most of the day.

T: Well, what time was the office party.

P: I don't remember.

T: Was it in the morning or afternoon?

P: Afternoon.

T: Were you feeling any anger or any strong emotion in the morning?

P: Nothing really. I just was working on labeling some of the files and was frustrated because we ran out of folders. I went out of my office to look for some, but really didn't want to see anyone. I hate going out in public.

T: I know you do, and I can understand why. People can be judgmental and you already feel like you don't fit in.

P: That's because I'm a total loser. [patient becomes visibly ashamed]

T: It looks like you might be feeling a little ashamed right now. I'm noticing how you are looking down at the floor. You know, it turns out that when people feel ashamed they often try to conceal themselves or hide. Are you feeling ashamed right now?

P: I don't know what I feel. ... I just know I feel like a piece of garbage.

T: Do you think you would be willing to look up toward me as we continue?

P: OK. [looks up]

T: Excellent. [leans in toward patient] My observation is that as we talk about yelling and slamming the door at the party, you are starting to feel terrible.

P: Like a loser. Like a total reject.

T: Exactly. I wonder if you felt this way when you were at the office party on Wednesday?

P: Probably.

T: Think about it for a second. What happened at the party?

P: I went in just to get some punch and was planning on leaving as soon as possible. But, JoAnn and Steve were there around the food and they started talking to me. They started complaining about the new computer system. JoAnn asked me what I thought of her memo about the new program to Richard, my boss.

T: What did you say?

P: I told her that I thought the memo maybe was too harsh, especially since the program had just been up and running about a week.

T: What happened next?

P: After I said that, I felt horrible.

T: What were you thinking about in that moment?

P: Ummm ... I felt like I had done something wrong.

T: It sounds like you felt guilty about giving her your opinion.

P: Yeah, that sort of fits.

T: What did you do next?

P: I told her I was sorry. She said that it was OK and that she was glad to hear my opinion. I guess that I then sort of felt better, but I also felt sort of vulnerable or, I don't know, embarrassed.

T: What were you thinking?

P: I don't know, I guess I was thinking: Why do I always have to be the one saying their sorry? Why do I always have to be the one that keeps the relationship smooth? Why couldn't JoAnn have apologized for asking my opinion in the first place? She shouldn't have done that. [clenching her fists]

T: Is this when you started feeling angry?

P: Yeah. But, then I started feeling like I was doing something wrong again. JoAnn and Steve kept staring at me, like I was a freak.

T: What did you do?

P: I told them that I was sorry for saying sorry. That I know it's OK to have an opinion. They said that it was OK. That I didn't need to apologize again.

T: What happened next?

P: I don't know. I just felt embarrassed and humiliated by this again. Then I felt furious. How dare they tell me how to behave. Why aren't they apologizing? Don't they know that asking people their opinion is annoying?

T: Is that when you ran out?

P: Yeah, I screamed at them both to shut up and threw my cup down on the table. Then I slammed the door. [looks sheepish]

T: You are doing a great job remembering the details. Now, let me ask you this. Is it OK for someone to give an opinion, especially when asked? What I mean is, if you heard a good friend give exactly the same opinion you did in the same tone of voice to JoAnn, would you say they should not have given their opinion or that giving their opinion was OK?

P: I guess, I might think they did OK.

T: So, we know that the guilt you felt was not justified for the situation. Even though it is understandable, after all your parents punished you whenever you had an opinion. But, we can be pretty sure that you did not do anything wrong in this situation. Therefore, we know that saying sorry was not necessary and it makes sense that you might feel a little embarrassed for apologizing for something that your wise mind knows was not really your fault. I wonder if your anger was at least partly directed at yourself?

Epilogue: It is important to note that there are numerous targets that emerged in this short transcript. The dialectical behavior therapist then proceeded to discuss with the patient skills that could have been used in the moment to prevent this type of problem from occurring again in the future. Some of these skills included cognitive restructuring of the thought that she had done something wrong (e.g., tell herself that it is OK to have an opinion and disagreement can help things work out better) or self-soothing (e.g., do a brief five-minute relaxation exercise before going to the party). It is important to note that the therapist was careful during the generation of solutions not to overly criticize or comment on her actual opinion giving. Because this patient has difficulty giving opinions, any (even mild) criticism could function to punish future opinion giving. Therefore, after ascertaining that the way the opinion was given was relatively reasonable, the therapist would work instead on reinforcing the patient's bravery (i.e., for having attempted to give an opinion). The most important solution the therapist used with this patient was to teach the patient to block automatic repairs when feeling guilty (i.e., always saying sorry). To help the patient with this reaction, particularly because early in treatment it was very difficult for the patient to discriminate when or when not to say she was sorry, the patient was given a rule that she could not apologize for at least one day following the experience of guilt. Because guilt was a common emotion for this patient, blocking automatic repairs helped keep her from experiencing embarrassment and shame (the precursors for anger). The idea here was to use a stall tactic (i.e., wait a day) so that she could have time to consider whether she had actually done something wrong. For most situations, giving an apology for egregious behavior will be effective even if done at a later time. Over time, this approach allowed the patient to learn how to give opinions, feel less ashamed, and prevented unnecessary anger.

RECOGNIZING AND EVALUATING PERSONALITY DISORDERS

Sometimes those diagnosed with depression or anxiety disorders are able to mask or control their symptoms in the workplace, but this is likely to be more challenging for personality-disordered individuals. Emotion and impulse control difficulties may impede job performance, which co-workers will often detect. For example, co-workers may notice how a narcissistic colleague routinely alienates others by behaving in an arrogant fashion or how a colleague with dependent traits consistently fails to initiate tasks without the help of others.

Although co-workers may notice the presence of traits that could indicate the presence of these disorders, those with the condition may not realize that they should seek treatment. Some of those with personality disorders may realize that their behavior complicates their life, but because the behaviors are so intertwined with their self-identity, they may not wish to change or may believe they are unable to. Because of these factors, many individuals may not seek treatment for these disorders. However, because other mood disorders often coexist with personality disorders, an affected individual may instead seek treatment for the comorbid mood condition.

Diagnosis can be made from self-report questionnaires, observation of clinical behavior and chart review, or structured interviews. The three most commonly used self-report measures are the Personality Disorder Questionnaire, the Millon Clinical Multiaxial Inventory, and the Minnesota Multiphasic Personality Inventory. The Minnesota Multiphasic Personality Inventory is a 550-item true–false questionnaire. It is probably the most commonly used questionnaire for assessing personality types, although it was not originally developed to diagnose personality disorders. The Millon Clinical Multiaxial Inventory and Personality Disorder Questionnaire can both diagnose specific personality disorders, but research suggests that these measures may be more accurate when used only as screening tools. In addition, because many personality disorder symptoms are not socially acceptable or because symptoms are ego-syntonic, many patients may not endorse personality disorder criteria. Structured interviews, like the Structured Clinical Interview for the *DSM-III-R* and the Personality Disorder Examination have the advantage of examining patients' beliefs and reports alongside their behavior. Raters can be trained to probe for an accurate understanding of questions and for additional clarification of ambiguous responses. However, while considered the best with regard to accuracy, these structured interviews are time-consuming and require specialized training. Here too patients may be reluctant to report undesirable traits or behavior, particularly when faced with a clinician.

Despite the wide availability of methods to assess personality disorders, no standardized way of diagnosing these disorders is commonly accepted, which highlights the difficulty inherent to the diagnosis of personality disorders. Researcher Spitzer (1983) recommended a combination of assessment approaches, known as the LEAD standard, to improve the quality of diagnostic efforts. LEAD is an acronym where *L* (longitudinal history) means that clinicians should consider the patient's history over his or her entire adult life span, *E* (expert opinion) means that clinicians should be well trained so that an expert is considering the diagnosis, and *AD* (all available data) means that multiple sources of information, including clinical interviews and self-report questionnaires, should be considered when making a diagnosis.

REFERRAL STRATEGIES

In general, individuals with personality disorders are more sensitive to criticism than is the average person and may be less likely than those with other disorders to self-refer to treatment. Because personality disorders are complex conditions, referrals given to employees with personality disorders should be able to provide multiple approaches to treatment. Although not a great deal is known about effective treatments for personality disorders, research has suggested that a combination of psychotherapeutic and pharmacologic treatments is more effective for those with other psychiatric diagnoses than either medication or therapy alone. It seems plausible that this finding would also apply to the treatment of personality disorders. In general, clinicians with experience treating personality disorders and comorbid conditions should be referred to the individual seeking treatment. Table 10.1 presents strategies for diagnosing and treating personality disorders.

TABLE 11.1
Considerations in Diagnosing and Treating Personality Disorders

1. Look for patterns of behavior while probing for specific events to support your diagnosis:
   - Does this person exhibit a long-standing pattern of interpersonal difficulties in a variety of contexts?
   - Does this person exhibit a long-standing pattern of problems with emotional and/or impulse control?
2. Consider social desirability factors when obtaining a self report. A nonjudgmental stance on the part of the clinician will likely help disclosure.
3. If the patient is willing, consider consulting family members or friends to clarify diagnostic issues.
4. Some patients avoid feedback about their problems as a way to reduce anxiety. Advise patients that change will likely involve some discomfort as they learn to cope differently (e.g., being assertive if normally avoidant).
5. In cases of comorbid Axis I disorders, try to establish personality pathology outside Axis I episodes.

WORKPLACE OR HOME STRESSORS WITH PARTICULAR RELEVANCE TO PERSONALITY DISORDERS

Stressful situations can exacerbate and reinforce the problematic behaviors that are hallmarks of individual personality disorders. Although these diagnoses are chronic and stable over time, stressors still can have a deleterious effect on the functioning of individuals with these diagnoses. This is especially so when a patient carries a comorbid mood disorder diagnosis. Stressors for a personality-disordered employee will vary depending on the individual diagnosis, but any stressor is likely to increase conflict levels and tension with co-workers and result in the individual behaving in ways harmful to the quality of his or her work duties.

For example, a stressor for an employee with borderline personality disorder might be when a close colleague gets laid off. This situation could elicit strong feelings of abandonment, betrayal, and anger in the individual, which may result in the individual having an emotional outburst in the workplace setting. A narcissistic employee, on the other hand, may find a situation where his or her superiority is questioned to be especially traumatic, such as during a yearly performance review. If certain aspects of job performance were criticized, the individual with this disorder may lash out and insult or demean a co-worker, resulting in a hostile work environment or even potential job loss. It is likely that the pathology of the individual determines the extent to which a situation serves as a stressor, so the success of a personality-disordered individual in an employment setting will largely depend on whether he or she is able to manage or minimize stressors through treatment or other means.

TREATING PERSONALITY DISORDERS

Mental health providers have traditionally viewed personality disorders as highly resistant to treatment, and perhaps because of this view few researchers have examined empirically supported treatments for these disorders. In recent years this trend has changed and researchers are beginning to apply systematic scientific inquiry to this topic. Despite improvements in research, much is still unknown about effective treatments for personality disorders. The conclusions one can reach from personality disorder research are limited by the wide variety of populations, methodologies, and assessment techniques that are used in personality disorder research, which calls into question the validity of findings and sometimes results in contradictory outcomes.

Conducting treatment outcome research studies for personality disorders are difficult not only because of inconsistencies in research design but also because these disorders are difficult and require time to successfully treat. Those with personality disorders frequently have other comorbid diagnoses, and studies indicate that treatment response is poorer for these individuals. Some studies and clinical observations suggested that those with personality disorders have more difficulty with treatment compliance and drop out at higher rates than those with other psychiatric diagnoses, in addition to doing less well in treatment. Because of the interpersonal skills deficits, those with personality disorders also may have difficulty establishing a strong connection with their clinician, which could have a deleterious impact on treatment outcome. Despite these complicating factors, research is emerging that suggests that treatment is beneficial for those with personality disorders, and more research should be conducted to illuminate specific information about type, duration, and outcome of treatment.

Pharmacologic Treatment

One type of treatment with potential benefit for personality disorders is the use of medications to target behaviors related to these disorders. Research consistently supports the notion that personality traits are mediated by neurotransmitter physiology, and it is believed that psychotropic medications act to influence the neurotransmitter systems. Hence, pharmacologic approaches to treating personality disorders could be effective in targeting specific symptoms related to these disorders. Researchers have used selective serotonin reuptake inhibitors antidepressants, atypical antipsychotics, antianxiety medications, tricyclic antidepressants, traditional neuroleptics, mood stabilizers, and monoamine oxidase inhibitors with personality-disordered patients. These medications have been shown to have some success in treating specific features of personality disorders. For example, a study by Goldberg et al. (1986) suggested that antipsychotics can effectively treat the paranoia associated with schizotypal and paranoid personality disorders, as well as the rage and agitation associated with antisocial and borderline personality disorders. Antidepressants, including fluoxetine, have been shown to reduce avoidant behaviors, as well as impulsive and angry behaviors characteristic of borderline and antisocial personality disorders (Coccaro, Astill, Herbert, & Schut, 1990).

Despite these promising results, we the authors are unaware of any randomized trials examining the efficacy of pharmacotherapy for histrionic, schizoid, narcissistic, dependent, or obsessive-compulsive personality disorders. Additional research into pharmacotherapy for personality disorders will provide frameworks specifying connections between individual medications and specific traits and behaviors involved in a personality disorder diagnosis. However, it is unlikely that a medication will ever be found that cures a personality disorder; instead medications may help alleviate some of the symptoms (e.g., anxiety).

Psychotherapeutic Treatment

Personality disorders are disorders of coping. Coping in this context refers to styles of dealing with stressors, either inside the person (e.g., intense emotion) or outside the person (e.g., interpersonal conflict). Psychotherapy is in essence a process that involves learning effective coping, through insight or explicit teaching. Studies of psychotherapy interventions also have been scarce, although initial research seems to suggest more uniformly positive results for psychotherapy. A meta-analysis by Perry, Banon, and Ianni (1999) examined 15 studies treating personality disorders with psychotherapy and found that virtually all studies reported statistically significant improvements at the end of treatment and at follow-up points, even though these studies varied greatly on methodology, assessment, and treatment types.

In the review Perry and his colleagues (1999) found that no particular theoretical orientation of therapy was superior overall. Six of these studies used a psychodynamic treatment format, three used cognitive-behavioral therapy (CBT), two compared these treatment types, one examined supportive psychotherapy, and two studied interpersonal group therapy. Although no significant differences were noted between the different types of treatment orientations in this study, other research has provided more specific information about which therapy types are effective for particular personality disorders; namely, borderline and avoidant personality disorders. Dialectical behavior therapy (DBT), a modified type of CBT developed at the University of Washington by Marsha Linehan (Linehan, Armstrong, Suarez, Allmon, & Heard, 1991), has been established as a beneficial and widely used treatment for borderline personality disorder (BPD) and has more recently been applied to other personality disorders and other multiproblem disorders. In sum, the literature suggests that for those parasuicidal patients with BPD, who receive DBT have less parasuicidal behavior, psychiatric hospitalizations, anger, and psychotropic medication use, and greater overall functioning, social adjustment, and retention in therapy compared with those who receive treatment as usual (Scheel, 2000). Several studies, including one by Alden (1989), indicated that the social skills training used in some CBTs are important to the success of treatment for avoidant personality disorder.

Results examining specific treatments for other individual personality disorders indicate that psychotherapy is possibly efficacious, but additional research is required to replicate initial findings. For example, one study (Karterud, Vaglum, Friis, & Irion 1992) showed a significant improvement in antisocial outpatients over a six-month course of intensive psychodynamic psychotherapy.

The studies included in the review by Perry and his colleagues (1999) include a varied range of treatment length, with a median of 28 weeks of therapy. Although these findings are by no means conclusive, this review reported 50 percent of the participants were classified as recovered after 1.3 years of treatment. This review also found that in studies relying on self-report of personality disorder symptoms, patients reported better results in shorter therapy types. The authors suggested several possible explanations for this finding, including the notion that the participants reported a more favorable response early in the treatment, or the possibility that longer treatment studies included the more severe patients than did the short formats.

Overall, researchers need to conduct more studies to compare types of psychotherapies with control groups and other treatments. Greater focus needs to be placed on the issue of symptom relapse in future studies by incorporating longer follow-up periods in these studies. By better understanding the relationship between specific personality disorders and treatment type, mental health professionals can better tailor therapy to individual combinations of traits and behaviors.

THERAPEUTIC BENEFITS OF WORK FOR THOSE WITH PERSONALITY DISORDERS

The therapeutic benefits of a work environment depend entirely on the characteristics of the individual employee and the context of the employment. A conflict-ridden workplace is detrimental to all of those involved, and a job that does not complement an employee's strengths can be similarly negative. Alternatively, a job that one can do well and enjoy completely may buffer many of the detrimental effects of stress. Positive employment experiences can provide a worker with a sense of competency and self-efficacy, a stable income, and a satisfying structure to one's life, which can mitigate the depression and anxiety that often accompany personality disorders.

Because interpersonal and occupational impairment may cause an individual to seek treatment for a personality disorder, employment situations can serve as useful targets in psychotherapy and assist a person in changing his or her behavior. For example, an obsessive-compulsive employee, accustomed to exerting excessive control in the workplace, might be assigned by his or her therapist to delegate work-related tasks more frequently or with less oversight. A therapist may have an avoidant client agree to initiate a social encounter in the workplace, such as extending a lunch invitation to a colleague.

It seems clear that the workplace is one of the most potentially stressful and problematic situations for an individual with a personality disorder. A positive and fulfilling work experience that is well matched to an individual's strengths can go a long way to minimize the problematic behaviors associated with personality disorders and comorbid diagnoses.

SUMMARY

Personality is a key factor in determining the quality of interpersonal relationships in the workplace, which in turn influences the overall work environment. Personality disorders by their very nature are diagnoses that result in negative interpersonal interactions and dysfunctional behaviors, which necessarily affect the workplace as a whole. Many questions persist regarding the validity of personality disorders as discrete diagnostic categories, and a multitude of conceptual and methodological questions about the assessment, treatment, and research of these disorders remain as well. Despite these questions, the large impact that personality disorder diagnoses have on those afflicted and those in their home and working environments necessitates further research on these conditions. The need is underscored by the high rates of personality disorder prevalence noted in research of community and clinical samples of individuals, and also the frequent comorbidity of Axis I disorders like depression, anxiety, and substance abuse.

Fortunately, this need is beginning to be addressed. Some promising work has examined the efficacy of psychopharmacological and psychotherapeutic approaches to treating certain personality disorders, such as borderline personality disorders, but for other personality disorders these is little research to guide or inform treatment decisions of mental health professionals when encountering individuals with these diagnoses. As research continues to provide us with information, which can be disseminated from the research community to the public as a whole, those with personality disorders will be identified and effectively treated with greater frequency. Certainly employers have a vested interest in joining with mental health professionals in addressing these disorders, which can have far-reaching effects on the quality of life for affected individuals, their co-workers, and the entire work environment.

References

Abrams, R. C., & Horowitz, S. V. (1996). Personality disorders after age 50: A meta-analysis. *Journal of Personality Disorders, 10,* 271-281.

Alden, L. (1989). Short-term structure treatment for avoidant personality disorder. *Journal of Consulting and Clinical Psychology, 56,* 756-764.

American Psychiatric Association. (2000). *Diagnostic and statistical manual of mental disorders* (4th ed., text revision). Washington, DC: Author.

Casey, P. R., & Tyrer, P. (1990). Personality disorder and psychiatric illness in general practice. *British Journal of Psychiatry, 156,* 261-265.

Cavaiola, A. A., & Lavender, N. J. (1999, March). *Personality disorders in the workplace.* Paper presented at the Work, Stress, and Health: Organization of Work in a Global Economy conference of the American Psychological Association and the National Institute for Safety and Health, Baltimore, MD.

Coccaro, E. F., Astill, J. L., Herbert, J. A., & Schut, A. (1990). Fluoxetine treatment of impulsive aggression in *DSM-III-R* personality disorder patients. *Journal of Clinical Psychopharmacology, 10,* 373-375.

Goldberg, S. C., Schulz, P. M., Resnick, R. J., Hamer, R. M., & Friedel, R. O. (1986). Borderline and schizotypal personality disorders treated with low-dose thiothixene vs. placebo. *Archives of General Psychiatry, 43,* 680-686.

Karterud, S., Vaglum, S., Friis, S., & Irion, T. (1992). Day hospital therapeutic community treatment for patients with personality disorders. *Journal of Nervous and Mental Disorders, 180,* 238-243.

Linehan, M. M., Armstrong, H. E., Suarez, A., Allmon, D., & Heard, H. L. (1991). Cognitive-behavioral treatment for chronically parasuicidal borderline patients. *Archives of General Psychiatry, 48,* 1060-1064.

Mellman, T. A., Leverich, G. S., Hauser, P., & Kramer, K. L. (1992). Axis II pathology in panic and affective disorders: Relationship to diagnosis, course of illness, and treatment response. *Journal of Personality Disorders, 6,* 53-63.

Pelham, B. W., & Swann, W. B. (1994). The juncture of intrapersonal and interpersonal knowledge: Self-certainty and interpersonal congruence. *Personality and Social Psychology Bulletin, 20,* 349-357.

Perry, J. C., Banon, E., & Ianni, F. (1999). Effectiveness of psychotherapy for personality disorders. *The American Journal of Psychiatry, 156,* 1312-1321.

Reich, J., Yates, W., & Nduaguba, M. (1989). Prevalence of *DSM-III* personality disorders in the community. *Social Psychiatry and Psychiatric Epidemiology, 24,* 12-16.

Rosowsky, E., & Gurian, B. (1991). Borderline personality disorder in late life. *International Psychogeriatrics, 3,* 39-52.

Scheel, K. R. (2000). The empirical basis of dialectical behavior therapy: Summary, critique, and implications. *Clinical Psychology—Science and Practice, 7,* 68-86.

Spitzer, R. L. (1983). Psychiatric diagnosis: Are clinicians still necessary? *Comprehensive Psychiatry, 24,* 399-411.

Swann, W. B., Jr. (1997). The trouble with change: Self-verification and allegiance to the self. *Current Directions in Psychological Science, 8,* 177-180.

Torgerson, S., Kringlen, E., & Cramer, V. (2001). The prevalence of personality disorders in a community sample. *Archives of General Psychiatry, 58,* 590-596.

Weissman, M. (1993). The epidemiology of personality disorders: A 1990 update. *Journal of Personality Disorders, 7* (Suppl.), 44-62.

Zimmerman, M., & Coryell, W. (1989). *DSM-III* personality disorder diagnoses in a nonpatient sample: Demographic correlates and comorbidity. *Archives of General Psychiatry, 46,* 682-689.

11

Schizophrenia

KIM T. MUESER
Dartmouth Medical School

SUSAN R. MCGURK
Mount Sinai School of Medicine

DESCRIPTION OF THE DISORDER

Schizophrenia (and the closely related schizoaffective disorder) is a major mental illness that has a profound effect on a wide range of different areas of functioning, including performance at work and school and the ability to parent, to have close relationships with others, and to care for oneself. While the characteristic impairments in day-to-day functioning are what most distinguish schizophrenia from other mental illnesses, it is important to understand the specific psychiatric symptoms present in the disorder in order to distinguish it from other major mental illnesses such as major depression and bipolar disorder. People with schizophrenia often have problems with hallucinations and delusions. Psychotic symptoms often are flagrant but they also tend to fluctuate over time and are present on a consistent basis for only a minority of clients. People with schizophrenia also have difficulties with high levels of apathy and social withdrawal, problems that can be quite persistent over time. Cognitive impairments are also a common manifestation of schizophrenia, which tend to be stable over time. In addition to these characteristic symptoms, people with schizophrenia often experience problems with depression throughout their lifetime, as well as high levels of anxiety and substance-use problems.

Schizophrenia may manifest itself in a variety of ways at the workplace. Because people with schizophrenia often have poor social competence, as reflected by difficulties they experience in social cognition (i.e., the ability to perceive important social information during interactions with others) (Penn, Corrigan, Bentall, Racenstein, & Newman, 1997) and social skill (Bellack, Morrison, Wixted, & Mueser, 1990), the disorder may be apparent in problematic social interactions at the workplace. Common ways in which these social impairments may present themselves include awkwardness when conversing with others (e.g., co-workers), apparent lack of responsiveness during social interactions (due to common symptoms in schizophrenia such as a blunted facial expression, a monotonous voice tone, and minimal amount of speech), difficulty picking up the nuances of nonverbal or paralinguistic communication (such as a customer who appears anxious about a product and needs reassurance), high levels of anxiety when talking with others (e.g., supervisors), and avoidance of social interactions, especially when a conflict or the possibility of a conflict is present (Mueser & Liberman, 1988). Misunderstandings may easily occur because of the diminished expressiveness of people with schizophrenia when others misinterpret this to mean they are less concerned and interested than they really are (J. J. Blanchard, Mueser, & Bellack, 1998). Social difficulties at the workplace may result in the individual, as well as others with whom the person interacts, feeling uncomfortable.

The psychotic symptoms of schizophrenia also may become apparent at the workplace, depending on the severity of the person's disorder and the stage of the illness. When psychotic symptoms are persistent, or when they occur during a symptom relapse, they may interfere with work functioning in several ways. The individual may become delusional and begin talking about his or her delusions or even acting on them. Delusions can take many different forms, such as paranoid (persecutory), somatic (bodily), or grandiose. Talking about or acting on such delusions can be distressful to others and disruptive to workplace performance. Hallucinations also can disrupt workplace performance. The individual may draw attention to himself or herself by talking back to auditory hallucinations. Even when the person does not respond overtly to the hallucinations, they can be distracting, resulting in deterioration in ability to fulfill work responsibilities. Fortunately, when psychotic symptoms are present at the workplace they often occur on a temporary basis, and they are a warning sign that the person is beginning to experience a relapse; rapid intervention as soon as psychotic symptoms emerge can be effective at preventing full-blown relapses and the ensuing loss of functioning.

Another common way in which schizophrenia can become apparent at the workplace is through the effects of impaired cognitive functioning (McGurk & Meltzer, 2000). Some degree of cognitive impairment relative to premorbid functioning is present in most people with schizophrenia (Heaton et al., 1994). Problems in cognitive functioning can manifest themselves in a number of ways, including increased difficulty paying attention to work-related tasks, reduced speed of work performance, increased difficulty learning new job tasks, and greater difficulty solving problems at work. Often, cognitive impairment results in a decrement in work performance, which may be noticeable to the employer.

A final way in which schizophrenia may manifest itself at the workplace is through decreased energy and drive to succeed at the job. People with schizophrenia often are easily fatigued and have attenuated social drive (Andreasen, 1982). This can make it more difficult for them to perform well in jobs that require high levels of personal initiative, stamina, and the will to get ahead. Employers can easily misunderstand low levels of social drive as laziness or lack of personal commitment to work. However, many individuals with these symptoms are in fact fully committed to work and are highly dependable employees despite their reduced energy and social drive.

EPIDEMIOLOGY

Schizophrenia usually develops in late adolescence or early adulthood, between the ages of 16 and 30 years, and is present throughout much, if not all, of the remaining life span. While much less common, schizophrenia also can have an onset later in life, after the age of 50 (Almeida, Howard, Levy, & David, 1995; Howard, Almeida, & Levy, 1994). Onset of schizophrenia in childhood is extremely rare and is considered a separate disorder than adult-onset schizophrenia. Although schizophrenia tends to persist through most of people's adult lives, significant numbers of people experience significant improvements in the severity of their symptoms and psychosocial functioning over the lifetime and many have full remissions of their symptoms (Harding & Keller, 1998).

Prevalence of schizophrenia in the general population is approximately 1 percent (Keith, Regier, & Rae, 1991). While the prevalence is essentially the same across genders, women tend to have a later age of onset and a more benign course of the illness, including fewer hospitalizations and better community functioning (Angermeyer, Kuhn, & Goldstein, 1990; Goldstein, 1988). Although a variety of explanations has been posited to account for the better course of illness among women than men, including differences in biology or social tolerance for deviant behavior (Lewine, Gulley, Risch, Jewart, & Houpt, 1990; Salokangas, 1983; Seeman & Lang, 1990), no single explanation has strong scientific support (Haas & Garratt, 1998). While rates of schizophrenia are fairly similar across different racial and ethnic groups (Jablensky, 1999), some evidence indicates higher rates among minority populations (Adams, Dworkin, & Rosenberg, 1984; Minsky, Vega, Miskimen, Gara, & Escobar, 2003). In addition, prevalence of schizophrenia is higher among individuals living in poverty (Bruce, Takeuchi, & Leaf, 1991). One possible explanation for these differences is that living in poverty or a social environment in which one is a member of an ethnic minority group may result in higher levels of stress, thus increasing vulnerability to the development of schizophrenia among individuals who are biologically predisposed to the disorder (see the stress-vulnerability model, discussed later in this chapter). Across different countries, prevalence of schizophrenia is quite similar, although the course of illness is more benign in nonindustrialized countries (Lo & Lo, 1977; Sartorius et al., 1986).

CASE ILLUSTRATION

Note that initials and descriptive information provided in this vignette have been altered to disguise the client's identity.

SB is a 32-year-old Caucasian male with a diagnosis of schizophrenia. He is thin, of medium height, with brown curly hair. He has an intense, serious demeanor and rarely smiles. His affect is slightly flattened. Prior to SB's first hospitalization his social functioning was marginal. He had a few friends, but none whom he thought of as close, and he was considered by many at his school to be a loner. Although SB had been an average student throughout his childhood and adolescence, he began to experience problems with his schoolwork due to difficulties with attention and concentration in his eleventh year of high school. After several months of declining academic performance SB was hospitalized when he reported hearing voices and believing that he was being controlled by "outside forces." SB was in the hospital on and off for the next two years and did not finish high school. He obtained his graduate equivalency diploma (GED) at the age of 22 through the education department of the community mental health center where he receives outpatient services.

Following receipt of his GED, SB sought vocational services and participated in some client-worker programs at the mental health center, including one in which he received training in janitorial services and another where he worked as a busboy at the center's cafeteria. After working in several of these jobs SB expressed an interest in learning computer skills, such as word processing. He was enrolled in a computer-training program offered at the vocational rehabilitation program. He did so well in this class that he became a teacher's assistant in the program. He then received funding through the State Department of Vocational and Educational Rehabilitation to enter a certificate program for television production, which he completed, and then followed up with college classes in desktop publishing and computer graphics. SB said he had always wanted to write screenplays, and he hoped that this experience would help in that direction. As SB tried his hand at writing a screenplay, and talked over his efforts with his counselor at the mental health center, he realized how difficult it was to accomplish this goal and decided that he would pursue it in his spare time. In the meanwhile, he decided that he wanted to get a competitive job so he could move into a nicer apartment and have something to do with his time. SB enrolled in a supported employment program to help him achieve this vocational goal.

During SB's initial meeting with his assigned employment specialist he told her that he wanted competitive work because "I just want to be like everybody else." To assess SB's symptoms and cognitive functioning, a clinical interview and neuropsychological evaluation were conducted. SB's symptoms were relatively mild and included occasional bouts of paranoia that led to feelings of anxiety in social situations. His negative symptoms included reduced energy and social withdrawal. SB's neuropsychological evaluation indicated intact attention and mild impairments in problem solving and verbal learning and memory. Some psychomotor slowing also was noted. Results of this clinical and cognitive evaluation were shared with SB and his employment specialist. SB expressed an interest in clerical work that would also provide opportunities to use his newly developed computer skills.

With help of his employment specialist, SB obtained a position as a clerk in a law firm. His duties included performing Internet searches and filing legal documents. Although he disclosed his illness to his employers, SB did not feel the need for on-the-job supports. Instead, he had weekly meetings with his employment specialist to discuss how his job was going and any difficulties he was encountering. Initially, SB had trouble fully understanding what his supervisor was asking him to do for the Internet searches. Even when he was unclear of what his supervisor wanted, SB's approach was to tackle the task without asking for further clarification because he did not want his supervisor to think he could not do the job. As a result of forging ahead before he was ready, SB often ended up doing the task wrong and wasting time. With input from his employment specialist, and some role playing with her, SB learned the strategy of paraphrasing back to his supervisor the nature of the task as he understood it and asking for confirmation or clarification as needed.

This allowed the supervisor to correct any misunderstandings SB had about the task before starting it. This strategy improved SB's work performance and he gained enough confidence to routinely ask for clarification when he had questions regarding a job task.

SB's job duties were fairly consistent from day to day. Thus, while SB was a little slower in learning his job tasks, once he had learned his job his memory impairment did not impact his job performance. Similarly, because of SB's computer training, his psychomotor speed impairments also did not affect his job performance. SB's pay started out at $6.50/hour, and over the next year it rose to $8.00/hour. SB reported that he really liked his job and the people with whom he works.

Another issue related to work that SB discussed with his employment specialist was his concern that he might offend or upset his boss or co-workers. SB said, "I don't want anyone mad at me." He said he sometimes thought people were looking at him "funny" and that he made people uncomfortable around him. Some of SB's concerns appeared to be related to his discomfort and awkwardness in social situations. SB never dated and had only a few casual friends. SB was frequently invited to company-sponsored social events, which he went to because he was glad to be included. However, at these events SB did not feel that he knew what to say, and he often felt flustered trying to make small talk with other co-workers, particularly women. SB's employment specialist helped him deal with these situations by engaging him in social skills training aimed at improving his conversational skills, such as being able to come up with good topics for conversations and showing the other person that he found them interesting. These sessions helped SB feel more confident around other people, including women, and to enjoy himself more at these informal company gatherings.

Over the several years since SB began working he enjoyed a modest improvement in his quality of life. He moved into his own apartment and made several closer friendships. SB continued to work on his screenplays but also expanded his activities to include art. He stated that one of his goals was "to share my art with the world and to entertain through the arts." While SB has expressed doubts as to whether he will be able to successfully write a screenplay, he also continued to be concerned that others would try to steal his ideas. Work continued to play an important role in SB's life, one that provided him with extra income and an enhanced sense of worth. SB still gets support from his employment specialist, whom he sees once every three to four weeks. SB described his work experience as follows: "I used to feel so different, like I wasn't as good as other people. Now I feel just like everybody else. I have a job to go to and I'm a part of my community. It feels good to fit in with other people."

RECOGNIZING AND EVALUATING PSYCHOPATHOLOGY

The core symptoms of schizophrenia can be divided into three major groups, including psychotic symptoms (also called positive symptoms), negative symptoms, and cognitive impairment (or disorganization). Psychotic symptoms primarily include hallucinations and delusions but also may be evident in the form of tangential speech, neologisms (making up new words), word salad (incomprehensible speech with disordered syntax), and bizarre behavior. Negative symptoms refer to diminution or loss of functions ordinarily present in individuals, such as blunted or flattened affect (reduced emotional expressiveness), anhedonia (reduced experience of pleasure), apathy (reduced social drive), avolution (difficulty initiating and following though on actions), and alogia (reduced amount and meaning of speech). Negative symptoms are very common and relatively stable over the course of schizophrenia. As previously described, people sometimes misunderstand negative symptoms as signs of laziness, which can be problematic, especially at the workplace. Cognitive impairments span the range of different cognitive functions, including reduced attention, psychomotor speed, memory and learning capacity, and executive functions (planning ability and abstract reasoning). Similar to negative symptoms, cognitive impairments relative to premorbid functioning are present in most people with schizophrenia and these impairments tend to be stable over time. However, it should be noted that for individuals whose intellectual functioning was above average before they developed schizophrenia, their cognitive functioning might remain above average or within the average range even after developing the illness. Therefore, while cognitive decline is common in schizophrenia, not all individuals have cognitive impairments compared with the general population.

Some of the symptoms of schizophrenia may be apparent to others at the workplace. However, the formal assessment of psychopathology is best accomplished using standardized clinical rating scales specifically designed to elicit these symptoms. Two general psychopathology rating scales that are commonly used in the assessment of schizophrenia are the Brief Psychiatric Rating Scale (BPRS) (Lukoff, Nuechterlein, & Ventura, 1986) and the Positive and Negative Syndrome Scale (PANSS) (Kay, Opler, & Fiszbein, 1987). Both of these measures, which contain many overlapping items, provide information about a range of different symptoms commonly present in schizophrenia, including psychotic symptoms, negative symptoms, disturbances in mood (e.g., depression, anxiety), and disturbances in activity level (e.g., motor retardation, excitement). One widely used scale for negative symptoms is the Scale for the Assessment of Negative Symptoms (SANS) (Andreasen, 1984). Each of these rating scales includes standardized probe questions and clearly anchored criteria for scoring responses on Likert-type scales. In addition, when administered by trained clinical interviewers, each of these scales has been shown to have excellent psychometric properties. A comprehensive assessment of the symptoms of schizophrenia can usually be accomplished with one or more of these scales in a 20- to 30-minute interview.

Some psychiatric rating scales (such as the PANSS and the SANS) include items to assess cognitive functioning in addition to other symptoms of schizophrenia. However, research shows that these rating scales fail to assess the full range of cognitive impairments typically found in schizophrenia (Harvey et al., 2001). As the unique pattern of impairments in different areas of cognitive functioning may vary from one individual to the next, a precise evaluation of specific areas of cognitive functioning is critical to understanding how cognition affects performance in the workplace and to taking steps to address specific areas of impairment. Assessment of cognitive functioning can be accomplished by administering selective neuropsychological tests. A comprehensive battery should include at least one test for each of the four areas of cognitive functioning: attention and concentration (e.g., the Digit Span subtest of Wechsler Adult Intelligence Scale–III [WAIS-III]) (Wechsler, 1998), psychomotor speed (e.g., WAIS-III Digit Symbol Substitution subtest), learning and memory (e.g., the California Verbal Learning Test) (Delis, Kramer, Kaplan, & Ober, 1987), and executive functions (e.g., the Wisconsin Card Sorting Test) (Berg, 1968). A brief neuropsychological battery can usually be administered in less than an hour.

In addition to assessing characteristic symptoms of schizophrenia, it is important to assess several other symptoms or problem areas. Depression is common in schizophrenia, with a mortality rate due to suicide of approximately 5 percent (Caldwell & Gottesman, 1990; Inskip, Harris, & Barraclough, 1998). Depression is distinct from the negative symptoms of schizophrenia and should be routinely assessed. Depression can be assessed through questions on the BPRS or PANSS. Self-report measures of depression also can be used, such as the Beck Depression Inventory (Beck, Steer, & Garbin, 1988).

In addition to depression, problems with anxiety also are common in schizophrenia. Anxiety symptoms also can be evaluated with questions from the BPRS or PANSS. A self-report measure of general anxiety is the Beck Anxiety Inventory (Beck & Steer, 1990). One particular anxiety disorder may be of special concern for people with schizophrenia: post-traumatic stress disorder (PTSD). Surveys indicate high rates of trauma and PTSD in people with schizophrenia and other severe mental illnesses, with 28 to 43 percent meeting criteria for PTSD (Mueser, Rosenberg, Goodman, & Trumbetta, 2002), compared with about 10 percent of people in the general population (Breslau, Davis, Andreski, & Peterson, 1991; Kessler, Sonnega, Bromet, Hughes, & Nelson, 1995). PTSD can be formally assessed with a structured interview, the Clinician Administered PTSD Scale (Blake et al., 1990). A brief screening instrument for PTSD is the PTSD Checklist (E. P. Blanchard, Jones-Alexander, Buckley, & Forneris, 1996). Both of these instruments have been shown to have good psychometric properties for people with severe mental illness (Mueser, Salyers, Rosenberg, et al., 2001).

A final associated problem area in people with schizophrenia is substance abuse. Approximately half the individuals with schizophrenia experience substance abuse or dependence at some point in their life, compared with about 16 percent of the general population (Regier et al., 1990). Because substance abuse can have a deleterious effect on all aspects of client functioning, including work performance, assessment of substance-use problems should be routinely conducted for all people with schizophrenia. Two screening instruments, which have been shown to be sensitive to detecting substance abuse in people with schizophrenia, are the Alcohol Use Identification Test (Saunders, Aasland, Babor, De La Fuente, & Grant, 1993) and the Dartmouth Assessment of Lifestyle Instrument (Rosenberg et al., 1998). Each of these instruments can be administered in a 10- to 15-minute period.

REFERRAL STRATEGIES

Because schizophrenia is a severe mental illness that often has pervasive effects on a wide range of different areas of functioning, people frequently receive treatment in the public sector at local community mental health centers. However, some individuals with schizophrenia receive treatment from private psychiatrists or primary health care providers. For individuals with schizophrenia who are not currently receiving treatment, referral will depend on whether they have private insurance or access to funds to purchase their care.

As discussed in more detail later, for many people with schizophrenia treatment includes both medication and rehabilitation services. Some individuals, however, are treated effectively with only medication. The choice of referral for treatment also depends on the individual's need for rehabilitation. Relatively few rehabilitation programs are available privately and those available are quite expensive. Local community mental health centers, on the other hand, charge on a sliding fee scale and typically offer a wide range of rehabilitation programs in addition to pharmacological treatment. Information concerning referrals for treatment can be obtained either at the local community mental health center or by contacting the National Alliance for Mental Illness, an advocacy organization for people with mental illness that has numerous local chapters throughout the country.

WORKPLACE OR HOME STRESSORS

People with schizophrenia are exquisitely sensitive to stress in their environments (Myin-Germeys, van Os, Schwartz, Stone, & Delespaul, 2001). Exposure to stress, in terms of either unpleasant life experiences (Bebbington & Kuipers, 1992) or strong levels of interpersonal stress in one's living environment (Butzlaff & Hooley, 1998), has been shown to precipitate relapses and rehospitalizations in people with schizophrenia. Therefore, awareness of potential stresses and minimization of stress at home and the workplace are important for maintaining optimal work performance and avoiding the disruptive effects of a relapse.

A variety of different factors may act as potent stresses for people with schizophrenia at work. Jobs that are highly demanding, such as those requiring high levels of productivity or completion of work at a rapid rate, may be stressful to people with schizophrenia and may increase their vulnerability to symptom relapses. Jobs that require long hours may induce high levels of stress because many individuals with the disorder have limited energy and require considerable sleep to meet their daily needs and responsibilities. People with schizophrenia also may experience difficulty with rapid changes in job expectations. To the extent that changes in job responsibilities must occur, it will be less stressful if they occur very gradually over time and if ample opportunities to learn the new skills are provided under low stress conditions.

Because many people with schizophrenia have cognitive impairments, their problem-solving skills often are deficient (Bellack, Sayers, Mueser, & Bennett, 1994). This can lead to difficulties on the job in spontaneously dealing with problems as they arise. Therefore, jobs that require strong, spontaneous decision-making skills and effective problem solving may be stressful because these skills often are underdeveloped.

A final common source of workplace stress involves social situations. People with schizophrenia often have impaired social skills, and this can make it more difficult for them to informally socialize with others on the job, to respond to customers, and to deal with supervisory feedback. Therefore, jobs that require high levels of social interaction, and especially social sensitivity to others, may be more stressful for people with schizophrenia.

EMPIRICALLY BASED TREATMENT

Tremendous advances have been made in the treatment of schizophrenia over the past two decades. Considering the complexities of the disorder and the many areas of life functioning it affects, comprehensive treatment of schizophrenia usually requires a variety of specific interventions. In this section we focus on those interventions that have been demonstrated to improve outcome in schizophrenia (i.e., evidence-based practices), beginning with effective vocational rehabilitation strategies. Following the discussion of strategies for improving employment outcomes, we briefly describe other evidence-based practices for improving outcomes of schizophrenia.

Vocational Rehabilitation

Brief Description

Traditional approaches to vocational rehabilitation in schizophrenia were typically based on the "train-place model." That is, these strategies were aimed at teaching people the requisite skills needed to perform in the workplace. Unfortunately, extensive research on the train-place model of vocational rehabilitation indicated that these approaches were not effective (Bond, 1992). At least one contributing factor to the lack of effectiveness was that most people with schizophrenia who want to work want employment as soon as possible, and their motivation to work may wane if the job search does not commence soon after joining a program.

Over the past decade, evidence has accumulated supporting a new model of vocational rehabilitation based on the "place-train" approach: supported employment. The underlying philosophy of supported employment is that the best way to help people with major mental illnesses get back to work is to help them find jobs and to then provide supports to enable them to be successful on the job. The core ingredients of supported employment programs include focus on competitive work that pays competitive wages in integrated community settings; rapid job search and attainment, with minimal prevocational assessment and no prevocational skills training; attention to clients' preferences in terms of the jobs they want and whether to disclose their psychiatric disorder to the employer; provision of follow-along supports to help clients succeed on the job or to facilitate a smooth transition of one job to another; and integration of vocational services with clinical services, preferably at the level of the team (Becker & Drake, 2003). Supported employment services are usually provided by an employment specialist who provides the full range of services for each client and who works in close coordination with the client's treatment team (and often serves as a member of that team). More than ten controlled studies document the effectiveness of supported employment over other models of vocational rehabilitation for people with schizophrenia and other severe mental illnesses (Bond, Becker, et al., 2001).

Although there is strong evidence for the supported employment approach, research also shows that the clinical features of schizophrenia are related to both work outcomes and supported employment services (McGurk & Mueser, 2003; McGurk, Mueser, Harvey, Marder, & LaPuglia, 2003). McGurk and Mueser (in press) recently developed a model to account for the interactions between the symptoms and cognitive impairment of schizophrenia, vocational outcomes, and supported employment services. According to this model, which is depicted in Figure 11.1, supported employment services are capable of compensating for the effects of some illness-related impairments on work but for not others. Specifically, negative symptoms of schizophrenia are predictive of vocational outcomes even in clients' receiving supported employment services (McGurk et al., 2003; Mueser, 2002), as such services are not able to compensate for the effects of negative symptoms on work. On the other hand, supported employment services can be effective at compensating for the effects of psychotic symptoms on work. Therefore, clients who have more severe psychotic symptoms may require more supported employment services but may nevertheless have just as good vocational outcomes as clients with less severe psychotic symptoms (McGurk et al., 2003).

A cascading model of cognitive functions is assumed, which reflects the fact that more complex cognitive abilities, such as learning and memory and executive functions, depend on intact lower cognitive functions, such as attention and psychomotor speed. Supported employment services are hypothesized to be able to compensate for the basic cognitive functions of poor attention and slowed psychomotor speed but are not able to fully compensate for the higher order cognitive functions of learning and memory and executive functions. Therefore, all of the different types of functioning are related to employment supported services (i.e., clients with more cognitive impairments require more supported employment services to compensate for the effects of those impairments), whereas only learning and memory and executive functions are related to work outcomes (McGurk et al., 2003).

The importance of this model is that it suggested that strategies designed either to remediate cognitive impairments in schizophrenia or to help people develop compensatory strategies will be effective at improving vocational outcomes and decreasing the intensity of supported employment services. Such improvements in cognitive functioning also may be necessary for clients to move from supported employment to independent work (McGurk & Mueser, 2003). Similarly, specific interventions may need to be aimed at reducing the effects of negative symptoms or psychotic symptoms in order to improve work outcomes or reduce the intensity of supported employment services.

Time Element

Most supported employment programs provide services to clients on a time-unlimited basis. Many clients appear to benefit from ongoing access to supported employ-

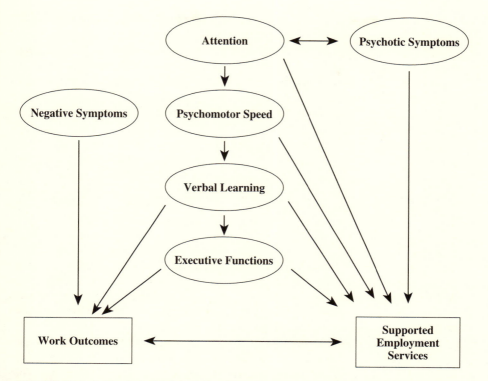

FIGURE 12.1 A Heuristic Model of Cognition, Symptoms, Work, and Supported Employment Services

ment services even after they have been stably employed for a considerable period of time. The nature of supports may be on-site or off-site supports, depending on whether the client has chosen to disclose his or her psychiatric illness to the employer and the nature of the supports needed. Some individuals are able to move from supported employment to independent employment. However, clients should not be pressured to move to independent employment before they are ready.

Side Effects of Treatment

There are no known side effects of supported employment.

Pharmacological Treatment

Brief Description

Pharmacological treatment with antipsychotic medications is the mainstay for the treatment of schizophrenia (Davis, Chen, & Glick, 2003; Herz & Marder, 2002). More than any other treatment, antipsychotics have been shown to decrease the severity of symptoms and prevent or delay relapses in individuals with schizophrenia. For such medications to be effective, they need to be taken routinely either by mouth or by depot (long-acting) injection. Without pharmacological treatment, most people with schizophrenia would be unable to work, care for themselves, or have good social relationships with others.

In addition to antipsychotic medications, selective use of other medications, such as antidepressants, benzodiazepines, and mood-stabilizing medications, also may be warranted (Herz & Marder, 2002). These medications are generally used to treat symptoms of depression, anxiety, or mania (decreased need for sleep, grandiosity, inflated self-esteem, and increased goal-directed behavior).

Time Element

For most people with schizophrenia, medications need to be taken on a regular basis throughout most of the lifetime. A relatively small percentage of people with schizophrenia does not require medications or requires them only intermittently (probably less than 10 percent).

Side Effects of Treatment

Although medications are the most potent treatment available for schizophrenia, they also can produce a wide range of different side effects. Some of the most common side effects of antipsychotic medications include muscle stiffness, akathisia (an inner feeling of restlessness), sedation, tremors, sexual difficulties, blurred vision, sensitivity to the sun, weight gain, akinesia (reduced affective expressiveness), sexual side effects (e.g., difficulty maintaining erection, reduced libido), and tardive dyskinesia (a long-term neurological syndrome associated with involuntary motor movements in the extremities, including the oral facial region, fingers, and toes). The advent of second-generation antipsychotic medications over the past decade has reduced severity of many of these side effects (especially the extrapyramidal side effects, such as muscle stiffness and akathisia), but these newer medications also have side effects that require monitoring and management.

Judicious prescription of antipsychotic medications at the lowest possible dosage level and use of other medications to address side effects are effective at minimizing the severity and disruptiveness of antipsychotic side effects. Problems at the workplace from high levels of fatigue either can be medication related or due to reduced energy, a common symptom of schizophrenia. The reasons for reduced energy may be difficult to discern, and modifications in medication dosage level or type may be useful in determining whether it is medication related.

Family Psychoeducation

Brief Description

Many people with schizophrenia live at home or have regular contact with their family members. As previously discussed, high levels of stress in family relationships can worsen the course of schizophrenia. At the same time, family support can play a critical role in minimizing stress, monitoring the illness, and supporting the client in pursuing personal goals. Family psychoeducation is aimed at helping families, including the client, learn how to more effectively manage schizophrenia in a loved one. Over the past 20 years, a variety of different family psychoeducational programs has been developed and empirically validated (Anderson, Reiss, & Hogarty, 1986; Barrowclough & Tarrier, 1992; Falloon, Boyd, & McGill, 1984; McFarlane, 2002; Mueser & Glynn, 1999). While these programs vary somewhat in their format and the nature of the therapeutic techniques involved, they share a number of core characteristics, including provision of basic educational information to family members, including the client, about the nature of schizophrenia and the principles of its treatment; focus on here and now and the future, rather than extensively talking about and dredging up the past; efforts to improve communication and problem-solving skills in the family, thereby reducing stress levels; and establishing a collaborative stance between the family and the treatment team so that the family in effect becomes a member of the treatment team. Extensive research on family psychoeducational programs shows that they are successful in reducing rates of relapse and rehospitalization over two years from approximately 60 percent to less than 30 percent in clients who also are receiving antipsychotic medications (Pitschel-Walz, Leucht, Bäuml, Kissling, & Engel, 2001).

Time Element

Family psychoeducational programs are most effective when they are delivered over an extended period of time of at least nine months. Treatment over a relatively long period of time is necessary to build an effective and genuinely collaborative relationship between the family and treatment team. However, people with schizophrenia and their families also may benefit from shorter term psychoeducational programs. It also should be noted that in addition to psychoeducational programs conducted by mental health professionals, most communities have local chapters of the National Alliance for the Mentally Ill. This family advocacy organization for persons with a major mental illness usually provides monthly support groups for clients with schizophrenia or another major mental illness and their relatives and offers a short-term educational program, the Family-to-Family program, which preliminary research suggests is beneficial to relatives (Dixon et al., 2001).

Side Effects of Treatment

There are no known side effects of family psychoeducation programs.

Training in Illness Self-Management

Brief Description

People with schizophrenia are capable of being partners in their own treatment and of learning skills to better manage their illness (Copeland, 1997; Gingerich & Mueser, 2002; Hogarty, 2002). Teaching clients illness self-management skills generally involves interventions focused on four topic areas: (1) providing basic educational material about the nature of schizophrenia and its treatment in order to facilitate informed decision making by clients about their illness, (2) teaching clients strategies designed to motivate them to take their medication regularly and to incorporate medication into their daily routines, (3) helping clients develop relapse prevention skills, and (4) teaching strategies for helping clients cope more effectively with persistent symptoms or stress. Training in illness self-management skills is usually done in conjunction with helping clients set personal recovery goals for improving their lives, including getting back to work or advancing on the job (Anthony, 2000).

Illness self-management skills can be taught either individually or in groups. Teaching is most effective when it employs cognitive-behavioral teaching strategies along with motivational enhancement aimed at helping people understand how to manage their psychiatric illness and providing them help in achieving personal goals. Numerous controlled studies document the effectiveness of illness self-management training in people with schizophrenia (Mueser, Corrigan, et al., 2002).

Time Element

Illness self-management training programs vary in their length from about four to eight months, although longer term programs also exist. The duration of the program is partly determined by its breadth, with more comprehensive programs requiring more time to teach illness self-management skills. Some clients may benefit from ongoing booster sessions to remind them or to provide additional opportunities to practice skills learned during the core-training phase.

Side Effects of Treatment

There are no established side effects of teaching clients illness self-management skills.

Social Skills Training

Brief Description

Social skills training is an intervention designed to improve the interpersonal effectiveness of people with mental illness. Problems with social functioning, both in the workplace and elsewhere, are common in schizophrenia and are part of the criteria for diagnosis of the disorder (American Psychiatric Association, 1994). Social skills training is the most empirically supported approach for helping people with schizophrenia improve their interpersonal functioning, including at the workplace.

Social skills training procedures are based on the principals of social learning theory (Bandura, 1969, 1986), and include modeling (demonstrating) social skills in role plays, engaging clients in frequent role plays to rehearse new social skills, providing ample positive feedback and corrective suggestions to improve performance following role plays and arranging for in vivo opportunities to help clients practice their new skills in naturally occurring situations (Bellack, Mueser, Gingerich, & Agresta, 1997). Social skills training is generally conducted in groups, although individual skills training is also feasible. A large research literature supports the effectiveness of social skills training for improving social functioning in schizophrenia (Heinssen, Liberman, & Kopelowicz, 2000).

Social skills training also has been shown to be effective at improving work-related social interactions, and some research indicates that skills training can improve vocational outcomes, even in the absence of supported employment (Tsang, 2001; Tsang & Pearson, 2001). For example, social skills training can be provided to help clients improve their job interviewing skills (Furman, Gleller, Simon, & Kelly, 1979) and to socialize more effectively with co-workers, deal with criticism from supervisors, and handle interactions with customers (Mueser, Foy, & Carter, 1986). Recently, a new social skills training program has been developed that is specifically tailored to address the needs of people with schizophrenia in the workplace (Wallace, Tauber, & Wilde, 1999). Preliminary evidence from one controlled study indicates that this program improves job retention (Wallace, 2003).

Time Element

Social skills training programs typically last between four and six months, although longer and more comprehensive programs may last longer, up to two years.

Side Effects of Treatment

There are no known side effects of social skills training for people with schizophrenia.

Cognitive-Behavior Therapy for Psychosis

Brief Description

Between 25 and 35 percent of the people with schizophrenia experience persistent psychotic symptoms (Carpenter & Buchanan, 1994; Curson, Patel, Liddle, & Barnes, 1988). These symptoms can be a source of significant distress and they can either interfere with work performance or require more supports so the client can perform effectively at the job. Cognitive-behavior therapy for psychosis involves developing a collaborative therapeutic alliance with the client and helping clients through this relationship to evaluate the evidence supporting and not supporting psychotic thought processes (Chadwick, Birchwood, & Trower, 1996; Fowler, Garety, & Kuipers, 1995; Kingdon & Turkington, 1994). When conducting cognitive-behavioral treatment for psychosis, the therapist is careful to avoid directly confronting clients with evidence contrary to their beliefs, because such confrontation can lead to increases in delusional thinking (Milton, Patwa, & Hafner, 1978). Rather, the therapist adopts a Socratic teaching style by asking numerous questions designed to help clients evaluate for themselves the evidence supporting their beliefs and to consider alternative explanations for their experiences.

Research on cognitive-behavior therapy for psychosis has emerged mainly over the past decade, with numerous controlled studies conducted (Gould, Mueser, Bolton, Mays, & Goff, 2001). Across the different studies, conclusions are quite similar: cognitive-behavior therapy is effective at reducing the severity of psychotic symptoms in schizophrenia. In addition, several of these studies also have found improvements in negative symptoms as well.

Time Element

Cognitive-behavioral programs for psychosis usually last four to six months, although booster sessions may be necessary to help some clients maintain the benefits of treatment.

Side Effects of Treatment

There are no known side effects of cognitive-behavior therapy for psychosis.

Integrated Treatment for Dual Disorders

Brief Description

The high rate of substance abuse in schizophrenia, and its contribution to poor outcome (Drake & Brunette, 1998), underscores the importance of treating it in this population. Previous efforts to treat substance abuse in people with severe mental illnesses employed separate clinicians at separate agencies treating each disorder in either a parallel or a sequential fashion. These traditional approaches to treating dual disorders have proved to be unsuccessful for a number of reasons (Polcin, 1992; Ridgely, Goldman, & Willenbring, 1990). Some clients have difficulty accessing both services, because of either eligibility requirements or failure to follow through on referrals. When both services are provided, there is often a failure to integrate the two treatments, leading to poor treatment coordination and even contradictory messages between different providers. Efforts to treat mental illness and substance abuse in a sequential fashion, by first treating one disorder and then treating the other, are doomed to failure because they do not take into account the interactive nature of the two disorders, making the successful treatment of either one alone more difficult.

To address the problem of dual disorders, clinicians have developed and empirically validated integrated treatment models (Drake, Mueser, Brunette, & McHugo, in press; Mueser, Noordsy, Drake, & Fox, 2003). The essence of integrated treatment is that the same clinician or team of clinicians assumes responsibility for treating the mental illness and the substance abuse at the same time. In addition, effective integrated dual disorder treatment programs share a number of other characteristics, including stage-wise interventions that recognize the importance of enhancing motivation to work on substance-use problems before making efforts to change substance-use behavior, comprehensive services that address the wide range of needs that clients with dual disorders have, assertive outreach in which services are provided in clients' natural settings to engage and retain them in treatment, concerted efforts to reduce the harmful effects of substance use on people's lives, and access to a variety of different psychotherapeutic modalities, including individual, group, and family therapy.

Time Element

For many individuals with schizophrenia, substance-use problems are a chronic and relapsing disorder. Therefore, artificial time constraints are generally not imposed on integrated dual disorder treatment programs. Some clients experience a rapid recovery from their substance abuse and within a year or two and are able to sustain their sobriety. Other clients may require years of integrated treatment to make significant progress.

Side Effects of Treatment

There are no established side effects of integrated dual disorder treatment programs.

RELAPSE PREVENTION

Prevention of relapses in schizophrenia can be guided by the stress-vulnerability model of the disease (Nuechterlein & Dawson, 1984; Zubin & Spring, 1977). According to this model, schizophrenia is caused by an underlying psychobiological vulnerability, which is determined early in life by a combination of genetic and early environmental (e.g., perinatal) influences. Once the psychobiological vulnerability is established, the onset of the illness and its course, including relapses, is determined by the dynamic interplay of several biological and psychosocial factors. Among the biological factors, antipsychotic medication and drug and alcohol abuse are the most critical. Antipsychotic medications can reduce symptom severity and vulnerability to relapses, while substance abuse can worsen symptoms and contribute to relapses. Among psychosocial factors that can influence the severity in course of schizophrenia, stress, coping skills, and social support are most important. Stress can impinge on biological vulnerability, worsening symptoms and triggering relapses. However, effective coping skills (e.g., problem-solving skills and relaxation skills) can mediate the noxious effects of stress. Finally, strong social support can reduce the noxious effects of stress on psychobiological vulnerability and enhance effective client coping.

There are several implications for preventing relapses according to the stress-vulnerability model. From the biological perspective, facilitating medication adherence and reducing substance abuse are important strategies for preventing relapses (Miner, Rosenthal, Hellerstein, & Muenz, 1997; Zygmunt, Olfson, Boyer, & Mechanic, 2002). From the psychosocial perspective, prevention of relapses can be facilitated by improving coping skills by strategies such as social and problem-solving skills training (Liberman et al., 1986), increasing social support by strategies such as family therapy (Mueser & Glynn, 1999), and decreasing stress by strategies such as family intervention. One potentially important source of stress in people with schizophrenia is the lack of engagement in meaningful, structured activities, which can contribute to higher levels of psychotic symptoms (Corrigan, Liberman, & Wong, 1993; Rosen, Sussman, Mueser, Lyons, & Davis, 1981). Thus, working a regular job that includes clear, realistic, and predictable expectations provides a meaningful structure that can reduce vulnerability to relapses.

In addition to taking steps to minimize the possibility of a relapse, it is also important to develop a relapse prevention plan to respond to the early signs of a relapse. When relapses occur, they tend to be preceded by a prodromal phase lasting several weeks or longer, which may include subtle signs of an impending relapse, such as increased anxiety or depression, social withdrawal, or concentration difficulties (Herz, 1984; Jørgensen, 1998). Even when a clear prodromal phase does not occur, full-blown relapses that include deterioration in psychosocial functioning (including work) often requiring hospitalization are usually preceded by the emergence of mild psychotic symptoms, such as auditory hallucinations. Gradual onset of a relapse provides opportunities to take preventative steps.

Relapse prevention is most successfully accomplished by developing a specific plan in advance. This plan, which is best developed in collaboration with the client and family members (Birchwood et al., 1989), begins with a discussion of previous relapses in order to identify the early warning signs of a relapse. After these signs have been noted, the steps of responding to the early warning signs are determined by consensus. Such steps generally involve evaluating the presence of acute stress in the client's environment, identifying coping strategies, and contacting a member of the treatment team to arrange for a special evaluation. Temporary increases in medication dosage level often are successful in preventing the occurrence of a full-blown relapse (Herz, Glazer, Mirza, Mostert, & Hafez, 1989). Early warning signs of a relapse and the steps of responding to those signs are recorded on a relapse prevention sheet. It also can be helpful to role-play the relapse prevention plan. Research shows that formulating such plans reduces the frequency of relapses (Mueser, Corrigan, et al., 2002).

THERAPEUTIC BENEFITS OF WORK

The benefits of work for people with schizophrenia have long been debated (Strauss, Harding, Silverman, Eichler, & Liberman, 1988). In the early years of institutional treatment for people with schizophrenia, the routine of work was believed to be therapeutic, which was exemplified by farms run by large state psychiatric hospitals and manned by psychiatric patients. In ensuing years, as agricultural work by patients at state hospitals began to be viewed as coercive and an abuse of patient rights, work opportunities for patients in state hospitals were eliminated. With no chances to work, and limited psychotherapeutic activities in which to engage, institutional care devolved into the unstructured and unstimulating warehousing of people, with a resultant deterioration in functioning for patients who had no sense of purpose in life (Wing & Brown, 1979).

The notion that work is not therapeutic, and is potentially harmful, was further reinforced during the early years of the deinstitutionalization movement, following discovery of antipsychotic medications. As research began to show that stress (e.g., life events, stressful relationships with others) could lead to relapses in schizophrenia, efforts to protect outpatients with schizophrenia from stress often included discouraging them from returning to work. There was a strong consensus that people with schizophrenia should not return to work until they had established a long period of symptom stability, and patients with persistent symptoms often were discouraged from working altogether. As previously described, a broader view of the stress-vulnerability model of schizophrenia suggests that lack of meaningful structure is actually stressful, and engaging in meaningful, purposeful work may reduce rather than increase stress.

In more recent years, there has been a swing back toward viewing work as potentially therapeutic and as a critical outcome by itself. Several factors have played a role in creating a new understanding of the importance of work for people with schizophrenia. First, rates of competitive employment in people with schizophrenia are low, usually between 10 and 20 percent (Anthony & Blanch, 1987; Mueser, Salyers, & Mueser, 2001). Because problems working are included in the *Diagnostic and Statistical Manual of Mental Disorders–Fourth Edition* (American Psychiatric Association, 1994) criteria for the diagnosis of schizophrenia, addressing these problems is by definition important for the treatment of the disorder. Second, the majority of people with schizophrenia and other severe mental illnesses is dissatisfied with unemployment and wants to work (Mueser, Salyers, & Mueser, 2001; Rogers, Walsh, Masotta, & Danley, 1991). Furthermore, the work most clients want is competitive work in integrated community settings, not sheltered workshops or extensive prevocational training programs. Encouraging findings from research on supported employment indicate that such goals can be achieved for the majority of people with schizophrenia who want to work (Bond, Becker, et al., 2001).

Third, there has been a growth in interest and excitement about the concept of recovery for people with schizophrenia and other severe mental illnesses (Anthony, 1993; Deegan, 1988; Mead & Copeland, 2000; Noordsy et al., 2000). Rather than recovery referring to absence of symptoms and characteristic impairments, most modern conceptualizations of recovery view it as an intensely personal process that involves coming to grips with and managing one's mental illness and getting on with one's life in ways that are most meaningful to that individual. Often the process of pursuing personal goals in recovery involves returning to work and becoming a productive member of society (Provencher, Gregg, Mead, & Mueser, 2002). Many consumers with mental illness have written eloquently about the concepts and meanings of recovery, and these writings have served to highlight the role of work in the recovery process.

Fourth and last, there is evidence that work is associated with modest benefits for people with schizophrenia. In addition to improved financial standing, competitive work is related to improvements in self-esteem, life satisfaction, and symptoms (Arns & Linney, 1993; Bell, Lysaker, & Milstein, 1996; Bond, Resnick, et al., 2001; Mueser et al., 1997). Of equal importance, concerns about the stressful effects of work on schizophrenia have not been supported; returning to work is not associated with an increased risk of relapse or rehospitalization (Lehman, 1995). An additional possible advantage of work may be its effects on stigma, both societal-based stigma and self-stigma (Wahl, 1997). Because the inability to work is one of the most stigmatizing aspects of mental illness (Farina, 1998), work may have the added advantage of countering these attitudes toward mental illness. Thus, work for people with schizophrenia may provide valuable opportunities for these individuals to be integrated into general society and to be perceived as valued and respected persons and accepted by others in the community.

SUMMARY

Schizophrenia is a major mental illness affecting about 1 percent of the population and characterized by psychotic symptoms (such as hallucinations and delusions), negative symptoms (such as social withdrawal and apathy), and cognitive impairment. Schizophrenia can have a profound impact on a wide range of functioning, including the ability to work, to have close and meaningful relationships, to meet role responsibilities, and to take care of oneself. The most common ways in which schizophrenia can affect work include low energy and work productivity, cognitive impairments that interfere with attention to work tasks and learning new responsibilities, and social difficulties interacting with others at the workplace. Psychotic symptoms are less common but also can interfere with effective work performance. Despite these potential problems, most people with schizophrenia want competitive work and many are capable of being excellent, reliable, and dependable workers. People with schizophrenia benefit from supported employment rehabilitation programs, which focus on helping them get and keep competitive jobs in the community with the ongoing help of a mental health employment specialist. Research shows that supported employment programs are capable of helping most people with schizophrenia who want to work obtain competitive jobs in the community. Work has modest clinical benefits, including some reductions in symptoms and increases in self-esteem. Perhaps more important, people with schizophrenia identify work as an important personal recovery goal, and therefore work is imbued with personal meaning for many individuals. In addition, work at typical competitive jobs located in natural community settings tends to increase community integration for people with schizophrenia, providing them with increased access to social support and a better standard of living.

References

Adams, G. L., Dworkin, R. J., & Rosenberg, S. D. (1984). Diagnosis and pharmacotherapy issues in the care of Hispanics in the public sector. *American Journal of Psychiatry, 141*, 970-974.

Almeida, O. P., Howard, R. J., Levy, R., & David, A. S. (1995). Psychotic states arising in late life (late paraphrenia): Psychopathology and nosology. *British Journal of Psychiatry, 166*, 205-214.

American Psychiatric Association. (1994). *Diagnostic and statistical manual of mental disorders* (4th ed.). Washington, DC: Author.

Anderson, C. M., Reiss, D. J., & Hogarty, G. E. (1986). *Schizophrenia and the family*. New York: Guilford.

Andreasen, N. C. (1982). Negative symptoms in schizophrenia. *Archives of General Psychiatry, 39*, 784-788.

Andreasen, N. C. (1984). *Modified Scale for the Assessment of Negative Symptoms*. Bethesda, MD: U.S. Department of Health and Human Services.

Angermeyer, M. C., Kuhn, L., & Goldstein, J. M. (1990). Gender and the course of schizophrenia: Differences in treated outcome. *Schizophrenia Bulletin, 16*, 293-307.

Anthony, W. A. (1993). Recovery from mental illness: The guiding vision of the mental health service system in the 1990s. *Psychosocial Rehabilitation Journal, 16*, 11-23.

Anthony, W. A. (2000). A recovery-oriented service system: Setting some system level standards. *Journal of Psychiatric Rehabilitation, 24,* 159-168.

Anthony, W. A., & Blanch, A. (1987). Supported employment for persons who are psychiatrically disabled: An historical and conceptual perspective. *Psychosocial Rehabilitation Journal, 11*(2), 5-23.

Arns, P. G., & Linney, J. A. (1993). Work, self, and life satisfaction for persons with severe and persistent mental disorders. *Psychosocial Rehabilitation Journal, 17,* 63-79.

Bandura, A. (1969). *Principles of behavior modification.* New York: Holt, Rinehart & Winston.

Bandura, A. (1986). *Social foundations of thought and action: A social cognitive theory.* Englewood Cliffs, NJ: Prentice Hall.

Barrowclough, C., & Tarrier, N. (1992). *Families of schizophrenic patients: Cognitive behavioural intervention.* London: Chapman & Hall.

Bebbington, P., & Kuipers, L. (1992). Life events and social factors. In D. J. Kavanagh (Ed.), *Schizophrenia: An overview and practical handbook* (pp. 126-144). London: Chapman & Hall.

Beck, A. T., & Steer, R. A. (1990). *Manual for the Beck Anxiety Inventory.* San Antonio, TX: Psychological Corporation.

Beck, A. T., Steer, R. A., & Garbin, M. G. (1988). Psychometric properties of the Beck Depression Inventory: Twenty-five years of evaluation. *Clinical Psychology Review, 8,* 77-100.

Becker, D. R., & Drake, R. E. (2003). *A working life for people with severe mental illness.* New York: Oxford University Press.

Bell, M. D., Lysaker, P. H., & Milstein, R. M. (1996). Clinical benefits of paid work activity in schizophrenia. *Schizophrenia Bulletin, 22,* 51-67.

Bellack, A. S., Morrison, R. L., Wixted, J. T., & Mueser, K. T. (1990). An analysis of social competence in schizophrenia. *British Journal of Psychiatry, 156,* 809-818.

Bellack, A. S., Mueser, K. T., Gingerich, S., & Agresta, J. (1997). *Social skills training for schizophrenia: A step-by-step guide.* New York: Guilford.

Bellack, A. S., Sayers, M., Mueser, K. T., & Bennett, M. (1994). An evaluation of social problem solving in schizophrenia. *Journal of Abnormal Psychology, 103,* 371-378.

Berg, E. A. (1968). A simple objective test for measuring flexibility in thinking. *Journal of General Psychology, 39,* 15-22.

Birchwood, M., Smith, J., MacMillan, F., Hogg, B., Prasad, R., Harvey, C., & Bering, S. (1989). Predicting relapse in schizophrenia: The development and implementation of an early signs monitoring system using patients and families as observers, a preliminary investigation. *Psychological Medicine, 19,* 649-656.

Blake, D. D., Weathers, F. W., Nagy, L. M., Kaloupek, D. G., Klauminzer, G., Charney, D. S., & Keane, T. M. (1990). A clinician rating scale for assessing current and lifetime PTSD: The CAPS-1. *Behavior Therapist, 13,* 187-188.

Blanchard, E. P., Jones-Alexander, J., Buckley, T. C., & Forneris, C. A. (1996). Psychometric properties of the PTSD Checklist. *Behavior Therapy, 34,* 669-673.

Blanchard, J. J., Mueser, K. T., & Bellack, A. S. (1998). Anhedonia, positive and negative affect, and social functioning in schizophrenia. *Schizophrenia Bulletin, 24,* 413-424.

Bond, G. R. (1992). Vocational rehabilitation. In R. P. Liberman (Ed.), *Handbook of psychiatric rehabilitation* (pp. 244-275). New York: Macmillan.

Bond, G. R., Becker, D. R., Drake, R. E., Rapp, C. A., Meisler, N., Lehman, A. F., Bell, M. D., & Blyler, C. R. (2001). Implementing supported employment as an evidence-based practice. *Psychiatric Services, 52,* 313-322.

Bond, G. R., Resnick, S. G., Drake, R. E., Xie, H., McHugo, G. J., & Bebout, R. R. (2001). Does competitive employment improve nonvocational outcomes for people with severe mental illness? *Journal of Consulting and Clinical Psychology, 69,* 489-501.

Breslau, N., Davis, G. C., Andreski, P., & Peterson, E. (1991). Traumatic events and post-traumatic stress disorder in an urban population of young adults. *Archives of General Psychiatry, 48,* 216-222.

Bruce, M. L., Takeuchi, D. T., & Leaf, P. J. (1991). Poverty and psychiatric status: Longitudinal evidence from the New Haven Epidemiologic Catchment Area study. *Archives of General Psychiatry, 48,* 470-474.

Butzlaff, R. L., & Hooley, J. M. (1998). Expressed emotion and psychiatric relapse. *Archives of General Psychiatry, 55,* 547-552.

Caldwell, C. B., & Gottesman, I. I. (1990). Schizophrenics kill themselves too: A review of risk factors for suicide. *Schizophrenia Bulletin, 16,* 571-589.

Carpenter, W. T., Jr., & Buchanan, R. W. (1994). Schizophrenia. *New England Journal of Medicine, 330,* 681-690.

Chadwick, P., Birchwood, M., & Trower, P. (1996). *Cognitive therapy for delusions, voices and paranoia.* Chichester, England: John Wiley.

Copeland, M. E. (1997). *Wellness recovery action plan.* Brattleboro, VT: Peach Press.

Corrigan, P. W., Liberman, R. P., & Wong, S. E. (1993). Recreational therapy and behavior management on inpatient units: Is recreational therapy therapeutic? *Journal of Nervous and Mental Disease, 181,* 644-646.

Curson, D. A., Patel, M., Liddle, P. F., & Barnes, T. R. E. (1988). Psychiatric morbidity of a long stay hospital population with chronic schizophrenia and implications for future community care. *British Medical Journal, 297,* 819-822.

Davis, J. M., Chen, N., & Glick, I. D. (2003). A meta-analysis of the efficacy of second-generation antipsychotics. *Archives of General Psychiatry, 60,* 553-564.

Deegan, P. E. (1988). Recovery: The lived experience of rehabilitation. *Psychosocial Rehabilitation Journal, 11,* 11-19.

Delis, D. C., Kramer, J. H., Kaplan, E., & Ober, B. A. (1987). *California Verbal Learning and Memory Test (manual).* San Antonio, TX: Psychological Corporation.

Dixon, L., Stewart, B., Burland, J., Delahanty, J., Lucksted, A., & Hoffman, M. (2001). Pilot study of the family-to-family education program. *Psychiatric Services, 52,* 965-967.

Drake, R. E., & Brunette, M. F. (1998). Complications of severe mental illness related to alcohol and other drug use disorders. In M. Galanter (Ed.), *Recent developments in alcoholism: Consequences of alcoholism* (Vol. 14, pp. 285-299). New York: Plenum.

Drake, R. E., Mueser, K. T., Brunette, M. F., & McHugo, G. J. (in press). A review of treatments for patients with severe mental illness and co-occurring substance use disorder. *Mental Health Services Research.*

Falloon, I. R. H., Boyd, J. L., & McGill, C. W. (1984). *Family care of schizophrenia: A problem-solving approach to the treatment of mental illness.* New York: Guilford.

Farina, A. (1998). Stigma. In K. T. Mueser & N. Tarrier (Eds.), *Handbook of social functioning in schizophrenia* (pp. 247-279). Boston: Allyn & Bacon.

Fowler, D., Garety, P., & Kuipers, E. (1995). *Cognitive behaviour therapy for psychosis: Theory and practice.* Chichester, England: John Wiley.

Furman, W., Gleller, M., Simon, S. J., & Kelly, J. A. (1979). The use of a behavioral rehearsal procedure for teaching job-interviewing skills to psychiatric patients. *Behavior Therapy, 10,* 157-167.

Gingerich, S., & Mueser, K. T. (2002). *Illness management and recovery.* Concord, NH: West Institute.

Goldstein, J. M. (1988). Gender differences in the course of schizophrenia. *American Journal of Psychiatry, 145,* 684-689.

Gould, R. A., Mueser, K. T., Bolton, E., Mays, V., & Goff, D. (2001). Cognitive therapy for psychosis in schizophrenia: An effect size analysis. *Schizophrenia Research, 48,* 335-342.

Haas, G. L., & Garratt, L. S. (1998). Gender differences in social functioning. In K. T. Mueser & N. Tarrier (Eds.), *Handbook of social functioning in schizophrenia* (pp. 149-180). Boston: Allyn & Bacon.

Harding, C. M., & Keller, A. B. (1998). Long-term outcome of social functioning. In K. T. Mueser & N. Tarrier (Eds.), *Handbook of social functioning in schizophrenia* (pp. 134-148). Boston: Allyn & Bacon.

Harvey, P. D., Serper, M. R., White, L., Parrella, M., McGurk, S. R., Moriarty, P. J., Bowie, C., Vadhan, N., Friedman, J., & Davis, K. L. (2001). The convergence of neuropsychological testing and clinical ratings of cognitive impairment in patients with schizophrenia. *Comprehensive Psychiatry, 42,* 306-313.

Heaton, R., Paulsen, J. S., McAdams, L. A., Kuck, J., Zisook, S., Braff, D., Harris, M. J., & Jeste, D. V. (1994). Neuropsychological deficits in schizophrenics: Relationship to age, chronicity, and dementia. *Archives of General Psychiatry, 51,* 469-476.

Heinssen, R. K., Liberman, R. P., & Kopelowicz, A. (2000). Psychosocial skills training for schizophrenia: Lessons from the laboratory. *Schizophrenia Bulletin, 26,* 21-46.

Herz, M. I. (1984). Recognizing and preventing relapse in patients with schizophrenia. *Hospital and Community Psychiatry, 35,* 344-349.

Herz, M. I., Glazer, W., Mirza, M., Mostert, M. A., & Hafez, H. (1989). Treating prodromal episodes to prevent relapse in schizophrenia. *British Journal of Psychiatry, 155*(Suppl. 5), 123-127.

Herz, M. I., & Marder, S. R. (2002). *Schizophrenia: Comprehensive treatment and management.* Philadelphia: Lippincott Williams & Wilkins.

Hogarty, G. E. (2002). *Personal therapy for schizophrenia and related disorders: A guide to individualized treatment.* New York: Guilford.

Howard, R., Almeida, O., & Levy, R. (1994). Phenomenology, demography and diagnosis in late paraphrenia. *Psychological Medicine, 24,* 397-410.

Inskip, H. M., Harris, E. C., & Barraclough, C. (1998). Lifetime risk of suicide for alcoholism, affective disorder and schizophrenia. *British Journal of Psychiatry, 172,* 35-37.

Jablensky, A. (1999). Schizophrenia: Epidemiology. *Current Opinion in Psychiatry, 12,* 9-28.

Jørgensen, P. (1998). Early signs of psychotic relapse in schizophrenia. *British Journal of Psychiatry, 172,* 327-330.

Kay, S. R., Opler, L. A., & Fiszbein, A. (1987). The Positive and Negative Syndrome Scale (PANSS) for schizophrenia. *Schizophrenia Bulletin, 13,* 261-276.

Keith, S. J., Regier, D. A., & Rae, D. S. (1991). Schizophrenic disorders. In L. N. Robins & D. A. Regier (Eds.), *Psychiatric disorders in America: The Epidemiologic Catchment Area study* (pp. 33-52). New York: Free Press.

Kessler, R. C., Sonnega, A., Bromet, E., Hughes, M., & Nelson, C. B. (1995). Posttraumatic stress disorder in the National Comorbidity Survey. *Archives of General Psychiatry, 52,* 1048-1060.

Kingdon, D. G., & Turkington, D. (1994). *Cognitive-behavioral therapy of schizophrenia.* New York: Guilford.

Lehman, A. F. (1995). Vocational rehabilitation in schizophrenia. *Schizophrenia Bulletin, 21,* 645-656.

Lewine, R. R. J., Gulley, L. R., Risch, S. C., Jewart, R., & Houpt, J. L. (1990). Sexual dimorphism, brain morphology, and schizophrenia. *Schizophrenia Bulletin, 16,* 195-203.

Liberman, R. P., Mueser, K. T., Wallace, C. J., Jacobs, H. E., Eckman, T., & Massel, H. K. (1986). Training skills in the psychiatrically disabled: Learning coping and competence. *Schizophrenia Bulletin, 12,* 631-647.

Lo, W. H., & Lo, T. (1977). A ten-year follow-up study of Chinese schizophrenics in Hong Kong. *British Journal of Psychiatry, 131,* 63-66.

Lukoff, D., Nuechterlein, K. H., & Ventura, J. (1986). Manual for the Expanded Brief Psychiatric Rating Scale (BPRS). *Schizophrenia Bulletin, 12,* 594-602.

McFarlane, W. R. (2002). *Multifamily groups in the treatment of severe psychiatric disorders.* New York: Guilford.

McGurk, S. R., & Meltzer, H. Y. (2000). The role of cognition in vocational functioning in schizophrenia. *Schizophrenia Research, 45,* 175-184.

McGurk, S. R., & Mueser, K. T. (in press). Cognitive functioning, symptoms, and work in supported employment: A review and heuristic model. *Schizophrenia Research.*

McGurk, S. R., & Mueser, K. T. (in press). Cognitive functioning and employment in severe mental illness. *Journal of Nervous and Mental Disease.*

McGurk, S. R., Mueser, K. T., Harvey, P. D., Marder, J., & LaPuglia, R. (2003). Cognitive and clinical predictors of work outcomes in clients with schizophrenia. *Psychiatric Services, 54,* 1129-1135.

Mead, S., & Copeland, M. E. (2000). What recovery means to us: Consumers' perspectives. *Community Mental Health Journal, 36,* 315-328.

Milton, F., Patwa, V. K., & Hafner, R. J. (1978). Confrontation vs. belief modification in persistently deluded patients. *British Journal of Medical Psychology, 51,* 127-130.

Miner, C. R., Rosenthal, R. N., Hellerstein, D. J., & Muenz, L. R. (1997). Prediction of compliance with outpatient referral in patients with schizophrenia and psychoactive substance use disorders. *Archives of General Psychiatry, 54,* 706-712.

Minsky, S., Vega, W., Miskimen, T., Gara, M., & Escobar, J. (2003). Diagnostic patterns in Latino, African American, and European American psychiatric patients. *Archives of General Psychiatry, 60,* 637-644.

Mueser, K. T. (2002). Cognitive impairment, symptoms, social functioning, and vocational rehabilitation in schizophrenia. In H. Kashima, I. R. H. Falloon, M. Mizuno, & M. Asai (Eds.), *Comprehensive treatment of schizophrenia: Linking neurobehavioral findings to psychosocial approaches* (pp. 344-351). Tokyo: Springer-Verlag.

Mueser, K. T., Becker, D. R., Torrey, W. C., Xie, H., Bond, G. R., Drake, R. E., & Dain, B. J. (1997). Work and nonvocational domains of functioning in persons with severe mental illness: A longitudinal analysis. *Journal of Nervous and Mental Disease, 185,* 419-426.

Mueser, K. T., Corrigan, P. W., Hilton, D., Tanzman, B., Schaub, A., Gingerich, S., Essock, S. M., Tarrier, N., Morey, B., Vogel-Scibilia, S., & Herz, M. I. (2002). Illness management and recovery for severe mental illness: A review of the research. *Psychiatric Services, 53,* 1272-1284.

Mueser, K. T., Foy, D. W., & Carter, M. J. (1986). Social skills training for job maintenance in a psychiatric patient. *Journal of Counseling Psychology, 33,* 360-362.

Mueser, K. T., & Glynn, S. M. (1999). *Behavioral family therapy for psychiatric disorders* (2nd ed.). Oakland, CA: New Harbinger.

Mueser, K., & Liberman, R. (1988). Skills training in vocational rehabilitation. In J. Ciardiello & M. Bell (Eds.), *Vocational rehabilitation of persons with prolonged psychiatric disorders* (pp. 81-103). Baltimore: Johns Hopkins Press.

Mueser, K. T., Noordsy, D. L., Drake, R. E., & Fox, L. (2003). *Integrated treatment for dual disorders: A guide to effective practice.* New York: Guilford.

Mueser, K. T., Rosenberg, S. D., Goodman, L. A., & Trumbetta, S. L. (2002). Trauma, PTSD, and the course of schizophrenia: An interactive model. *Schizophrenia Research, 53,* 123-143.

Mueser, K. T., Salyers, M. P., & Mueser, P. R. (2001). A prospective analysis of work in schizophrenia. *Schizophrenia Bulletin, 27,* 281-296.

Mueser, K. T., Salyers, M. P., Rosenberg, S. D., Ford, J. D., Fox, L., & Cardy, P. (2001). A psychometric evaluation of trauma and PTSD assessments in persons with severe mental illness. *Psychological Assessment, 13,* 110-117.

Myin-Germeys, I., van Os, J., Schwartz, J. E., Stone, A. A., & Delespaul, P. S. (2001). Emotional reactivity to daily life stress in psychosis. *Archives of General Psychiatry, 58,* 1137-1144.

Noordsy, D. L., Torrey, W. C., Mead, S., Brunette, M., Potenza, D., & Copeland, M. E. (2000). Recovery-oriented pharmacology: Redefining the goals of antipsychotic treatment. *Journal of Clinical Psychiatry, 61*(Suppl. 3), 22-29.

Nuechterlein, K. H., & Dawson, M. E. (1984). A heuristic vulnerability/stress model of schizophrenic episodes. *Schizophrenia Bulletin, 10,* 300-312.

Penn, D. L., Corrigan, P. W., Bentall, R. P., Racenstein, J. M., & Newman, L. (1997). Social cognition in schizophrenia. *Psychological Bulletin, 121,* 114-132.

Pitschel-Walz, G., Leucht, S., Bäuml, J., Kissling, W., & Engel, R. R. (2001). The effect of family interventions on relapse and rehospitalization in schizophrenia: A meta-analysis. *Schizophrenia Bulletin, 27,* 73-92.

Polcin, D. L. (1992). Issues in the treatment of dual diagnosis clients who have chronic mental illness. *Professional Psychology: Research and Practice, 23,* 30-37.

Provencher, H. P., Gregg, R., Mead, S., & Mueser, K. T. (2002). The role of work in recovery of persons with psychiatric disabilities. *Psychiatric Rehabilitation Journal, 26,* 132-144.

Regier, D. A., Farmer, M. E., Rae, D. S., Locke, B. Z., Keith, S. J., Judd, L. L., & Goodwin, F. K. (1990). Comorbidity of mental disorders with alcohol and other drug abuse: Results from the Epidemiologic Catchment Area (ECA) study. *Journal of the American Medical Association, 264,* 2511-2518.

Ridgely, M. S., Goldman, H. H., & Willenbring, M. (1990). Barriers to the care of persons with dual diagnoses: Organizational and financing issues. *Schizophrenia Bulletin, 16,* 123-132.

Rogers, E. S., Walsh, D., Masotta, L., & Danley, K. (1991). *Massachusetts survey of client preferences for community support services (final report).* Boston: Center for Psychiatric Rehabilitation.

Rosen, A. J., Sussman, S., Mueser, K. T., Lyons, J. S., & Davis, J. M. (1981). Behavioral assessment of psychiatric inpatients and normal controls across different environmental contexts. *Journal of Behavioral Assessment, 3,* 25-36.

Rosenberg, S. D., Drake, R. E., Wolford, G. L., Mueser, K. T., Oxman, T. E., Vidaver, R. M., Carrieri, K. L., & Luckoor, R. (1998). The Dartmouth Assessment of Lifestyle Instrument (DALI): A substance use disorder screen for people with severe mental illness. *American Journal of Psychiatry, 155,* 232-238.

Salokangas, R. K. (1983). Prognostic implications of the sex of schizophrenic patients. *British Journal of Psychiatry, 142,* 145-151.

Sartorius, N., Jablensky, A., Korten, A., Ernberg, G., Anker, M., Cooper, J. E., & Day, R. (1986). Early manifestations and first-contact incidence of schizophrenia in different cultures. *Psychological Medicine, 16,* 909-928.

Saunders, J. B., Aasland, O. G., Babor, T. F., De La Fuente, J. R., & Grant, M. (1993). Development of the Alcohol Use Disorders Identification Test (AUDIT): WHO collaborative project on early detection of persons with harmful alcohol Cconsumption II. *Addiction, 88,* 791-804.

Seeman, M. V., & Lang, M. (1990). The role of estrogens in schizophrenia gender differences. *Schizophrenia Bulletin, 16,* 185-194.

Strauss, J. S., Harding, C. M., Silverman, M., Eichler, A., & Liberman, M. (1988). Work as treatment for psychiatric disorder: A puzzle in pieces. In J. A. Ciardiello & M. D. Bell (Eds.), *Vocational rehabilitation of persons with prolonged psychiatric disorders* (pp. 47-55). Baltimore: Johns Hopkins University Press.

Tsang, H. W. (2001). Applying social skills training in the context of vocational rehabilitation for people with schizophrenia. *Journal of Nervous and Mental Disease, 189,* 90-98.

Tsang, H. W., & Pearson, V. (2001). Work-related social skills training for people with schizophrenia in Hong Kong. *Schizophrenia Bulletin, 27,* 139-148.

Wahl, O. (1997). *Consumer experience of stigma.* Fairfax, VA: George Mason University.

Wallace, C. J. (2003). *Final report to the National Institute of Mental Health on Project 1RO1MH57029: A clinical pilot of the workplace fundamentals module.* Los Angeles: University of California at Los Angeles.

Wallace, C. J., Tauber, R., & Wilde, J. (1999). Teaching fundamental workplace skills to persons with serious mental illness. *Psychiatric Services, 50,* 1147-1153.

Wechsler, D. (1998). *Wechsler Adult Intelligence Scale–Revised (WAIS-III manual).* New York: Psychological Corporation.

Wing, J. K., & Brown, G. W. (1979). *Institutionalism and schizophrenia: A comparative study of three mental hospitals.* London: Cambridge University Press.

Zubin, J., & Spring, B. (1977). Vulnerability: A new view of schizophrenia. *Journal of Abnormal Psychology, 86,* 103-126.

Zygmunt, A., Olfson, M., Boyer, C. A., & Mechanic, D. (2002). Interventions to improve medication adherence in schizophrenia. *American Journal of Psychiatry, 159,* 1653-1664.

12

Eating Disorders

DREW A. ANDERSON, JENNIFER D. LUNDGREN, AND RACHEL G. MORIER

University at Albany, State University of New York

EATING DISORDERS IN THE WORKPLACE

*L*ittle is known about eating disorders in the workplace. With the exception of certain types of work constituting a risk factor for the development of eating disorders, there is very little research on the topic. We do know a great deal about the nature of eating disorders, however, and what treatments are effective for these disorders. This chapter provides a general overview of the eating disorders and how they might manifest in, and be affected by, the workplace environment.

DESCRIPTION OF EATING DISORDERS AND WORKPLACE MANIFESTATIONS

The current *Diagnostic and Statistical Manual of Mental Disorders–Fourth Edition–Text Revision* (*DSM-IV-TR*) (American Psychiatric Association [APA], 2000) recognizes two eating disorders, anorexia nervosa (AN) and bulimia nervosa (BN). A third disorder, binge eating disorder (BED), while not yet accepted as an independent diagnosis, is widely recognized. Currently, BED is classified as a specific example of "eating disorder not otherwise specified."

While these three diagnoses share some common features, they are distinct disorders. The key variables that help differentiate the disorders are (1) body weight, (2) the presence or absence of binge eating, and (3) the presence or absence of compensatory behaviors such as vomiting (Walsh & Garner, 1997). The current diagnostic criteria for these diagnoses are reviewed later. It should be noted that the current criteria for the eating disorders exclude large numbers of individuals who have significant eating pathology but do not quite meet full diagnostic criteria for any disorder (Anderson & Paulosky, 2003).

Anorexia Nervosa

Table 12.1 gives current *DSM-IV-TR* (APA, 2000) criteria for AN. Persons with AN often are secretive about their disorder, but there are a number of symptoms that can manifest in the workplace. First, the symptom of AN that is most likely to be noticed in the workplace is an abnormally low body weight. This low body weight goes beyond mere thinness and is the hallmark of AN. Second, abnormal patterns of eating may be noticed. Because persons with AN generally eat very little to achieve a low body weight, they may avoid occasions or circumstances at work in which food is likely to be served. Also, if they do eat, approximately half of those with AN will purge (i.e., vomit). Although purging is usually done in private, co-workers may accidentally come into a bathroom where an individual is purging. Finally, persons with AN are body focused and may spend a great deal of time talking about weight- and body shape–related topics, such as dieting and complaining about body size.

Bulimia Nervosa

Table 12.2 gives current *DSM-IV-TR* (APA, 2000) criteria for BN. Although BN often is thought of as a disorder of "binge eating and purging," this is not strictly true. Instead, persons with BN binge eat and engage in some sort of inappropriate compensatory behavior to prevent weight gain. These compensatory behaviors are

---

TABLE 13.1
***DSM-IV-TR* Diagnostic Criteria for Anorexia Nervosa**

A. Refusal to maintain body weight at or above a minimally normal weight for age and height (e.g., weight loss leading to maintenance of body weight less than 85 percent of that expected or failure to make expected weight gain during period of growth, leading to body weight less than 85 percent of that expected).

B. Intense fear of gaining weight or becoming fat, even though underweight.

C. Disturbance in the way in which one's body weight or shape is experienced, undue influence of body weight or shape on self-evaluation, or denial of the seriousness of the current low body weight.

D. In postmenarcheal women, amenorrhea, that is, the absence of at least three consecutive menstrual cycles. (A woman is considered to have amenorrhea if her periods occur only following hormone, for example, estrogen administration.)

Specify type
Restricting type: During the current episode of anorexia nervosa, the person has not regularly engaged in binge eating or purging behavior (i.e., self-induced vomiting or the misuse of laxatives, diuretics, or enemas).
Binge eating or purging type: During the current episode of anorexia nervosa, the person has regularly engaged in binge eating or purging behavior (i.e., self-induced vomiting or the misuse of laxatives, diuretics, or enemas).

Note. From the *Diagnostic and Statistical Manual of Mental Disorders,* 4th ed., text revision, by American Psychiatric Association, 2000, Washington, DC: Author. Reproduced with permission.

TABLE 13.2
DSM-IV-TR **Diagnostic Criteria for Bulimia Nervosa**

A.   Recurrent episodes of binge eating. An episode of binge eating is characterized by both of the following:

   1. eating, in a discrete period of time (e.g., within any 2-hour period), an amount of food that is definitely larger than most people would eat during a similar period of time and under similar circumstances; and

   2. a sense of lack of control over eating during the episode (e.g., a feeling that one cannot stop eating or control what or how much one is eating)

B.   Recurrent or inappropriate compensatory behavior to prevent weight gain, such as self-induced vomiting; misuse of laxatives, diuretics, enemas, or other medications; fasting; or excessive exercise.

C.   The binge eating and inappropriate compensatory behaviors both occur, on average, at least twice a week for three months.

D.   Self-evaluation is unduly influenced by body shape and weight.

E.   The disturbance does not occur exclusively during episodes of anorexia nervosa.

Specify type
Purging type: During the current episode of bulimia nervosa, the person has regularly engaged in self-induced vomiting or the misuse of laxatives, diuretics, or enemas.
Nonpurging type: During the current episode of bulimia nervosa, the person has used other compensatory behaviors, such as fasting or excessive exercise, but has not regularly engaged in self-induced vomiting or the misuse of laxatives, diuretics, or enemas.

Note. From the *Diagnostic and Statistical Manual of Mental Disorders,* 4th ed., text revision, by American Psychiatric Association, 2000, Washington, DC: Author. Reproduced with permission.

---

classified as purgative (including self-induced vomiting, laxative use, diuretic use, or use of enemas) or nonpurgative (including excessive exercise and extreme dieting or fasting). Thus, a person does not need to vomit to be diagnosed with BN; they must simply use some sort of inappropriate method to try to eliminate the calories they have eaten during a binge episode.

Overt symptoms of BN may be difficult to detect in a workplace setting. Unlike persons with AN, most persons with BN are normal weight to slightly overweight. However, like those with AN, persons with BN are usually secretive about their disorder (Anderson & Paulosky, 2003). Thus, they are unlikely to engage in binge eating or engage in purging while at work, although it is possible that co-workers may accidentally come into a bathroom where an individual is purging. It is more likely, however, that they will engage in other, nonpurging forms of compensatory behavior at work, such as excessive exercise and extreme dieting. These behaviors are easier to disguise as normal, because dieting and exercise are common in the workplace and it can be difficult to draw a line between "normal" and "excessive" exercise and dieting. Finally, like persons with AN, persons with BN are body focused and also may spend a great deal of time talking about body weight–related topics.

Binge Eating Disorder

Table 12.3 gives current *DSM-IV-TR* (APA, 2000) criteria for BED. Persons with BED binge eat but do not engage in regular compensatory behavior to prevent weight gain. As a result, most persons with BED are overweight or obese. Workplace manifestations of BED are extremely difficult to detect. Weight is not a reliable indicator of BED, as most obese persons do not have BED (see following discussion). Also, as with other eating disorders, binge episodes are generally secretive.

EPIDEMIOLOGY

Anorexia Nervosa

The overwhelming majority of those with AN are female (90 to 95 percent), with adolescent and young adult females at highest risk for the disorder (Pawluck & Gorey, 1998). AN is relatively rare; the average figure for point prevalence is 280

TABLE 13.3
DSM-IV-TR Research Criteria for Binge Eating Disorder

A. Recurrent episodes of binge eating. An episode of binge eating is characterized by both of the following:
    1. eating, in a discrete period of time (e.g., within any 2-hour period), an amount of food that is definitely larger than most people would eat during a similar period of time and under similar circumstances; and
    2. a sense of lack of control over eating during the episode (e.g., a feeling that one cannot stop eating or control what or how much one is eating).

B. The binge eating episodes are associated with three (or more) of the following:
    1. eating much more rapidly than usual:
    2. eating until feeling uncomfortably full;
    3. eating large amounts of food when not feeling physically hungry;
    4. eating alone because of being embarrassed by how much one is eating; or
    5. feeling disgusted with oneself, depressed, or very guilty after overeating.

C. Marked distress regarding binge eating is present.

D. The binge eating occurs, on average, at least 2 days a week for 6 months.

Note: The method of determining frequency differs from that used for bulimia nervosa; future research should address whether the preferred method of setting a frequency threshold is counting the number of days on which binges occur or counting the number of episodes of binge eating.

E. The binge eating is not associated with the regular use of inappropriate compensatory behaviors (e.g., purging, fasting, excessive exercise) and does not occur exclusively during the course of anorexia nervosa or bulimia nervosa.

Note: From the *Diagnostic and Statistical Manual of Mental Disorders,* 4th ed., text revision, by American Psychiatric Association, 2000, Washington, DC: Author. Reproduced with permission.

---

per 100,000 young females (Hoek, 2002). There is some indication that although the overall incidence of AN has remained stable over the past 40 years, it is increasing in women in their 20s and 30s (Pawluck & Gorey, 1998).

AN is an extremely serious disorder. It is associated with numerous medical complications, including dehydration, electrolyte imbalance, gastrointestinal disturbances, osteoporosis, and cardiac abnormalities including arrhythmia, cerebral atrophy, and seizures (Mitchell, Pomeroy, & Adson, 1997). In fact, it has been estimated that AN has one of the highests rate of mortality of any psychiatric disorder, roughly 6 percent per decade (Sullivan, 2002). Death is usually due to medical complications or suicide (Mitchell et al., 1997; Sullivan, 2002).

AN also is associated with high levels of psychiatric comorbidity. Major depression is the most commonly diagnosed comorbid disorder, with some studies finding that a majority of those with AN also are depressed. It is not clear which disorder develops first; there is some evidence that starvation can precipitate depression, but some persons with AN report developing depression before the eating disorder (O'Brien & Vincent, 2003). Anxiety disorders, particularly obsessive-compulsive disorder (OCD), appear to be associated with AN as well. While the relationship between OCD and AN is complex, it appears likely that the starvation associated with AN plays a role in the development of obsessive symptoms (O'Brien & Vincent, 2003). AN also is associated with personality disorders, particularly obsessive-compulsive personality disorder and avoidant personality disorder (O'Brien & Vincent, 2003).

Finally, it should be noted that the high-risk period for the onset of AN (for the teens to 30s age range) coincides with entry into the workplace for most women, and symptoms can significantly interfere with ability to function in a workplace environment. Moreover, inpatient treatment often is required. Thus, among other concerns, AN may have an extremely negative impact on work and career development.

Reviews of the literature suggest that, over the long term, roughly 50 percent of those with AN who receive treatment will recover, 15 to 25 percent will continue to show some symptoms of the disorder or will crossover to BN (50 percent will meet criteria for BN at some point), and 10 percent will develop chronic AN (Sullivan, 2002). Moreover, many of those who recover will continue to be thin and have elevated concerns with body weight and shape, and the risk of other psychiatric disorders can persist even if AN is treated successfully (O'Brien & Vincent, 2003; Sullivan, 2002).

Bulimia Nervosa

Like AN, up to 95 percent of those with BN are female, and adolescence and young adulthood also represent high-risk periods for developing the disorder. The incidence of BN has been stable over the past twenty years (Fombonne, 1996), and the prevalence is roughly four times that of AN, with an average point prevalence of 1,000 per 100,000 young females (Hoek, 2002).

BN is associated with a number of medical complications, including salivary gland enlargement, eroded dental enamel, gastrointestinal problems, electrolyte abnormalities, dehydration, and cardiac abnormalities; however, these problems are rarely fatal in those with BN (Mitchell et al., 1997; Sullivan, 2002).

BN also is associated with high levels of psychiatric comorbidity. As with AN, depression is the most common comorbid disorder, and it is not clear if depression precedes or is the result of the eating disorder (O'Brien & Vincent, 2003). BN also is associated with anxiety disorders and personality disorders, particularly borderline personality disorder (BPD) (O'Brien & Vincent, 2003). Individuals with BN who have comorbid depression and BPD also are at high risk for developing alcohol abuse or dependence (O'Brien & Vincent, 2003).

Also, as with AN, the critical period for development of the eating disorder coincides with entry into the workplace for most women. BN is less likely to be life threatening or require inpatient treatment than AN, however, and is less likely to cause as significant problems with work or career development.

Outcome for BN is somewhat better than that of AN. Reviews of the literature suggest that, over time, up to 70 percent of those who are treated for BN will recover, 20 percent will continue to show some symptoms of the disorder, and 10 percent will develop chronic BN (Sullivan, 2002). However, many of those who recover will show residual problems with body image and self-esteem, have elevated concerns with shape and weight, and may still occasionally overeat and purge when under stress (Sullivan, 2002).

Binge Eating Disorder

Unlike AN and BN, BED affects men and women much more equally (1.5 female-to-male ratio) and has an older age of onset (Grilo, 2002).

While it was originally thought that a significant minority of obese persons seeking weight loss treatment had BED, newer estimates suggest that the prevalence is much lower than originally thought. Current estimates suggest a prevalence of 2 to 3 percent of the general adult population, 8 percent of the adult obese population, and 5 to 10 percent of obese persons seeking treatment (Grilo, 2002).

Medical comorbidities associated with BED are generally related to weight status. While obesity is strongly associated with medical problems and major risk factors for poor health such as diabetes and heart disease, binge eating increases the probability of these risk factors (Bulik, Sullivan, & Kendler, 2002). BED also is associated with elevated rates of psychiatric comorbidity, including Axis I and Axis II disorders, with depression being the most common comorbid disorder (Grilo, 2002).

The course of BED is more favorable than those of AN and BN; it appears that the majority of persons with BED will recover even without receiving treatment (Fairburn, Cooper, Doll, Norman, & O'Connor, 2000). Also, BED does not appear to be a significant impediment to work or career development.

CASE ILLUSTRATION

The following case illustration is a compilation of a number of clients we have seen. The onset and course of the disorder are fairly typical.

Marie is a 22-year-old white female who lives alone in a large metropolitan area in the northeast United States. She is five feet, four inches tall and weighs 140 pounds.

Marie reports first becoming concerned with her weight at the age of eleven. She says that she was always "a little heavy" as a child but that this did not disturb her until some classmates began to tease her about her size. These concerns became stronger when she began puberty at age thirteen. At this time she says she began to be teased a great deal about the size of her breasts and her hips, and she began to be called "fat" by other children at school. Marie responded by dieting and exercising a great deal. These efforts were successful; she lost approximately 15 pounds and began to receive positive attention from classmates. She says that she did not tell her parents about either the teasing or her dieting, but that they commented favorably on her weight loss, saying she looked much more attractive.

Although she had an active social life and dated during this time, Marie says that she still "felt fat" and was under intense pressure to maintain her body weight and shape. She was able to do so with intermittent bouts of dieting and exercise. She denies any bulimic behaviors during this time, although it is not clear if her bouts of dieting and exercise during this period met the criteria for bulimia nervosa, nonpurging type.

Marie began college in another state immediately after high school. She reports gaining approximately seven to ten pounds her first semester because of poor eating habits and a busy schedule that kept her from exercising. She says that she began to feel extremely self-conscious and upset about her body at this time and that she became depressed about her weight; as a result she began to attempt to severely restrict her caloric intake. She frequently "gave in," however, and ate.

Marie's inability to maintain her dietary restraint (and her inability to lose weight) frustrated her greatly. Weight loss and dieting were common topics among her friends, and occasionally one of her friends would jokingly refer to purging as a method of weight loss. Marie reports that in the beginning of her sophomore year of college she made herself vomit "out of desperation"; she found it disgusting but reported that it made her feel "empty," which she did like. She began purging occasionally, usually after large dinner meals when her roommate was away. By the end of the semester she had settled into a pattern of skipping breakfast, eating a small salad with no dressing for lunch, and eating a very large dinner. She vomited following dinner and occasionally after lunch; she vomited at least once per day, and sometimes as often as three times per day. Marie reports that she realized that this was not healthy but was not able to stop the cycle. Her weight remained stable during this time.

This basic pattern of restricting and purging continued throughout college. Because of her negative body image Marie reports that she did not date very much, and she also tended to isolate herself from friends because so many college activities revolved around eating. Marie reports she was moderately depressed and did not want to continue her problematic eating patterns but was not able to stop.

After college, Marie got a job as a salesperson at a local designer clothing store, where she is currently employed. She says that no one at work has discussed her weight, but that she feels pressure to "be elegant" at work, and that includes being thin. She also says that she would be a better salesperson if she lost weight. She continues to be socially isolated and depressed, and she feels trapped in her current pattern of life circumstances. She presented for treatment because she is "fed up with my vomiting." However, she wants to be able to become thin without having to resort to vomiting and has a goal of losing 10 to 15 pounds.

RECOGNIZING AND EVALUATING PSYCHOPATHOLOGY

As mentioned previously, with the exception of the extremely low body weight seen in AN, it is difficult to recognize eating disorders in a workplace environment. The most obvious symptoms of eating disorders (i.e., binge eating and purging) are usually done in private. Moreover, other behaviors common in persons with eating disorders (e.g., skipping meals, talking disparagingly about one's weight and shape) are common in Western culture and thus often are overlooked. What is likely to be noticed, however, are comorbid symptoms such as depression and anxiety (see the chapters on mood disorders (Chapter 9) and anxiety disorders (Chapters 7 and 8) for more information on workplace manifestations of these disorders). Unfortunately, there is no way for the casual observer to determine whether these are comorbid with an eating disorder, particularly if no eating disorder is suspected. Thus, when present, comorbid disorders such as anxiety and mood disorders are more likely to be the target of intervention than the eating disorder. Complicating this issue is the fact that it is extremely common for individuals with eating disorders to deny or minimize their problems, even if confronted (Anderson & Paulosky, 2003). Thus, it may take a trained professional to accurately assess an eating disorder unless strong evidence is apparent.

REFERRAL STRATEGIES

Treatment of eating disorders, particularly AN, requires resources beyond what can be provided by most employee assistance programs (EAPs). Moreover, treatment providers need specific expertise and experience in assessment and treatment of eating disorders (Kaplan, 2002). Thus, it is critical to make appropriate referrals for persons with these disorders. There are a number of organizations whose members specialize in the treatment of eating disorders, such as the Academy for Eating Disorders (http://www.aedweb.org), the National Eating Disorders Association (http://www.nationaleatingdisorders.org), and the International Eating Disorder Referral Organization (http://www.edreferral.com). Employers or EAP staff can contact these organizations for names of local professionals with expertise in treating eating disorders.

Unfortunately, as noted previously, a significant proportion of individuals with eating disorders will deny or minimize their problems or will refuse treatment. This creates a difficult situation for employers and co-workers who are aware of or suspect an eating disorder.

WORKPLACE OR HOME STRESSORS WITH PARTICULAR RELEVANCE TO EATING DISORDERS

It has long been suggested that certain professions and activities place individuals at higher risk for eating disorders. In particular, there is some evidence that individuals in professions that place an emphasis on appearance or body size (such athletes, dancers, models, and entertainers) have an elevated risk for eating disorders (Byrne, 2002). Thus, employers or coaches involved in these professions should be particularly alert for the presence of eating disorder symptoms and have appropriate referrals available (see previous discussion). Beyond these professions, however, there is little research demonstrating that other work factors are particularly associated with eating disorders.

Certain home stressors also have been shown to have an impact on eating behaviors and eating disorders. Because of the age of onset of eating disorders (i.e., adolescence or young adulthood), most research has examined the quality of familial or parental relationships and eating pathology. These studies have found eating disorders and problematic eating behavior to be associated with low levels of familial support and high levels of familial conflict, dysfunction, and abuse; conversely, positive familial interactions, communication, and closeness are protective factors (Fonseca, Ireland, & Resnick, 2002). Very little research has been done on home stressors of older individuals with eating disorders.

EMPIRICALLY BASED TREATMENTS FOR EATING DISORDERS

Brief Description

Anorexia Nervosa

There is currently no widely accepted, empirically based treatment for AN. In terms of psychological approaches, behavioral therapy, cognitive-behavioral therapy (CBT), psychodynamic treatment, and family-based interventions all have been recommended, but research studies on their efficacy have been limited (Garner & Needleman, 1997). Given the success of CBT for BN and BED (see following discussions), CBT for AN holds particular promise (Garner, Vitousek, & Pike, 1997). Regardless of the psychological approach taken, it is generally accepted that the seriousness of the disorder requires a multifaceted approach, with a number of specialists working as part of a treatment team (Garner & Needleman, 1997; Kaplan, 2002). Pharmacotherapy appears to have little value in treating AN, however (Garner & Needleman, 1997).

Bulimia Nervosa

Two psychological approaches have been shown to be effective in the treatment of BN; CBT and interpersonal therapy (IPT). CBT (Fairburn, Marcus, & Wilson, 1993) is composed of three phases. Phase one is designed to normalize eating behavior with self-monitoring, education about weight and eating, and strategies to regulate meal patterning. Phase two uses cognitive and behavioral techniques to challenge maladaptive attitudes toward body image, weight, and self-esteem; reduce dietary restraint; and further prevent binge eating. Phase three focuses on relapse prevention. The recommended length of treatment is 20 weeks and typically occurs in an outpatient setting. CBT can be conducted in both group and individual formats.

In contrast to CBT, the goal of IPT (Fairburn, 2002) is to improve interpersonal functioning, not reduce eating disorder symptoms per se. However, IPT appears to be an effective treatment for BN. IPT has three phases. In the first phase, areas of interpersonal difficulty are identified and the ways in which they might affect eating are discussed. In phase two, the patient thinks of solutions to the interpersonal difficulties identified in phase one and tries to implement them. In phase three, the focus switches to relapse prevention. Treatment generally involves 12 to 20 sessions over three to five months. Treatment is generally conducted in an outpatient setting and is done one-on-one.

CBT appears to work more quickly than IPT, but both treatments are equally effective over the longer term (i.e., six months after treatment and longer) (Fairburn, 2002). Because it works more quickly, CBT is generally favored over IPT (Fairburn, 2002; Garner & Needleman, 1997).

In addition to CBT and IPT, pharmacotherapy has been shown to have some benefit in treating BN, particularly as an adjunct to psychological treatment. It is usually not the first treatment of choice for the disorder, however (Garner & Needleman, 1997). Antidepressants have shown the most promise in the treatment of BN (Garner & Needleman, 1997).

Binge Eating Disorder

Both CBT and IPT have been found to be effective psychological treatments for BED. Treatment is generally similar to the treatment for BN, with the exception that regular compensatory behavior does not occur in BED. Both approaches reduce binge eating and improve associated comorbidities equally well; however, unlike the treatment of BN, both approaches work equally quickly for BED (Wilfley, 2002).

One problem with CBT and IPT, however, is that neither produces clinically significant weight loss in obese persons with BED (Wilfley, 2002). Behavioral weight loss treatment thus has been recommended as an alternative to psychological treatment of BED. Behavioral weight loss appears to produce short-term effects similar to CBT and IPT but also may result in significantly greater weight losses, at least over the short term (Wilfley, 2002).

Time Element

CBT and IPT for BN and BED are short-term therapies; they are designed to be completed in 12 to 20 weeks (Fairburn, 2002; Fairburn et al., 1993; Wilfley, 2002). However, given the complex and serious nature of AN, it is not surprising that treatment for this disorder can take much longer than treatment of BN and BED, even when similar treatment modalities are used (Garner & Needleman, 1997).

Side Effects of Treatment

Psychological treatments generally represent the front-line treatment for the eating disorders. These interventions do not produce side effects in the traditional sense of the term; at worst, they appear to be merely ineffective. This, however, does produce a negative side effect in the sense that as long as an ineffective treatment strategy is pursued, other potentially successful treatment strategies are not likely to be instituted. To minimize this possibility, researchers have developed a number of strategies for sequencing and integrating treatments for the eating disorders. Interested readers should refer to Garner and Needleman (1997) for an extensive discussion of these issues.

The various prescription medications used in treating eating disorders have well-established side-effect profiles that are generally minor. Issues of side effects of medications should be discussed with the prescribing professional.

RELAPSE PREVENTION

Relapse prevention strategies are explicitly included in the CBT and IPT treatments for BN and BED (Fairburn, 2002; Fairburn et al., 1993; Wilfley, 2002) and in the CBT treatment of AN (Garner et al., 1997). Techniques include developing realistic expectations for future progress, identifying high-risk situations and triggers for binge eating, and developing strategies for dealing with difficult situations.

THERAPEUTIC BENEFITS OF WORK

If the work environment does not involve an emphasis on appearance or body size (see previous discussion), work can serve many useful functions for persons with eating disorders. First, work can provide ways to improve self-esteem that do not rely on body weight or shape. Second, co-workers can be a valuable source of social support and encouragement. Third, continuing to work provides a sense of being able to maintain a "normal life" while dealing with an eating disorder, and if an individual has received inpatient or day patient treatment, the return to work can be part of a return to normalcy.

SUMMARY

Eating disorders can affect all areas of life, including the work environment. They typically develop before or at the beginning of an individual's career and can have a significant impact on one's ability to work. The workplace environment can play a role in the development of eating disorders but also can help in the recovery process.

AN is associated with severe disruptions in all aspects of life and is extremely dangerous. BN and BED, while serious, do not appear to be as dangerous or disruptive as AN. All of the eating disorders are associated with other disorders, particularly depression and anxiety disorders, and these other disordres can have their own consequences.

Fortunately, a substantial proportion of those who develop eating disorders can be treated successfully, but accurate diagnosis and quick referral are critical. It is difficult to identify eating disorders in the workplace because of their secretive nature, however. Employers, EAP programs, and the like should be prepared to refer individuals with eating disorders to a specialist as soon as it is detected.

References

American Psychiatric Association. (2000). *Diagnostic and statistical manual of mental disorders* (4th ed., text rev.). Washington, DC: Author.

Anderson, D. A., & Paulosky, C. A. (2003). Psychological assessment of eating disorders and related features. In J. K. Thompson (Ed.), *Handbook of eating disorders and obesity,* pp. 12-129. New York: Wiley.

Bulik, C. M., Sullivan, P. F., & Kendler, K. S. (2002). Medical and psychiatric morbidity in obese women with and without binge eating. *International Journal of Eating Disorders, 32,* 72-78.

Byrne, S. M. (2002). Sport, occupation, and eating disorders. In C. G. Fairburn & K. D. Brownell (Eds.), *Eating disorders and obesity: A comprehensive handbook* (2nd ed., pp. 256-259). New York: Guilford.

Fairburn, C. G. (2002). Interpersonal psychotherapy for eating disorders. In C. G. Fairburn & K. D. Brownell (Eds.), *Eating disorders and obesity: A comprehensive handbook* (2nd ed., pp. 320-324). New York: Guilford.

Fairburn, C. G., Cooper, Z., Doll, H. A., Norman, P., & O'Connor, M. (2000). The natural course of bulimia nervosa and binge eating disorder in young women. *Archives of General Psychiatry, 57,* 659-665.

Fairburn, C. G., Marcus, M. D., & Wilson, G. T. (1993). Cognitive-behavioral therapy for binge eating and bulimia nervosa: A comprehensive treatment manual. In C. G. Fairburn & G. T. Wilson (Eds.), *Binge eating: Nature, assessment, and treatment* (pp. 361-404). New York: Guilford.

Fombonne, E. (1996). Is bulimia nervosa increasing in frequency? *International Journal of Eating Disorders, 19,* 287-296.

Fonseca, H., Ireland, M., & Resnick, M. D. (2002). Familial correlates of extreme weight control behaviors among adolescents. *International Journal of Eating Disorders, 32,* 441-448.

Garner, D. M., & Needleman, L. D. (1997). Sequencing and integration of treatments. In D. M. Garner & P. E. Garfinkel (Eds.), *Handbook of treatment for eating disorders* (2nd ed., pp. 50-63). New York: Guilford.

Garner, D. M., Vitousek, K. M., & Pike, K. M. (1997). Cognitive-behavioral therapy for anorexia nervosa. In D. M. Garner & P. E. Garfinkel (Eds.), *Handbook of treatment for eating disorders* (2nd ed., pp. 94-144). New York: Guilford.

Grilo, C. M. (2002). Binge eating disorder. In C. G. Fairburn & K. D. Brownell (Eds.), *Eating disorders and obesity: A comprehensive handbook.* (2nd ed., pp. 178-182). New York: Guilford.

Hoek, H. W. (2002). Distribution of eating disorders. In C. G. Fairburn & K. D. Brownell (Eds.), *Eating disorders and obesity: A comprehensive handbook* (2nd ed., pp. 233-237). New York: Guilford.

Kaplan, A. S. (2002). Eating disorder services. In C. G. Fairburn & K. D. Brownell (Eds.), *Eating disorders and obesity: A comprehensive handbook* (2nd ed., pp. 293-297). New York: Guilford.

Mitchell, J. E., Pomeroy, C., & Adson, D. E. (1997). Managing medical complications. In D. M. Garner & P. E. Garfinkel (Eds.), *Handbook of treatment for eating disorders* (2nd ed., pp. 383-393). New York: Guilford.

O'Brien, K. M., & Vincent, N. K. (2003). Psychiatric comorbidity in anorexia and bulimia nervosa: Nature, prevalence, and causal relationships. *Clinical Psychology Review, 23,* 57-74.

Pawluck, D. E., & Gorey, K. M. (1998). Secular trends in the incidence of anorexia nervosa: Integrative review of population-based studies. *International Journal of Eating Disorders, 23,* 347-352.

Sullivan, P. F. (2002). Course and outcome of anorexia nervosa and bulimia nervosa. In C. G. Fairburn & K. D. Brownell (Eds.), *Eating disorders and obesity: A comprehensive handbook* (2nd ed., pp. 226-230). New York: Guilford.

Walsh, B. T., & Garner, D. M. (1997). Diagnostic issues. In D. M. Garner & P. E. Garfinkel (Eds.), *Handbook of treatment for eating disorders* (2nd ed., pp. 25-33). New York: Guilford.

Wilfley, D. E. (2002). Psychological treatment of binge eating disorder. In C. G. Fairburn & K. D. Brownell (Eds.), *Eating disorders and obesity: A comprehensive handbook* (2nd ed., pp. 350-353). New York: Guilford.

13

Learning Disabilities and Attention Deficits in the Workplace

BENSON SCHAEFFER
Pacific University

Work is beneficial for most of us, a positive force for emotionally satisfying engagement in life; enjoyable and supportive relations with others; organization of the day, and prevention of social isolation and disengagement, anomie, and involution; and generation of the financial wherewithal to do what we wish when we are not at work. This is the case for individuals with learning disabilities (LDs) and attention-deficit/hyperactivity disorders (ADHDs) as much as it is for those who do not have cognitive deficits. Whether work is, in some sense, even more beneficial for individuals with cognitive deficits than for other people must remain an open question. A good argument can be made, however, that work may be especially beneficial for individuals with LDs and ADHDs. Specifically, winning the struggle for success in the world of work may do more to strengthen the self-concept, improve the self-esteem, and increase the sense of self-efficacy and personal agency of individuals with LDs and ADHDs than of people who do not have to struggle for work success nearly as much. A victory over great odds can be extremely empowering and conducive to the development of a sense of personal well-being and security in the world.

In this chapter, I discuss the effects of LDs and ADHDs on workplace function; specifically, how the cognitive, academic, social, and self-management difficulties, and in some instances strengths, associated with them affect workplace performance. I then outline and discuss ways to promote workplace success. The analytic framework I use takes into consideration individuals' self-regulation skills, their ability to manage their own behavior in the workplace, their co-regulation needs and skills, their need and ability to rely on others for assistance dealing with some of their difficulties, and their need for environmental structure, when they must depend on environmental structures and supports to succeed at their jobs. In most of the sections of the chapter this framework is implicit; in the section on empirically based treatments, it is explicit. There is not a wealth of hard data on the effects of LDs and ADHDs in the workplace, despite the many studies that have been done, because of methodological issues and the difficulties of gathering follow-up data, and no broadly agreed upon set of procedures for helping people, because of the breadth of the problems and varied ages and issues faced by the people affected, despite the many good descriptions of and attempts to organize assistive strategies and treatment. I offer an integration and overview based on an integration of my own clinical knowledge and experience with the information in the relevant literature.

DESCRIPTION OF LDS, ADHDS, AND WORKPLACE MANIFESTATIONS

Learning Disabilities

Researchers typically define LDs by the discrepancies between measures of intellectual function and measures of academic function, the differences between IQs or other cognitive function scores, and achievement test scores. When an individual's discrepancy and difference scores in a particular academic domain, expressed as standard scores, are so large that they would be very unlikely to occur by chance, the individual is said to have an LD in that domain, such as reading, mathematics, or written language. Although the impact of an LD can be enormous, defining an LD in a precise and unbiased fashion is extremely difficult. Among the reasons for this are that an individual with a very high IQ whose reading achievement scores are only average can be said to have an LD; it is often difficult to distinguish between the effects on academic function of the specific cognitive deficits thought to underlie LDs, low level of cognitive function, and attentional problems (more about this in the section on ADHDs); and also cognitive ability and academic achievement discrepancies can be a function of emotional difficulties that may or may not have been adequately assessed, or of poor instruction, or of lack of learning opportunities. Whether an individual has a technically definable LD, he or she may nevertheless suffer greatly on the job from the effects of academic deficits. A full account of these assessment and diagnostic difficulties is beyond the scope of this chapter.

What then are the effects of LDs in the workplace? The data regarding the effects take two forms: descriptions of the specific problems workers experience and the longer term effects of LDs on employment success. At one level the effects are obvious: difficulties reading instructions or orders; understanding and remembering work-related information; doing work-related calculations and mathematical problems; and difficulties writing down work-related data, messages, or orders all have a direct effect on job performance. At another level, we can speak of the cognitive difficulties presumed to underlie LDs, such as memory problems; problems understanding spoken information, especially in amounts that exceed immediate memory span; problems with organization; fine motor skill problems; and physical awkwardness or clumsiness. And at an even higher level, we can talk about social issues, including difficulties getting along with others, organizational citizenship behavior (Van Dyne, Cummings, & Parks, 1995), career maturity (Ohler, Levinson, & Sanders, 1995), ambition, and personality function. A complete listing of mutually exclusive and clearly hierarchically arranged problems related to LDs would be hard to develop, but the outlines are clear: academic problems related to essential job tasks (more on this in the following sections), problems related to the specific cognitive and fine and gross motor deficits associated with LDs, and social and organizational citizenship and job advancement problems.

Regarding the long-term effects of LDs on success in the workplace, the relevant data available are incomplete. The studies do reasonably clearly indicate, however, although not 100 percent conclusively, that young people, especially young women, with LDs transitioning from high school to the workplace generally attain lower levels of employment in terms of job ranking and occupational status, earn lower hourly wages, and have curtailed job longevity and more frequent job changes (Goldstein, Murray, & Edgar, 1998; Haring, Lovett, & Smith, 1990; Levine & Nourse, 1998; Murray, Goldstein, & Edgar, 1997; Scuccimarra & Speece, 1990; Sitlington, Frank, & Carson, 1992). For individuals transitioning from college to the workplace, very few data are available, particularly with LD and non-LD comparisons (but see Greenbaum, Graham, & Scales, 1996), and for older individuals, especially those identified as having LDs well after completing school, the data set is almost nonexistent, beyond the descriptions of the clinicians who work with them. For post–high school adults with LDs, the major problematic issues appear to be related to the cumulative impact that unresolved problems and failure experiences have on self-concept (Ratey, Hallowell, & Miller, 1997).

Further complicating matters, it is clear that the overall level of cognitive function of an individual with an LD has a large effect on outcome. For the most part, individuals functioning at high cognitive levels are likely to be more able to self-regulate and co-regulate in relation to LDs and so can learn skills to help them deal with their difficulties, seek assistance from others, and reorganize their work environments than are individuals functioning at low cognitive levels. In fact, Gerber, Ginsberg, and Reiff (1992) proposed a model for the attainment of vocational and professional success for individuals with LDs based on their gaining an understanding of the nature of their difficulties and then exercising a high degree of personal control dealing with the myriad issues related to them; that is, becoming excellent self-regulators. The model is based on comparisons between the thinking and behavior patterns of highly successful individuals with LDs and those of less successful individuals with LDs. I discuss the model later in the chapter, but note here that its implementation by an individual with an LD, without assistance from others, presupposes a reasonably high overall level of cognitive function.

And then there is the legal domain; specifically, the Americans with Disabilities Act of 1990 (ADA) and the Individuals with Disabilities Education Act of 1990 (IDEA) (Brown, 2000; Wyld, 1997). The ADA states, in summary, that an individual whose LD substantially limits a major life activity but who can perform essential job functions and is otherwise qualified for the job cannot be discriminated against and is entitled to those reasonable accommodations that will allow him or her to do the job. The IDEA specifies that an individual with an LD is entitled to high school–level Special Education services through age 21, including a carefully developed and executed Transition Plan that helps the individual move from high school, often through a vocational training program, to the world of work.

Attention-Deficit/Hyperactivity Disorders

Previously I outlined the linkages between LDs and workplace problems. The same issues are relevant to individuals with ADHDs, but with perhaps a slightly different emphasis because of the differences between ADHDs and LDs; that is, the different problems associated with each. Individuals with ADHDs may not experience academic skill–related job difficulties to quite the degree that individuals with LDs do, a claim I would make but cannot support directly on the basis of research data, but they certainly experience workplace problems related to ADHD-linked cognitive problems. These problems include inattention and distractibility, impulsivity, hyperactivity, the need for stimulation, memory difficulties, time management problems, and difficulties getting along with others (Nadeau, 1997). The last difficulties listed may be a function of the individuals' cognitive problems, but nevertheless, they have a large impact on organizational citizenship and job maintenance (Nadeau, 1997).

Regarding long-term outcome, the research data indicate that adults with ADHDs, as compared with controls, exhibit more oppositional-defiant behaviors on the job, quit or are fired more often, have shorter durations of employment, change jobs more frequently and have lower average occupational rankings, experience greater psychological distress and maladjustment, report committing more antisocial acts, are more likely to abuse drugs and alcohol, and are arrested more often (Barkley, Murphy, & Kwasnik, 1996; Mannuzza, Klein, Bessler, Malloy, & Hynes, 1997; Mannuzza, Klein, Bessler, Malloy, & LaPadula, 1993; Murphy & Barkley, 1996; Weiss & Hechtman, 1993). These data suggest that individuals with ADHDs, in addition to experiencing cognitive difficulties that affect job performance, may be more prone than individuals with LDs to experience problems related to getting along with co-workers and organizational citizenship.

EPIDEMIOLOGY

The incidence of LDs and ADHDs in the adult population is difficult to assess accurately. LDs have been estimated to be present in 9.4 percent of college freshmen (Henderson, 1999) and ADHDs are present in up to 3.5 percent of post-college adults (Silver, 2000). However, given the great variability in diagnostic procedures used to evaluate LDs and ADHDs, the variability in age at diagnosis, and the vicissitudes of on-and-off remission, at least for ADHD, all estimates of incidence must be taken with a grain of salt. That there are data suggestive of components of heritability and abnormalities of brain structure and function associated with LDs and ADHDs has not yet made diagnosis easier (Pennington, 1991). Perhaps a statistical estimate based on the likelihood of occurrence by chance of data supportive of an LD or ADHD diagnosis is not unreasonable. By this argument, the typical statistical significance level of 5 percent would be a reasonable estimate of the incidence of LDs and ADHDs separately in the adult population; because of not infrequent comorbidity, the total incidence for the two together would then be less than 10 percent. Making a 5 percent estimate by assumption does not solve the problem of establishing true incidence, but it could serve as a preliminary basis for setting priorities for the allocation of educational and treatment resources and might provide a statistical bulwark against overdiagnosis.

CASE ILLUSTRATIONS

In this section I briefly summarize two evaluation reports on individuals with overall normal range measured intelligence to illustrate some of the issues and problems related to the impact of LD-related and other cognitive problems on workplace performance and success. The great variety of possible LD and ADHD effects on adaptive function, great variation in cognitive level among individuals experiencing workplace problems, and the possible presence of comorbid emotional disorders would make an attempt to illustrate the full range of possible impacts of LDs and ADHDs a gargantuan task, which I do not attempt. I present summary descriptions and explanations of the two individuals' psychological and work problems and the recommendations made for reducing them. In the section on empirically based treatment, I discuss treatment issues more broadly.

Mr. X

A vocational counselor referred Mr. X, a man in his 40s, for an LD evaluation. He was contemplating a return to school for training that would enable him to obtain a more satisfying and higher paying job than the ones he has had. Mr. X has a lifelong history of difficulties with reading and writing and of anxiety problems as well. The evaluation indicated normal range overall intelligence with relative strengths in speeded hand-eye coordination, a relative weakness in verbal-linguistic information processing, consistent with his reading and writing difficulties, a functional but not statistically significant LD in reading, and a formally diagnosable, statistically significant LD in written language, with a significant anxiety disorder and depression. Mr. X's reading problems appeared to be a function of a speech sound analysis (phonemic awareness) weakness, a short-term auditory-verbal memory weakness, and real difficulty sustaining attention (though not to the level of formal ADHD diagnosis) to long reading passages over time, compounded by anxiety about his level of performance. His difficulties translating thoughts, which he can express well enough in words, into written form appeared to be a function of the negative effects of his short-term auditory-verbal memory weakness and anxiety on writing-related organizational skills.

The recommendations offered to help Mr. X were as follows:

1. individual tutoring in reading and writing with a tutor familiar with adult literacy issues;
2. continued individual psychotherapy to address anxiety, depression, and harsh self-judgment;
3. medication reevaluation to assess the effectiveness of current medications and to explore the possible benefits of medications to help reduce inattentiveness;
4. education about LDs and support from an organization such as Learning Disabilities Association of America;
5. participation in a support group such as those offered by the Orton-Gillingham Society, which focuses on reading and other LDs;
6. contact with a study skills center at a community college for accommodations based on his LDs if Mr. X decides to seek further education (A light initial courseload at a community college would be a good idea.); and
7. careful fine motor skills assessment if Mr. X chooses to seek a job where fine motor skills are critical (although motor skills appear to be strong).

Ms. Y

Her employer referred Ms. Y, a woman in her 30s, for assessment because of concerns about work performance, and Ms. Y is very concerned about job maintenance and advancement. In her job at a securities trading firm she was transposing numbers and leaving digits out of numbers, transposing letters in words, and substituting one number or word for another. The evaluation indicated normal range overall intelligence, with strengths in auditory-verbal memorization and learning skills and the completion of routine visual-motor tasks, and academic skills commensurate with her measured intelligence, therefore no LDs were evident, but she had weaknesses in reading-related speech sound analysis, the accurate perception of visual-spatial and shape information, and the execution of mathematical calculations in short-term memory, coupled with a tendency to become overwhelmed and anxious under stress, but not to the degree of a formal anxiety disorder. Her information processing weaknesses, and tendency to become overwhelmed, are consistent with and help explain the difficulties she is experiencing at her job.

The recommendations offered to help Ms. Y were as follows:

1. structuring the work environment in a way that is well organized and minimizes clutter, distraction, and stress;
2. working with a coach or mentor over a three- to six-month period to obtain assistance in developing and ingraining the most efficient procedures for accomplishing the tasks involved in her job, with "booster" meetings with her coach or mentor every six months to troubleshoot problems that arise;
3. providing access to an easily understandable manual of job procedures, including examples and forms for tasks, to help her routinize work tasks and prevent mistakes;

4. consistently using a notepad to write down orders and asking for clarification of the accuracy of the orders she records at the time they are given;
5. consistently and routinely repeating back numbers and spellings of accounts and orders to ensure accuracy;
6. using a daily calendar with a detailed checklist to ensure all tasks for the day are completed; and.
7. continuing psychotherapy, incorporating a focus on work-related stresses.

It also might be possible for Ms. Y to discuss with her employer whether she might change jobs within the company to a position that would not stress her weaknesses, but the clinician would probably not want to put this in the report as a recommendation.

As can be seen from the two examples above, the effects of LDs and cognitive and emotional problems in the workplace are varied and remediating them is a complex process that involves implementation of a variety of assistive strategies, some of which the individual can do on his or her own, but many of which, even for individuals of normal intelligence, depend on obtaining help from others.

RECOGNIZING AND EVALUATING PSYCHOPATHOLOGY

Most of what could be called psychopathology related to LDs and ADHDs in the workplace appears to be a result of the impact of individuals' academic and cognitive deficits on job performance and on interactions with co-workers and supervisors, not primarily of emotional or personality disorders. This is not to say that no individuals with LDs and ADHDs have emotional or personality disorders; some do, and emotional and personality issues need to be carefully assessed in evaluating the impact of LDs and ADHDs, and where there is an impact, the problems created need to be carefully dealt with. Nevertheless, my clinical experience suggests that it would be fair to say that more of the emotional problems related to LDs and ADHDs have to do with the cumulative impact of lack of work success and negative self-concept than with comorbid emotional disorders.

The evaluation process is complex. Individuals come to psychologists for evaluation self-referred because of concern about workplace difficulties or are referred by an employer or agency, such as the Department of Vocational Rehabilitation, or by their physician. Whatever the referral source, though, there is often a subtext that lies beneath the request for evaluation of the specific problem and its possible sources. Subtext questions could include the following: Will I be fired? Can I be promoted? How can I explain my difficulties to my friends, or to my wife and children? And questions from the employer's side include: Would it be best for us to let this person go? Switch him or her to a different job? Provide specific accommodations to make the job doable? Such subtext issues sometimes become part of the formal evaluation, sometimes not, but they always need to be taken into account, because if they are not considered the information about the presenting problem and treatment recommendations will be less likely to be understood, accepted, and acted on.

Regarding the evaluation itself, it is usually best to attempt to generate as complete a picture as possible of the presenting problem, or in other words to do a comprehensive psychological assessment. This assessment would include evaluation of overall level of intellectual function, language, memory, problem solving, fine motor skills, academic skills, emotional function and personality structure, developmental history, trauma and medical history, and living situation, and review of any records or previous evaluations available. A special attempt should be made by the assessor, too, to gather collateral information about the presenting problem from a reliable informant other than the individual, such as a spouse or supervisor, to develop as broad a perspective as possible on the relevant issues and reduce the likelihood of not obtaining important information. This is very much needed, but may be difficult because of confidentiality issues.

In practice what the preceding means is a careful clinical interview with the individual being evaluated and administration of a standard intelligence test, such as the Wechsler Adult Intelligence Scales–III, subtests from a memory battery, such as the Wechsler Memory Scales–III, several tests of executive function, perhaps subtests from Delis–Kaplan Executive Function System, a fine motor skill test or two, such as the Purdue Pegboard Test and Finger Tapping Test, subtests from an academic achievement batter, such as the Woodcock-Johnson–III, a broad-gauge personality test, such as the Minnesota Multiphastic Personality Inventory–2, and if possible, an interview with a reliable informant.

The result of the evaluation process would then include a thorough written report, including a succinct, integrated conceptualization of the cognitive, academic, and possibly emotional components of the problem; a set of very personally tailored treatment recommendations for reducing, remediating, or bypassing the problem; and a caring, careful, thorough debriefing with the individual evaluated.

REFERRAL STRATEGIES

The assessor typically writes in the evaluation report, and includes as part of the debriefing process a referral for the individual for treatment and assistance in dealing with his or her workplace problems. Referrals could be made for therapy, vocational counseling, or training and retraining; further assessment; discussions with the individual's employer, and so forth. During the referral process, when the assessor endeavors to make certain that the individual benefits from having been evaluated, it is particularly important that overall level of cognitive function and the resources the individual has available to him or her, or can access, be taken into account. Individuals with low levels of cognitive function need assistance in implementing treatment recommendations, that is, connecting with the professionals, programs, and agencies that could help them; individuals with few financial resources and weak social support systems need assistance obtaining resources for treatment in the form of workmen's compensation or state- or county-funded retraining or other services, Supplemental Security Income, assistance from family, and so on. A solely self-regulation–based approach is not likely to be sufficient. People with relatively high levels of cognitive function, good financial resources, and strong social support systems can do more for themselves: Gerber et al.'s (1992) model of how to work toward success by taking control of life might be appropriate for such individuals. A primarily self-regulation–based approach may then succeed.

Furthermore, the form of the referral process will be different for younger individuals still in the process of transitioning out of their families of origin to a job and living on their own than for individuals who have been in the workplace and out of school for years and are living independently. If the individual is below the age of 21 years and was on an Individualized Educational Plan (IEP), he or she will still likely be receiving assistive services as part of a Transition Plan; through vocational counseling, a job training program, job and life skills coaching; through instruction related to employment arranged through the state department or division of vocational rehabilitation, and so forth. For older individuals, the referral process may involve assistance from workmen's compensation programs, state- or county-level retraining programs, support group and job club participation, and, more often than for younger individuals in my experience, the recommendation that the individual seek therapy.

As can be seen, the referral process must be tailored to the specific needs of each individual. This means that referring professionals must be aware and have information about the wide but often not well-accessed resources available to individuals with LDs and ADHDs.

WORKPLACE OR HOME STRESSORS

Individuals with LDs and ADHDs experience the same workplace and home stressors as do other individuals but may, because of their cognitive deficits and history of nonsuccess, react to them more strongly than do other individuals; that is, with anxiety, depressive feelings, anger, behavioral and emotional disorganization, and losses of self-confidence. On the job, dealing with difficult colleagues and supervisors, attempting to master difficult new tasks, having the need to multitask (do components of a number of tasks in interleaved fashion), and doing jobs in disorganized work environments full of distractions can pose serious difficulties. At home, all of the pressures and stresses attendant on being a fully functional family member also can pose problems, especially when things are not going well. Marital difficulties, a child with problems of his or her own that require attention, illness, financial difficulties, and so on create difficulties that must be dealt with and take energy away from managing problems in the workplace.

Of particular importance is whether the family and workplace function as social and job support systems for the individual with an LD or ADHD. Although taking control of life may be the goal, and the individual may feel that he or she should be able handle problems on his or her own or at least corral the resources necessary to do so on his or her own, this is in practice not often the case and could, in fact, be viewed as a dysfunctional schema, a way of thinking more likely to interfere with problem solving than facilitate it. Now, it may be that the individual's family and workplace, particularly the person in charge or a boss, function naturally, without having to be asked, as support systems. In this case, the individual can focus primarily on dealing with the workplace stresses and problems he or she faces and secondarily, only with a view to keeping a watchful eye on them, on the normally expectable assistance and consideration he or she needs to do so. When it is not the case, however, when background stressors interfere or prevent others from providing support and help, or when the implicit assumptions and usual interaction patterns in the family and workplace do not include the special assistance an individual with an LD or ADHD may need, the individual will have to ask for it explicitly, search it out deliberately, organize its implementation, and in some instances, show family members, co-workers, and colleagues how to provide it. This raises the issue of self-advocacy, the need for the individual to be able advocate for him- or herself, or in other words, recognize the need for particular types of assistance and ask or press for them to be provided. I will not discuss self-advocacy at length here, but I note that is an essential skill for the individual with an LD or ADHD (Skelton & Moore, 1999).

EMPIRICALLY BASED TREATMENTS

There is a reasonably well-developed literature on the subject of empirically based treatments for reducing workplace problems arising from the effects of LDs and ADHDs, with a variety of reasonably well-spelled-out treatment and training techniques and recommendations, but the literature has not yet been integrated and organized for optimal therapeutic and educational use. Furthermore, we do not have a highly analytic outcome database that would allow for the evaluation of the effects on job performance and retention of use of the treatment and training techniques. Most of the outcome studies that have been done ask about the effectiveness of vocational training programs for individuals with LDs and ADHDs who are high school age or early post–high school age, who were on IEPs and who received vocational training as part of their transition plans, as mandated by IDEA. These studies suggest, but not necessarily conclusively, that vocational training programs have positive effects on employment outcome (Evers, 1996), that positive effects depend on the presence of follow-up assistance on the job after termination of training (Neubert, Tilson, & Ianacone, 1989), and that positive effects are more likely when the training received is specifically related to the job obtained subsequently (Sitlington, Frank, & Carson, 1994) and, for young adults, when parents participate in the education and job training process (Furqurean, Meisgeier, Swank, & Williams, 1991). There is virtually no outcome data, however, on the treatment of older adults who are well out of school and experience LD- and ADHD-related problems in the workplace.

At the start of this chapter I outlined a framework for discussing and analyzing treatment. I talked about three ways in which workplace difficulties could be managed: by self-regulation, where the individual acts mostly on his or her own to reduce problems; by co-regulation, where others help the individual reduce problems; and through environmental restructuring, where the structure of the workplace is altered or assistive technology is provided to help the individual succeed on the job. In this section I consider four approaches to treatment and training in the light of the self-regulation, co-regulation, environmental restructuring framework: The Gerber et al. (1992) take-control-of-your-life model; self-help books whose goal is to provide guidance and advice for individuals with LDs and ADHDs; the assistance provided to young individuals in high school and college in the form of vocational training and job support that is often a part of IDEA Transition Plans; and specifically for older adults, schema-based cognitive therapy. The most important subsection is that on assistance provided to young individuals: the literature on such assistance, in my view, can be used to provide an integrated framework for dealing with the larger problem and has important things to say about how to assist individuals of any age experiencing LD- and ADHD-related problems in the workplace. Furthermore, it highlights what I see as the most important issue that needs to be addressed by treatment programs; namely, the interface between self-regulation and co-regulation, how to make certain that an individual with an LD or ADHD is well assessed regarding how much assistance from others he or she needs, and that carefully formulated plans for providing such assistance are made and actually implemented. Most of the individuals we are considering need more co-regulatory assistance than they know and receive less than they need.

I end the section by briefly outlining possible links between the problems individuals with LDs and ADHDs experience in the workplace, organizational citizenship behavior, and the industrial-organizational psychology literature on task performance and contextual performance (Motowidlo, Borman, & Schmit, 1997).

Gerber et al. (1992) Model

The model Gerber et al. (1992) offered outlining the path to professional and job and career success for individuals with LDs and ADHDs proposed that to succeed in the workplace the individual with an LD needs to take control his or her life and workplace problems, as the highly successful individuals with LDs in their study did, through what the investigators term internal decisions and external manifestations. Highly successful individuals with LDs viewed their efforts to gain and exercise control over the different components of their life, especially their professional life, as crucial to the successes they achieved. In the following paragraphs I draw directly from Gerber et al.'s article to describe their model.

The internal decisions that highly successful individuals with LDs made to obtain control over their life took the form of desire, goal orientation, and reframing. Desire refers to the desire to excel, to get ahead, a burning determination to succeed. Gerber et al. viewed such desire as an internal decision, essentially a choice the individual makes, not a choice independent of the choices and actions related to other elements of the model but a choice nevertheless, an act of will. Goal orientation refers to the conscious setting of goals, particularly the goal of succeeding in the chosen field of endeavor. The individuals set such goals because they desire to succeed and are anxious about failure, though their anxieties remain secondary to their drive to succeed. Setting goals, both short term and long term, permits them to develop realistic, potentially achievable aspirations and a sharper focus than they would otherwise have on the difficulties they face learning new skills, and goal setting feeds on itself, with accomplishment of initial goals feeding into the setting and accomplishment of future goals. Reframing refers to the reinterpretation of the LD (or ADHD) experience in a more positive and productive manner by the individuals than they had previously. There are four stages in the reframing process: recognition, acceptance, understanding, and action. Recognition means recognition of the LD and all of its components, or that the individuals do things differently from others. Acceptance means acceptance of the reality of the disabilities, or the fact that the disabilities would likely not disappear and would require them to make extra efforts to succeed, over and above what they might otherwise expect of themselves or others, and that despite their disabilities they are good people. Understanding means understanding their strengths and weaknesses, so that they will be able to capitalize on the strengths and work toward reducing the effects of their weaknesses. And action refers to the decision and the act of taking specific actions to achieve the goals the individuals set.

The external manifestations of the drive to obtain control, related to the internal decisions but separate from them, refer to the translation of internal decisions into actual behaviors, including persistence, goodness of fit with one's environment, learned creativity, and social ecologies. Persistence means the willingness to do whatever is required to achieve the goals set, over whatever period of time necessary; that is, working harder than other people, doing extra work when necessary, and spending longer hours at work. Goodness of fit refers to the individuals' attempts to fit themselves into and work in environments where they could succeed, where use of their skills could be optimized. Goodness of fit allowed them, by dint of making good choices, to work with passion at tasks they enjoyed. Learned creativity refers to the development of strategies, techniques, and systems to enhance their ability to perform well, which included using divergent problem-solving tools to deal with difficult tasks; that is, solving problems in ways that capitalized on their strengths, as well as using modern conveniences and technologies, such as word processors, dictaphones, and so forth. Last, social ecologies mean that the individuals surrounded themselves with supportive and helpful people and upgraded their skills by designing personal improvement programs.

To help others use their model, Reiff, Gerber, and Ginsberg (1997) outlined ways of turning their model into a teaching tool and offered thoughts on self-advocacy skills for individuals with LDs (and ADHDs) and general advice. They talked in terms of alterable variables, which they did not define specifically, and implied that the internal decisions and external manifestations posited in their model of success correspond to alterable variables, that is, can be taught. The instructional overview they presented applies to the instruction of children and adolescents in the schools and describes ways in which the specific components of their take-control-of-your-life process for achieving success can be taught to students through a wide variety of teaching exercises that use a wide variety of curriculum materials. For young adults making the transition from school and family of origin to the world of work, living on their own, and having families of their own, some of the instructional strategies Reiff et al. described for younger students are applicable, but some are not. Regarding self-advocacy and general advice, Reiff et al. did not present strategies for developing skills but presented descriptions of skill components, information relevant to skill use, general guidelines for raising children with LDs, and suggestions as to how individuals with LDs can deal effectively with prototypical dilemmas and life adjustment issues.

As the reader can see, the Gerber–Reiff model has heuristic value and is intrinsically interesting (to my way of thinking), helps us understand the inner world of individuals with LDs, and has the potential to stimulate creative thinking about and the development of ways of dealing more effectively than mental health professionals and educators do now with LD-related problems. From the point of view of the self-regulation, co-regulation, environmental restructuring framework, however, the model has real limitations. Reiff et al. (1997) and Gerber et al. (1992) briefly acknowledged in discussing the implications of their model for educational practice that character, cognition, and coincidence play a large role in whether an individual with an LD will succeed in the work world. This is actually a stronger statement than it appears and when more closely examined it has important implications for practice.

Gerber et al. (1992) and Reiff et al.'s (1997) emphasis on the need for an individual with an LD (or ADHD) to take control of his or her life is admirable and in line with notions of personal empowerment but does not do justice to the large effects of cognitive level on performance in the workplace. Individuals who function at relatively high cognitive levels are more able to take and to exercise control over problems related to job skill learning, the need for assistance from others, and the restructuring of the work environment to reduce stress than are individuals who function at low cognitive levels. Their capacity for self-regulation is likely to be greater. What this means is that it will be important for those who assess LDs and ADHDs and their impact on workplace performance to make specific recommendations about how much and what type of assistance from others a particular individual is likely to need, to outline specific methods for obtaining that assistance, and to make specific recommendations about what environmental restructuring and technological or other supports and accommodations the individual needs, and to outline methods for working toward their implementation. Assistance and support are essential.

Regarding character and coincidence, the Gerber–Reiff model is also silent, and this too likely overestimates the ability of some individuals to take control of the problematic aspects of their work life. Individuals with LDs and ADHDs may lack self-confidence, experience anxieties and depressive reactions, and feel demoralized as a result of the cumulative effects of the failures they have experienced and may therefore need much help developing a positive view of themselves and a sufficiently future-oriented motivation to even begin attacking the problem of taking control of their work life. Furthermore, lack of access to financial, therapeutic, and training resources and lack of an adequate social support system also may interfere significantly with, or even preclude, their obtaining the assistance they need, even when they function at high enough cognitive levels to potentially take on the task of taking control. Poverty, lack of education, and the unavailability of resources and social support have profound effects on individuals with LDs and ADHDs. This means that if an individual with little in the way of financial and social capital is lucky enough to receive a careful assessment, it will be important for the evaluator to make explicit recommendations regarding how to develop the resources the individual will need to have a chance of accessing assistance for dealing with workplace difficulties. In fact, it may be doing a disservice to the individual to overemphasize his or her ability to take control of problems related to the workplace or to foster go-it-alone, individualistic expectations that he or she will find impossible to meet. Take-control motivation is needed, but it should be carefully titrated with the help of others so individuals can achieve a balance between self-regulation and co-regulation, especially for people who are unsure of their abilities, lacking in financial and social resources, and fearful of exposing their inadequacies.

Self-Help Books

Brown (2000) on LDs in the Workplace

Moving from the Gerber–Reiff model, I now consider books whose aim is to provide advice and guidance to individuals with LDs and ADHDs as they go about dealing with workplace issues and problems. The books I examine and whose aims and suggestions I analyze are one by Brown (2000), which is addressed primarily to individuals with LDs, and one by Nadeau (1997), which is addressed primarily to individuals with ADHDs. Brown wrote as an individual with an LD and his book is a self-help guide with a wealth of good information. It outlined strategies and practical recommendations for addressing many of the issues faced by individuals with LDs. The list of topics he considered on a chapter-by-chapter basis is relatively long and includes making job or career choices; benefiting from high school; benefiting from trade school, college, and graduate school; obtaining accommodations in education and training; developing social skills; developing self-esteem and motivation; obtaining work experience; finding a job; interviewing for a job; obtaining assistance from career counselors and vocational rehabilitation and other helping professionals; preventing discrimination and protecting civil rights through the ADA; obtaining appropriate job accommodations; and working for job or career advancement and success.

As this list demonstrates, an individual with an LD needs to amass considerable knowledge about a large number of work- and disability-related issues to succeed in a job or career. This knowledge base defies a simple summarization. It would take an individual functioning at a relatively high cognitive level with reasonable reading skills a significant amount of time to learn the information and the strategies outlined for acting on that information. Now, some individuals with LDs function at a relatively high cognitive level but many do not, and probably less than a majority of them read easily and well. What this means is that for many individuals, unaided self-directed study of the material in the book and self-directed implementation of the strategies, or self-regulation, is not possible.

If an individual with an LD wants to use Brown's book, he or she will likely need to read and study it with a tutor, coach, or other helping professional, or in a group with other individuals with LDs; in other words, coregulate. Assisted self-help will need to be the watchword of the day and the watchword for the months during which the individual works his or her way, with others' help and support, through all of the book or parts of it. Let me emphasize again, though, that Brown's book offers much excellent information; the issue is how to help the individual with an LD benefit maximally from that information.

Nadeau (1997) on ADHDs in the Workplace

Nadeau (1997) wrote as a professional with extensive experience helping individuals with ADHDs deal with workplace issues. Her book, like Brown's, is a self-help manual and offers much excellent information. The chapter topics include seeking an adult ADHD career or workplace assessment, gaining control over job performance (note the emphasis on control), gaining control of social skills on the job, discussing characteristics of ADHDs and LDs, capitalizing on positive ADHD traits, implementing strategies for workplace success, structuring the work environment, finding an ideal (really "good") boss, obtaining reasonable workplace accommodations, finding alternatives to a "9-to-5" job (individuals with ADHDs are restless), women in the workplace, discussing ADHD difficulties and the ADA, and achieving success in the workplace.

As can be seen, there is considerable overlap between Nadeau's list of topics for individuals with ADHDs and Brown's list for individuals with LDs. It is important to note as well that there is much potential overlap between LDs and ADHDs in terms of comorbidity and in terms of potential negative effects on workplace performance. The likelihood of negative effects in the workplace is particularly high when individuals with LDs and ADHDs must process amounts of information that exceed immediate memory span, and perform tasks that demand the effective use of organizational strategies, that require study and practice, that depend on efficient time management, and that assume the ability to ignore highly distracting stimulation. It also is important to note that, like Brown's list, Nadeau's list of job-relevant information and strategies is long and the body of material an individual needs to master or at least gain familiarity with is large, and that to be able to use Nadeau's excellent book on his or her own, the individual must function at a relatively high cognitive level and be able to read reasonably well. Because this will likely not be the case for many individuals with ADHDs, as was true for individuals with LDs, completely self-directed study and use of the book by an individual on his or her own is not likely to work out; that is, self-regulation alone will not suffice. Rather, as was the case with Brown's book, study with a tutor, coach, or other helping professional or in a group with other individuals with ADHDs will likely be needed for a given individual to benefit maximally from the excellent information and strategies Nadeau offered.

Toward an Integrated Framework: Assistance to Young Individuals

Although there do not appear to be research-based data that conclusively demonstrate that assistance, in the form of vocational training, work experience, and follow-along or follow-up supervision, provided to young individuals during the transition from school to the world of work uniformly make a positive difference, the overall picture is encouraging, especially and not surprisingly, for the benefit of vocational training that matches the job at which the individual starts working and of prior summer and other job experience (Sitlington et al., 1994). Next I discuss frameworks for and considerations related to the education and treatment strategies that have been used by number of investigators who have written about assisting young individuals with LDs and ADHDs in dealing with job or career development and workplace problems. The view I take is that these frameworks strike a good balance between self-regulation and co-regulation, present a useful self-regulation–co-regulation interface and are applicable to individuals of all ages who are facing LD- and ADHD-related workplace issues.

I believe young individuals receiving vocational training, job supervision, and job accommodations related to Transition Plans likely function at a lower average cognitive level than do the individuals to whom self-help books are addressed, read less well, have access to fewer financial and social support resources, and likely also have less self-confidence and lower self-esteem. In other words, they need more assistance: on the self-regulation, co-regulation, environmental restructuring continuum, they can exercise self-regulation only in the context of much co-regulation and environmental restructuring. Therefore plans for assistance developed for them are likely to provide a good base for the development of assistance plans for individuals who function at higher cognitive levels and have access to more financial and social resources.

Ohler et al. (1995) noted that young adults with LDs tend to have lower levels of career maturity than do individuals without LDs, because of impaired progress through the developmental sequence of life and vocational tasks that enable individuals to deal with the career choices they confront. Then, at the end their article, Ohler et al. outlined a framework for the provision of assistance to young individuals with LDs. I like their framework: I believe that it can serve as a generic plan for the provision of help to all individuals with an LD or ADHD when individualized in ways that take into account each individual's unique strengths, weaknesses, and life situation and that it strikes an appropriate self-regulation–co-regulation balance.

The successive steps in Ohler et al.'s (1995) plan are as follows:

1. a transdisciplinary assessment of intellectual and academic skills, personality, interests, and career maturity;
2. guided awareness and exploratory career activities, including reading, informational interviewing, job shadowing, and job simulation;
3. academic and career counseling to develop a plan geared to the individual's goals and assets;
4. hands-on experience (experiential learning), part-time and summer jobs, volunteer work, supervised internships, and cooperative education, that is, job pretraining;
5. social skills training emphasizing interpersonal communication, self-awareness, and job-seeking skills;
6. shared monitoring of career development needs and progress by employment counselors, parents (or spouse or friend, when appropriate), training personnel, and school personnel (and the individual's employer);

7. appropriate placement assistance, job development, instruction in job-seeking (and job-maintenance) skills, and follow-up assistance to promote success in the transition to and later in the world of work; and
8. consultation as needed by professionals familiar with the effects of LDs (and ADHDs) on workplace performance.

Assuming appropriate individualization that takes into account the person's unique strengths and weaknesses and life situation, this framework would appear applicable to the development and implementation of a plan of assistance for any individual with an LD or ADHD, especially if a strong emphasis is maintained on on-the-job training and supervision and psychotherapy can be offered when needed.

To give the reader more of a sense of how the Ohler et al. (1995) framework might be implemented in practice, I now consider recommendations for the provision of assistance to individuals with LDs and ADHDs other writers have made. Reisman and Reisman (1993) presented suggestions for the on-the-job supervision of individuals with LDs (and ADHDs). The problems they described that individuals with LD and low average intelligence have, beyond specifically academic ones, include inability to abstract and generalize, social immaturity, short attention span, distractibility, (specific) information processing difficulties, memory problems, perseveration (on errors and maladaptive responses), and inappropriate social responses, along with insecurity about their job roles and low self-esteem; that is, much the same problems I listed earlier in the chapter, with great overlap between the problems of individuals with LDs and ADHDs. They then discussed the results of their experience with the Threshold Program for training young individuals with specific LDs for independent living and employment through academic and practical experience.

What they reported to be of particular value to the individuals whom they assisted were regularly scheduled on-site supervision; discussions between the individual and supervisor as part of the on-site supervision; immediate feedback regarding job performance; supervisory intervention especially when and if job retention became an issue; encouragement of the individuals to ask questions and advocate for themselves, that is, self-advocacy (see also Skelton & Moore, 1999); and the supervisor's offering concrete ways to provide the individual with help on the job.

Consistent with Reisman and Reisman's (1993) suggestions, Neubert et al. (1989) noted that individuals with LDs and mild mental handicaps benefited from periodic ongoing support for the maintenance of employment and for job retention and advancement and that the individuals requested support, of a minimal variety, when negotiating job changes in the work world. The task-related difficulties they reported the individuals experienced included inadequate performance of assigned job tasks, inadequate production rate, and difficulties following directions (an aspect of difficulty in processing spoken information). The work adjustment skills they reported the individuals were at times deficient in included attendance and punctuality, personal adjustment (grooming and hygiene), and social and interpersonal adjustment. Last, they stated that it would be helpful for the individuals if companies' human resources departments took on part of the task of developing and implementing accommodations for individuals with LDs and other handicaps.

Also for the purpose of developing a larger framework for the provision of assistance, we can look at job accommodations made for individuals with LDs, ADHDs, and psychiatric problems. Means, Stewart, and Dowler (1997) presented data they obtained from the Job Accommodation Network on accommodations obtained by individuals with these problems. The most frequently offered and used accommodation was an assistive device, which the investigators defined as any object or item that helps the individual perform the job. In this category, they listed computer hardware and software, and modifications to them, tape recorders, color-coding systems, note-taking systems, telephone adaptations, white noise machines, timers and alarms, spell checkers, glare guards, and data bank watches.

The next two types of accommodation in frequency were training and retraining and environmental changes. Training and retraining refers to instruction that helps the individual learn to do his or her job more effectively or to relearn job tasks and procedures, including tutoring, mentoring, and test-taking accommodations (oral rather than written format, extra time, etc.). Environmental changes refer to ways of altering the work environment to make it easier for the individual to do his or her job, such as rearranging the workstation to screen out potential distractions, the use of sound-reducing cubicles, giving an employee his or her own office, and displaying written instructions prominently to cue the worker to the next task and to remind him or her of task components. Last in frequency of use, the investigators listed policy changes and medical accommodations. Policy changes could include restructured job duties, especially nonessential ones (consistent with the ADA), flexible scheduling, and frequent break periods. Medical accommodations included medication, opportunities for exercise, and release time for counseling, psychotherapy, and other behavior interventions.

To expand the assistance framework even further, I also consider the work of Jacobs and Hendricks (1992). These investigators stated that in helping individuals with LDs, it is important also to assist their employers in developing an understanding of LD-related workplace problems, which in part could be provided by published materials. Employers often do not understand the implications for workplace performance of cognitive as opposed to more visible physical disabilities, or they lack experience with individuals with LDs (and ADHDs). Regarding issues related specifically to job accommodations, the investigators noted the need for knowledge of job task requirements and for assistance at times from local professionals able to assess the individual, the job, and the organization. They also mentioned that the decision needs to be carefully made regarding specific workplace problems as whether to try to develop an accommodation or attempt to remediate the deficit underlying the problem; they suggested accommodations for severe deficits and remediation for nonsevere deficits. Last, they noted that an accommodation provided to a specific individual, such as reducing workplace distractions, often benefits his or her co-workers, and that the development of accommodations demands careful analysis, creative thinking, and a willingness to try novel approaches.

Finally, I note that Okolo (1988) stated there is the expectation in vocational training laboratories and workshops that trainees will display a high level of independence, specifically, self-motivated, appropriate work habits, and the self-monitoring of on-task behavior. For individuals with a history of lack of success in the workplace, poor self-concept, and low self-esteem, meeting this expectation can be very difficult.

Schema-Based Cognitive Therapy

Clinicians who work with adults who are many years removed from school and experience LD- and ADHD-related workplace difficulties talk of the need to help the individuals overcome demoralization and develop positive self-concepts, self-esteem, and a sense of self-efficacy and personal agency. They note, too, such growth can be very difficult for the individuals to make, given their often long histories of nonsuccess in the workplace and the infiltration of the negative emotional effects of these shortcomings into every aspect of their personalities, every cell of their psychological beings. Ratey et al. (1997), discussing such issues, noted that individuals with ADHDs (and individuals with LDs as well, though I have observed perhaps less so on some counts) often underachieve in educational and educational settings, have difficulties related to initiating tasks and procrastination, have problems with intimacy and trouble with authority, are impatient and may engage in patterns of self-defeating behaviors, may have impulsive outbursts and tantrums, may engage in risk-taking behaviors, and have low self-esteem and self-worth. I believe, on the basis of my own experience and the experience of other clinical psychologists who work with adults with LDs and ADHDs, that self-confidence and a sense of self-efficacy are basic and important components self-regulatory competence, that their growth needs to be actively fostered, that therapy can be of great help in this regard, and that the other problems listed by Ratey et al. are exacerbated by a lack of self-confidence and sense of self-efficacy. I also suggest that schema-focused cognitive therapy (Young, 1999) might provide a good set of techniques for helping individuals with LDs and ADHDs overcome their history-based demoralization.

Young (1999) presented schema-focused cognitive therapy as a set of techniques for treating personality disorders. I view it as applicable to individuals with LDs and ADHDs as well, because their history-based poor self-concepts, demoralization, and lack of a sense of self-efficacy are pervasive, if not personality, traits, and demand the use of tools powerful enough to alter personality traits. These traits are allied to dysfunctional patterns of maladaptive behavior that can be seen as having dysfunctional schemas both as important sources and as points of potential therapeutic leverage. In regard to personality, Young discussed rigidity, avoidance, and interpersonal difficulties, terms assuredly applicable to the behavioral and emotional functioning of many individuals with LDs and ADHDs. He then talked of early maladaptive schema domains related to disconnection and rejection, impaired autonomy and performance, impaired limits, other-directedness and overvigilance, and inhibition; again terms that are applicable to many individuals with LDs and ADHDs. Next, Young discussed the processes of schema maintenance, schema avoidance, and schema compensation; that is, the ways individuals with dysfunctional schemas organize their actions in the service of the schemas. Last, he outlined cognitive, experiential, and interpersonal techniques for altering schema-driven behavior and emotional reactions. Among the cognitive techniques, he listed memory and self-management aids, review of the evidence in support of the schemas, critical examination of the evidence, review of the evidence contradicting the schemas, the illustration of how the individual discounts contradictory evidence, and the development of flash cards that contradict the schemas.

In my view, schema-focused cognitive therapy as outlined by Young (1999) presents a set of organized tools for problem analysis and therapeutic techniques that will likely prove useful in helping individuals with LDs and ADHDs relinquish their reliance on dysfunctional schemas, create growth-promoting schemas and reorganize their actions around them, and develop positive self-concepts, self-esteem, self-confidence, and a sense of self-efficacy and personal agency. The latter positive-sense-of-self characteristics are especially important because of the individuals' cognitive difficulties and their need to become, given the likelihood that their cognitive difficulties will not disappear completely, excellent whistlers in the dark; that is, capable of continuing to perform despite experiencing difficulties and a level of personal insecurity not faced by people without their cognitive difficulties.

I suggest that what will be crucial for developing and implementing an integrated counseling and psychotherapy, vocational training and retraining, on-site job supervision, and follow-up treatment and educational plan for a specific individual, with appropriate job accommodations, will be the careful consideration of the interface between self-regulation, co-regulation, and environmental restructuring. In particular, it will important to clearly delineate exactly what the individual is likely to be able to do for him- or herself, what he or she will need direct assistance from others to accomplish, what form that assistance should take, and how that assistance can be obtained and implemented. Individuals with LDs and ADHDs need both powerful capacities for self-regulation and the ongoing availability of others' help. Essentially, I am suggesting that every individual with an LD or ADHD, no matter his or her age, will benefit from a carefully developed, clearly specified Individual Transition Plan, analogous to IDEA Transition Plans for young adults leaving high school, implemented by a team of helpers and focused, as noted, on the interface between self-regulation and co-regulation, including the financial and social support resources the plan demands.

RELAPSE PREVENTION

As the preceding section implies, the most effective forms of relapse prevention for individuals who experience workplace problems related to LDs and ADHDs are likely to be booster shots of on-site supervision, training and retraining, psychotherapy, and so forth, the components of the Individual Transition Plan, by supervisors or consultants, to maintain the quality of or improve the individual's performance of work tasks and relations with co-workers, to assess the possible need for job reorganization or change, to help with training on new tasks or retraining on old or altered tasks, and to promote the maintenance of acceptable organizational citizenship behaviors. The point is that even with good initial counseling and job training, individuals with LD and ADHDs are likely to need ongoing assistance to maintain their job over time. The interface between self-regulation and co-regulation does not maintain itself of its own accord: it needs the ongoing attention of the individual him- or herself and of supervisors, trainers, counselors, consultants, and others interested in the individual's welfare.

Links to the Industrial/Organizational Psychology Literature

Before closing, let us look at the individual with an LD or ADHD in the workplace from an organizational perspective. In the industrial/organizational psychology literature, the distinction is made between task and contextual performance in the workplace (Motowidlo et al., 1997). Task performance constitutes those actions directly related to and involved in the performance of essential job tasks and transforms raw materials into the goods and services that are the organization's products; contextual performance constitutes those actions only indirectly related to job essentials but possibly very important for promoting the interests and continued existence of the company or organization in which the job is done and for job maintenance and advancement. The problems individuals with LDs and ADHDs have in the workplace relate to task performance and contextual performance, with cognitive difficulties more likely to compromise task performance and social-emotional difficulties (which could be a function of the cognitive difficulties or be separate from them) more likely to compromise contextual performance.

In the preceding discussion of assistance for individuals with LDs and ADHDs in the workplace, I emphasized difficulties related to task performance more than difficulties related to contextual performance. Allow me to perhaps slightly redress the balance. The two major constructs related to contextual performance in the industrial/organizational psychology literature are organizational citizenship behavior (Podsakoff & MacKenzie, 1997) and counterproductive job performance (Collins & Griffin, 1998). Organizational citizenship behaviors include, but are not limited to, all of those extra-role behaviors that benefit the organization or are so intended, are discretionary, and go beyond existing role expectations (Van Dyne et al., 1995); extra-role behaviors are distinguished from in-role, or normally expectable, behaviors. Counterproductive job performance constitutes those actions that are detrimental, in the short term but more often in the long term, to the interests and continued existence of the company or organization; such performance tends to be egocentrically self-serving and often undermines others' efforts or reputations. There are two major points I want to make regarding organizational citizenship behaviors and counterproductive job performance. First, individuals with LDs and ADHDs often are lacking in an understanding and appreciation of what organizational citizenship behavior entails and they fail to engage in it, which works against job retention and advancement; often they also are unaware of when they are engaging, for the most part inadvertently, in counterproductive job performance, which also works against job retention and advancement; and often they do not know that appropriate self-advocacy can be a potent form of organizational citizenship behavior. Therefore, it is a good idea to include a mini-course in organizational citizenship behavior in vocational and career training for individuals with LDs and ADHDs.

SUMMARY

In this chapter I presented information on the effects of LDs and ADHDs on individuals' performance and level of success in the workplace and a framework for dealing with the problems they experience there. The central point I attempted to make, within a self-regulation, co-regulation, environmental restructuring framework, was that individuals with LD and ADHDs need more assistance from others to succeed in the world of work than do other people, and although the maximal possible self-regulation may be desirable, co-regulation will need to be the primary vehicle for lessening the individual's difficulties in the workplace. What this means is the assessment of their strengths and weaknesses must include a careful evaluation of exactly what assistance they will need to succeed and a carefully formulated plan for and implementation of that assistance. I considered LDs first, outlining the characteristic cognitive deficits associated with them and their impact on workplace success. For the most part, individuals with LDs are less successful than their peers in the world of work: they earn less, stay in jobs for shorter periods of time, change jobs more often, and do not, on average, obtain jobs of high occupational status and rank. Next I outlined analogous data on the cognitive characteristics and low level of workplace success of individuals with ADHDs.

Then I proceeded to what I consider the most important section of the chapter, the section on empirically based treatments. I discussed first the Gerber–Reiff model of the path to success for individuals with LDs and ADHDs, a model based on the individual's striving to understand his or her cognitive deficits and to take control of his or her life in ways that allow him or her to overcome, bypass, or compensate for career and workplace problems and to strive for success. Next I talked about self-help books for individuals with LDs and ADHDs and what they offer in the way of advice and guidance. Following that, I presented material on a framework for the empirically based treatment of the workplace problems experienced by individuals with LDs and ADHDs. The framework derives from the strategies, techniques, and support programs used to provide an education, vocational training, and on-the-job supervision to young individuals in the process of making the transition from high school or college to work and from the psychotherapy done with older individuals with LDs and ADHDs experiencing workplace problems related to their cognitive deficits, particularly schema-focused cognitive therapy. First and foremost, the framework stresses the need for the provision of assistance, which I termed an Individual Transition Plan, for individuals with LDs and ADHDs by qualified professionals, including educators, mental health professionals, supervisors, and employers. The need to carefully formulate and maintain the interface between self-regulation, so necessary for personal empowerment, and co-regulation is the sine qua non of success in the workplace. No individual with an LD or an ADHD can be an island, especially in the workplace ocean.

I can envision a comprehensive decision tree for designing an Individual Transition Plan for a specific individual, based on his or her cognitive level, particular cognitive and academic deficits, age, pattern of emotional reactivity, financial and social support resources, and so forth, and a comprehensive set of manualized education and treatment materials to draw from for implementation of the plan. Of course, it will then be important to gather hard research data on whether individuals actually benefit from the plans and in what ways the plans can be improved.

References

Barkley, R. A., Murphy, K., & Kwasnik, D. (1996). Psychological adjustment and adaptive impairments in young adults with ADHD. *Journal of Attention Disorders, 1,* 41-54.

Brown, D. S. (2000). *Learning a living.* Bethesda, MD: Woodbine House.

Collins, J. M., & Griffin, R. W. (1998). The psychology of counterproductive job performance. In R. W. Griffin, A. O'Leary-Kelly, & J. M. Collins (Eds.), *Monographs in organizational behavior and relations, Vol. 23: Dysfunctional behavior in organizations: Non-violent dysfunctional behavior.* Stamford, CT: JAI.

Evers, R. B. (1996). The positive force of vocational education: Transition opportunities for youth with learning disabilities. *Journal of Learning Disabilities, 29,* 69-78.

Furqurean, J. M., Meisgeier, C., Swank, P. R., & Williams, R. E. (1991). Correlates of post-secondary employment outcomes for young adults with learning disabilities. *Journal of Learning Disabilities, 24,* 400-405.

Gerber, P. J., Ginsberg, R., & Reiff, H. B. (1992). Identifying alterable patterns in employment success for highly successful adults with learning disabilities. *Journal of Learning Disabilities, 25,* 475-487.

Goldstein, D. E., Murray, C., & Edgar, E. (1998). Employment earnings and hours of high school graduates with learning disabilities through the first decade after graduation. *Learning Disabilities Research and Practice, 13,* 53-64.

Greenbaum, B., Graham, S., & Scales, W. (1996). Adults with learning disabilities: Occupational and social status after college. *Journal of Learning Disabilities, 29,* 167-173.

Haring, K. A., Lovett, D. L., & Smith, D. D. (1990). A follow-up study of recent special education graduates of learning disabilities programs. *Journal of Learning Disabilities, 23,* 108-113.

Henderson, C. (1999). *College freshmen with disabilities: A biennial statistical profile.* Washington, DC: American Council on Education, HEATH Resource Center.

Jacobs, A. E., & Hendricks, D. J. (1992). Job accommodations for adults with learning disabilities. *Learning Disability Quarterly, 15,* 274-285.

Levine, P., & Nourse, S. W. (1998). What follow-up studies say about postschool life for young men and women with learning disabilities: A critical look at the literature. *Journal of Learning Disabilities, 31,* 212-233.

Mannuzza, S., Klein, R. G., Bessler, A., Malloy, P., & Hynes, M. (1997). Educational and occupational outcome of hyperactive boys grown up. *Journal of the American Academy of Child and Adolescent Psychiatry, 36,* 1222-1227.

Mannuzza, S., Klein, R. G., Bessler, A., Malloy, P., & LaPadula, M. (1993). Adult outcome of hyperactive boys. *Archives of General Psychiatry, 50,* 565-576.

Means, C. D., Stewart, S. L., & Dowler, D. L. (1997). Job accommodations that work: A follow-up study of adults with attention deficit disorder. *Journal of Applied Rehabilitation Counseling, 28,* 13-17.

Motowidlo, S. J., Borman, W. C., & Schmit, M. J. (1997). A theory of individual differences in task and contextual performance. *Human Performance, 10,* 71-83.

Murphy, K., & Barkley, R. A. (1996). Attention deficit hyperactivity disorder in adults: Comorbidities and adaptive impairments. *Comprehensive Psychiatry, 37,* 393-401.

Murray, C., Goldstein, D. E., & Edgar, E. (1997). The employment and engagement status of high school graduates with learning disabilities through the first decade after graduation. *Learning Disabilities Research and Practice, 12,* 151-160.

Nadeau, K.G. (1997). *ADD in the workplace: Choices, changes and challenges.* New York: Brunner/Mazel.

Neubert, D. A., Tilson, G. P., & Ianacone, R. N. (1989). Postsecondary transition needs and employment patterns of individuals with mild disabilities. *Exceptional Children, 55,* 494-500.

Ohler, D. L., Levinson, E. M., & Sanders, P. (1995). Career maturity in young with learning disabilities: What employment counselors should know. *Journal of Employment Counseling, 32,* 64-78.

Okolo, C. M. (1988). Instructional environments in secondary vocational education programs: Implications for LD adolescents. *Learning Disability Quarterly, 11,* I36-148.

Pennington, B. F. (1991). *Diagnosing learning disorders: A neuropsychological framework.* New York: Guilford.

Podsakoff, P. M., & MacKenzie, S. B. (1997). Impact of organizational citizenship behavior on organizational performance: A review and suggestions for future research. *Human Performance, 10,* 133-151.

Ratey, J. J., Hallowell, E., & Miller, A. (1997). Psychosocial issues and psychotherapy with adults with attention deficit disorder. *Psychiatric Annals, 27,* 582-587.

Reiff, H. B., Gerber, P., & Ginsberg, R. (1997). *Exceeding expectations: Successful adults with learning disabilities.* Austin, TX: PRO-ED.

Reisman, E., & Reisman, J. I. (1993). Supervision of employees with moderate special needs. *Journal of Learning Disabilities, 26,* 199-206.

Scuccimarra, D., & Speece, D. (1990). Employment outcomes and social integration of students with mild handicaps: The quality of life two years after high school. *Journal of Learning Disabilities, 23,* 213-219.

Silver, L. B. (2000). Attention-deficit/hyperactivity disorder in adult life. *Child and Adolescent Clinics of North America, 9,* 511-523.

Sitlington, P. L., Frank, A. R., & Carson, R. (1992). Adult adjustment among high school graduates with mild disabilities. *Exceptional Children, 59,* 221-233.

Sitlington, P. L., Frank, A. R., & Carson, R. (1994). Postsecondary vocational education—Does it really make a difference? *Issues in Special Education and Rehabilitation, 9,* 89-100.

Skelton, J., & Moore, M. (1999). The role of self-efficacy in work for people with learning difficulties. *Community, Work and Family, 2,* 133-145.

Van Dyne, L., Cummings, L. L., & Parks, J. M. (1995). Extra-role behaviors: In pursuit of construct and definitional clarity (a bridge over muddied waters). *Research in Organizational Behavior, 17,* 215-285.

Weiss, G., & Hechtman, L. T. (1993). *Hyperactive children grown up* (2nd ed.). New York: Guilford.

Wyld, D. C. (1997). Attention deficit/hyperactivity disorder in adults: Will this be the greatest challenge for employment discrimination law? *Employee Responsibilities and Rights Journal, 10,* 103-125.

Young, J. E. (1999). *Cognitive therapy for personality disorders: A schema-focused approach.* Sarasota, FL: Professional Resource Press.

14

Traumatic Brain Injury

CHARLES J. GOLDEN AND ZARABETH L. GOLDEN
Nova Southeastern University

DESCRIPTION OF THE DISORDER

Traumatic brain injury (TBI), also referred to as head injury or acquired brain injury, is a dysfunction of the brain that results from a physical force outside of the individual that causes an alteration in the way the brain functions at a structural, biochemical, or behavioral level. These changes will result in a diminished or altered state of consciousness, disturbances of behavior, emotional problems such as irritability or depression, or specific cognitive deficits. The most common mechanism for TBI is to hit the skull with a large force whose shockwaves are transmitted through the skull to the brain itself, causing lasting or temporary damage (C. J. Golden, Zillmer, & Spiers, 1992).

Symptoms may include a wide range of problems that differ in intensity and duration depending on the injury and the individual. These deficits can include short-term memory loss, long-term memory loss, slowed ability to process information, trouble concentrating or paying attention over sustained periods of time, difficulty keeping up with a conversation, word-finding problems, problems in understanding language, loss of a second (acquired) language, spatial disorientation, driving difficulties, impulsivity, inflexibility, time disorientation, organizational problems, impaired judgment, problems doing more than one thing at a time, seizures, muscle spasticity, double vision, impaired visual fields, loss of smell or taste, slow or slurred speech, headaches or migraines, fatigue, a lack of initiating activities, difficulty completing tasks without reminders, increased anxiety, depression and mood swings, denial of deficits, impulsive behavior, lack of insight, agitation, egocentricity (inability to see how behaviors affect others), explosive behavior, erratic behavior, sensory losses, inability to deal with novel or new material, and impairment in reading, writing, or arithmetic.

In all cases of TBI, there is a physical alteration of the brain. However, this alteration may not be evident on standard neurological tests (CT scan, MRI, X-rays, SPECT, PET, physical examination). In other cases, TBI is accompanied by other serious injuries (back injuries, chest injuries, broken bones, respiratory problems) that may cause the TBI to be missed. Although TBI is due to a physical change in the brain, the head does not need to be affected by any object for a TBI to occur. It can be caused by sudden acceleration or deceleration (such as an accident in which a car is stopped by a wall but the head is not affected but rather slams against the inside of the skull because of inertia).

Most cases of TBI are classified as concussions. In such cases there is no loss of consciousness or the length of unconsciousness is usually less than thirty minutes. Symptoms from a concussion may last only minutes but can stretch in some individuals up to three months. More serious cases of TBI are labeled as contusions. In such cases there is bruising or bleeding in the brain itself. Deficits from contusions may be permanent although in many cases the brain "reorganizes" so that long-term symptoms are not apparent. More serious contusions, which produce definite evidence of focal injuries in a specific area of the brain, often are called lacerations.

In milder head injuries, problems may arise from what has been labeled a diffuse axonal injury (DAI). DAI occurs when there is a sudden change in the acceleration of the brain, usually from sudden stops. In such cases, rate of slowing is different for the cortex (outside of the brain) and the deep structures within the brain. This difference in rates causes the cortex to pull away from the deeper structures, causing stretching, ripping, or tearing of the axons that connect these structures together. The stretching causes the axons to break or tear. Because axons are responsible for the communication between different areas of the brain, such breaks or tears cause an impairment of communication in the brain resulting in problems in attention, focusing, emotions, and cognitive skills. DAI may occur whether or not there is a physical blow to the head.

There are other conditions that result in complications of TBI. The most common is when the skull is fractured. In such cases a piece of the skull or a foreign object (such as a bullet) may pierce the brain, causing destruction of brain tissue. Interestingly, in some cases where the skull is fractured but the brain is not pierced, the overall injury may be less because the skull absorbs the impact of the injury to a greater degree than when the skull is intact. In cases when the skull is penetrated, veins and arteries within the brain may be torn causing the release of blood into the brain. In other cases, the force of a blow may cause a weak spot in an artery or vein to rupture, again resulting in the release of blood into brain tissue. Blood is toxic to the brain, so such cases result in the death of neurons, which process the messages within the brain.

Another major complication is edema. Edema represents swelling of the brain, which is the result of the blow to the brain, much as swelling occurs when an ankle or knee is struck with a significant force. However, unlike the knee or ankle, swelling within the brain occurs within a closed contained vessel (the skull). Thus swelling causes pressure to build up in the brain. Such pressure may act to cause brain tissue to compress, causing injury to the brain calls called neurons. In other cases, the buildup of pressure may result in the closing off of arteries providing blood to the brain, much as flow in a hose is cut off if enough pressure is applied to the hose. This will result in hypoxia, which is the loss of adequate oxygenation to the brain cells, or anoxia, which is the complete loss of oxygen to the neurons. These conditions result in neuronal injury or death, depending on how long the condition persists and how serious it is. It is not unusual to see cases of TBI in which the person seems normal at first only to go into a coma later as the result of building pressure in the brain. Increases of pressure within the brain may impair blood flow, much as water through a hose is restricted when one pinches on the hose. This can result in partial (hypoxia) or total (anoxia) loss of oxygen and nutrients to specific parts of the brain, resulting in neuronal damage or death.

MANIFESTATIONS

Manifestations of head injury in the workplace take several forms. In more serious cases, there are obvious alterations of physical abilities including paralysis or loss of the ability to speak, which most often preclude return to work at all. In some of these severe cases, there can be a partial return to work, which usually occurs with major revisions of job responsibilities and hours. These cases are usually worked out in conjunction with rehabilitation settings and are not the emphasis of this chapter.

Much more common are the effects of more subtle or milder cases of head injury. In these cases, motor skills and motor speech appear to be within normal limits although those who knew the worker well may note mild changes. The major changes of importance lie in the area of cognition and personality. Cognitively, the individual may think in a slower or more concrete manner. They may have more difficulty with solving problems, especially those that they have not encountered before. Problem solving for routine difficulties with which they are familiar are generally not a challenge. Jobs that are routine and repetitive, which were well performed before the injury, are least likely to be affected.

Situations that require new ways of doing things or adapting old ways will be more of a difficulty. Such workers may appear adequate in most situations, with the problems arising only when a novel circumstance arises that they must solve on their own. Such workers will do better when someone else is there to give advice on changes but they still may have trouble adapting, falling back into old routines easily even when they are not appropriate.

For higher level jobs, abstract thinking may be affected. This is serious when the job requires the worker to make subtle distinctions between different circumstances and when the worker has a large number of alternative procedures to choose between when dealing with an issue. Managers, customer service workers, problem solvers, and supervisors are especially affected by these abstract problems. They will fail to discriminate between situations that require different responses, unable to recognize subtle individual differences in a timely manner.

Personality problems take a wide range of expressions, but the major problems reported by employers are irritability, a loss of motivation, inability to tolerate stress, depression, and anxiety. These problems often can be much harder to deal with than cognitive problems. Individuals' irritability can arise from multiple sources: frustration at themselves for not being able to do things they expect they can do, frustration at others for what they see as inappropriate demands, and a general loss of self-control. In the first two cases, the demands of work are too much for the individual as a result of cognitive losses and the individual is aware of his or her failure or is in denial. In the last case, the individual may simply be expressing feelings that previously existed but that were (wisely) not expressed openly. When impulse control is lost, these feelings and ideas may simply tumble out without any editing or control.

Loss of motivation comes from higher level losses that may reflect a change in attitude characterized by less ambition or by an apparent inability or refusal to see that work quality is inadequate. In the first case, injuries simply result in a loss of the impulse to do well. The individual's attitude becomes more immature and more oriented toward the "here and now" rather than working for the future or for future goals. Traditional motivators such as a paycheck or praise may fail to work, and punishments are more likely to generate a feeling that work is unfair rather than to motivate better work.

In the second case, the individuals may lose the cognitive ability to evaluate the quality of their own work. They may not lack the desire to do well, but they are unable to see that the work they are doing is poor. This is often referred to as a loss of evaluative skills. Corrections for their errors may lead to irritation that the demands being made are unfair and aimed at them because of their disability. Workers may see behavior as discriminatory, which is a growing area because of federal and state laws regarding accommodations.

EPIDEMIOLOGY

An estimated 5.3 million Americans—a little more than 2 percent of the U.S. population—currently live with disabilities resulting from brain injury. These individuals, however, may not be aware of their condition, may be in denial about their condition, or may fail to report their condition. About 1 million people in the United States are treated for TBI and released from hospital emergency rooms every year. In many cases, they are released the same day without recognition of the long-term seriousness of their condition, thus returning to work too early and without awareness of the safety and functional impact of their disability.

Each year, eighty thousand Americans experience the onset of long-term disability following TBI. Motor vehicle crashes are the leading cause of brain injury. They account for 50 percent of all TBIs. Crashes involving smaller cars and motorcycles are typically most serious. Younger people, especially males, are most likely to get a head injury from a motor vehicle accident, but the impact of such injuries are often more serious in the elderly whose brains are more vulnerable to injury as the result of the natural changes associated with aging as well as the impact of such illnesses as high blood pressure, high cholesterol, arteriosclerosis, diabetes, and breathing difficulties. Falls are the second leading cause and are most common among the elderly. The overall risk of TBI is highest among adolescents, young adults, and those older than 65 years.

Individuals may appear to recover from an initial brain injury. However, such individuals are much more likely to have a second injury. After two brain injuries, the risk for a third injury is eight times greater than normal. The cost of TBI in the United States is estimated to be $48.3 billion annually. Hospitalization accounts for $31.7 billion, and fatal brain injuries cost the nation $16.6 billion each year, resulting in substantially higher costs for medical insurance. The cost to the workplace in terms of lost days, impaired level of work, additional accidents, poor decisions and judgment, and shoddy work has never been calculated but is likely in the billions as well. All employees, no matter what their age or gender or background, are at risk for head trauma. Such accidents may occur in the workplace (especially falls and accidents by employees who drive as part of the job) but often occur outside of the workplace as well. Outcome of TBI cases will depend on how quickly help is provided for the victim. Complications such as edema develop over time so effective early treatment may prevent otherwise serious long-term problems.

CASE ILLUSTRATIONS

Case 1

AK was a successful executive with a major telecommunications company. He had been a middle-level manager and had been recently promoted to a higher level job. As a result of drinking at a celebration party for the promotion with co-workers, he was in an automobile accident in which he hit his head on the windshield and was unconscious for approximately one hour. He was taken to the hospital where he stayed for three days. He appeared to be fully recovered with no evident motor or sensory difficulties. He was able to communicate without any apparent difficulties. On the basis of the medical reports, he returned to work one week after the accident.

In his new job, he seemed to do as expected but over the course of the first month a pattern of deficits emerged. He was having difficulty dealing with direct personnel issues in which he was expected to counsel and advise people under him who were having difficulties with job performance. He seemed uncharacteristically short tempered and irritable with co-workers. He had difficulty adjusting when "crisis" situations arose which he was expected to handle, despite a history of doing well in such situations in the past. When he yelled at a superior after a confrontation about his performance, he was referred for a neuropsychological evaluation.

The comprehensive evaluation revealed that the client was showing symptoms of problems dealing with ambiguity and problems dealing with abstractions. While he did very well on routine tasks and tasks that were clearly and concretely described in terms of expectations, he did poorly with tasks in which he had to figure out what to do based on limited feedback or that required him to figure out rules for solving complex situations, both verbally and nonverbally. He was depressed and angry, alternately blaming himself for handling situations badly and others for expecting him to do things that he saw as impossible. While he recognized he was not doing well, his insight as to why this occurred was very limited. He denied any connection between his head injury and the problems he was having.

The findings were consistent with a mild head injury affecting higher level functions, impairing his ability to deal with the demands of his new position. He was unable to adapt well and was likely to overreact with frustration and anger.

Given that his long-term functioning and his ability to do well with situations that he understood well, the evaluators suggested that rather than stress him with the demands of a new position that he be allowed to return to his former position to see if he could do better. When this was attempted, his level of performance improved considerably. He was much more comfortable with the demands of his old job and was able to return to the routine that he had previously established. While he still had problems with unusual situations and demands, these were much more rare in the lower level management position. A system was set up with his supervisor so that he would be available to help when such situations occurred, at the instigation of either the client or the supervisor. With this additional supervision, the client was able to maintain himself in his old position and he gradually improved over a period of nine months so that problems were rare.

At this point, the employer decided that the client had returned to normal and offered him the promotion he had previously been granted. When this occurred, the same problems reappeared and another neuropsychological evaluation was eventually requested. The same problems the evaluators had previously identified were seen again. It was clear that while the client was able to settle back into the job that he knew well, his ability to learn new material and adapt was still impaired, although this was not evident when the job was one that was overlearned and routine. Interestingly, this time the employer balked at returning the client to the former job and insisted he stay in the new position or take medical retirement at full retirement pay. As the client was sixty-three, he decided to take the full retirement rather than continue to stress himself at a job he was unable to do.

This case illustrates several important points. First, the deficits that arise from a head injury may be very subtle. A physician who does not know the client can easily miss such subtle symptoms, as most of the deficits are seen in people who are otherwise normal. What makes them deficits is the fact that they did not exist in the individual premorbidly. Thus, while there are undoubtedly immature people who cannot handle stress, the sudden appearance of such symptoms in a person who did not display such behavior points to a neuropsychological or psychological problem. Many of the behaviors displayed after subtle injury are not out of the range of what is possible in normal people but rather are out of the range of what is expected for a single individual.

While diagnosis that a head injury may have occurred is not difficult, the diagnosis of sequelae is therefore a much more significant problem. While many of these deficits could be identified in comprehensive neuropsychological testing, such testing in mild cases often is ordered only after there have been complaints from the family or co-workers. Thus, it is important that those close to the client observe the person for signs of changes in behavior that may be related to the injury. (It should be noted that in some cases these changes are not due to brain injury per se but rather by to the trauma of having a serious accident, including feelings of near-death or fear of serious injury.) If such changes are noted, then evaluations can be requested.

The case illustrates a common problem after a successful return to work. Employers reasonably like to reward employees with promotions or additional responsibilities. In the case of the client with a head injury, what appears to be recovery may simply be adaptation to an appropriate job situation. Placing the client in a new job situation may lead to the original symptoms again becoming more obvious. This may then require a new (longer than normal) period of adaptation in some cases or make it impossible for the client to succeed (as in this case). In many cases, as this one, the willingness of the employer to bend regular rules and procedures regarding promotion and expectations also plays a substantial role in whether a client becomes disabled or continues at work.

Case 2

ZX was a 22-year-old male mechanic who was injured in a one-car accident when his car left the road and hit a tree. He was unconscious for a period of two weeks. In addition to a severe injury, he suffered multiple broken bones and internal injuries, all of which healed well. He was treated initially in an acute hospital, then moved to an inpatient rehabilitation center, and finally to a community-based reintegration program for head-injured clients. He made an excellent physical recovery but continued to have serious cognitive problems. Interestingly, because he was unaware of his problems because of his cognitive deficits, he was relatively pleasant and seemingly unaware that he was not performing at his prior level. As a result, he was rarely frustrated and showed few signs of irritability and anger. After he had reestablished all his basic living skills (dressing himself, basic home care, meal preparation, etc.), which took one year, his former employer was contacted regarding devising a job he could return to.

It was evident that he was unable to continue as a general mechanic, as he needed a fixed routine that required relatively few decisions on his own. With the cooperation of the owner of the firm he worked for, it was decided that he could return with the job of placing new tires on cars. He began at work initially two hours a day with a job coach to ensure that the work was done correctly. He had known how to replace tires since he was a young teenager, so the skills came back to him readily. He had more difficulty with recognizing the need for speed and the need to stick to task. With the help of the job coach, these skills were developed and his workday was extended one hour at a time until he was working a full workweek.

At this point, it was evident that there was not enough business in replacing tires for him to keep busy for 40 hours. Again, working with a job coach, he began training on another task he had done well: replacing brake pads. With the aid of the job coach, he learned these tasks well. He eventually was able to "fade out" the job coach and continue to work on his own. Follow-ups a year later showed that he had continued successfully at work.

This case illustrates the impact of a more severe brain injury. The use of a job coach or mentor is often important in these cases to ensure that the job is initially learned and done correctly without unduly affecting the employer. With cooperation, the individual can be phased back into an old job or learn an appropriate new job. Such workers can become very productive although they may be unable to do the specific job or all the duties they once were able to do.

RECOGNIZING AND EVALUATING HEAD TRAUMA

The assessment of TBI is a difficult and complex process. This arises from several factors: symptoms are not always evident to casual interaction with the client, neurological tests are relatively insensitive to mild and moderate instances of brain injury, and patients may be unable or unwilling to report the symptoms that they have because of either a lack of awareness (called neglect) or a need to appear strong and not complain about "minor" symptoms (seen more often in young men.) While cases with mild or moderate injury are more difficult to identify, it is these individuals who most likely to return to work and cause problems in the workplace.

In nearly all cases, the employer or co-workers are aware that an accident has occurred, as people are usually quite willing to relate stories of auto accidents or falls from mountains. In more complex cases, professionals and those who knew the person previously can immediately and easily recognize the severity of the problems, which can include paralysis, loss of memory, loss of language skills, slowness of thinking, disorientation, confusion, and other similar problems.

In more subtle cases, the problems become apparent only after observation of the client in the work setting or at home. It is important for an employer to be observant of the returning employee initially, as workers will return before they are fully recovered either because of lack of insight, denial, lack of awareness, a desire to return to work, a fear of losing their job, or other pressure from a spouse or the employer. This observation should focus on changes in the employees' work abilities and performance. These changes can be more diagnostically accurate and useful than any neurological or neuropsychological test (Sachs & Redd, 1993).

Such observations should be done by a supervisor familiar with the individual's level of performance. If it is discovered or suspected that the client cannot properly return to work because of cognitive or emotional reasons, further neurological and neuropsychological evaluation is indicated. (It should be noted that in many cases of suspected TBI there also might be ancillary physical injuries that can cause pain, slowness, emotional reactivity, and poor performance, which are not related in any way to head injury.) The impact of a brain injury may be in almost any area, so the key issue is change from previous levels of functioning after the injury rather than any specific sign or symptom.

REFERRAL STRATEGIES

In most every case, an individual with a head injury has at least seen a physician previously, although this may not always be true in the milder injuries. Unlike other neuropsychiatric disorders, where workers may see the referral as an insult ("You think I am crazy!"), referral for the effects of head injury are better accepted. One can approach the worker and express concern for the effects of the accident and suggest the need to see the doctor to make sure "everything is OK." When possible, the doctor or physician should receive a call or letter specifying the specific problems that the client is having, as the problems may not be evident on a physical exam and may not be reported by the client.

If a physical evaluation yields nothing, then there is a need for a neuropsychological evaluation. This may generate more resistance (the word *psychological* raises fears, especially when the client is unaware of the problems). Neuropsychologists can provide comprehensive cognitive and personality evaluations that focus on the specific problems seen in the work setting. The evaluation is most helpful when the employer provides a detailed list of what the client should be doing on the job and the changes in performance that have arisen since the accident. Many of these exams are less useful than they can be because the neuropsychologist works in a vacuum where information comes solely from the client and consequently does not understand the workplace demands or performance problems.

Clients who return to work but have problems should be treated as if they have an illness with time off for medical leave or reduced duties based on communication between the employer and the worker until the examinations are concluded. This is a tricky process for many clients when they fail to recognize or admit their own problems. This is discussed in more detail in the section on treatment considerations.

WORKPLACE OR HOME STRESSORS

While disorders such as depression can be triggered by events at work, head traumas are not the result of work (or home) pressures but rather are the end result of a traumatic injury. However, the symptoms of head injury will become more evident when work or home places emphasis on those cognitive or personality areas that highlight the client's weaknesses, which can lead to depression, anxiety, a sense of failure, irritability, and anger as a result of the client being forced to acknowledge problems. Indeed, avoiding such situations is a central aspect of successful return to work, as illustrated in the case examples. This is discussed in more detail in the section on treatments.

TREATMENTS

Treatments and intervention can be divided into two areas: (1) those that are done outside the workplace and require nothing other than time off and flexible scheduling, and (2) those that reflect changes in the workplace that accommodate the deficits seen in the client. Although the traditional emphasis has always been on those treatments done outside the workplace, which are focused immediately after an injury, the ability to return to work often depends more on the long-term changes that are addressed under the workplace accommodations.

External Changes

Medication

Many patients with TBI will be given medications (Perna, Bordini, & Newman, 2001; Zasler, 1997). These medications fall into several classes: seizure medication, pain medication, medication for fatigue or alertness, and medication for psychiatric symptoms. Medication monitoring is very important because the damaged brain may not react to these drugs as expected, as the drugs are from models based on normal individuals (Bleecker & Hansen, 1994).

Time element. Medications often start at the time of injury and are added as symptoms become clear. Physicians may prescribe seizure medication as a prophylaxis even in the absence of any overt seizures. Such medication may be continued for 3 to 12 months depending on the physician's judgment if no seizures occur. If they do occur, treatment may be for long periods of time depending on the course of the disorder.

Pain medications are a particularly challenging area. TBI patients may complain of headaches that may or may not be related directly to the brain injury. In many cases the pains is due to injuries to the neck, back, or scalp area rather than to the brain. The length of use of these medications is related to the time of the persistence of the pain problems, which is often indeterminate. Another relevant issue is the presence of hysterical or psychosomatic pain that is related to the client's anxiety and depression rather than to an actual physical pain. Head injury clients may prefer to complain of pain rather than of an inability to move or of confusion. It is essential that pain medications not be used to treat psychiatric problems because of the pain medication's potential side effects on cognition and arousal, so detailed psychiatric and physical evaluations often are necessary in determining the proper course. When this does not occur, patients may become psychologically addicted to the pain medication as a method of handling their psychological problems.

Medications for arousal problems may be helpful in cases when the client shows low attentional abilities or excessive fatigue. As with the other medications, time course is indeterminate. Medication for associated psychiatric symptoms typically do not begin unless the client or others complain of depression, anxiety, anger, or other psychiatric disorders. Time course is also indeterminate in these disorders.

Side effects of medication. Side effects are a major problem with each of these classes of medication in the workplace. It is important that the employer be aware of side effects and that this information be made available to the employee, his or her family, and his or her physician. (This is unfortunately rarely done in an organized and effective fashion.) The most common side effects of all of these medications are fatigue, loss of concentration and attention, memory problems, and slowness. It should be noted that each of these side effects is similar to the symptoms of the TBI itself. This should not be surprising, as the medication may impair the brain just as the TBI does and the effects are in similar areas of the brain. Balancing the positive and negative effects of medication in this population is difficult and is complicated by frequent atypical responses to medication caused by the disrupted brain neuro-chemistry that arises from the head trauma.

These side effects will clearly have an impact on work much as the original symptoms do. In some cases, because of overreaction by the employee's brain, these symptoms may be worse than the TBI symptoms. The employer should alert the physician to these effects, as they may be modified or eliminated by changing doses of medication or changing the medication itself. The employer should be alert to signs of psychological or physical dependence on the medications as well, especially many of the pain medications.

Physical and Occupational Therapy

In cases when the TBI is accompanied by motor deficits, either physical or occupational therapy or both may be necessary. Physical therapy traditionally deals with gross motor impairment, while occupational therapy deals with fine motor impairment such as writing or putting things together. Either therapy can have major impacts on jobs the client is able to complete successfully.

Time element. These therapies typically start soon after the TBI and last anywhere from three to twelve months (although longer periods of treatment are possible.) The length of treatment depends on the severity and recovery rate of any motor impairment.

Speech Therapy

Speech therapy deals with impairment in the understanding or expression of speech. Such therapy is very rarely needed in mild TBI, but is more common in moderate and severe TBI.

Time element. This therapy typically starts soon after the TBI and last anywhere from 3 to 12 months (although longer periods of treatment are possible). The length of treatment depends on the severity and recovery rate of any speech impairment.

Side effects. There are no serious side effects to this treatment.

Cognitive Therapy

Cognitive therapy deals with changes in the worker's memory, concentration, attention, judgment, insight, reasoning, visual-spatial, achievement, and abstract skills. This therapy may be given in conjunction with occupational or speech therapy or may come from a separate cognitive therapist. It may be one-to-one therapy or may involve computerized training (Glisky, 1992; Glisky & Schacter, 1988; Kreutzer & Wehman, 1991; Wehman, 1991; Wehman, Kreutzer, Sale, & West, 1989). Computerized training works best with basic, fundamental skills (visual recognition or rote memory) and less well with higher level skills such as judgment or abstractive skills or creativity.

Time element. This therapy typically starts soon after the TBI and last anywhere from 3 to 12 months (although longer periods of treatment are possible). The length of treatment depends on the severity and recovery rate of any cognitive impairment.

Psychological Therapy

Psychological therapy addresses both the emotional impact of the organic injury as well as the adjustment of the client to the injury. This is particularly important, as clients may develop anxiety, depression, anger, and paranoia toward the employer or insurance company as a reaction to their injury. Early therapy and monitoring can eliminate or at least reduce the seriousness of these symptoms.

In cases of severe injuries, clients must be taught to accept their deficits and find ways to work around them. Injuries may be responded to in much the same way one responds to the death or loss of a loved one. Indeed, some TBI survivors will speak of the death of the person they used to be. As in other grief reactions, the individual often goes through five stages: denial, anger, bargaining, depression, and acceptance. Many individuals who could return to work successfully get stuck at the earlier stages. Such individuals never reach the level of acceptance that allows them to get on with their life successfully, often because they receive no counseling or support. In some cases, therapy is denied because clinicians believe the problems are organic, a result of brain damage rather than emotional, or a result of the reaction to the damage or, even worse, clinicians provide therapy that emphasizes the organic etiology, making the patient essentially helpless to do anything for him- or herself. However, in most cases the emotional issues are as important or more important than organic changes in emotional status. (Golden & Golden, 2003). An essential issue is for the clients to reach acceptance and to take responsibility for their behavior and for making their lives better. Clients who simply blame their problems on the head injury but take no responsibility for their problems generally do poorly.

Another important aspect of psychological intervention early on is to make the client with mild head injury aware of what deficits and problems are expected after a head injury. They need to be told that it is normal for them to feel fatigue, to want to sleep more, to have some difficulty concentrating, to be irritable, to be afraid of the situation in which they were injured, and to have difficulties trying to do more than one thing at a time or dealing with groups of people. These deficits and the general course of the deficits should be explained in detail: that many people feel better in just a few days and almost everyone recovers within 3 to 6 months at the longest. They also should be told to return cautiously to their day-to-day activities and not to overdo it at first, just as if they had the flu or some other more easily seen medical disorder. It is equally useful for the employer to become aware of what problems that a given individual has so as to handle them in a way that maximizes work productivity and minimizes emotional reactions to failure.

Time element. This therapy typically starts soon after the TBI and last anywhere from 3 to 12 months (although longer periods of treatment are possible). The length of treatment depends on the severity and recovery rate of psychological problems.

Workplace Accommodations

An integral part of many treatments is accommodations by the workplace to the TBI. These accommodations allow the worker to return to productive work as early as possible and show that the employer is supportive of the injured worker. This is especially important in the many cases of TBI that occur from work-related injuries or on the way to or from work. Inflexibility on the part of the employer often will result in anger that further deepens the client's condition and creates a sense of entitlement in the worker. These accommodations take many forms, and they may last from a few weeks to months to years depending on the seriousness of the injuries. In many cases, the response of the workplace often can be the difference between an individual returning to productive work or ending up disabled. These accommodations may include workplace modifications as well as the use of assistive devices (Bricout, 1999; Gale & Christie, 1987; Michaels & Risucci, 1993; Warren, 2000; West, 1995).

Initial Return to Work

There is a tendency for clients to return to work too soon after a head injury. In the cases of subtle injuries, clients may be released from the hospital emergency room the same day or after a very short period. Because they are released, they feel compelled to return immediately to work because of economic reasons and employer pressures. They also may be in denial about the presence or extent of any problems they may have. Such clients, however, may not be ready to return: they may have mild concentration problems, attentional problems, fatigue, irritability, interpersonal problems, and impaired judgment. These problems may last in most cases from a few days to a few months, with 90 percent of the individuals returning to normal within 6 months or often less.

Problems arise when too many demands are placed on the employee by the employer or by the employee himself or herself. These demands highlight the employee's temporary symptoms, causing the employee to focus on these changes and also may result in negative feedback from co-workers and supervisors. This in turn leads to what Goldstein (1939) called a "catastrophic reaction," one in which the client overreacts to the magnitude of the deficits and becomes convinced that he or she has a serious and lasting deficit. This leads to depression and anxiety and a sense of failure that in turns leads to additional fatigue, attentional problems, irritability, and poor judgment, resulting in a "biopsychosocial circle" in which the psychiatric reaction magnifies the neurological symptoms. Over time, the symptoms due to the brain injury and those due to the psychiatric component become so intertwined that one cannot be separated from the other.

This catastrophic reaction is not caused by the severity of the injuries. Golden and Golden (in press) found that this reaction was more likely to occur in those with mild to moderate injuries rather than in those with severe injuries. This occurrence may be due to the fact that those with severe injuries are less aware of their problems or that they are accommodated more readily because their symptoms are obvious. In the milder injuries, clients are more aware of their problems, but others are less likely to notice the changes and the clients are less likely to be offered helped. (A similar problem may be seen in mild to moderate pain disorders where the existence of the pain disorder is difficult to establish objectively, as is the case with mild brain injury.) The failure of home and work to recognize that there may be problems from the TBI is a key factor in setting off this reaction.

The proper response from an employer to this situation lies in two areas. One is determining when someone should return to work, and the second deals with what duties the person should have when they return. Unfortunately, there is no single answer to these questions, with each case needing individualized decision making. However, we can describe some general guidelines.

In terms of if the employee should return to work, two issues arise: when is the client physically and mentally ready to return, and when it will be most useful for his or her recovery to return. In more serious injuries, physicians and other treatment providers will generally provide the answer for when the client is ready. However, such decisions often are made incorrectly for several reasons. First, there is a tendency to ignore deficits that cannot be objectively determined or measured by a physical test. Many of the problems arising from head injury fall into this group, resulting in clients' returning to work too soon. On the other extreme, physicians may fail to realize the importance of returning to work for the self-esteem of the individual, leading them to keep the patient at home until he or she is more fully recovered. Unfortunately, after head injury, this inability to return to some productive work can cause secondary psychiatric problems, as discussed previously.

For the employer, the best thing to do is to be in communication with the worker regarding his or her recovery. Placing pressure on the worker to return before he or she is ready or cleared should never be done, as this routinely leads to disaster. While most patients need a few days off to rest and recover even in a mild injury, they may be able to return in a short time but not as a full-time employee. Employer policies that do not allow part-time return or punish part-time returning patients economically are potentially very detrimental in these cases. Policies that offer clients only full disability or part-time pay are detrimental to recovery, while those that offer the same pay whether the employee is disabled or has partially returned to work are better. Once the worker indicates a readiness to return and is cleared medically then the actual reintegration of the worker can begin. It should be noted that policies that allow part-time return to limited work will allow a physician to clear a worker at an earlier date when there is a concern.

Once the worker is medically cleared, gradual return to work is the ideal situation if it can be arranged. Such gradual return may lead rapidly to full-time work in several days or a week in some cases but in other cases it may be months or never if the injuries are severe enough. Once the worker is cleared, he or she should be encouraged to come in for a half day and be observed by the supervisor to see how the employee performs across the full range of required job skills. The purpose of the observation must clearly be in the roll of a job coach, someone who aids the injured worker rather than criticizes or complains or interferes when it is unnecessary. Such individuals must be patient and recognize the impact to self-esteem when someone is unable to do something he or she could previously accomplish. If all goes well, time at work can be expanded rapidly to full time.

The issue is clearly more complicated when things do not go easily or as expected. In such cases, the employer should be sensitive to the problems that are present and work with the employee to modify the job temporarily as the worker recovers. This should be an active process in which the employer and employee negotiate such issues as hours, days per week, and duties based on the mutual best interest of both parties. This often is best accomplished with a neutral mediator who understands head injuries and works out a solution with both parties. Allowing active involvement with the client and showing concern for the worker's welfare generally results in much better long-term results, while making decisions by fiat or by hard and fast rules risk a catastrophic reaction.

In cases of milder injuries, return to completely normal work occurs within 1 week to 3 months, with 95 percent recovery by 6 months. In a small percentage of the mild cases and a larger percentage of moderate and severe injuries, some workplace changes are necessary on a permanent basis. These changes must be negotiated on an individual basis but include accommodation to physical impairment, shorter work hours, limited workweek, change in responsibilities, change in expectations, reduction of stressful interpersonal situations, reductions of judgment decisions, increased routine and structure, and specific alterations in tasks consistent with specific cognitive deficits.

RELAPSE PREVENTION

Unlike many other mental health disorders, relapse is unlikely unless another TBI occurs, although those who have had one TBI are generally at higher risk to react poorly to a second TBI. However, there are several errors that can be made by the employer that can cause regression in behavioral symptoms that should be discussed.

The foremost problem is after finding a job that the employee is able to do after TBI (whether this is a former job or a modified job), the employer chooses to switch the employee to another job either as a reward for good work or because of work demands. The most long-lasting symptom after TBI is difficulty in learning new material. Thus, switching the client to a similar job may result in some initial problems but ones that can be worked out with patience or training.

However, switching the worker to an entirely new position may result in severe problems and even failure. While the employer does not need to avoid all such attempts nor is it advisable not to allow the worker to try a more difficult position, it is important to make it clear to the employee that he or she can return to the former (successful) job if the attempt fails. Flexibility becomes the key concept in working with TBI survivors. In those patients who do not have complete recovery, any new jobs may need to be modified in light of residual symptoms. Employers should carefully monitor changes, keeping in mind that recommendations from physicians or psychologists may not recognize the full extent of the client's problems in adapting to a new position or, on the other hand, may underestimate the potential of the client to learn new jobs.

A related problem is not listening to the worker's descriptions of problems. Patients with TBI are in some cases seen as whiners whose complaints are ignored unless there is hard medical evidence to support the employee's complaints. Unfortunately, not all of the symptoms reported by TBI survivors can be documented in a medical or even neuropsychological examination with any certainty. Demanding such proof in all cases is neither fair nor accurate. The employer and the employer's insurance company need to work with the employee and physician to reach reasonable accommodations and requirements. Failure to do this leads to multiple problems which make what would have been relatively simple cases extremely complex and in the long term very costly in human and economic terms.

Finally, because workers who have had one TBI are more likely to get another, sending employees back to dangerous jobs after an injury may not be the most effective response, both in terms of the safety of the employee and the liability of the employer. While in many cases this may not be a problem, careful consideration and consultation (involving the employee as well) must be included as part of the work assignment process. Failure to do so may lead to future, more serious problems.

THERAPEUTIC BENEFITS OF WORK

After a brain injury, individuals often suffer serious problems with self-esteem, depression, and anxiety because they feel they are no longer as effective or as smart or as useful as they once were. In many cases, roles within families change with spouses and children taking over more responsibility from the injured client. Similar things happen in the work setting, which routinely lead to exacerbation of these problems. Thus, the degree to which the individual can succeed at work is an extremely important factor in preventing this exacerbation and in building up and reestablishing the person's self-esteem. Just the process of being occupied at a job prevents clients from being preoccupied with their physical, cognitive, and personal losses and instead focuses them on productive work and what they can do.

As a result, work is seen as essential in getting the injured worker back to normal in an economic and psychological sense. The closer the current job can resemble the preinjury job, the easier it is for the TBI survivor to feel recovered. However, any level of work is clearly associated with better outcomes and better psychological health.

SUMMARY

TBI is a significant challenge to the workplace. TBIs are common in work settings and outside work and primarily are due to falls and motor vehicle accidents. However, while many TBI survivors may have residual symptoms, nearly all, except the most severe, remain employable on at least a part-time or modified job basis, with many able to return to their former positions without difficulty. Symptoms may include a wide range of problems that differ in intensity and duration depending on the injury and the individual. The deficits from TBI can include short-term memory loss, long-term memory loss, slowed ability to process information, trouble concentrating or paying attention over sustained periods of time, difficulty keeping up with a conversation, word-finding problems, problems in understanding language, loss of a second (acquired) language, spatial disorientation, driving difficulties, impulsivity, inflexibility, time disorientation, organizational problems, impaired judgement, problems doing more than one thing at a time, seizures, muscle spasticity, double vision, impaired visual fields, loss of smell or taste, slow or slurred speech, headaches or migraines, fatigue, a lack of initiating activities, difficulty completing tasks without reminders, increased anxiety, depression and mood swings, denial of deficits, impulsive behavior, lack of insight, agitation, egocentricity (inability to see how behaviors affect others), explosive behavior, erratic behavior, sensory losses, inability to deal with novel or new material, and impairment in reading, writing, or arithmetic.

The symptoms of mild TBI may be more evident in the workplace rather than in the emergency room, so the employer may be the first to notice many of the effects of these injuries. In most cases, careful handling of the worker will allow the worker to complete recovery while maintaining a reasonable work schedule. Coordination of accommodations with the worker's physician and neuropsychologist is important so that the worker does not have emotional blowups, failure at work, or further injuries because of work demands. Most cases, when handled properly, will improve within a six-month period or less. Therapies, which may need to be ongoing, may typically include physical therapy, occupational therapy, speech therapy, medication, seizure treatment, pain medication, psychotropic medication, cognitive therapy, psychological therapy, and workplace and job accommodations.

Unlike many other mental health disorders, relapse is unlikely unless another TBI occurs, although those who have had one TBI are generally at higher risk for a second TBI. However, there are several errors that can be made by the employer that can cause regression in behavioral symptoms that should be discussed. The foremost problem is after finding a job that the employee is able to do after TBI (whether this is the employee's former job or a modified job), the employer chooses to switch the employee to another job that puts stress on the worker's residual weaknesses. A related problem is not listening to the worker's descriptions of problems. Not all of the symptoms reported by TBI survivors can be documented in a medical or even neuropsychological examination with any certainty, so listening to the worker as well as making observations is essential. Finally, because workers who have had one TBI are more likely to get another, sending employees back to dangerous jobs after an injury may not be the most effective response. Careful consideration and consultation (involving the employee as well) must be included as part of the work assignment process.

References

Bleecker, M. L., & Hansen, J. A. (1994). *Occupational neurology and clinical neurotoxicology.* Baltimore: Williams & Wilkins.

Bricout, J. C. (1999). The relationship between employers' perceived organizational context and their impressions of the employability of job applicants with either a severe psychiatric or physical disability. *Dissertation Abstracts International, 60*(1-A), 247.

Gale, A., & Christie, B. (1987). *Psychophysiology and the electronic workplace.* New York: John Wiley.

Glisky, E. L. (1992). Computer-assisted instruction for patients with traumatic brain injury: Teaching of domain-specific knowledge. *Journal of Head Trauma Rehabilitation, 7*(3), 1-12.

Glisky, E. L., & Schacter, D. L. (1988). Acquisition of domain-specific knowledge in patients with organic memory disorders. *Journal of Learning Disabilities, 21*(6), 333-339, 351 .

Golden, C. J., Zillmer, E., & Spiers, M. (1992). *Neuropsychological diagnosis and intervention.* Springfield, IL: Charles C. Thomas.

Golden, Z., & Golden, C. (2003, August). *Impact of physical and neurological trauma on personality.* Paper presented at the annual meeting of the American Psychological Association, Toronto, Canada.

Golden, Z. L., & Golden, C. J. (in press). Impact of trauma severity on personality. *International Journal of Neuroscience.*

Goldstein, K. (1939). *The organism.* New York: Zone Books.

Kreutzer, J. S., & Wehman, P. H. (1991). *Cognitive rehabilitation for persons with traumatic brain injury: A functional approach.* Baltimore: Brookes.

Michaels, C. A., & Risucci, D. A. (1993). Employer and counselor perceptions of workplace accommodations for persons with traumatic brain injury. *Journal of Applied Rehabilitation Counseling, 24*(1), 38-46.

Perna, R. B., Bordini, E. J., & Newman, S. (2001). Pharmacological treatments considerations in brain injury. *Journal of Cognitive Rehabilitation, 19*(1), 4-7.

Sachs, P. R., & Redd, C. A. (1993). The Americans with Disabilities Act and individuals with neurological impairments. *Rehabilitation Psychology, 38*(2), 87-101.

Warren, C. G. (2000). Use of assistive technology in vocational rehabilitation of persons with traumatic brain injury. In R. Fraser & D. Clemmons (Eds.), *Traumatic brain injury rehabilitation: Practical vocational, neuropsychological, and psychotherapy intervention* (pp. 129-160). Boca Raton, FL: CRC Press.

Wehman, P. H. (1991). Cognitive rehabilitation in the workplace. In J. Kreutzer & P. H. Wehman (Eds.), *Cognitive rehabilitation for persons with traumatic brain injury: A functional approach* (pp. 269-288). Baltimore: Brookes.

Wehman, P., Kreutzer, J. S., Sale, P., & West, M. (1989). Cognitive impairment and remediation: Implications for employment following traumatic brain injury. *Journal of Head Trauma Rehabilitation, 4*(3), 66-75.

West, M. D. (1995). Aspects of the workplace and return to work for persons with brain injury in supported employment. *Brain Injury, 9*(3), 301-313.

Zasler, N. D. (1997). The role of medical rehabilitation in vocational reentry. *Journal of Head Trauma Rehabilitation, 12*(5), 42-56.

15

Social Skills Deficits

EILEEN GAMBRILL
University of California, Berkeley

A lack of effective social behavior has been implicated in a wide range of problems, including depression, antisocial aggressive behavior, and substance abuse. The role of anxiety and social skills deficits in interfering with effective social exchanges has long been recognized. For example, Wolpe (1958) considered effective social behavior to be related to well-being and emphasized the inhibiting role of anxiety and the role of effective social skills in decreasing anxiety. Effective social behavior avoids problematic situations or alters situations so that they are no longer problematic and at the same time offers a maximum of other positive consequences and a minimum of negative ones. Most work settings require social interaction, which may range from jobs in which employees are involved in almost continuous social interaction throughout the day to those requiring few social exchanges. Effective supervision requires a range of interpersonal skills, including offering feedback, handling emotional outbursts and complaints effectively, mediating conflicts, responding to criticism, making and refusing requests, and helping staff find solutions to work-related interpersonal dilemmas. Other skills include delegating responsibility, persisting in the face of resistance, persuading others, building consensus, conducting effective meetings, anticipating and removing obstacles to communication, handling difficult people, and offering clear instructions. Effective team participation also requires a variety of social skills for effective collaboration, including offering constructive feedback and providing reinforcement for creative ideas.

DESCRIPTION OF SOCIAL SKILLS DEFICITS AND WORKPLACE EXAMPLES

Even in jobs that require little social interaction, ineffective social skills may create problems. Social skills deficits are not a disorder, although they may contribute to consequences that are labeled as a disorder. Deficits in social skills may lead to a variety of problems, including those reflected in diagnostic categories described in the *Diagnostic and Statistical Manual of Mental Disorders-IV-TR* (APA, 2002). For example, lack of social skills in refusing unwanted requests may result in a feeling of having little control over one's work life, stress, and burnout, which may result in the employee being fired, leaving a job, or remaining in the job but not functioning well. Lack of effective social skills lies behind many problems in the workplace that affect work-related behaviors. Related skills include managing anger and anxiety in interpersonal exchanges; for example, avoiding excesses such as inappropriate display of anger that may escalate into violence (see e.g., Gardner & Martinko, 1998). Opportunities are lost and unpleasant events tolerated because of ineffective social skills. A coveted promotion may be foregone because of an employee's inability to ask an employer for a higher position. Resentment and anger may accumulate, until finally one more precipitating event sets off an inappropriately strong reaction. Behavior that reduces anxiety, disappointment, or anger may occur, such as drinking, social isolation, or excessive attention to physical symptoms. Lack of effective social skills in responding to harassment may prolong such negative events. Many social skills of value in maintaining positive relationships with friends and partners and dealing with strangers come into play in work situations. These skills include basic greeting behaviors, initiating and ending conversations, requesting favors, refusing requests, offering corrective feedback, and responding to criticism (e.g., Baron & Greenberg, 1990). Lack of effective social skills may result in emotional reactions that dampen the amount and creativity of work. Indeed it could be argued that the greater the need for creativity in one's job, the more damaging certain kinds of social skills deficits may be. For example if an employee is not able to refuse requests that intrude on his or her time, there will be less time available for a creative free flow of ideas that contribute to innovations. Kinds of social skills deficits that may influence work-related behaviors include behaviors that enable one to develop social support systems that may dampen stressors, social skills that allow one to control the flow of work, and skills that contribute to the quality of work.

EPIDEMIOLOGY

As discussed earlier, social skills deficits are not a disorder, although they may contribute to reactions that are labeled as a disorder. "Counterproductive work behaviors" range from product theft to hitting other people and trying to look busy when there is work to be done, being nasty or rude to a client or customer, and starting arguments with co-workers (Spector, 2001). Fox, Spector, & Miles (2001) suggest that some of these responses are directly related to work stress. Four personality characteristics that increase the likelihood of counterproductive work behaviors include trait anger and trait anxiety, which decrease the threshold for these reactions. Perceived lack of control and narcissism also have been found to be associated with counterproductive work behavior. "The narcissist is a person with an exaggerated sense of esteem with a fragile ego. In other words, he or she has an inflated opinion of himself or herself and is easily insulted or angered when someone challenges that view" (Spector, 2001, p. 9). Forty-two percent of a sample of 10,648 women working for the federal government in 1988 said they had been harassed (cited in Petrocelli & Repa, 1992, p. 4/37). These incidents involved unwanted sexual remarks (35 percent), leers and suggestive looks (28 percent), being touched (26 percent), being pressured to date and to provide sexual favors (15 percent and 9 percent, respectively), and rape or sexual assault (8 percent). The sources of the reported harassment were co-workers (41 percent), other employees (33 percent), and higher level (19 percent) or immediate (12 percent) superiors (see also NiCarthy, Gottlieb, & Coffman, 1993). Ineffective reactions to bullying at work may decrease work productivity (e.g., Einarsen, 2000).

The components of effective social behavior correspond to the ways in which things can go wrong (see Table 15.1). Both verbal and nonverbal behaviors are important in social behavior. *How* something is said may be more important than *what* is said. Goals, plans, and feedback are important. Behavior may be ineffective because people have inappropriate social goals in a situation or because they have not identified their goals. Their goals may be appropriate, but they may fail to make plans or make inappropriate plans. Effective plans require effective problem-solving skills, and include a clear description of the situation, a description of alternatives, and then choosing the best alternative, trying it out, evaluating the results, and changing what is done in similar situations in the future based on the outcomes of a plan. Social behavior may be ineffective because of lack of attention to feedback provided by others or distortion of feedback.

TABLE 16.1
Factors Related to Ineffective Social Behavior

Problem	Remedy
1. Lack of knowledge about social rules/norms	1. Acquire knowledge
2. Lack of needed skills	2. Acquire skills
3. Interfering behavior (aggressive reactions)	3. Replace with behaviors that result in more benefits and fewer costs
4. Inappropriate or inadequate stimulus control (e.g., skills are available but not used)	4. Develop effective stimulus control
5. Interfering emotional reactions (anxiety, anger)	5. Identify related factors (e.g., lack of skills or knowledge, taking things personally, fear of negative evaluation, unrealistic expectations) and make needed changes
6. Fear of negative evaluation	6. Decrease sensitivity to social disapproval
7. Unrealistic performance standards	7. Moderate standards, identify unrealistic expectations (e.g., "I must please everyone") and replace them with realistic ones (e.g., "I can't please everyone")
8. Lack of respect for others	8. Increase empathy for others
9. A focus on "winning"	9. Focus on shared goals (e.g., to help clients)
10. Few settings that encourage positive exchanges	10. Increase access to such settings
11. Dysfunctional agency culture	11. Rearrange contingencies

Note. From *Social Work Practice: A Critical Thinker's Guide* (p. 343), by E. Gambrill, 1997, New York: Oxford University Press. Adapted with permission.

Effective behavior is situationally specific; what will be effective in one situation may not be in another. Knowledge of norms concerning acceptable and unacceptable behavior in given situations is important and should contribute to effective social behavior. Different sources of influence may be successful in different situations. French and Raven (1959) suggested five sources of influence, including reward power (the ability to reward others), coercive power (the ability to punish others), expert power (others believe that you possess knowledge that is useful to them), referent power (influence based on people's liking you), and legitimate power (possessing influence to encourage others to comply because they believe they should). There are gender differences in what will be effective in different situations. Porter and Geis (1981) found that women who sit at the head of a table are not as likely as are men to be perceived as the leader of a group. Many situations require special skills—skills that are somewhat unique to that situation. For example, conducting an employment interview requires skills that are different from those involved in having an enjoyable social conversation. The ability to reward others is a key skill. People differ in how supportive they are of other people's behavior and how much they show liking rather than dislike of others. Other components of effective social behavior include self-presentation, the ability to take the role of others, and flexibility and creativity in drawing on social skills and combining old skills in new ways (e.g., Trower, 1982).

Social skill deficits on the part of supervisors are a major concern in the workplace. Many supervisors do not know how or do not believe in offering positive feedback for effective work behavior but rather just criticize their employees when they do something wrong. This punitive pattern of supervisory (and administrative) behavior may be related to a lack of social skills or lack of knowledge regarding the effectiveness of positive feedback compared with punishing feedback. One could have the social skills to give positive feedback but have a belief that employees "should know what to do" and not need (or deserve) such feedback. Excessive concern about disagreeing with others or raising important but unpopular points may create anxiety, which prevents these behaviors from occurring or hinders the effectiveness with which they are expressed. For example, "groupthink" (Janis, 1982) may go unchallenged in team meetings because of social skill deficits. Thus social skills deficits may result in a variety of undesired consequences, as illustrated next.

CASE ILLUSTRATION

Instructions and rapid performance feedback were successful in increasing the assertive behaviors of two patients who were residents of a Veterans Administration hospital (Eisler, Hersen, & Miller, 1973). One patient, a 28-year-old house painter, had been admitted after he fired a shotgun into the ceiling of his home. His history revealed periodic rages following a consistent failure to express anger in social situations. His behavior was assessed by asking him to role-play interpersonal situations related to the current life experiences in which he was unable to express anger. These situations included being criticized by a fellow employee at work, disagreeing with his wife about her inviting company over to their home without checking this with him first, and his lack of ability to refuse requests by his eight-year-old son. An assistant played the complementary role in each situation: his wife, son, or fellow employee. The client's reactions were videotaped as well as observed through a one-way mirror. Assessment of his reactions revealed expressive deficits in four components of assertiveness, including eye contact (he did not look at his partner when speaking to him), loudness of his voice (one could barely hear what he said), speech duration (his responses were very short, consisting of one- or two-word replies), and behavioral requests of his partner (he was unable to ask his partner to change his behavior). He was informed that during training sessions, he would learn how to respond more effectively in these interpersonal situations. Twelve situations that were unrelated to the client's problem areas but that required assertive behavior were employed during training sessions. Each was role-played five times in different order over the training sessions.

The counselor offered instructions to the client through a miniature radio receiver. Instructions related to only one of the four response areas at any one time. Thus, during the initial scenes he was coached to look at his partner when speaking to him, and during the second series he was coached to increase the loudness of his voice but received no instructions concerning any other response. During the fourth series, he was coached to speak longer, and during the last series, he was instructed to ask his partner for a behavior change. He received feedback concerning his performance after each role play. This procedure permitted a multiple-baseline analysis of the four behaviors, in which intervention was applied to only one behavior at a time; meanwhile, information was gathered concerning the frequency or duration of all behaviors. Each response increased after specific instructions were given regarding this, and effects were generalized to the specific situations that were problematic for this client. The counselor rated his behavior in reviewing videotapes of his performance.

A similar training procedure was successful in increasing the assertive behavior of a 34-year-old man with a history of alcoholism. His current admission had been related to an inability to handle increased responsibility at work after he was promoted to a managerial position at a small motel. It was difficult for him to confront those who worked for him when they performed poorly, he complied with unreasonable demands made on him by his employer as well as by his motel guests, and he was unable to resist pressure from salespersons.

RECOGNIZING AND EVALUATING SOCIAL SKILLS DEFICITS

Effective social skills (assertive behaviors) are differentiated from both aggressive and submissive behaviors. Some people are passive (e.g., say nothing) when they must speak up to attain valued outcomes. Other people are aggressive, and they put people down and harshly criticize them. Assertion is essentially effective social behavior; for example, the calm expression of preferences in a way that encourages others to consider them. Assertive behavior involves expressing preferences without undue anxiety in a manner that encourages others to take them into account and that does not infringe on other people's rights (Alberti & Emmons, 2001). There is a focus on the situation rather than on the person. Aggression refers to the hostile expression of preferences in a manner that takes away the rights of another person. The aggressive person puts down, hurts, or humiliates people and achieves goals at the expense of causing bad feelings in others. Anger is expressed at the other person rather than at the situation and reactions express intention of hostile action. Punitive or aggressive responses may involve ridicule, disparagement, shouting, and violent gestures or other threatening or belligerent body expressions. Research on anger shows that inappropriate expression of anger usually results in negative feelings on the part of the expressor and often decreases the chance of attaining valued goals (e.g., Averill, 1982). Alternatives to aggressive reactions include calming self-talk, polite requests, reframing situations (e.g., as unimportant), and emphasizing common interests. Submission involves allowing one's rights to be ignored, and yielding humbly to the wishes of others. Submissive individuals allow others to choose for them. They do not achieve desired goals, and their reactions suggest that they are in the wrong and others are right.

Ineffective social behavior is typically situational. That is, we usually experience difficulty only in certain situations. A client may be appropriately assertive (effective) in some situations (e.g., initiating conversations), passive in others (e.g., refusing requests), and aggressive in other contexts (e.g., requesting changes in behavior). The effect of a given behavior will often differ depending on the unique relationship involved. Each person differs in his or her social skill repertoires. An employee with a certain pattern of social skills may do better (e.g., display less dysfunctional behavior) in a job that reflected a better match with his or her particular pattern of social skills. Positive feelings may be appropriately expressed but difficulty encountered when expressing negative feelings. Factors that affect social competence include (1) the degree of intimacy involved; (2) whether the feeling to be expressed is positive or negative; (3) various characteristics of relevant people including their status, age, and gender; (4) perceived status of self in the situation; and (5) number of people present. Ineffective behavior may occur only in interactions with people in positions of authority such as supervisors at work. Women tend to be less aggressive and less dominant than men, and goals reported by women in social exchanges often differ from those of men: women often pursue interpersonal rather than task-completion goals (e.g., Wilson & Gallois, 1993). Cultural differences influence the effectiveness of given behaviors in situations.

Some social behaviors occur in response to an overture made by another person. Other behaviors require initiative; for example, responding to someone initiating a conversation in contrast to initiating a conversation. A second variable is the valence of the affect involved; is it negative or positive? Situations involving negative assertion include refusing requests, responding to criticism, discouraging unwanted interactions, requesting a change in someone else's behavior, disagreeing with others, and resisting interruptions. In each case, difficulties may be only in relation to specific individuals (strangers, acquaintances, intimates) or contexts (service related—as in stores and restaurants—authority, family). Situations involving negative assertion have received greater emphasis in the literature compared with those situations involving positive assertive behaviors. For example, in *Assertive Behavior,* Rakos (1991) devoted three chapters to conflict assertion. Positive assertion includes initiating and maintaining conversations and small talk, admitting personal short-comings, giving and receiving compliments, and expressing positive emotions. The particular goals a client wishes to pursue are important to consider in selecting response components. Both long-term and short-term personal and social goals should be considered. The specific components of effective social behavior depend on the situation involved. The components of effective social skills can be divided into three areas: (1) content (what is said), (2) paralinguistic features (how it is said), and (3) nonverbal behaviors such as eye contact and posture. Timing and persistence is often important. Effective timing will require self-management skills as well as selection of facilitating contexts.

There has been a movement away from a component model of social skills in which attention is focused on specific verbal or nonverbal behaviors toward a process model in which cognitions (covert behaviors) such as goal setting and knowledge of rules are viewed as integral to social competence. McFall (1982) used an information processing model emphasizing the importance of (1) decoding skills (the reception, perception, and interpretation of social stimuli), (2) decision-making skills (used to generate and select an appropriate response), and (3) enacting skills (translation of the alternative selected into action [execution] and following the impact of the response [self-monitoring]). For example, excessive anger may result in the misinterpretation of social signals, the decision to use an aggressive response option, the enactment of an aggressive response, and misinterpretation of the effect of the action as positive (when it is negative). A reluctance to refuse unreasonable requests may be due to a past history of punishment for such refusals. Cognitive surfeits (self-doubts) and deficits (lack of encouraging thoughts) may interfere with effective use of social skills. Cognitive-behavior therapists emphasize the role of dysfunctional attributions, negative self-statements, and unrealistic expectations in inhibiting effective social behavior, including the role of such thoughts in preventing corrective exposure to feared situations. The finding that the addition of cognitive treatment methods to social skills training improves success suggests the value of addressing interfering thoughts.

Differences in social skills have been found to be related to a variety of cognitive skills, including perception and translation of social cues, interpersonal problem solving and self-monitoring, affect regulation, use of positive self-statements, and realistic expectations and beliefs. Accurate perception and translation of social cues is required for effective social behavior. People who are ineffective in social situations are not as sensitive to social cues. People who are not assertive have deficits in problem recognition and assessment as well as in the skill in selecting an appropriate response (Chiauzzi & Heimberg, 1986). Social problem-solving models include the steps of generating behavioral alternatives, selecting one that will be effective, trying it out, and evaluating the outcome (e.g., Nezu & D'Zurilla, 1979).

Unassertive individuals often have unrealistic expectations such as "Everyone should like me," "I should never make mistakes," and "Other people should do what I want them to." They often are overly self-critical and inaccurately label aggressive and assertive behavior. Assertive compared with nonassertive individuals have an internal locus of control. Schwartz and Gottman (1976) found that less assertive men had more negative self-statements and fewer positive self-statements than did more assertive men but did not differ from more assertive men in their knowledge of appropriate behaviors. Other studies have found differences in content knowledge between high and low assertion participants (Bruch, 1981). Even though observers indicated no differences among assertive and nonassertive individuals, nonassertive compared with assertive college students rated themselves as less assertive, less effective, and more anxious and were more likely to endorse irrational beliefs than were assertive students (Alden & Cappe, 1981). Beliefs may result in distortion of social feedback. For example, if an employee believes she is not competent, she may misinterpret social signals and positive feedback from a supervisor as negative. Excessive fears of negative evaluation increase scanning for negative cues. People who differ in assertion also differ in their predictions about the consequences of different courses of action. For example, people who decided not to act assertively predicted more bad consequences and fewer positive consequences from assertion than did people who decided to act assertively (Fiedler & Beach, 1978). Compared with participants rated low in assertion, participants rated high in assertion expect more positive reactions from others and have less of a discrepancy between what they think they should do and what they actually do (Eisler, Frederiksen, & Peterson, 1978). Assertive individuals expect positive outcomes to follow refusal of requests, compared with nonassertive individuals who expect positive outcomes to follow compliance. The opposite pattern was found in relation to negative consequences. However, differences in values given to positive and negative consequences in these two different groups have been found: the assertive clients rated the positive consequences of refusal as more desirable and the negative consequences of compliance as more undesirable than did the nonassertive clients.

REFERRAL STRATEGIES

Professionals differ in their competencies in offering certain kinds of services in a way that maximizes the likelihood of success. For example, they may not be skilled in carrying out an individualized, contextually oriented assessment that attends to personal and environmental factors that may be related to social skill deficits such as lack of needed supervisory training and monitoring. They may refer staff members to employee assistance programs in which staff focus on individual pathology and ignore environmental factors that contribute to lack of expected social behaviors such as excessive workloads. Selecting referral sources in which staff members are skilled in assessment and provision of social skills training will contribute to achieving hoped-for outcomes.

WORKPLACE OR HOME STRESSORS

Sources of stress either at work or at home may compromise the use of effective skills; for example, by decreasing thresholds for anxiety or angry outbursts. Lack of sleep may decrease fine-grained discrimination skills required for effective social behavior and alter nonverbal behaviors in less rewarding directions. Lack of expected social behaviors may be due to a unique work culture and climate in an organization

(Glisson, 2000). Performance difficulties (including lack of facilitating social behaviors) may be due "to a host of nonworker factors such as unclear agency policies, resource limitations, vague work priorities or performance standards, poor supervision, caseload demands, and assignments of inappropriate cases" (Pecora & Wagner, 2000, p. 416). Degree of autonomy and control at work seems to be related to activity outside of work hours; that is, the greater the autonomy the more activity outside of work that may decrease overall stress and facilitate use of effective social skills (e.g., Karasek & Theorell, 1990). Employees may be overburdened and have few, if any, ways to make appropriate complaints to alter dysfunctional work cultures and climates. Nothing may be said because of fear of losing one's job. Employers may label complainers as troublesome employees who suffer from "mental illnesses" rather than altering dysfunctional or unfair conditions of employment that contribute to social skill deficits.

EMPIRICALLY BASED TREATMENTS

Both social skills and assertion training have been used to address social skills deficits. The terms "assertive behavior" and "assertive training" have been replaced by the terms "effective/competent social behavior" and "social skills training."

Social Skills Training

Both single-case and group designs have been used to evaluate the success of social skills training. Single-case designs are uniquely suited for evaluating progress with an individual, as suggested in the case illustration. Generalization has been a persistent problem; that is, new behavior may not generalize to other situations including real-life situations. For example, responses to situations requiring negative assertion do not necessarily generalize to those requiring positive assertion. Relevant skills include effective use of a variety of assessment tools, familiarity with and skill in correctly implementing related intervention methods, and skill in selecting relevant, clear progress indicators.

Clients have used social skills training to develop a wide variety of behaviors related to a wide variety of goals (O'Donohue & Krasner, 1995). Examples of relevant behaviors include offering positive feedback to others (empathy and listening), expressing feelings, disclosing personal information,requesting behavior changes, negotiating, and refusing requests. Natural contexts provide many opportunities to enhance valued skills. Social skills training is designed to enhance effective social behavior. It is used to empower people by increasing their influence over their environments. For example, people with physical disabilities learn how to identity and report issues at group meetings (Balcazar, Seekins, Fawcett, & Hopkins, 1990). Training may be carried out in either individual or group settings. The main goal of enhancing social skills may be to prevent problems.

Selection of intervention programs should be based on an individualized assessment, which will suggest factors related to ineffective social behavior. For example, clients may have required skills to attain desired outcomes and to avoid unwanted consequences at work such as conflicts with other employees, but they may not use them. That is, it is important to distinguish between motivational and behavioral deficits. Assessment should indicate the particular situations of concern. Exactly what situations are involved, who is involved, and where do relevant exchanges occur? What are the clients' goals? Social behavior is situationally specific in terms of what is effective. A behavior that is effective in achieving a given outcome in one situation may not be successful in another, which highlights the importance of clearly describing situations of concern. Socially valid data describing what specific behaviors are necessary and sufficient to be effective in specific situations often are absent.

Social skills training should be preceded by a contextual assessment. Only through a careful assessment can the role of skills deficits be determined. Careful assessment allows individual tailoring of intervention programs to the unique goals and related assets and deficits and contributing factors of each individual. Clients may have skills but not use them. They may not be motivated to do so; for example, no positive incentives may follow related behaviors or they may be punished or they may forget to use them (there is a cuing problem). Assessment should indicate the client's goals, what situations are involved, who is involved, and where relevant exchanges occur. Behaviors required for success should be clearly described. The behaviors that make up an effective reaction differ in different situations. Definitions of socially effective behavior differ in the extent to which personal outcomes (effects on oneself) as well as social outcomes (effects on others) are considered. Most definitions emphasize providing reinforcing consequences in a way that is socially acceptable and that does not harm others. Practice-related literature may offer guidelines about what is effective. Each client's relevant entering repertoire should be clearly described. This step requires identifying what skills clients already possess. The gap between current skill levels and required skills can then be accurately assessed. In addition, possible obstacles should be identified. What obstacles, such as negative thoughts, unrealistic expectations, or excessive anxiety or anger, interfere with success? Excessive anger or anxiety may be related to negative self-statements (e.g., "I'm no good") or inappropriate expectations (e.g., "I should always get my way"). Unique socialization patterns may pose an obstacle, such as the belief that "I must please everyone." Clients may have inappropriate goals (those that cannot be met or are met at a high cost such as social rejection).

An explain-demonstrate-practice-feedback model is used in which explanations are first offered about why certain skills are of value and the situations in which they can be used are identified. Training may be more effective if it is individually tailored to each person's unique entry-level skills and obstacles that may interfere with acquiring and using skills. The more extensive the lack of skills, the more likely model presentation, rehearsal, feedback, and instructions will be needed to develop skills. In other cases, practice or instructions alone may be sufficient to achieve desired outcomes. Behavioral rehearsal involves the practice of behaviors. For example, a client who has difficulty during job interviews can practice effective ways of acting after watching a model. Coaching (e.g., signals during role plays) and prompting may be used to encourage desired behaviors, and written prompts may describe specific verbal and nonverbal behaviors. Prompts and guidance are faded as skills increase. The "minimally effective response" is encouraged, which refers to behavior that is likely to succeed with a minimum of effort, negative emotion, and negative consequences. Norms of politeness are followed and negative labels are avoided.

Description of initial skill levels allows programming of change in which available skills are built on in a step-by-step manner. Specific feedback based on clearly defined criteria will help clients to identify what to do to enhance their effectiveness. Homework assignments provide opportunities for practice of skills in real-life settings after criterion-level skills and comfort levels have been achieved in role plays. A contextual understanding of the situations involved is vital for preparing clients for negative outcomes. Change may be slow and new reactions may initially create negative feelings and consequences. For example, job interviewers may be rude. If such reactions may occur, help clients to develop coping skills for handling them before they try out new behaviors in real life. Special arrangements may be needed to encourage generalization.

Assertion Training

Assertion training differs from social skills training in emphasizing individual rights and obligations and encouraging participants to alter norms and stereotypes that limit options (Gambrill, 1995). It is identical to social skills training in encouraging social behaviors that enhance positive social consequences. A respect for rights, one's own as well as those of others, is integral to the philosophy underlying assertion training. It is not a "do your own thing" approach in which preferences are expressed regardless of their effects on others. Nor does it guarantee that valued goals will be achieved. An advantage of the phrase "assertive behavior" for some groups, such as women, is the emphasis on taking the initiative to enhance opportunities.

HELPING CLIENTS CHANGE COGNITIONS

Cognitive and affect management skills may be in need of refinement or development. What clients say to themselves (their self-statements), which may be due to unique socialization patterns such as a norm that it is rude to question authorities, may contribute to social skills deficits. Programs focused on altering cognitions believed to be related to ineffective behavior have sometimes been found to be as effective as those focused on altering overt behavior (Rosenfarb, Hayes, & Linehan, 1989). Clients may have dysfunctional rules about how to act or what consequences to expect in certain situations. A client may believe that if he or she does not get what he or she wants in a situation, "It is a disaster" (e.g., Ellis & Blau, 1998). People who have angry outbursts may relive imagined slights and exaggerate their importance. The term "cognitive restructuring" refers to methods that focus on changing what people say to themselves. Reframing refers to encouraging a different way of viewing events and can be used to alter views of problems. Cognitive-restructuring may require identifying the themes (e.g., beliefs) underlying negative self-statements (e.g., "I am worthless"). Without identifying the themes, change efforts maybe of little value because core beliefs remain untouched. Enhancing self-reinforcement skills is valuable when support will not be offered in real life. Clients may increase positive self-statements as well as access to specific reinforcers contingent on desired behaviors. Problem-solving training also has been used to enhance effective social skills. Clients are encouraged to clearly identify problems, alternative ways to resolve them, and the consequences of each. Clients may benefit from learning how to carry out small cost-benefit analyses as a guide to how to act.

ENHANCING SKILLS IN MANAGING EMOTIONS

Enhancing skills in managing emotions may be needed to increase effective social behaviors. Feelings can be altered by changing related overt and covert (i.e., thoughts) behaviors. Programs have been developed to help clients with anger and social anxiety (e.g., Heimberg, Liebowitz, Hope, & Schneider, 1995; Novaco, 1995). Coleman (1995) used the term "emotional intelligence" to refer to skills in recognizing and managing emotions (see also Salovey, Hesse, & Mayer, 1993; Weisinger, 2000). Education is a component of cognitive-behavioral programs that are designed to help clients manage their emotions. Clients learn how feelings and thoughts influence their behavior and how their behavior influences what they think and feel. In stress management training, clients learn to identify feelings and thoughts associated with emotional reactions such as anxiety and anger and to use them as cues for constructive thoughts and actions. They learn how to carry out a situational analysis of arousal-provoking thoughts. The relationship between thoughts, feelings, and behavior is emphasized. Clients are encouraged to view emotions as reactions they can influence rather than as feelings that are out of their control. They are encouraged to identify low levels of unpleasant arousal so they can use mood-altering skills at an early point to prevent escalation. Clients may benefit from acquiring relaxation skills that help them handle stressful situations.

RELAPSE PREVENTION

Social skills training typically includes an educational component that may be of value in maintaining valuable social skills (see Table 15.1). Including a troubleshooting guide for specific concerns such as increasing participation may be of value in recovering from negative events (see Gambrill, 1997). Practicing skills until they flow easily in particular social situations should decrease cuing problems as hoped-for behaviors come under the influence of relevant situational contexts.

THERAPEUTIC BENEFITS OF WORK

Work settings potentially provide clients with multiple opportunities to develop, use, and benefit from effective social skills. Employees may acquire new social behaviors by observing employees who model such behaviors. They can gain the personal satisfaction of helping others and, at the same time, contributing to the overall success of the organization. Many hours are spent at work. To the extent to which such hours are rewarding, unnecessary stress is avoided.

SUMMARY

Work environments require social interactions. It is inevitable that these will go awry in various ways for various reasons, only some of which may be related to the unique characteristics of employees, including their social skill deficits and related factors. Lack of training in the social skills required for certain positions such as supervisory or administrative roles may increase the likelihood of dysfunctional reactions. Consequences of social skill deficits include low productivity and unhappy, stressed employees. Fortunately, there is a rich literature related to social skills and assertion training that can be drawn on to help employees to enhance effective social behaviors. Such training is typically individually focused. Assertion and social skills training may do little to alter organizational factors that contribute to dysfunctional social behaviors that may reflect societal sources of inequity such as discrimination based on gender or color. (See, for example, Martinko, Gundlach, & Douglas, 2002.) There is thus the danger of blaming clients for problems that do not originate with them. As Hollin and Trower (1988) noted, "Potential environmental influences are being minimized if not ignored, and individual training slips toward a 'medical model' in which the person is to be 'cured' rather than the environment modified … an accurate behavior analysis would make such issues clear" (p. 1983). The ideology of success through mind power that is especially prevalent in the United States, where assertion training flowered, requires vigilance for discouraging programs that offer only the illusion of greater influence over one's environment. Attention should be paid to altering environmental circumstances (work climate and cultural variables) that interfere with job satisfaction and work productivity such as fostering an organizational culture that discourages harassment and bullying and fosters positive working relationships.

References

Alberti, R., & Emmons, M. (2001). *Your perfect right: Assertiveness and quality in your life and relationships* (8th ed.). Atascadero, CA: Impact.

Alden, L., & Cappe, R. (1981). Nonassertiveness: Skill deficit or selective self-evaluation. *Behavior Therapy, 12,* 107-114.

American Psychiatric Association (2000). *Diagnostic and statistical manual of mental disorders* (4th ed., text rev.). Washington, DC: Author.

Averill, J. (1982). *Anger and aggression: Implications for theories of emotion.* New York: Springer-Verlag.

Balcazar, F. E., Seekins, T. L., Fawcett, S. B., & Hopkins, B. L. (1990). Empowering people with physical disabilities through advocacy skills training. *American Journal of Community Psychology, 18*(2), 281-296.

Baron, R. A., & Greenberg, J. (1990). *Behavior in organizations: Understanding and managing the human side of work* (3rd ed.). Boston: Allyn & Bacon.

Bruch, M. A. (1981). A task analysis of assertive behavior revisited: Replication and extension. *Behavior Therapy, 12,* 217-230.

Chiauzzi, E., & Heimberg, R. G. (1986). Legitimacy of request and social problem-solving: A study of assertive and non-assertive subjects. *Behavior Modification, 10,* 3-18.

Coleman, D. (1995). *Emotional intelligence.* New York: Bantam.

Einarsen, S. (2000). Harassment and bullying at work: A review of the Scandinavian approach. *Aggression and Violent Behavior, 5,* 379-402.

Eisler, R. M., Frederiksen, L. W., & Peterson, G. L. (1978). The relationship of cognitive variables to the expression of assertiveness. *Behavior Therapy, 9,* 419-427.

Eisler, R. M., Hersen, M., & Miller, P. M. (1973). Effects of modeling on components of assertive behavior. *Journal of Behavior Therapy and Experimental Psychiatry, 4,* 1-6.

Ellis, A., & Blau, S. (Eds.). (1998). *The Albert Ellis reader: A guide to well-being using rational emotive behavior therapy.* Secaucus, NJ: Citadel Trade.

Fiedler, D., & Beach, L. R. (1978). On the decision to be assertive. *Journal of Consulting and Clinical Psychology, 46,* 537-546.

Fox, S., Spector, P. E., & Miles, D. (2001). Counterproductive work behavior (CWB) in response to job stressors and organizational justice: Some mediator and moderator tests for autonomy and emotions. *Journal of Vocational Behavior, 59,* 291-309.

French, J. R. P., Jr., & Raven, B. (1959). The bases of social power. In D. Cartwright (Ed.), *Studies in social power.* Ann Arbor: University of Michigan.

Gambrill, E. (1995). Assertion skills training. In W. O'Donohue & L. Krasner (Eds.), *Handbook of psychological skills training: Clinical techniques and applications* (pp. 81-118). Boston: Allyn & Bacon.

Gambrill, E. (1997). *Social work practice: A critical thinker's guide.* New York: Oxford University Press.

Gardner, W. L., III, & Martinko, M. J. (1998). An organizational perspective of the effects of dysfunctional impression management. In R. W. Griffin, A. O'Leary-Kelly, & J. M. Collins (Eds.), *Dysfunctional behavior in organizations: Non-violent dysfunctional behavior* (Vol. 23, Part B, pp. 69-125. Stamford, CT: JAI Press.

Glisson, C. (2000). Organizational climate and culture. In R. J. Patti (Ed.), *The handbook of social welfare management* (pp. 395-423). Thousand Oaks, CA: Sage.

Heimberg, R. G., Liebowitz, M. R., Hope, D. A., & Schneider, F. R. (1995). *Social phobia: Diagnosis, assessment and treatment.* New York: Guilford.

Hollin, C. R., & Trower, P. (1988). Development and applications of social skills training: A review and critique. In M. Hersen, R. Eisler, & P. Miller (Eds.), *Progress in behavior modification* (Vol. 22, pp. 166-201). New York: Academic Press.

Janis, I. L. (1982). *Group think: Psychological studies of policy decisions and fiascos* (2nd ed.). Boston: Houghton Mifflin.

Karasek, R. A., & Theorell, T. (1990). *Healthy work.* New York: Basic Books.

Martinko, M. J., Gundlach, M. J., & Douglas, S. C. (2002). Toward an integrative theory of counterproductive workplace behavior: A causal reasoning perspective. *International Journal of Selection and Assessment, 10,* 36-50.

McFall, R. M. (1982). A review and reformulation of the concept of social skills. *Behavioral Assessment, 4,* 1-33.

Nezu, A., & D'Zurilla, T. J. (1979). An experimental evaluation of the decision-making process in social problem solving. *Cognitive Therapy and Research, 3,* 269-277.

NiCarthy, G., Gottleib, N., & Coffman, S. (1993). *You don't have to take it!: A woman's guide to confronting emotional abuse at work.* Seattle, WA: Seal Press.

Novaco, R. W. (1995). Clinical problems of anger and assessment and regulation through a stress coping skills approach. In W. O'Donohue & L. Krasner (Eds.), *Handbook of psychological skills training: Clinical techniques and applications* (pp. 320-338). Boston: Allyn & Bacon.

O'Donohue, W., & Krasner, L. (Eds.). (1995). *Handbook of psychological skill training: Clinical techniques and applications.* Boston: Allyn & Bacon.

Pecora, P. J., & Wagner, M. (2000). Managing personnel. In R. J. Patti (Ed.), *The handbook of social welfare management* (pp. 395-423). Thousand Oaks, CA: Sage.

Petrocelli, W., & Repa, B. K. (1992). *Sexual harassment on the job.* Berkeley, CA: Nolo Press.

Porter, N., & Geis, F. (1981). Women and nonverbal leadership cues: When seeing is not believing. In C. Mayo & N. M. Henley (Eds.), *Gender and non-verbal behavior.* New York: Springer-Verlag.

Rakos, R. F. (1991). *Assertive behavior: Theory, research and training.* New York: Routledge.

Rosenfarb, I. S., Hayes, S. C., & Linehan, M. M. (1989). Instructions and experimental feedback in the treatment of social skills deficits in adults. *Psychotherapy, 26,* 242-251.

Salovey, P., Hesse, C. K., & Mayer, J. D. (1993). Emotional intelligence and the self-regulation of affect. In D. M. Wegner & J. W. Pennebaker (Eds.), *Handbook of mental control* (pp. 258-277). Englewood Cliffs, NJ: Prentice Hall.

Schwartz, R., & Gottman, J. (1976). Toward a task analysis of assertive behavior, *Journal of Consulting and Clinical Psychology,* 44, 910-920.

Spector, P. E. (2001, May-June). Science briefs: Counterproductive work behavior: The secret side of organizational life. *Psychological Science Agenda, 14,* 8-9.

Trower, P. (1982). Toward a generation model of social skills: A critique and synthesis. In J. P. Curran & P. M. Monti (Eds.), *Social skills training.* New York: Guilford. (pp. 397-427)

Weisinger, H. (2000). *Emotional intelligence at work: The untapped edge for success.* San Francisco: Jossey-Bass.

Wilson, K., & Gallois, C. (1993). *Assertion and its social context.* New York: Pergamon.

Wolpe, J. (1958). *Psychotherapy by reciprocal inhibition.* Stanford, CA: Stanford University Press.

16

Marital and Family Problems

GARY R. BIRCHLER
University of California, San Diego

WILLIAM FALS-STEWART
State University of New York, Buffalo

KRISTEN G. ANDERSON
University of California, San Diego

DESCRIPTION OF THE DISORDER AND WORKPLACE MANIFESTATIONS

*S*ocial roles required for participation in marriage, family, and occupation are, for most people, the most important domains of life function. Given the structure of Western society, participation in work and nonwork roles significantly defines who we are, what we do with our time, and the associated quality of life for our families and ourselves. Investigators interested in the balance between work and family roles have conducted a considerable amount of research. Moreover, an imbalance between these particular social roles can be an important stressor influencing individuals' health outcomes and affecting family development.

The influential relationship between work and family is bidirectional and bivalent (Frone, 2003). That is, what goes on at work can influence what goes on in the family and vice versa. Moreover, the effects transmitted from one setting to the other may be positive or negative. Accordingly, the literature in this field refers to work-to-family conflict, family-to-work conflict, work-to-family facilitation, and family-to-work facilitation. Most of the research over four decades has focused on work-to-family conflict or "interference," less focus has been placed on family-to-work conflict, and even less work has been done on the facilitative and interactive effects of work and family roles (Lambert, 1990). On the basis of a major literature review, Frone (2003) described six basic models regarding the work-to-family interface: First, the segmentation model suggests that work and family life represent separate domains that do not influence one another. People somehow compartmentalize their life in one sphere that seems to have little or no overlap with the other sphere. Second, the congruence model suggests that although either a positive or a negative relationship may be found between work and family, the relationship is spurious because it is caused by a third common factor (e.g., one's personality style may cause one to have problems in both areas). Third, the identity or integrative model suggests that these two roles are so intertwined that they become indistinguishable, as might be exemplified by a family-owned and -operated business. Fourth, the spillover model postulates a positive correlation between work and family; the status of one domain spills over and similarly affects the other domain. Fifth, the compensation model posits a negative correlation between work and family, such that a resource shift made in one domain adds or takes away resources to engage in activity in the other domain; for example, if one experiences dissatisfaction at work, one would reduce effort there and devote more time and energy to family activities. Sixth, the resource drain model also suggests a negative correlation between family and work domains, such that there is a finite amount of personal resources to be expended and more activity in one domain, by definition, takes away from resources that could be expended in the other domain. In light of available empirical support, Frone (2003) noted that none of these models by itself can account for the dynamics of work-to-family balance. On the contrary, all of these mechanisms exist and may operate separately or simultaneously (Lambert, 1990).

When an imbalance between work and family persists, there is potential for marital and family problems. The difficulties could reach the level of disorder if marital or family discord becomes persistent and severe enough to cause mental or physical health problems in one or more family members. Likewise, the level of disorder is reached if sufficient intraindividual dissatisfaction exists such that one's interpersonal relationships are significantly and adversely affected. Recall that the influential effects of these two realms of activity are bidirectional. Indeed, research has demonstrated that the causes of work-to-family problems tend to be found in the workplace and the causes of family-to-work conflict tend to be found in the home (Frone, 2000). Therefore, in this chapter, when considering marital and family problems, there may be several possible explanations for them and for any workplace manifestations related to them.

At this point, it might be useful for the reader to consider a number of basic scenarios that illustrate problematic situations in which employees and families find themselves. Imagine that a marital dyad experiences relationship discord to such an extent that the couple is considering separation or divorce. The developments that might lead to this unfortunate circumstance can be outlined according to the work-to-family balance models previously described. That is, any of the following scenarios could cause the marital problem:

1. one partner's devotion to work that results in significant neglect of the other partner and the family (i.e., work-to-family resource drain model),
2. the existence of relationship-based conflicts that have nothing to do with either partner's work and their marital problems do not have any effect on their work performances (i.e., segmentation model),

3. one partner's recurrent major depressive disorder has negatively affected both the marriage and that partner's work performance (i.e., congruence model),

4. relationship-based conflicts about an affair that result in relationship withdrawal by the one partner and therefore that partner ends up doing more and better work on the job (i.e., compensation model),

5. one partner's failing job performance and related personal distress affect his or her interest and ability to perform spousal or parental roles (i.e., work-to-family conflict spillover model), or

6. one partner's role as home-based day care center operator is causing significant problems for the marriage because of confusion about that person's role identity and performance in the family (i.e., identity or integrative model).

There are significant workplace manifestations in five out of these six scenarios: situations 1 and 4 likely have positive effects at work; 3, 5, and 6 have negative effects at work; and situation 2 possibly has no implications for the workplace.

EPIDEMIOLOGY

The limited quantity and generally low level of methodological sophistication of the research in this area has restricted the conclusions that can be made regarding the amount of work-to-family imbalance. However, on the basis of a number of comparison studies, researchers have identified certain aspects of epidemiology. First, estimates of the prevalence of significant work-to-family conflict vary from 34 percent of all workers to 54 percent of parents of dual-earner families (Hughes, Galinsky, & Morris, 1992). Second, we know something about the relative frequency and amount of work-to-family compared with family-to-work conflict (Frone, Yardley, & Markle, 1997). Consistently, research has shown that the prevalence of work-to-family conflict is greater than the prevalence of family-to-work conflict. Thus, it appears that work can have a more deleterious effect on the family than vice versa. Interestingly, although more recent studies of work-to-family facilitation are few, the opposite phenomenon has been found. When comparing work-to-family facilitation with family-to-work facilitation, positive transfer from home to work seems more powerful in the lives of employees (Grzywacz & Marks, 2000b).

Third, research has been conducted regarding gender differences regarding work-to-family balance (Frone, 2000; Grzywacz & Marks, 2000b). Given the long tradition of gender roles regarding work and family in the United States, one would expect there to be significant gender differences when it comes to work-to-family balance. However, because most families now require two wage earners and more women are entering the career-oriented workforce, the short answer is that there are few gender differences. Some findings are mentioned later in the Workplace or Home Stressors section. Overall, however, men and women report similar levels of work-to-family and family-to-work conflict and facilitation.

CASE ILLUSTRATION

Phil, age 57, was divorced with two grown and married daughters and working for a large midwest machinery and equipment manufacturer when he met Susan, a fellow employee in the information technology department. Susan, age 48, also was divorced, and was single-handedly raising Jack, a 17-year-old boy who was starting his senior year in high school. Soon after the couple started dating, Phil was offered a six-month job assignment at a company subdivision in California. It was such a good opportunity that the couple decided to keep dating and commuting in order to maintain their courtship and respective jobs. During this period Susan was laid off as part of company downsizing. The couple liked California and made a plan for Phil to seek a permanent position there. Susan and her son would join him and she would seek employment in the new locale. Indeed, Phil was offered a permanent position and just before moving out west, Susan and Phil got married. Within a few months, several factors increased the stress level of members of this new stepfamily. First, Phil's new employer had expectations for long working hours and high productivity. This company also was facing downsizing and fewer employees were expected to be more productive. Second, Susan had difficulties finding a job in her career area of computer training; she even got a job that lasted only a few weeks before the company went out of business. Her lack of employment and income were very frustrating and stressful for the family. Third, Jack was a good athlete, an attribute that helped him adapt to his new school during his senior year, but he soon got in with the wrong crowd and began, repeatedly, to get in trouble with school authorities. His parents also caught him engaging in marijuana use. As is often the case in such stepfamily situations, Phil tended to be a strict disciplinarian, Susan was more protective and permissive, and Jack learned how to split his mother and stepfather as they attempted to bring his behavior under control. This combination of two stressful work situations and family conflict persisted for almost a year.

Over time, family function deteriorated individually and collectively. Family conflict combined with pressure at work was making Phil more and more irritable and withdrawn. Intermittent work and disciplinary struggles with her acting-out son made Susan frustrated and depressed. Despite some fairly remarkable success in baseball, Jack was behaving poorly at home and began failing in junior college academics. Everything came to a head when Phil was diagnosed with advanced colitis that required surgery and a colostomy (for many years he had occasionally suffered from an intestinal problem that was exacerbated by stress). Something had to change, on several fronts, or this family would break apart. Phil decided to seek assistance from his company's highly reputable employee assistance program (EAP). After just two counseling sessions, Phil went to his supervisor and negotiated a part-time position. Phil's department leadership skills were quite valued, even though the quality of his work had been slipping recently. This work reduction plan would begin immediately and extend for an indefinite period of time after his major surgery. His health became the highest priority. Fortunately, he had some accessible retirement plan savings to augment his income. Susan responded to the crisis by seeking guidance and support for herself from a psychotherapist in the community. Actually, the referral for a therapist came from Phil's EAP counselor. Within weeks she (and Phil) asked her son to move out and to establish his own residence. They also told Jack to get a part-time job to help pay for his bills. Finally, the couple made it clear that Jack's monetary support would be cut off if he continued to get into trouble. This ultimatum represented a significant shift in attitude for Susan. She realized from her husband's health crisis and from her own counseling that her son needed to become more independent and responsible. She decided to make her marriage a higher priority.

Phil's surgery went well and his recovery was slow but sure. After a bit of a struggle and more financial support than the couple planned, Jack began to function fairly well, sharing an apartment with two fellow teammates. With the pressure off from Phil's work and with her son doing better, Susan was able to get a flexible job working nearly full-time at home using the computer. On the basis of Phil's positive EAP contact and Susan's brief counseling experience, the couple sought evaluation and treatment from the senior author. They wanted to be sure that they were heading in a compatible direction. On the plus side, Phil's health crisis served as a wake-up call for these two people to review and to substantially reorganize their work and family priorities. The couple therapy lasted only five sessions over two months. Phil not only recovered from his surgery, he decided to take an early retirement benefit from the company, after working for 26 years. Susan's computer software development job was stable and very portable. Indeed, to live more frugally on less income, the couple made plans to move to Florida and into a modest new home that was custom built for them. Phil was interested in getting a real estate license and working part-time.

This case illustration is an example of the important interplay that work-to-family interactions can have. Problems at and regarding the pursuit of work can adversely impact family function; reciprocally, marital and family conflict can affect work performance. In this particular case, a health crisis shocked the couple into making significant changes. The company's EAP was instrumental in supporting evaluation and change and referring the partners, as appropriate, for additional mental health services. In this interesting case, the partners made changes that were bidirectional; presumably some relief would have been realized if either work or family pressures had improved toward a more satisfactory work-to-family balance.

RECOGNIZING AND EVALUATING PSYCHOPATHOLOGY

A fairly large body of research exists that has explored the predictors of work-to-family conflict; however, as mentioned previously, most of the work has investigated the direction of work-to-family. In general, predictors of work-to-family conflict can be grouped into role environment and personality influences. One aspect of role environment is behavioral involvement: the amount of time devoted to work and family roles. Studies have found that, according to the resource drain model described previously, the number of hours engaged in work is positively related to work-to-family conflict; similarly, the number of weekly hours devoted to family chores and activities is positively related to family-to-work conflict. Therefore, in families where either one partner or both partners are excessively (and especially if stressfully) engaged in one setting compared to the other, there may be negative implications for members' well-being and performances in the other setting (Frone et al., 1997).

A second aspect of role environment is psychological involvement: the degree to which people identify with a social role and regard it as important to their self-concept. Consistent with the resource drain model of work-to-family balance, excessive psychological involvement with work (i.e., workaholism) has been found to be related to increased work-to-family conflict. Also, researchers have found that excessive psychological involvement with family is related to increased family-to-work conflict (Carlson & Kacmar, 2000). A third aspect of role environment concerns the level of work and family stressors, dissatisfaction, and distress, as they may cause conflict in the work-to-family interface. Role-related distress and dissatisfaction are believed to consume and possibly to distort one's cognitive processes, resulting in a reduction of psychological and physical energy that is available for other work or family tasks. Indeed, past research suggested that reports of excessive work demands, work-role conflict, work-role ambiguity, or job distress are related significantly to levels of work-to-family conflict. Similarly, a parallel pattern holds that levels of family-to-work conflict are related to excessive family demands, family-role conflict, family-role ambiguity, and relationship distress (Carlson & Kacmar, 2000; Frone et al., 1997).

Finally, role environment includes aspects of work and family social support. Social support is expected to reduce work-to-family conflict. For example, a co-worker may pitch in and help an employee with a project that otherwise would be very stressful and cause stressful effects that would spillover to cause problems at home. Alternatively, a spouse may willingly take on additional chores at home to compensate for his or her partner being unusually busy at work. Indeed, these suppositions about the effects of positive social support were upheld in the research reviewed to date (e.g., Bernas & Major, 2000).

The second major category of causes of work-to-family imbalance is personality. Recent studies have considered personality disposition as possibly having a significant influence on work-to-family conflict. Bernas and Major (2000) and Grzywacz and Marks (2000a) found that high levels of hardiness, extraversion, and self-esteem were associated with lower levels of work-to-family conflict, in both directions. Grzywacz and Marks (2000a) also found that higher levels of negative affectivity and neuroticism were associated with higher levels of work-to-family conflict, again in both directions. Apparently, one's predominant personality disposition may enhance (or exacerbate) one's abilities to function in work and family settings, which is similar to the congruence model mentioned previously. Moreover, personality variables may set an upper limit on the availability of individual coping resources during times of stress.

In work settings, co-workers and supervisors are the people most likely to recognize that a given employee is suffering from work-to-family imbalance. Recognition may occur because the employee is performing poorly in his or her job, he or she may appear at work significantly upset, anxious, or depressed or may show excessive irritation and anger. Some employees fall silent and choose not to reveal the nature of their interpersonal problems; others may appear to waste time complaining about their problems at home. In addition, troubled individuals often reveal work-to-family problems by being excessively tardy or absent from work. In a caring and attentive work setting, co-workers and supervisors will notice the problems and encourage the employee to seek assistance. Unfortunately, many work settings are not as helpful and empathetic regarding troubled employees. For example, supervisors may ignore or neglect the symptoms until the time comes for performance evaluation. Worse yet, in some job settings people are relatively intolerant of family (or other) problems being brought to work and the insensitive responses to a stressed employee may significantly exacerbate the symptoms. An employee's physical and mental health status can deteriorate significantly when problems in the work or home setting interact with and serve to exacerbate problems in the other setting. Despite certain difficulties regarding early recognition and assistance with family-to-work problems in many work settings, early detection and evaluation of the marital and family problems are recommended.

When work problems spill over into the family, there also may be a long latency period between the start of the problems and the development of relationship distress that causes someone to seek relief or others to recommend treatment. Working partners usually are able to share their work-related concerns with one another. Many married couples, for example, can compensate for ongoing work stresses by supporting each another, psychologically and behaviorally. Other couples, who have fewer or poorer coping strategies, tend to suffer insidiously from the work-to-family spillover effect of the unresolved problems. In such cases, family members may be affected by increased stress and distress in multiple settings. One or more family members may break down or exhibit physical or mental symptoms of the developing psychopathology, and they may therefore come to the attention of extended family, friends, teachers, or other community contacts.

Regardless of the route or the process of developing marital or family problems (i.e., work-to-family conflict or family-to-work conflict), once these problems come to the attention of the employee, the supervisor, or the family, an evaluation of the problems should occur. The evaluation would include an analysis of the nature of the problems, the relative severity of the problems, the likely causes for the relationship distress, and possible solutions. More specifics regarding the types of stressors are discussed in the following section.

WORKPLACE OR HOME STRESSORS

The most prevalent kind of stressor is work overload at home, at work, or both. A second kind of stressor is interpersonal conflict: at work, conflict may occur with supervisors, co-workers, subordinates, and even the customers; at home, conflict may occur with spouses, children, extended family members, and friends (Bolger, DeLongis, Kessler, & Wethington, 1989). Arguments are more likely to occur at home than at work and they are more likely to influence individuals' psychological moods than their physical health status. There appear to be some reliable gender effects, but documenting these effects consistently across studies has been elusive.

Men seem more likely to experience overloads at work; women are more likely to experience overloads at home. Home-based arguments spill over to work more often for men than for women. And women are more likely to compensate at home for their mate's work overload than are men.

Work-to-home negative spillover can affect individuals' time, energy, and moods, whereas home-to-work negative spillover seems to affect attendance, job perfor-mance, and co-worker relationships. More specific stressors at work include low rewards and pay for the work required, depersonalization in large institutions or assembly-line operations, and various kinds of discrimination and harassment: age, gender, sexual, racial, and those based on physical or mental disabilities (Hughes et al., 1992). More specific stressors at home typically include couple and family conflicts regarding jobs or work activity per se, communication, money, sex and affection, substance use, quality time together, housework, parenting responsibilities, and engaging in outside relationships (i.e., family, in-laws, friends, and lovers).

There is some interesting research looking at differential stressors related to full-time versus part-time work and for dual-career versus dual-earner families. In gen-eral, men seem to be more stressed if they have only part-time employment versus full-time employment, whereas women who work full time and have children show more stress than do part-time working women with children or full-time working women without children (Almeida, Wethington, & Chandler, 1999). Viers and Prouty (2001) made a distinction between dual-earner and dual-career couples and their respective stresses and strains. Dual-earner families have two workers; dual-career families have two workers, both of who are establishing and maintaining careers. On one hand, the dual-career families do relatively better than dual-earner families because of increased income, status, and the sense of well-being associated with career development. On the other hand, because of extra time and energy demands required to maintain two careers, dual-career couples may have more role conflicts regarding sharing and accomplishing responsibilities and they may be more socially isolated than their various counterparts. However, in both types of two-worker families, there is a tendency for women to be more stressed than men by the burdens associated with maintaining work and home roles. However, if the wives are working full time, husbands seem more socially isolated from friends and family as they too may struggle with performance demands at home and at work.

In conclusion, in our contemporary society, there seems to be no substitute for an appropriate balance between work and home activities. Too little work causes economic and social stress for the family; too much work also definitely has a negative impact on personal and family health (Robinson, Flowers, & Carroll, 2001). When a major imbalance persists, eventually significant marital and family problems develop and they may require professional attention to remediate them.

REFERRAL STRATEGIES

As suggested earlier, despite the contemporary prevalence of work-to-family imbal-ance, most employees (and in this case family members) fail to recognize a problem until others bring it to their attention. The question then becomes whether the observer can provide the appropriate assistance or intervene in such a way to help resolve the problem. Certainly, in some instances and in high-quality companies, an employee's supervisor may recognize and provide problem-solving counseling on his or her own. Demonstrating positive encouragement and support or even pointing out to the worker the eventual negative job consequences from not making improvements in the work-to-family conflict can be very helpful. Often, however, the supervisor or co-workers may need to make a referral for the employee to get appropriate assistance. If the company has an EAP, several options may be available. Some EAPs provide assessment but not extended treatment. The employee may be seen for a couple of sessions and recommendations are made to help resolve the problem. If the problem is primarily related to personal issues, marital, or family problems, recommendations may include referral to HMOs, community agencies, and even private practitioners, depending on the outside services available and needed. Some EAPs provide limited in-house group or individual treatment for certain problems once they are identified. For example, the employee may be offered classes focusing on stress management, anger management, or health and wellness education. If the problem involves primarily people at work, many EAPs offer counselor-facilitated meetings with supervisors, co-workers, or both to help resolve any interpersonal problems or organizational conflicts. Mediation programs can mitigate major work-related organizational conflicts, which certainly can spill over and cause stress at home. Typically, large companies employ or can access trained mediators to help resolve equal employment opportunity, sexual harassment, gender, and other job discrimination complaints.

When work-to-family conflicts are noticed by friends and family, the referral process is much more unstructured and employee or family member follow-through tends to be much more unreliable. In general, work settings have more influence and control over employees' treatment-seeking behavior than do family members or friends. Given the nature of close relationships in the nonwork environment, problems tend to reach moderate to severe levels of intensity before effective referral strategies come into play. Although in some cases family members and close friends can get a loved one to seek treatment by using positive encouragement, more typically, coercion, threats, and even ultimatums may be required to get a poorly functioning or underfunctioning individual to admit to his or her problems and to seek help.

Once the initial contact is made with a health care provider, the well-trained provider can use psychoeducation and motivational interviewing strategies to encourage the employee or family member to consider an assessment and treatment program to help remediate the identified problems. Unfortunately, when these referral and intervention strategies fail, an individual may end up losing one's job, one's marriage, or both, before he or she decides to get help. By this time, the individuals' problems are multiple and even more distressing than before the more serious adverse events occurred. As is the case with other health care endeavors, it behooves all of us in the field to encourage prevention, early recognition, and early intervention strategies to minimize work-to-family conflicts and their consequences.

EMPIRICALLY BASED TREATMENTS

There are a limited number of empirically based treatments for marital and family problems (Baucom, Shoham, Mueser, Daiuto, & Stickle, 1998). Behavioral marital therapy (BMT) (Jacobson & Addis, 1993) has the most studies supporting its effectiveness; emotionally focused couple therapy (EFT) (Johnson & Denton, 2002) has a sufficient number to meet the criteria for empirically based treatments. Two other approaches, insight-oriented marital therapy (IOMT) (Snyder & Wills, 1989) and integrative behavioral couple therapy (IBCT) (Dimidjian, Martell, & Christensen, 2002) have limited evidence supporting effectiveness. In addition, the clinician in search of empirically supported treatments for marital and family problems associated with specific disorders can find literature suggesting effective treatments for alcohol and substance abuse; depression; bipolar disorder; domestic violence; anxiety disorders, including post-traumatic stress disorder (PTSD); problems with children and adolescents; and sexual dysfunction (Sprenkle, 2002). Details of these disorder-specific interventions are beyond the scope of this chapter; here we present a brief and basic description of BMT, EFT, IOMT, and IBCT.

BRIEF DESCRIPTION, TIME ELEMENT, AND SIDE EFFECTS OF TREATMENT

Behavioral Marital Therapy

BMT has been developed over the past 40 years and features a social learning approach to the assessment and treatment of couple dysfunction (Birchler, 2002). The two major components of intervention are behavioral exchange, and communication and problem-solving training. Couples are taught to identify positive and negative behaviors that are characteristic of or appropriate for their relationship and to increase positive behavioral exchanges while reducing or eliminating problem behaviors. Similarly, communication and problem-solving training consists of a psychoeducational, skill-acquisition, intervention component that helps couples to improve understanding and support for one another and to practice effective strategies for solving marital problems and reducing associated conflicts. Therapists employ a number of methods to help couples achieve their goals: (1) the administration of relationship assessment instruments to help define the problems, relationship strengths, and treatment goals and to provide baseline and outcome measures of change; (2) assertiveness and negotiation training; (3) coaching and feedback; (4) videotaped feedback of couple interactions; (5) modeling effective communication skills; and (6) systematic, often observational homework assignments.

BMT is conceptualized as a brief, here-and-now, directive treatment that typically lasts ten to twenty sessions. Regarding side effects of treatment, the relevant discussion on this point relates to what is known about any iatrogenic effects of treatment and any treatment-matching information that may be available. All couple therapies can have adverse iatrogenic effects, treatment failures, couple separations, and divorce outcomes. Most conjoint approaches are contraindicated for the treatment of moderate to severe domestic violence. Some couples, by entering into treatment, and perhaps through the influence and bias of the therapist, take actions that might not have been taken had treatment not been initiated. There are no good data regarding the prevalence of this phenomenon nor are there data on differential adverse effects due to type of treatment. That said, it is believed that, relative to EFT, IOMT, and IBCT, BMT may have a somewhat greater degree of relapse within one year following the end of formal treatment. Regarding suggestions for treatment matching, research to date suggests that BMT is particularly suited to younger couples who espouse an egalitarian relationship philosophy, who present with mild to moderate marital distress, who are committed to the relationship, and who are interactive and engaged enough to examine and carry out behavior change assignments in the home environment (Jacobson & Addis, 1993).

Emotionally Focused Couple Therapy

EFT is based on the attachment model of adult intimacy and focuses on restructuring key emotional responses and couple interactions to create a more secure bond between the partners (Johnson & Denton, 2002). EFT was developed in the early 1980s, emanating from earlier experiential and gestalt theory and practice. The EFT therapist acts as a process consultant, exhibiting unconditional positive regard, often working in a conjoint session with one partner at a time. Individual partners are helped to access and explore primary emotions (e.g., fear, hurt, need for attachment, etc.) and to identify and possibly relabel or eliminate secondary emotions (e.g., anger, defensiveness, etc.) that are more likely to lead to negative couple interactions. When EFT is successful, partners gain an understanding of their own and their partner's attachment histories and subsequent perceived needs. They learn to form an improved attachment bond with their mate that features positive and relatively softened interaction cycles. The therapist promotes empathy, acceptance, and mutual goal setting. Change is achieved not through insight into the past, catharsis, negotiation, communication and problem-solving training, or behavior exchange but through new emotional experiences learned in the present context of attachment-salient interactions. Most of the work is done in the weekly sessions; very little paper-and-pencil assessment or behavioral homework is assigned.

The length of treatment ranges from 8 to 15 sessions, unless one of the partners carries a diagnosis of PTSD; then the length of treatment is left open because moving through the stages of treatment takes longer. Regarding negative side effects, aside from the general phenomenon of iatrogenesis mentioned previously, EFT has not been found to be successful in cases of spouse abuse. Relatively speaking, EFT is particularly effective with couples older than the age of 35, from low income and low education levels, and with couples in which the woman believes that her mate still cares for her but whom she labels as "inexpressive." EFT also has been effective with families who are dealing with stress or grief reactions or where one partner has the diagnosis of PTSD (Johnson & Denton, 2002).

Insight-Oriented Marital Therapy

IOMT gained some status as an empirically supported marital treatment in 1989 when it was compared directly with BMT. Considerable notoriety has been related to this initial investigation and a follow-up study four years later. IOMT features a process called "affective reconstruction," whereby developmental origins of interpersonal themes and their manifestation in a couple's relationship are explored (Snyder & Schneider, 2002). The authors maintained that there is not one approach to IOMT, but many. The common objectives are to examine the affective and developmental components of couples' distress characterized by recurrent maladaptive relationship patterns based on early interpersonal experiences either in the partners' families of origin or as a function of other significant emotional relationships. Methods of intervention employed to accomplish this task range on a continuum from traditional psychoanalytic techniques rooted in object-relations theory to schema-based interventions derived from more traditional cognitive theory. The basic idea is that couples' maladaptive relationship patterns of interaction will continue until they are understood in a developmental context. Compared with skill acquisition methods featured in BMT, for example, proponents of IOMT argue that individuals' negative views of their partners' behavior are modified to a greater degree once they come to understand and resolve emotional conflicts they bring to the relationship from their own family and intimate relationship histories. For assessment, practitioners may use paper-and-pencil instruments, family genograms, and extended individual-based history-taking sessions. Techniques of affective reconstruction include therapists making interpretations relating partners' individual developmental relationship themes to current relationship conflict and promoting alternative relationship behaviors (including but not limited to basic behavior exchange techniques). Most of the insight-oriented work is done in session, with interpretive guidance provided by the therapist.

The length of therapy varies from 15 to 30 sessions, with an average of about twenty sessions. The approach may be best used for cases where developmental relationship experiences of one or both partners are causally related to the maladaptive interaction patterns that they are experiencing and when they are disposed to working on their problems by using an uncovering and interpretive psychotherapeutic approach. Moreover, this approach works best when it is quite possible to establish an atmosphere of safety, empathy, and mutual support. Given that these conditions are met, there is some evidence that the treatment gains made in IOMT are more profound and longer lasting than with BMT. On the other hand, IOMT may be less effective for persistently angry couples and for those couples who simply experience difficulties due to situational stressors or interpersonal skill deficits (Snyder & Schneider, 2002).

Integrative Behavioral Couple Therapy

IBCT is the newest kid on the block; empirical support for its effectiveness is emerging (Dimidjian et al., 2002). IBCT was conceived in the mid-1990s by behaviorally oriented marital therapists as a response to consistent research findings that BMT had a greater relapse rate than was desirable. In general, while the majority of couples treated with BMT significantly improved as a function of the therapy, about half relapsed at one-year follow-up (Jacobson & Addis, 1993). In addition, there was a desire by BMT practitioners to incorporate interventions targeting affect, as well as the previously developed treatments that targeted partners' behaviors and cognitions. IBCT basically adds acceptance strategies as a precursor to employing traditional BMT techniques. In certain cases, in lieu of BMT, the therapist employs acceptance strategies in an attempt to improve couple functioning.

Acceptance theory presumes that couples struggle over their differences (i.e., persistent conflict themes) and reach levels of polarization. Often, partners' persistent attempts to change unchangeable aspects of the relationship can trap both of them into maladaptive and ineffective patterns of relating. Accordingly, assessment strategies include the use of paper-and-pencil instruments to identify strengths and problems and to measure acceptance and change in these variables over time. Clinical interviewing is employed to discover and to explore the partners' presenting complaints and their typical conflict themes (e.g., closeness-distance, independence-dependence, introversion-extroversion, etc.). Moreover, if and when behavior-change strategies are used, training in the acquisition of communication and problem-solving skills and homework assignments are employed. The basic interventions used to promote partner and relationship acceptance (i.e., an intellectual and emotional understanding of what aspects of the relationship can and cannot be changed) include (1) empathic joining (i.e., teaching partners to express their pain and complaints in ways that elicit empathy versus making accusations), (2) unified detachment (i.e., helping partners to develop psychological distance from their conflicts by encouraging intellectualized analysis of the problem), and (3) tolerance building (i.e., reframing negative aspects of the problem into positives, practicing negative behavior in the therapy session and faking it at home, and self-care as an appropriate diversion from making unrealistic demands on the relationship).

Typically, up to 25 weekly sessions have been employed to achieve couples' goals. Although there appear to be no unique contraindications for the use of IBCT, it appears to work best with committed couples who, despite their struggles, have retained a measure of caring. Moreover, the approach, like most couples therapy, is not used in cases of domestic violence, active substance abuse, or severe psychopathology. In these latter cases, referrals for affected individuals need to be made to appropriate health care providers (Dimidjian et al., 2002).

These four empirically based marital treatments, by virtue of their inherent diversity, offer the couple therapist and the clients a variety of approaches to address marital and family problems. Ongoing research will suggest further treatment-matching guidelines so that the appropriate therapist may offer the appropriate treatment for a given couple with certain kinds of problems.

RELAPSE PREVENTION

Once couple or family therapy has been conducted and certain treatment gains achieved, there are basically two strategies that may be employed to prevent relapse in marital and family problems. Of course, relapse may be detected at home, in the workplace, or both. The most effective prevention strategy is to teach the employee and his or her partner directly how to recognize the potential risk factors or signs of relapse and what to do about them. For example, partners can be taught to recognize slippage in identified treatment gains and to take action to prevent further deterioration within the individual or within the relationship. Because the four therapy approaches described are relatively brief in duration, planned follow-up or booster sessions may be advised. It is recommended that the therapist encourage the couple to return to treatment at the earliest signs that they cannot maintain gains or whenever new problems persist.

The second strategy to help prevent relapse is used in the work setting. If family-to-work spillover occurred and the supervisor or co-workers were instrumental in recognizing and intervening on the employees' behalf then these people may be recruited to help be on guard for any signs of relapse as detected in the work setting. For example, for a period of follow-up, therapists may schedule supervisor-supervisee checkups. Similarly, at periodic performance-appraisal meetings, interactive review of the previous problems and reinforcement of ongoing prevention strategies can be very helpful. The objective is to provide an interpersonal mechanism for early detection and prevention of future difficulties. If the supervisors, co-workers, family members, and friends of an employee can be included in the knowledgeable and caring support group, success at relapse prevention can be achieved.

THERAPEUTIC BENEFITS OF WORK

There is little doubt that, apart from the basic economic survival and well-being of the family, participating in productive work is a desirable and meaningful life activity for most people. Moreover, adult participation in work also benefits the family (Piotrkowski, 1979). Certainly, it is the rare individual who does not do better and feel better when he or she is engaged in meaningful vocational or avocational pursuits. There is an increasing body of research that suggests that marriage and work go well together in terms of basic health status (Barnett, Brennan, Raudenbush, & Marshall, 1994). Men in our society, a society that expects men to work, generally have better physical and mental health when they are working (Carlson & Kacmar, 2000). Moreover, research conducted over the past few years also suggests that married women, compared with single women or homemakers, tend to be less depressed and more self-satisfied when engaged at least in part-time work (Almeida et al., 1999). There is little doubt that work is therapeutic. Productive activity can prevent health deterioration and work can help individuals to recover from a variety of mental health disorders (Montrey, 2000). It should be noted, however, that the key to mental and physical well-being of the family is a healthy work-to-family balance. Too much working, as in the case of workaholism, can be detrimental to marriages and to all family members' functioning (Robinson et al., 2001).

SUMMARY

Work and family, for most people, are two of the most rewarding and demanding social roles in life. A considerable amount of research has been conducted that suggests that work-to-family balance, or imbalance, as the case may be, plays a key role in individual and family health. Over the past few decades, socioeconomic factors have increased the requirement that both partners (or parents) in the family work. For many dual-earner families, this necessity has served to increase work-to-family stress factors and conflicts. On the other hand, changing aspirations, roles, and opportunities for women have increased dramatically their opportunity to establish careers along with their mates (i.e., dual-career families). These families gain certain benefits, but some pay a high price in terms of work-to-family work overload and social isolation outside of the work setting. This chapter described the relationship between work-to-family interactions, the bidirectional nature of setting influences, problem recognition, evaluation, referral strategies, and existing empirically based treatments for marital and family problems. A case illustration was included to exemplify typical development and possible resolution of problems related to work-to-family imbalance. More research is needed in this emerging area of concern so that appropriate people in work and home settings can understand the potential risks of work-to-family imbalance, recognize associated problems, and refer to or offer interventions that are appropriate to restore a health-promoting work-to-family balance.

References

Almeida, D. M., Wethington, E., & Chandler, A. L. (1999). Daily transition of tensions between marital dyads and parent-child dyads. *Journal of Marriage and the Family, 61,* 49-61.

Barnett, R. C., Brennan, R. T., Raudenbush, S. W., & Marshall, N. L. (1994). Gender and the relationship between marital-role quality and psychological distress: A study of dual-earner couples. *Psychology of Women Quarterly, 18,* 105-127.

Baucom, D., Shoham, V., Mueser, K., Daiuto, A., & Stickle, T. (1998). Empirically supported couple and family interventions for marital distress and mental health problems. *Journal of Consulting and Clinical Psychology, 66,* 53-88.

Bernas, K. H., & Major, D. A. (2000). Contributors to stress resistance: Testing a model of women's work-family conflict. *Psychology of Women Quarterly, 24,* 170-178.

Birchler, G. R. (2002). Behavioral marital therapy. In M. Hersen & W. Sledge (Eds.), *The encyclopedia of psychotherapy* (pp. 223-231). New York: Academic Press.

Bolger, N., DeLongis, A., Kessler, R. C., & Wethington, E. (1989). The contagion of stress across multiple roles. *Journal of Marriage and the Family, 51,* 175-183.

Carlson, D. S., & Kacmar, K. M. (2000). Work-family conflict in the organization: Do life role values make a difference? *Journal of Management, 26,* 1031-1054.

Dimidjian, S., Martell, C. R., & Christensen, A. (2002). Integrative behavioral couple therapy. In A. S. Gurman & N. S. Jacobson (Eds.), *Clinical handbook of couple therapy* (3rd ed., pp. 251-280). New York: Guilford.

Frone, M. R. (2000). Work-family conflict and employee psychiatric disorders: The national comorbidity survey. *Journal of Applied Psychology, 85,* 888-895.

Frone, M. R. (2003). Work-family balance. In J. C. Quick & L. E. Tetrick (Eds.), *Occupational health psychology.* Washington, DC: American Psychological Association.

Frone, M. R., Yardley, J. K., & Markle, K. (1997). Developing and testing an integrated model of the work-family interface. *Journal of Vocational Behavior, 50,* 145-167.

Grzywacz, J. G., & Marks, N. F. (2000a). Family, work, work-family spillover, and problem drinking during midlife. *Journal of Marriage and the Family, 62,* 336-348.

Grzywacz, J. G., & Marks, N. F. (2000b). Reconceptualizing the work-family interface: An ecological perspective on the correlates of positive and negative spillover between work and family. *Journal of Occupational Health Psychology, 5,* 111-126.

Hughes, D., Galinsky, E., & Morris, A. (1992). The effects of job characteristics on marital quality: Specifying linking mechanisms. *Journal of Marriage and the Family, 54,* 31-42.

Jacobson, N. S., & Addis, M. (1993). Research on couples and couples therapy: What do we know? *Journal of Consulting and Clinical Psychology, 61,* 85-93.

Johnson, S. M., & Denton, W. (2002). Emotionally focused couple therapy: Creating secure connections. In A. S. Gurman & N. S. Jacobson (Eds.), *Clinical handbook of couple therapy* (3rd ed., pp. 221-250). New York: Guilford.

Lambert, S. J. (1990). Processes linking work and family: A critical review and research agenda. *Human Relations, 43,* 239-257.

Montrey, J. S. (2000, April). The therapeutic value of work. *Veterans Health System Journal,* 25-28.

Piotrkowski, C. S. (1979). *Work and the family system.* New York: Macmillan.

Robinson, B. E., Flowers, C., & Carroll, J. (2001). Work stress and marriage: A theoretical model examining the relationship between workaholism and marital cohesion. *International Journal of Stress Management, 8,* 165-175.

Snyder, D. K., & Schneider, W. J. (2002). Affective reconstruction: A pluralistic, developmental approach. In A. S. Gurman & N. S. Jacobson (Eds.), *Clinical handbook of couple therapy* (3rd ed., pp. 151-179). New York: Guilford.

Snyder, D., & Wills, R. (1989). Behavioral versus insight oriented marital therapy: Effects on individual and interspousal functioning. *Journal of Consulting and Clinical Psychology, 57,* 39-46.

Sprenkle, D. H. (2002). *Effectiveness research in marriage and family therapy.* Alexandria, VA: American Association for Marriage and Family Therapy.

Viers, D., & Prouty, A. M. (2001). We've come a long way? An overview of research of dual-career couples' stressors and strengths. *Journal of Feminist Family Therapy, 13,* 169-190.

Part III

Environmental and Managerial Interventions

17

Workplace Accommodations for Psychopathology

LEAH TONEY PODRATZ
Shell Oil Company

LOIS E. TETRICK
George Mason University

*E*mployment is an important source of self-worth, meaning, and well-being for many people. Being excluded from productive work leads to social stigmatization and devaluation as well as poor individual health (Mechanic, 1998). According to epidemiological studies, in the United States within a one-year period approximately 28 percent of the adult population can be expected to experience some form of psychopathology (Milazzo-Sayre, Henderson, & Manderscheid, 1997, as cited in Thomas & Hite, 2002). Mental health disability is a common result of psychopathology and is costly to individuals and employers. The cost of mental illness has been estimated to be second only to heart disease in terms of total cost to employers (including cost of treatment, absenteeism, lost productivity, and mortality costs due to suicide) and in terms of lost years of healthy life. Thus, it is not unrealistic to say that most workplaces will be affected in some way by mental health concerns (Thomas & Hite, 2002). For legal, social, and business reasons, employers cannot afford to do nothing in response to needs of individuals with mental health disability, and they need to make accommodations. Accommodations are changes in the work structure or work environment that allow an individual with a disability to compete equally with nondisabled persons (Miller, 1997). Because mental illnesses are usually manifest through individuals' behavior, they call for accommodations that are different than those needed for physical disabilities. The goal of this chapter is to aid students, human resource professionals, and service providers in understanding the rationale for providing accommodations for psychopathology, barriers to accommodation, and the development of accommodations for individuals with mental health disabilities.

RATIONALES FOR ACCOMMODATION

Three primary rationales for accommodating individuals with mental health disability have been explicated by Cleveland, Barnes-Farrell, and Ratz (1997) and include legal mandates (i.e., "We must accommodate to be compliant with the law"), social or moral mandates (i.e., "We should accommodate in the best interest of our employees and society"), and business or economic principles (i.e., "Accommodation is an investment from which we will receive a return"). In this section we examine the nature and implications of these three forces behind employers' decisions to accommodate individuals experiencing psychopathology.

Legal Mandates

The Americans with Disabilities Act (ADA) of 1990 prohibits employment discrimination against qualified persons with disabilities, in an attempt to provide disabled persons with equal opportunities to experience the benefits of productive employment, to participate fully in society, and to live independently (Wasserbauer, 1997). The ADA requires employers with fifteen or more employees to accommodate individuals with physical or mental disabilities who can perform the essential functions of the job with reasonable accommodation. Employers are required to accommodate an individual whether the disability is a condition that exists prior to employment or one that develops during employment (Crist & Stoffel, 1992). Implications of this mandate are that employers will first have to determine who qualifies for disabled status under the ADA, whether they can perform the essential functions of the job (not to mention what the essential functions of the job are), and whether the requested accommodations are, in fact, reasonable. A considerable amount of ambiguity exists around these determinations, which is likely to make this task a difficult one and possibly lead to frustration on the part of the employee and the employer. (However, guides to compliance with the ADA are available; see the end of this chapter for resources.) In addition, as pointed out by Stone and Colella (1996), although legislation is likely to increase the access of disabled individuals to organizations, it may elicit negative reactions due to a feeling of being coerced to give special treatment to a target group, which may result in resentment toward disabled individuals, less challenging job assignments, or negatively biased performance appraisals.

On the other hand, a positive outcome of legislation surrounding accommodation (other than disabled individuals having equal opportunity in the workplace) may be a sense on the part of employers that there are an increasing number of protected groups and a willingness to accommodate a wide variety of employee needs and requests, regardless of whether an individual is protected by legislation (Cleveland et al., 1997). Evidence as to whether this positive reaction is indeed occurring is mixed. Although more companies are offering flexible benefits plans and work schedules, the psychological literature suggests that attributions about the individual employee and his or her disability (such as the origin of the disability and whether it is partially caused by the employee) affect the extent to which an employer is willing to fulfill an accommodation request (Cleveland et al., 1997; Stone & Colella, 1996). For example, employers may be less willing to accommodate an individual recovering from substance dependence than an individual experiencing depression, because substance dependence is often viewed as caused by the employee rather than by a disease process, whereas depression is more often thought of as a neurological disorder.

Social or Moral Mandates

The foundational concept for disability rights in general is that disability is the result of an interaction between the individual's impairments and environmental factors (Pope & Tarlov, 1991, as cited in Mechanic, 1998). Thus, individuals with impairments can participate in society to the extent that the environment is structured so as to not impose obstacles to participation. This idea along with the notion that employing organizations have a social obligation to provide for workers' needs and in doing so give back to employees and the larger society in which they conduct business makes up the social or moral rationale for accommodation. The degree to which an organization operates under these principles will likely influence the extent to which they offer accommodations for individuals with mental health disability.

However, norms surrounding justice and equal treatment of all employees may pose a conflict to the social impetus for accommodating specific groups of people. In other words, employers may feel that granting special accommodations to individuals with mental disability will cause resentment and negatively affect justice perceptions of other employees (employees who may feel that the organization's social obligations take a backseat to equal treatment). In this case an organization may be hesitant to grant accommodations even if doing so would fulfill a social or moral mandate (Cleveland et al., 1997). An alternative possibility is again that organizations seeking to fulfill social or moral obligations to accommodate individuals with disabilities (but also to avoid negatively affecting other employees' justice perceptions) should endeavor to create a flexible environment and management practices that provide for and accommodate the needs of all individuals. For example, as opposed to providing scheduling flexibility only for those employees who request it because of a disability, providing scheduling flexibility (e.g., flextime) to all employees would accommodate individuals with disabilities as well as decrease the risk of unfavorable justice perceptions on the part of nondisabled employees.

Business or Economic Considerations

Finally, business considerations may influence the extent to which employers accommodate individuals with mental health disabilities. Since the early 1990s there has been a growing understanding of the changing nature of the workforce and a sense of fierce competition for talent (Offerman & Gowing, 1990). Thus, many organizations conceptualize recruitment and selection activities as a two-way process, and attraction of potential employees to the organization has become a primary goal. One way in which organizations have attempted to attract the best employees is by providing appealing benefits and rewards packages. Thus, offering accommodations to qualified individuals with disabilities is one way that organizations can attract and retain good employees, and thus compete in the "war for talent." In addition, providing accommodations that facilitate the performance of essential job functions is likely to boost productivity. In other words, the process of accommodation can be viewed as a way of removing barriers to job performance and thus serves as an integral part of performance management (Brannick, Brannick, & Levine, 1992). Finally, federal tax incentives exist to encourage the employment of people with disabilities. For each of these reasons, providing accommodations to individuals experiencing psychopathology can be viewed as a good business practice.

BARRIERS TO PROVIDING ACCOMMODATIONS

We have made a case for accommodation of individuals with mental health disabilities according to legal, social or moral, and business or economic factors. Nevertheless, the ADA was implemented in 1992 and there appears to be some mixed findings as to how well the United States is doing in accommodating people with disabilities (Schall, 1998). Mental illness is the second most common charge of discrimination filed with Equal Employment Opportunity Commission (EEOC) under the ADA (Scheid, 1998). Therefore, it appears that the general business community may be hesitant to provide accommodations for people with mental health disabilities. Tetrick and Toney (2002) discussed that this hesitancy may stem from two sources: concerns about compliance with the ADA and the effect of reasonable accommodations on organizational functioning, and concerns about people with mental health disabilities.

Concerns about Compliance with the ADA

As noted previously, the ADA is ambiguous in that it does not offer concrete guidelines regarding whether a particular disability necessarily constitutes a disability covered by the ADA, making this process potentially frustrating for employers. In addition, employers may be concerned that individuals may misuse the ADA to get accommodations for disabilities they do not have. This concern should be somewhat alleviated in that the ADA does allow an employer to request medical documentation of the disability. Nevertheless, there are not explicit guidelines as to whether a particular accommodation is or is not appropriate for a particular disability or even what constitutes an undue hardship on an organization in making an accommodation. Essentially, each individual's request for accommodation under the ADA needs to be handled on a case-by-case basis. This reflects a shift in human resources thinking, in that previous EEOC recommendations indicated that an organization is expected to treat people the same or at least equally (Tetrick & Toney, 2002). The ambiguity resulting from a lack of specific guidelines also increased organizations' concerns about litigation under the ADA and the costs inherent in such litigation (Moore & Crimando, 1995).

In addition to the costs of litigation, employers have been concerned about the costs of accommodations (Moore & Crimando, 1995). However, several studies have indicated that the cost of accommodating employees with mental illnesses is low. The Job Accommodation Network reported that the cost of more than two-thirds of the accommodations for individuals with physical or mental health disabilities is less than $500 (Zuckerman, 1993). Meltsner (1998) found that 80 percent of accommodations for people with psychiatric disabilities cost nothing. While these concerns may not have disappeared, the data available suggest that most accommodations for physical and mental disabilities are not costly (Berry & Meyer, 1995).

Concerns about Hiring People with Mental Illness

Although the media and the public often associate mental health disabilities with aggressive and unsafe behavior, most individuals with mental health disabilities do not pose a greater threat to the safety of employees than does the general population (Monahan, 1992). Furthermore, the literature indicates that many people including employers and managers experience discomfort being around people with disabilities (Berry & Meyer, 1995), with the greatest stigma being associated with mental illness (Mechanic, 1998). Overcoming these negative stereotypes and attitudes toward individuals with mental health disabilities is a key component to an effective accommodation process. Recommendations regarding overcoming negative attitudes toward individuals with disabilities are discussed later in the Developing Accommodations section.

Another concern with making accommodations for people with mental health disabilities may stem from the type of accommodations needed. Accommodations for people with physical disabilities are usually accomplished by changing the physical environment (e.g., adjusting furniture so as to accommodate wheelchairs). Accommodations for people with mental health disabilities are not as straightforward because the disability is usually manifested in behaviors, therefore requiring behavioral accommodations (Kaufmann, 1993). According to the ADA, such accommodations might include job restructuring; part-time or modified work schedules; reassignment to another position; appropriate adjustment or modification of examinations, training materials, or policies; and provision of qualified readers or interpreters and other similar accommodations for persons with disabilities. The need to make such accommodations is often viewed by managers and co-workers as inconsistent with the behaviors of a "good employee," which adds to the stigma of having a mental illness (Mechanic, 1998).

Employee Self-Advocacy and Self-Identification

The ADA has the potential to help millions of Americans succeed in the workplace. However, people with mental health disabilities must first understand their rights under the ADA, identify barriers and accommodation strategies, initiate requests with the employer for reasonable accommodations, and implement accommodations collaboratively with their employers in order to benefit from the legislation (Roessler & Rumrill, 1995). Studies have shown that individuals with psychiatric conditions often do not know about their rights, and those who are well informed do not always feel confident in discussing arrangements for job accommodations with an employer (Granger, 2000). Furthermore, disclosure may be embarrassing to the individual and result in negative co-worker attitudes and stigmatization (Granger, 2000). Thus, mental health and human resource professionals should seek to develop employees' advocacy skills. For example, professionals should make available books and resources on the ADA, as well as teach advocacy skills through role play, group discussions, and *in vivo* skill application. A tool that may be helpful in helping individuals identify and request accommodations is the Work Experience Survey (Roessler & Gottcent, 1994). The Work Experience Survey is a structured interview that can be used by mental health professionals to facilitate individuals' identification of barriers to job performance and potential reasonable accommodations. Roessler and Gottcent (1994) suggested that use of the Work Experience Survey allows employees to limit the intrusiveness of the accommodation process and enhance their sense of control over the process and outcomes of the process.

Furthermore, it is important for employees to develop social support relationships at work, and they also may want to consider joining a support group for emotional and informational support outside of the workplace. Human resource professionals should provide employees with a reference library of books, Web sites, and contact information for such support groups, and make it possible for employees to access such information anonymously (such as on the organization's Web site). Of course, for employees to use this resource, the human resources department needs to advertise it so that employees know it is available. One potential way to disseminate such information is to include it as a note on pay stubs (Tetrick & Toney, 2002).

DEVELOPING ACCOMMODATIONS

Theoretical Frameworks for Developing Accommodations

Tetrick and Toney (2002) cited two frequently used theoretical approaches for developing accommodations for people with mental health disabilities. They are behavior analysis and self-efficacy.

Behavior Analysis

The behavior analysis approach, also referred to as the performance management approach, "seeks to systematically identify and reinforce successful work behavior, as well as the work environments which occasion it" (Hantula & Reilly, 1996, p. 114). Performance management has been shown to be highly effective in increasing a wide variety of positive work behaviors. Thus, performance management can be used as a foundation from which to design, implement, and evaluate reasonable work accommodations for persons with mental health disabilities. Using a behavior analysis framework, Hantula and Reilly (1996) stated that behavior is a function of the environment, and therefore there are no disabled persons but rather particular environments that are either enabling or disabling of a behavior. They proposed that it is the interaction between an individual and the individual's environment that determines whether a person has a "disability." The goal of reasonable accommodation, then, is to arrange the environment so that the probability of the occurrence of essential job-related behaviors is increased.

This framework is useful when developing accommodations, as it encourages the practitioner or employee to consider the specific situation at hand and how to best construct the environment to maximize important job behaviors, instead of choosing an accommodation from a published list (Tetrick & Toney, 2002). Because the primary causal factors of behavior in the workplace are social reinforcement contingencies, the majority of accommodations for mental health disabilities will involve a permanent and ongoing change in management style and technique, instead of a one-time engineering or mechanical change, as is frequently done to accommodate individuals with physical disabilities (Hantula & Reilly, 1996; Mancuso, 1990).

Self-Efficacy

Crist and Stoffel (1992) used Bandura's theory on self-efficacy as a basis to understanding the purpose of the accommodation, facilitating individuals in work roles. *Self-efficacy* is the term used by Bandura to refer to an individual's judgment about his or her own skills or abilities to perform a task or to succeed in a particular situation and has been found to predict subsequent behavior better than performance skills (Bandura, 1982). The authors described employability as a match between work-related skills, one's beliefs regarding job-related competence, and the job itself. Crist and Stoffel (1992) cited Bandura's four sources of self-efficacy judgments (emotional arousal, verbal or social persuasion, vicarious experience, and performance accomplishments) and noted that performance accomplishments appear to have the strongest effect on behavior. Thus, from a self-efficacy point of view, the purpose of reasonable accommodation is to give employees the opportunities to experience performance accomplishments. These experiences will in turn increase self-efficacy and lead to the successful performance of essential job-related behaviors.

Procedures Surrounding the Development of Accommodations

Job Analysis

Job analysis is a foundation to many human resource and management functions, not excluding the development of accommodations (Gatewood & Field, 2001). The ADA requires reasonable accommodation for individuals who can perform the essential functions of the job. Essential job functions are tasks and responsibilities necessary to the successful performance of the job, and if not performed they change the fundamental nature of the job (Wasserbauer, 1997). A thorough job analysis includes the identification of essential functions. According to the ADA, the following criteria can be used to assess the essential functions of a job: (1) Does the job exist to perform the function? (2) Which employees can perform the function? (3) What special skills are needed to perform the function? Essential job functions should then be documented in a written job description before a job is posted or candidates are interviewed. An important task especially relevant to accommodations for mental health disabilities is defining essential job functions related to emotional and psychosocial performance and differentiating the essential functions from the marginal functions (Crist & Stoffel, 1992). It is critically important for employers to include all essential job functions, including psychosocial performance, in a written job description. Court decisions also have included implicitly essential functions that do not appear in the ADA but are central functions of most jobs. These implicitly essential functions include being able to follow orders of supervisors, control behavior on the job, refrain from engaging in physical violence while at work, and attend work regularly (Schwartz, Post, & Simonetti, 2000).

The job analysis also should include the identification of knowledge, skills, and abilities required to perform job functions. According to Fine and Cronshaw (1999, as cited in Cronshaw & Kenyon, 2002), these skills can be grouped into three broad categories: adaptive skills (related to the ability to manage oneself in relation to the demands of conformity, change, or both), functional skills (related to the ability to appropriately process things, data, and people on simple to complex levels), and specific content skills (related to the ability to perform a specific job to predetermined standards using specific equipment, technology, and procedures and relying on functional skills).

Organizational Policies Regarding Accommodations

Developing, highlighting, and providing employees with a written policy on accom-modations for disabilities will likely increase the success of such programs. The literature suggests that to improve attitudes toward individuals with disabilities, first organizations need a policy on compliance with the ADA (Scheid, 1998). EEOC (2002) recommended that employers indicate in employee handbooks and on job applications that the employer will provide reasonable accommodations for the application process and during employment. Furthermore, employers should have written procedures regarding whom to contact with accommodation requests, a time frame for responses, and external resources for the identification of accommodations (for a list of resources, please see the last section in this chapter). Of course, employers need to supplement these written procedures with action and education of existing employees. Last, to foster an organizational culture that is supportive of developing accommodations, employers should coordinate various workplace sys-tems and programs such as employee assistance programs, wellness programs, coaching and mentoring, and training programs that facilitate job performance (Kirsh, 2000).

The Accommodation Process

From an employer's perspective, the process of developing accommodations can be viewed as a type of mediation process in the framework of alternative dispute resolution, as observed by Blanck, Andersen, Wallach, and Tenney (1994). Blanck and his colleagues demonstrated how this process could be used to ensure equality of job opportunity by outlining eight crucial decision points in the accommodation process: (1) address the disability, (2) get the facts, (3) identify reasonable accommodations, (4) assess the need for expertise, (5) assess cost factors and potential undue hardship, (6) initiate a problem-solving dialog, (7) develop an accommodation plan, and (8) evaluate the accommodation plan.

Blanck and colleagues (1994) suggested that the first step in developing accommodations is identifying or addressing the disability. An employer is not required to accommodate a disability until the employee identifies him- or herself as having a disability and needing reasonable accommodation. Second, employers should gather facts about whether the employee's condition qualifies as a disability under the ADA, in what ways the disability limits the employee's work, and whether the employee can perform the essential functions of the job with or without reasonable accommodation (Blanck et al., 1994). After facts have been gathered about the disability and the employee's particular challenges, an assessment of threat should be made; that is, whether the employee's disability poses a direct threat to him- or herself or co-workers under the ADA. Next, the employer should compare the employee's abilities and limitations with the essential job functions by reviewing the employee's written job description and job analysis information. According to Blanck and colleagues (1994), the next task is to identify the type and scope of potential reasonable accommodations and whether the costs of any accommodations would cause undue hardship to the employer.

During this accommodation negotiation process, the employer or employee may wish to use a consultant or job coach. If a consultant or job coach is to be used, according to alternative dispute resolution he or she should function as a neutral problem solver by finding solutions that work for both parties (Blanck et al., 1994). The consultant or job coach (or the employee if a consultant or job coach is not being used) should provide a list of accommodations that are agreeable to the employee, and the employer should select those accommodations he or she is willing to implement and provide a business-related reason for rejecting any potential accommodations. The employer should then initiate a meeting with the employee. During this meeting, the employer and employee together with the consultant (if one is being use) should develop an accommodation plan and establish a time line for the implementation of short- and long-term reasonable accommodations. It is important to note that consent from the employee must be obtained to include additional individuals in any discussion of the employee's condition, and confidentiality of the disability and accommodation plan should be maintained (EEOC, 2002; Mechanic, 1998). Blanck et al. (1994) suggested putting the plan in writing as "a road map" and signing it to make the plan specific and thorough, tangible, and substantiated. Plans for accommodations should include an open-door policy that empowers the employee and employer to modify the plan when necessary. Finally, Blanck and colleagues (1994) pointed out the need to evaluate the accommodation plan periodically. With the episodic nature of many mental illnesses, accommodations may have to be modified to match the individual's ability to perform various job responsibilities. The most important characteristics of the development and evaluation of accommodations are collaboration, flexibility, and documentation.

TYPES AND EFFICACY OF ACCOMMODATIONS

Accommodations Targeting Common Functional Limitations

Mental health disabilities often present recurrent functional challenges to employees. Mancuso (1990) categorized these potential challenges in terms of difficulties in one or more of the following: (1) duration of concentration, (2) screening out environmental stimuli, (3) maintaining stamina throughout the workday, (4) managing time pressure and deadlines, (5) initiating personal contact, (6) focusing on multiple tasks simultaneously, (7) responding to negative feedback, and (8) identifying physical and emotional side effects of psychotropic medications. Accommodations are likely to target aspects of the work environment that would ameliorate these difficulties. Crist and Stoffel (1992) developed a thorough list of potential reasonable accommodations for each of Mancuso's (1990) functional limitation categories. A few examples from their article are as follows: to accommodate difficulties with maintaining concentration, Crist and Stoffel (1992) suggested reducing interruptions by putting requests in writing and leaving them in a "to do" box, providing directive guidance on a regular basis, and reducing the noise level. To accommodate difficulties with maintaining stamina during the workday, Crist and Stoffel (1992) recommended providing additional breaks or a shortened workday, teaching on-the-job relaxation and stress-reduction techniques, and assistance with work organization and prioritization. In terms of accommodating difficulties with managing pressure and deadlines, Crist and Stoffel (1992) suggested daily assistance with structuring the workday such that small goals are set (with a short time frame) and reinforcement when goals are completed within the time frame.

Accommodations listed elsewhere in the literature typically involve flexibility with work schedules and the work environment, job duties modification, emotional support, effective supervision, and co-worker education. Some potential examples are as follows: flexible scheduling that allows time off for therapy followed by incremental increases in job responsibility; restructuring of office space (Blanck et al., 1994) or testing space (Zuriff, 1997) such as providing a private space, purchasing room dividers, and allowing employees to work from home; increased supervision including goal setting along with positive feedback (Mancuso, 1990); reassignment to a vacant position, part-time status, or both (Kaufmann, 1993); auxillary aids and services such as job coaches or readers; redelegation or restructuring of job assignments; and modification of training or testing materials and methods, including extension of time limits and provision of readers (Nester, 1993). Furthermore, because some individuals with mental health disabilities have difficulty with social skills and social interaction, helpful accommodations might include time off for social skills training or inclusion of feedback and guidance regarding appropriate job-related social interaction skills (Tetrick & Toney, 2002). Employers are encouraged to be creative and collaborate with the employee to develop individualized accommodations.

On-Site Emotional Support

In a survey of employers of individuals with psychiatric disability, most of whom were providing peer and other support services through NIMH Community Support Program, Parrish (1991) reported that many respondents found emotional supports helpful. Emotional supports included identifying co-workers willing to provide support on the job, making employee assistance programs available, providing on-site crisis intervention programs, and allowing telephone calls for support during work hours. A job coach is also an on-site source of support for an employee (Finkle, 1995). A job coach typically determines the type and quality of duties that are expected from the employee, reads or completes a performance contract for the employee, monitors the employee as he or she performs job duties, and then makes accommodation recommendations. Granger (2000), in a study of twenty focus groups with persons with psychiatric disabilities, found that in general, those individuals with job coaches reported that the most valued support in getting job accommodations was their job coach or job developer. However, Parrish (1991) recommended that employers encourage the use of on-site supports, but not to promote continued use of these supports any longer than necessary, because of the stigmatization that can occur when such visible on-site supports are used.

Effective Supervision

Employees with mental health disabilities often may be accommodated through the use of increased and more effective supervision. Hantula and Reilly (1996) defined effective supervision as "supervisory and management practices or systems which maximize individual performance and protect the dignity of the individual" (p. 114). Accommodations that increase effective supervision are likely to be beneficial for all employees, not just those with disabilities. Not only should increased monitoring and reinforcement increase the performance of employees with mental health disabilities (Mancuso, 1990) but also monitoring and reinforcement should communicate clear and unambiguous performance standards. Czajka and DeNisi (1988) found that specified performance standards eliminated the perception of employees with disabilities as members of an outgroup needing special favors and resulted in individuals with disabilities receiving comparable performance ratings as individuals without disabilities. Thus, it appears that good management practices such as clear performance goals, regular monitoring and feedback, and positive reinforcement should be included as important aspects of an accommodation plan.

Evaluating the Efficacy of Accommodations

Very few studies exist that empirically examine the efficacy of specific accommodations for specific disabilities and are sorely needed (Tetrick & Toney, 2002). Nevertheless, we can infer characteristics of effective accommodations from the clinical treatment literature. As discussed in earlier chapters, cognitive-behavioral therapy has received considerable empirical support in the clinical treatment literature, especially for anxiety and mood disorders (cf. Roth, Marx, & Coffey, 2002; Truax & McDonald, 2002). The primary mechanism of cognitive-behavioral therapy that may generalize to work accommodations is the process of changing individuals' thoughts, behaviors, or both. Many of the accommodations discussed previously have the potential to help the individual change nonproductive thoughts and behaviors—effective supervision, mentoring, coaching, and social skills training can all provide structured feedback on job-relevant behaviors and thought processes. Also, because psychotropic medications have been shown to be effective in ameliorating symptoms of psychopathology, work accommodations that facilitate employees' sticking to their medication regimen (e.g., time off for doctor's visits) as well as those that allow the employee to manage medication side effects (e.g., breaks during the day or flexible work schedules) also should be effective accommodations.

Regardless of the specific accommodations, the intended results of workplace accommodations should be evaluated and monitored to know whether the accommodation is effective. Furthermore, based on the performance management or behavioral analysis approach, accommodations can be evaluated by simply examining the employee's ability to perform the job. If an assumption of developing an accommodation plan is that it will facilitate the employee's successful performance of the job, then an examination of job performance should be one indication of the efficacy of the accommodation.

SUMMARY

Making accommodations for individuals with mental health disabilities serves to enhance employers' pools of talented employees, enhance employees' ability to perform their jobs, and meet the legal requirements of the ADA. Accommodations for individuals with mental health disabilities tend to be behavioral and ongoing compared with the one-time change of the physical work environment associated with many workplace accommodations for people with physical disabilities. Successful accommodations appear to be those that are developed collaboratively (i.e., between the individual employee and the employer) and are flexible and clearly specified. Further periodic reevaluation of the effectiveness of accommodations is required.

INFORMATION AND RESOURCES ON WORKPLACE ACCOMMODATIONS

Equal Employment Opportunity Commission
1801 L. Street NW
Washington, DC 20507
(800) 669-4000
www.eeoc.gov

Job Accommodation Network
P.O. Box 6080
Morgantown, WV 26506-6080
(800) 526-7234 or (304) 293-7184
www.jan.wvu.edu

U.S. Department of Labor
For written materials: (800) 959-3652 (voice); (800) 326-2577 (TTY)
To ask questions: (202) 219-8412
www.dol.gov

ADA Disability and Business Technical Assistance Centers (DBTACs)
(800) 949-4232

RESNA Technical Assistance Project (technology-related services for individuals
with disabilities)
(703) 524-6686 (voice); (703) 524-6639 (TTY)
www.resna.org

Access for All Program on Employment and Disability
School of Industrial and Labor Relations
106ILR Extension
Ithaca, NY 14853-3901
(607) 255-7727 (voice); (607) 255-2891 (TTY)
ilr_ped@cornell.edu

Business Leadership Network
1331 F Street, NW
Washington, DC 20004-1107
(202) 376-6200, ext. 35 (voice); (202) 376-6205 (TTY)
dunlap-carol@dol.gov
www.usbln.com

References

Americans with Disabilities Act of 1990, 42 U.S.C.A. § 12101 *et seq.* (West 1993).
Bandura, A. (1982). Self-efficacy mechanism in human agency. *American Psychologist, 37,*
    122-147.
Berry, J. O., & Meyer, J. A. (1995). Employing people with disabilities: Impact of attitude
    and situation. *Rehabilitation Psychology, 40,* 211-222.
Blanck, P. D., Andersen, J. H., Wallach, E. J., & Tenney, J. P. (1994). Implementing reasonable
    accommodations using ADR under the ADA: The case of a white-collar employee
    with bipolar mental illness. *Mental and Physical Disability Law Reporter, 18*(4), 458-
    464.
Brannick, M. T., Brannick, J. P., & Levine, E. L. (1992). Job analysis, personnel selection
    and the ADA. *Human Resource Management Review, 2,* 171-182.
Cleveland, J. N., Barnes-Farrell, J. L., & Ratz, J. M. (1997). Accommodation in the workplace.
    Human Resource Management Review, 7, 77-107.
Crist, P. A., & Stoffel, V. C. (1992). The Americans with Disabilities Act of 1990 and
    employees with mental impairments: Personal efficacy and the environment. *Ameri-
    can Journal of Occupational Therapy, 46,* 434-443.

Cronshaw, S. F., & Kenyon, B. L. (2002). An application model relating the essential functions of a job to mental disabilities. In J. C. Thomas & M. Hersen (Eds.), *Handbook of mental health in the workplace* (pp. 501-518). Thousand Oaks, CA: Sage.

Czajka, J. M., & DeNisi, A. S. (1988). Effects of emotional disability and clear performance standards on performance ratings. *Academy of Management Journal, 31*(2), 394-404.

Equal Employment Opportunity Commission. (2002). *The Americans with Disabilities Act: A primer for small business.* Washington, DC: Author.

Finkle, A. L. (1995). Reasonable accommodation obligation: Some practical tips. *Employee Assistance Quarterly, 10*(3), 1-20.

Gatewood, R. D., & Field, H. S. (2001). *Human resource selection* (5th ed.). Fort Worth, TX: Dryden Press.

Granger, B. (2000). The role of psychiatric rehabilitation practitioners in assisting people in understanding how to best assert their ADA rights and arrange accommodations. *Psychiatric Rehabilitation Journal, 23*(3), 215-223.

Hantula, D. A., & Reilly, N. A. (1996). Reasonable accommodation for employees with mental disabilities: A mandate for effective supervision? *Behavioral Sciences and the Law, 14,* 107-120.

Kaufmann, C. L. (1993). Reasonable accommodations to mental health disabilities at work: Legal constructs and practical applications. *Journal of Psychiatry and Law, 21*(2), 153-174.

Kirsh, B. (2000). Factors associated with employment for mental health consumers. *Psychiatric Rehabilitation Journal, 24,* 13-21.

Mancuso, L. (1990). Reasonable accommodations for workers with psychiatric disabilities. *Psychosocial Rehabilitation Journal, 14*(2), 3-19.

Mechanic, D. (1998). Cultural and organizational aspects of application of the Americans with Disabilities Act to persons with psychiatric disabilities. *Milbank Quarterly, 76,* 5-23.

Meltsner, S. (1998, June). Psychiatric disabilities: What's real, what's protected. *Business and Health, 16*(6), 46-53 .

Miller, S. P. (1997). Keeping the promise: The ADA and employment discrimination on the basis of psychiatric disability. *California Law Review, 85,* 701.

Monahan, J. (1992). Mental disorder and violent behavior: Perceptions and evidence. *American Psychologist, 47,* 511-521.

Moore, T. J., & Crimando, W. (1995). Attitudes toward Title I of the Americans with Disabilities Act. *Rehabilitation Counseling Bulletin, 38,* 232-247.

Nester, M. A. (1993). Psychometric testing and reasonable accommodation for persons with disabilities. *Rehabilitation Psychology, 38*(2), 75-85.

Offerman, L., & Gowing, M. (1990). Organizations of the future: Changes and challenges. *American Psychologist, 2,* 95-105.

Parrish, J. (1991). *Reasonable accommodations for people with psychiatric disabilities* (Informal survey report). Rockville, MD: National Institute of Mental Health.

Roessler, R., & Gottcent, J. (1994). The Work Experience Survey: A reasonable accommodations/career development strategy. *Journal of Applied Rehabilitation Counseling, 25*(3), 16-21.

Roessler, R. T., & Rumrill, P. D. (1995). Promoting reasonable accommodations: An essential postemployment service. *Journal of Applied Rehabilitation Counseling, 26*(4), 1-7.

Roth, D. A., Marx, B. P., & Coffey, S. F. (2002). Social anxiety disorder, specific phobias, and panic disorder. In J. C. Thomas & M. Hersen (Eds.), *Handbook of mental health in the workplace* (pp. 193-213). Thousand Oaks, CA: Sage.

Schall, C. M. (1998). The Americans with Disabilities Act: Are we keeping our promise? An analysis of the effect of the ADA on the employment of persons with disabilities. *Journal of Vocational Rehabilitation, 10*(3), 191-203.

Scheid, T. K. (1998). The Americans with Disabilities Act, mental disability, and employment practices. *Journal of Behavioral Health Services and Research, 25,* 312-324.

Schwartz, R. H., Post, F. R., & Simonetti, J. L. (2000). The ADA and the mentally disabled: What must firms do? *Business Horizons, 43,* 52-60.

Stone, D., & Colella, A. (1996). A model of factors affecting the treatment of disabled individuals in organizations. *Academy of Management Review, 21,* 352-401.

Tetrick, L. E., & Toney, L. P. (2002). Job accommodations for mental health disabilities. In J. C. Thomas & M. Hersen (Eds.), *Handbook of mental health in the workplace* (pp. 509-534). Thousand Oaks, CA: Sage.

Thomas, J. C., & Hite, J. (2002). Mental health in the workplace: Toward an integration of organizational and clinical theory, research, and practice. In J. C. Thomas & M. Hersen (Eds.), *Handbook of mental health in the workplace* (pp. 3-14). Thousand Oaks, CA: Sage.

Truax, P., & McDonald, T. (2002). Depression in the workplace. In J. C. Thomas & M. Hersen (Eds.), *Handbook of mental health in the workplace* (pp. 123-154). Thousand Oaks, CA: Sage.

Wasserbauer, L. I. (1997). Mental illness and the Americans with Disabilities Act: Understanding the fundamentals. *Journal of Psychosocial Nursing, 35*(1), 22-26.

Zuckerman, D. (1993). Reasonable accommodations for people with mental illness under the ADA. *Mental and Physical Disability Law Reporter, 17*(3), 311-320.

Zuriff, G. E. (1997). Accommodations for test anxiety under ADA? *Journal of the American Academy of Psychiatry and the Law, 25*(2), 197-206.

18

Motivating and Leading Dysfunctional Employees

JON FREW
Pacific University

*O*nce upon a time, the roles and responsibilities of the manager were unadorned and straightforward. In 1971, this author was hired as the personnel specialist at a manufacturing facility. In those days, if the foreman had problems with an employee, the foreman would simply send him (occasionally her) to the "kid upstairs" who would handle the "head cases." We were all working in the land of X.

Fifteen years later, Hunsaker and Alessandra (1986, p. XI) wrote, "The art of managing others is a dynamic process that is ever changing and evolving. Many of the managerial concepts proposed only a few years ago cannot and will not work in today's environment. People have changed. Government has changed. The world economy has changed." Into the 1980s and 1990s, the fundamental fabric of the management role has been torn away. Managers who were once expected to command, control, and persuade others to engage in activities they would not do if not closely watched were now required to be leaders, to be forward thinking, to have people skills, and to build self-managed teams. The land of X was being slowly transformed into the land of Y.

Hunter, Schmidt, Rauschenberger, and Jayne (2000, p. 294) described this shift as a "new social contract" between management and workers, "with new implications for understanding managerial and supervisory perceptions of intelligence and motivation as causal agents of objective measures of job performance and ratings of that performance." Workers, tired of being cogs in hierarchical wheels in organizations with assembly-line mentalities, were invited to become partners and to participate in efforts to increase productivity and competiveness. Supervisors were confronted with the daunting task of changing their worldview and their skill set.

In this new millennium, a new wrinkle has been added to the fabric. Organizational theory always has been conceived and developed with the assumption that the individuals who populate the workplace are rational and psychologically fit. But Thomas and Hite (2002, p. 5) made a convincing case that this notion of a mentally healthy workplace is moribund. According to these authors, "Mental illness is pervasive in American society," and because most of us go to work, in the workplace as well. They assert that in the days of X, workplaces could eliminate this problem simply by eliminating the dysfunctional employee. In this new era, however, "Organizations will find it in their own interests, as well as the employees, to accommodate the needs of an individual experiencing mental distress" (p. 3).

Svyantek and Brown (2002, p. 490) corroborated this trend in the workplace and stated that management must make a decision to "ignore the increase in dysfunctional behavior(s) and hope the behavior goes away, or take actions to decrease the dysfunctional behavior." Clearly dysfunctional behavior does not just go away. The critical question that this chapter addresses is, What are the approaches managers can take to motivate, lead, and communicate sensitively with employees who are experiencing moderate to high levels of distress that leads to dysfunctional behavior?

THE DYSFUNCTIONAL EMPLOYEE—A CLARIFICATION

In the title of this book is the term *psychopathology*. In the title of this article is the *dysfunctional employee*. I must examine and sharpen these terms before this chapter proceeds.

Psychopathology means literally some type of sickness of the brain. In their previous book, Thomas and Hersen (2002) devoted a section to effects of psychopathology on work and included eleven chapters on specific forms of psychopathology like bipolor disorders, depression, and schizophrenia. In this book, the language has changed to "categories of dysfunction" and eleven chapters have been included in that section of the book. There is significant overlap in topics, but in this book, the authors of the chapters have reviewed additional categories like martial and family problems and social skills deficits, which are not types of sickness of the brain. Although there are syndromes that are clearly psychopathological in nature, this author favors the term *dysfunction* and proposes two types of dysfunction that managers will confront and be required to address.

Lowman (1993, p. 4) defined "worak dysfunction" as "psychological conditions in which there is a significant impairment in the capacity to work caused by characteristics of the person or by an interaction between personal characteristics and working conditions." This definition delineates the core of the two general types of work dysfunction. I call the first category "individual dysfunction." Individual dysfunction refers to an impairment in the capacity to work that is related primarily to psychological distress which has nothing or very little to do with the workplace itself. Examples are mental health conditions such as depression, post-traumatic stress disorder, anxiety, and panic attacks or "life" conditions such as marital problems, a death in the family, or conflicts with a child. Employees dealing with these types of issues bring their residue into the workplace and can be significantly impaired as they attempt to carry out their job responsibilities. Certainly workplace dynamics can exacerbate these conditions, but they did not originate or develop in the workplace as a result of the individual's interaction with the work environment.

The second category of work dysfunction is dysfunction that arises primarily because of the nature of the ongoing contact between and employee and some element(s) of his or her work environment. This type of dysfunction is not solely the domain of the individual but is a product of the dynamic relationship between the individual and the environment. For the purpose of this chapter, I call the second category "systemic dysfunction." Examples are psychological distress related primarily to conflict with a boss, a transfer to a job that does not challenge the employee, sexual harassment, or a poor fit between an employee and the values or culture of that organization.

Managing and leading employees who exhibit individual or systemic dysfunction is a challenge. Being able to diagnose the etiology or primary source and cause of the distress is critical in choosing effective strategies to respond to the employee. Managers generally speaking have more authority, expertise, and power to respond to employees who are experiencing work-related difficulties. Employees who demonstrate individual dysfunction, however, must be managed as well, and the next section of this chapter focuses on this category.

THE CASE OF INDIVIDUAL DYSFUNCTION

A manager becomes aware of an employee's dysfunctional behavior. This employee may be late for work several days a week, may be tearful or agitated, may sit and stare into space, and may not be getting the work done. These behaviors are not consistent with this employee's past record. Something has changed. Something is wrong. What is the manager's role and responsibility in terms of intervention with this employee?

For the purposes of this section, this employee's dysfunctional behavior is directly linked to a type of mental illness or to an acute situational stressor such as a divorce or a seriously ill child. This employee is as disabled as his co-worker who suffered a mild heart attack and is back at work on light duty. In this era following the Americans with Disabilities Act (ADA) of 1990, the organization's responsibility is clear. Some type of accommodation must be struck that will balance the need of the employee and the needs of the organization. There are at least three compelling reasons for the organization to work with this employee. The first reason is legal, and ADA guidelines are outlined in the next paragraph. The second reason is human. This employee needs support from his employer to weather the acute phase of the mental health illness or family crisis. The third reason is on the business side. Thomas and Hite (2002, p. 6) pointed out that there are a number of sound business reasons to find an accommodation.

ADA CONSIDERATIONS

Bernardin and Lee (2002, pp. 27-28) reviewed the ADA and related case law and made the following recommendations for employers dealing with an employee with a mental disability. I have modified or expanded on the recommendations listed by Bernardin and Lee but not altered the core point they made.

1. The employee can decide to disclose that there is a mental condition or not but must make this disclosure to be covered under the ADA.
2. If the disclosure is made, information about the nature of the mental disability must be provided to the human resources (HR) manager or someone who performs in that capacity in the organization.
3. The HR manager and the employee decide whether to let others (co-workers, supervisors) know about the disability. The employee can choose to have the information remain confidential with only the HR manager in the loop.
4. It is generally to the employee's benefit to give others information about the disability. Information can curtail rumors and false perceptions, increase co-workers' comfort with the acceptance of the employee, and attack the stigma that is so often associated with mental illness.
5. According to the ADA, performance expectations do not need to be changed by the employer.
6. Regular contact and meetings should occur between the HR manager, the employee, the mental health therapist involved, and any relevant employees (e.g., the supervisor) to evaluate how well the accommodation is serving the needs of all parties involved.

Given these recommendations, how does the supervisor manage, motivate, and lead this employee with a mental disability? The following section will address these concerns.

GUIDELINES AND STEPS FOR MANAGERS

The following guidelines outline the necessary steps and potential actions that apply to the case scenario of individual dysfunction.

Assessment and Disclosure

The first step occurs when information about the individual dysfunction comes to the attention of the manager. In the best case scenario, the employee initiates a conversation with the manager about the illness or acute situation. Workers often are reluctant to make this disclosure, however, fearing that they will be stigmatized or lose their job. If the employee does not come forward, the manager will surmise there is a problem because of the dysfunction related to the condition is evident to the manager or is brought to his or her attention through the report of co-workers. There are many warning signs but listing them is beyond the scope of this chapter. A key red flag, however, is a relatively sudden change in the employee's appearance, demeanor, interpersonal style, work habits, or level of productivity.

If the employee does not disclose, the manager must conduct some type of assessment to objectively measure the manifest dysfunctional behavior. The assessment tools will vary widely by job context but may include attendance records, tardiness reports, a performance review, or productivity measures.

After sufficient data are collected to document the change in the employee's behavior, the manager can initiate a meeting with the employee. It is strongly recommended that the manager approach the employee sensitively and compassionately rather than critically and dispassionately. An employee who is struggling with a mental illness or family crisis and is confronted in a caring way by the boss will generally be willing to begin the disclosure process, which will lead to the following steps.

Work or Leave Determination

After the manager and HR manager have information about the nature and severity of an employee's mental disability, a decision must be made regarding whether the employee is best served by remaining at work (in full or limited capacity) or going on leave. Most organizations have provisions for medical leave and in some situations time away may be the best option.

There are a number of individuals who must communicate and collaboratively make the decision about the disabled employee's job status. It is critical that the employee be in treatment with a health professional who can provide the expert information to organization representatives about the type of mental illness or acute situational stressor and its severity and prognosis. The manager or supervisor's role is not to diagnosis and treat the employee. The health professional(s) involved in the case will typically be an employee assistance program counselor, an independent psychotherapist, a psychiatrist, or a general medical practitioner. The other "players" who need to be part of the decision are the employee, the immediate supervisor, and the HR manager. Collaboration is crucial because different individuals have different pieces of the puzzle that must be put together to reach the best recommendations regarding the employee's ability to work and whether continuing to work will be likely to exacerbate or attenuate the presenting condition and circumstances.

This author has been in two of these important roles. As a manager, I have supervised individuals who became mentally impaired by issues not related to the job. As a psychologist, I have worked with HR departments and supervisors to devise accommodations for patients under my care or to arrange temporary medical leave. I can attest that the welfare of the individual employee and the needs of the organization are best served when there is an open dialogue between mental health professionals and the organization. The best prognosis for a speedy return to work or recovery when working occurs when organization officials are genuinely concerned about the employee's health, open to the input of health professionals and willing to be educated at least at a basic level about the particular mental illness or life crisis involved. It is also very helpful if the clinician(s) involved have a working understanding of how organizations work, the roles of leaders, and the dynamics of discrimination and harassment and any other features of the workplace that may come into play as decisions are being made (see Thomas & Hite, 2002, p. 10).

Designated Implementation and Follow-up of a Plan of Action

The next step is the design and implementation of a plan. For example, the employee will be on leave until the end of the month and at that time the ability to work will be revisited, or the employee will continue to work in the same job, or the employee will be transferred temporarily to other duties, part-time employment, or both. If the employee remains at work, the plan should include regular communication points between the employee, the supervisor, HR, and the treating clinician. Performance expectations (according to the ADA) do not need to be modified, although realistically they usually are modified as supervisors and co-workers give the employee time and a wider berth while the disability condition is ameliorated.

If the vast majority of cases are handled sensitively and follow the steps above, the dysfunctional behavior that was the red flag that set off the series of steps and actions will disappear or decrease sufficiently. The combination of effective mental health interventions (including counseling and often medication), the support of family and friends, and a workplace that is responsive, flexible, and caring will create the conditions that allow the employee to return to work or continue to work and regain status of a productive and valued member of the organization.

Motivation and Leadership in the Case of Individual Dysfunction

Issues of motivation and leadership are discussed in more detail in the next section of this chapter. In the case of individual dysfunction, the following actions and behaviors will serve the manager well.

Contemporary leadership theory (see, for example, Robbins, 2002, p. 74) emphasizes trust. Workers will not follow leaders they do not trust. Trust is critical in any supervisory relationship but perhaps is even more important when an employee is experiencing an acute mental or life crisis. To engender trust, managers must be open and fair, show consistency, fulfill promises made, and maintain confidences. Managers often are caught in a tricky triangle between their bosses who want the employee to "get well now" and the employee and health professionals who are asking for time and patience. To be trustworthy, managers must speak the truth and not make deals with the employee that they must later rescind. The key is to be open and fair while accurately representing the organization's bottom lines.

Employees who are in distress will appreciate the opportunity to tell their story to their manager. This relatively simply yet powerful action requires only that the manager create time and space to listen to the employee's description of the illness or life crisis without judgment or criticism. Ideally, this is a very "human" conversation with work consideration bracketed off temporarily. The manager should not probe for details the employee does not want to provide. These types of dialogues in which the employee feels accepted and affirmed despite the disturbing current circumstance are healing (without the manager attempting to be a counselor) and will motivate the employee to work with the organization to reach the appropriate accommodations that serve both parties.

The manager will demonstrate effective leadership and motivate the employee by holding the employee accountable to whatever conditions are arranged in the plan of action. If the performance expectations are not being met, the plan of action can be renegotiated. Renegotiation is a better solution than "letting the employee slide," which sends the wrong message and can be demotivating.

THE CASE OF SYSTEMIC DYSFUNCTION

One early leading theorist in the field of organization behavior, Chris Argyris (1957) recognized that the nature of a job or the effect of a company's social organization (e.g., autocratic management) could impede an employee's development and ultimately interfere with the attainment of full mental health. Lowman (1993, p. 9) wrote, "It is the failure to find, implement, or sustain a satisfactory work role ... that creates psychological difficulties." Thomas and Hite (2002, p. 7) said, "The workplace itself may contribute to distress, and ultimately, to mental disorders." Svyantek and Brown (2002) reviewed the literature that addresses dysfunctional behavior in the workplace and concluded that although most explanations favor individual pathology over organizational characteristics, systematic factors are frequently the culprit. They described the potential influence of variables such as structure, design, climate, and particularly culture on individual behavior. Robbins (2002, p. 26) picked up on the importance of the employee–culture fit and urged managers to hire only individuals who they think will fit into the organization's culture. He cautioned that a poor fit will lead to "hires who lack motivation and commitment and who are dissatisfied with their jobs and the organization."

In this section of this chapter the challenges of managing, motivating, and leading the employee who is exhibiting dysfunction related to his or her relationship with aspects of the workplace are considered. Authors and observers of individual behavior in the workplace from the days of the Hawthorne studies (and earlier) to the most contemporary literature recognize that it is frequently the case that an employee's so-called mental illness or work dysfunction is an obvious result of factors that reside exclusively or primarily in the workplace. It is well beyond the scope of this chapter to develop a thorough taxonomy of those factors. Common issues that arise between an employee and the workplace are interpersonal conflicts with supervisors or co-workers, the perception (or reality) of unfair treatment by an employer such as being passed over for promotion or not getting a raise, a poor fit between the employee and job content, team or group dynamics that ostracize an employee, and a poor fit between employee and organizational culture. For the purposes of the chapter, I assume that the systemic dysfunction has not always been present. The employee and his or her relationship with the organization was in some balance, and because of a change in the environment, dysfunctional behavior emerged; for example, there was merger and the organization's culture was dramatically altered, there was a new job assignment, there was a new supervisor, or the organization shifted to a team-based philosophy.

Why is there less written and known about these circumstances of systemic dysfunction? This author's opinion is that these types of situations are far more complex to clearly conceptualize and even more difficult to find successful approaches to remediate. The situation of the worker who has an active episode of a mental illness like manic depression, though tragic and disruptive for the organization, is relatively straightforward and simple. The "problem" is not work related so members of the organization are not required to examine "their piece of the action" that contributed to the illness or dysfunction. It is the employee who must change, not the workplace.

In the case of systemic dysfunction, the manager must follow a series of steps that are not dissimilar to the ones outlined that addressed individual dysfunction. The process begins when the dysfunctional behavior is extreme enough, prolonged enough, and sufficiently out of the ordinary for that employee to come to the manager's attention. The dysfunctional behavior is merely a symptom of a state of "dis-ease" or the tip of an iceberg. To make sense out of the behavior(s), managers must analyze the entire iceberg above and below the water, and that will involve an assessment phase, which will require a close examination of the relationship between the employee and elements of the work environment.

The primary source of information for this assessment phase will be the employee. Managers must document the dysfunctional behavior and then initiate a meeting with the employee. (It is assumed that other employees may have approached the manager as well about the change in this employee's behavior.) In this meeting, it is advisable for the manager to present the information in the form of objective data and observation rather than as interpretation and criticism. For example, the manager may say, "Sam, you have been late for work five times in the past two weeks and your daily reports are not being turned in. You have an excellent record of being on time and meeting deadlines so I am wondering what's up?" Contrast that approach with "Sam you are always late for work, and I can't remember the last time you got a report to me on time. Obviously you don't give a shit about my expectations or this company anymore."

In the first scenario, Sam is less likely to be defensive and is given the opportunity to comment on the factors that are creating the work dysfunction. In the second case scenario, Sam is being criticized and blamed, and the boss who, at this point does not have a clue about what the behaviors mean, imposes an explanation for the behavior. Sam will undoubtedly clam up or become defensive. Instead of a dialogue between Sam and his boss that would uncover the underlying factors that are directly connected to the dysfunctional behavior, a power struggle has already begun, which will be difficult to undo. The manager will not elicit Sam's cooperation, the true causes of Sam's problem will not be revealed, and the dysfunction will continue or worsen.

A final factor that often comes into play in this phase is the degree of safety the employee feels to "speak the truth." Even if the manager invites this conversation in a supportive, nonaccusatory way, Sam may be reluctant to speak up, fearing sanctions given the political context. Maybe his problem is with the very supervisor who is asking him what is wrong, or maybe it is with another employee who is the supervisor's best friend, or perhaps he fears if he says he cannot stand his new job assignment that he will get a pink slip in the next wave of layoffs. These types of situations are delicate, but the goal is to increase the employee's sense of safety and security so that the core factors involved can be uncovered and a determination can be made about making modifications and accommodations that can mediate the employee's work environment misalignment and ultimately reduce or eliminate the dysfunctional behavior.

This assessment phase is the key to success. The manager must have accurate information about the workplace factors that are causing the dysfunctional employee such distress. Later in this chapter, several examples of types of factors are described in a case study format, including recommendations for managerial interventions that will restore motivation and model effective leadership.

Unlike cases of individual dysfunction, rarely is there a decision to be made about whether to continue to work or to leave. Ideally, the organization is flexible enough to make some changes and the employee, appreciating that flexibility, is willing to make certain compromises as well. Over time, the situation is modified enough that the employee's job satisfaction improves. If the poor fit between the employee and the germane organizational factors cannot be modified, the employee will be expected to modify the dysfunctional behavior or be terminated.

The final step of the process is designing and implementing an action plan that takes into consideration individual and organizational characteristics and contains proposals for modifications to make changes which would lead to a decrease in the dysfunctional behavior. As in the case of individual dysfunction, after the plan is agreed on by all parties and is implemented, regular communication points are built in at which the effectiveness of the change is evaluated.

Motivation and Leadership in the Case of Systemic Dysfunction

Managers are not mental health specialists and are not qualified to diagnose symptoms or treat employees who are manifesting dysfunctional behavior in the case of individual dysfunction. Managers are qualified, if not well trained, to address and intervene with employees whose psychological distress is related to work factors.

Arguably, there has been more written about motivation and leadership than any other topic in the field of organizational behavior. In this section, a brief review of selected topics about motivation and leadership are presented.

As theories of motivation have evolved over the past 50 years, there have been many attempts to test and validate these theories. Despite differences among these theories, there is general agreement that motivation is not a trait that an individual either may or may not possess. Rather, motivation is a more complex and sophisticated concept that is embedded in the relationship between the individual and the work environment. In Theory X days, little attention was paid to organizational factors that contribute to motivation. Motivated or not, employees were expected to produce because, if they didn't, there were many others ready to take their place.

Theoretically, there will be certain situations in which the lack of motivation can be traced exclusively to the individual employee. The first section of this chapter describing the case of individual dysfunction offers a good example of this situation. Generally, however, the vast majority of cases of low motivation are the result of a lack of engagement between the individual and some aspect of the environment.

The literature began to acknowledge the "relationship" dimensions of motivation when studies begin to appear on job enrichment or job redesign (see, for example, Hackman & Oldham, 1976).

For the purposes of this chapter, the assumption is made that the employee who is exhibiting dysfunctional behavior related primarily to workplace factors also is experiencing a decrease in motivation to perform his or her job duties, or "an individual's intensity, direction and persistence of effort in attaining a goal" (Robbins, 2001, p. 156) is diminished. The task of leadership is to influence a group (and individuals) toward achievement of goals. A manager or leader must therefore be able to diagnose the processes and factors that are contributing to a loss of motivation in an attempt to restore the individual's intensity, direction, and persistence toward the goals. Is the emergence of dysfunctional behavior and coinciding loss of motivation related to the employee's current job content, the employee's relationship with a supervisor or co-worker, the employee's membership status in a group or team, or the fit (or lack thereof) between the employee's values and the values espoused by the organization's mission and culture?

An enhanced classic theory of motivation can be a very useful framework for a manager who is responsible for finding solutions to systemic motivational problems. Maslow (1954) proposed that our happiness and life satisfaction can be understood quite simply as related to the degree that our needs for safety, social relationships, self-esteem, and self-actualization are met by the environment. Most of us spend approximately one-quarter of our time in the work environment. Maslow, Stephens, and Heil (1998) discussed these basic needs and how they are addressed at work. In the ideal situation, the employee is safe and secure (free from harassassment, threat of layoff, etc.), has positive social relationships with co-workers, is well respected, is recognized and valued, and has opportunities for meaningful work and promotion. When the work environment consistently meets these needs, employees' motivation will not generally be an issue and dysfunctional behavior due to workplace factors will not be evident.

Maslow's hierarchy of needs theory and its application to motivation holds intuitive appeal. It is simple, straightforward, and often quoted across many disciplines. Unfortunately it has little or no empirical support. Alderfer (1972) recast Maslow's model and proposed three essential needs: existence, relatedness, and growth (ERG theory). These three sets of needs do not occur in an orderly sequential way. Rather, multiple needs can be operating at the same time. The most salient need for an employee is individually and culturally based. Needs are not ranked by importance. The ERG theory of motivation is a "more valid version of need hierarchy" (Robbins, 2001, p. 162) and has slightly better empirical support (see, for example, Wanous & Zwany, 1977).

For the manager charged with the tasks of understanding and remediating an employee's lack of motivation, a needs-based framework can be very helpful. Specifically when an employee is exhibiting dysfunctional behavior (related to work factors) and is not motivated (there is decrease in effort to attain goals), then the employee's needs are not being met. The manager's goal then is to identify which need or needs are not being met, pinpoint which aspect or aspects of the work environment are involved and preventing these needs from being met, and explore possible modifications in the work environment that might increase the likelihood of the needs being met.

This approach is a dramatic departure from the era when low motivation was seen as the employee's problem. Instead, the lack or loss of motivation is not the employee's or the employer's problem alone; it is a problem related to the relationship between the individual and the environment and it can be solved only if both parties are willing to communicate, dialogue (understand the other's perspective and limitations), and make accommodations.

Modern leadership theory supports the basic premise of this approach. Aditya, House, and Kerr (2000) conducted a meta-analysis of many studies on leadership. They cited leader flexibility and social sensitivity as critical factors in successful leaders (p. 143). Social sensitivity refers to the ability to perceive and anticipate variances in constituents, group situations, and the environment. Flexibility is the ability to modify one's own behavior in response to these perceptions and variances. In the case of the dysfunctional employee, the manager must be able to perceive changes in an employee's behavior, accurately assess the individual needs that are not being met and the related workplace factors, and be willing to modify his or her behavior (as well as other work elements) to address the circumstances contributing to the loss of motivation and dysfunctional behavior.

On the basis of many years of counseling and coaching experience it is this author's opinion that one of the steps described previously is the most critical to a successful outcome. A successful outcome in these situations is a decrease in dysfunctional behavior, an increased level of motivation, or, in some cases, an amicable parting of the employee and the work organization. The most critical element of the diagnosis and interventions process is the assessment phase. In almost every case, this step involves a face-to-face conversation between the manager and the employee who is exhibiting dysfunctional behavior.

There are two primary goals for the manager in this assessment phase. First is to get the "whole story." Dysfunctional behavior is merely the tip of a much larger complex iceberg. The behavior is above the water and can be seen. Understanding the behavior, however, requires being able to see the behavior in relation to the entire iceberg. What are the needs that are not being met, what are the work dynamics and elements that are preventing the employee from being satisfied and productive? Second, the manager is striving to elicit the employees' trust. Robbins (2001, p. 340) stated that trust is a primary attribute associated in leadership: "It appears increasingly evident that you cannot lead people who do not trust you." Kouzes and Posner (1995) surveyed more than 20,000 employees in the United States and several other countries about the leadership characteristic they most admire. The characteristic that received the highest ranking was honesty. Employees follow only those "worthy of our trust" (Kouzes & Posner, 1995, p. 22). Trust is particularly important in resolving workplace situations that involve dysfunctional behavior.

Managers who are confronted with these cases of dysfunctional behavior and loss of motivation due to work factors have a difficult task. They must design strategies to proceed that will address the needs of the individual employee and the needs of the manager, department, or organization. Getting the employee's story and fully understanding the employee's perspective and point of view is an essential first step. In some situations, the employee will be reticent to open up to "the boss." The manager must enter these conversations with an attitude of concern and curiosity (not impatience and criticism about the poor work performance) and convey to the employee that solutions to the problem being encountered at work can be explored through collaboration and dialogue. The information that is shared in this conversation about needs not being met and the reasons why will be used to find solutions and not used against the employee. If the employee trusts the manager and believes that the organization is genuinely concerned about his or her health and happiness, a successful outcome is likely.

The motivational theories of Maslow and Alderfer were cited earlier in this chapter. Needs-based theories are appealing but are incomplete, focusing only on the individual. This author proposed in an article (Frew, 1992) that relationships of all kinds can be viewed as the intersection of two sets of needs. When we are in the position of being a "need satisfier" for others, we can adopt a number of stances. We can put our needs aside for the time being and meet the other's need, we can impose our needs on others and not listen to or meet the other's need, or we can engage in a friendly competition between conflicting needs and a compromise can be struck so that each party gets some needs met. In this assessment conversation, the proper and most effective stance is for the manager to set aside his or her needs (e.g., "You are always late for work. I need you to be on time.") and to discern what the needs of the employee are that are no longer being met in the workplace. The needs of the manager, the department, and the organization will be folded into the process later. Now is the time to learn as much as possible about what happened that led to the employee's dysfunctional behavior and loss of motivation.

After the manager has completed this assessment phase, a plan must be developed that will involve changes in the employee's work environment. The type of changes and authority a manager has to initiate changes will vary across situations. In many cases, an organization can be responsive to the needs of an employee and changes can be made that will resolve the situation. In other cases, the factors contributing to an individual's dysfunctional behavior cannot or will not be changed and that employee usually will leave the organization.

CASE ILLUSTRATIONS

The following scenarios briefly outline several cases of systematic dysfunctional behavior and the steps taken to assess and respond to the circumstances that led to the behavior and the outcome of the interventions attempted. Each of these vignettes were drawn from this author's consulting or management experience. Names, gender, and the type of organization in each vignette have been changed to ensure that confidentiality and privacy are protected.

Vignette 1: The Promotion

The Story

Michael was hired by a large manufacturing organization to be an employee relations specialist in one of the departments. In that capacity, he had the opportunity to screen potential employees carefully, sending only top candidates to the foreman for interviews. The foreman did not have the time or the expertise to screen potential employees and therefore really came to appreciate Michael's work. Only on rare occasions did they fail to hire an individual he sent to them for a final interview.

Two years into the job, Michael was "promoted." The company was in a downturn and had to lay off a number of employees. Michael's counterpart in another department, which was twice the size of Michael's, was terminated. Michael was told he should be honored the company chose to retain him. Suddenly, however, he was doing three times as much work with no increase in salary.

The Dysfunctional Behavior

Michael tried to continue to take time to screen potential employees. Soon, as business improved, it became evident that the exploding number of new hires to review had radically changed the fundamental nature of his job. He became a paper shuffler and sent all new candidates to the foreman for him to screen and interview. He no longer had time to do the part of the job he loved—talking and connecting with candidates. He began to get negative feedback from the foreman because he was creating work for him by not doing the work he used to do. Michael's attitude went south. He disliked his job. He stopped writing reports. He missed work or came in late. He felt used by the company. He isolated himself at work to avoid others.

Assessment and Intervention

Michael's boss saw the warning signals and called him in. Michael laid out the story and said his needs were no longer being met. His job content had lost its meaning and he had a number of co-workers upset with him. Michael's manager knew he was about to quit. He compared his past work record with his current performance level. He wanted to retain Michael. After a number of calls and conversations, the manager was able to offer Michael his old job back by finding another employee relations specialist who was willing to pick up the two departments that had been added to Michael's job. That specialist was keen on climbing the corporate ladder and thought it would look good if she had three departments to run, not just one.

The Outcome

Michael gratefully downsized to his previous one-department position and his motivation and job satisfaction were quickly restored. The foreman was delighted to have the "old" Michael back.

Vignette 2: The Bounced Check

The Story

Jamie was a 16-year employee with a flawless work record. She was employed by a county government organization and worked at a neighborhood community center that served primarily low socioeconomic status families. She had a very positive relationship with her boss, Daniel. Jamie's primary duties were to greet children and parents who came to the center for classes or to swim, and to collect fees. By all accounts, she was beloved by co-workers and the families being served. She was known for her big heart, which eventually created the problem. Jamie would occasionally help out moms or kids who did not have sufficient funds to pay their fees. She would put some of her own cash into the cash drawer. One day a family she had known for years was $10 short to sign up for swim lessons. Jamie had no cash that day so she wrote a check to the county and put that in her drawer. Jamie's own funds were tight that month and the check bounced, which came to the attention of the central accounting office. Daniel was notified and confronted Jamie. Jamie, not aware that she had been violating several policies by helping her customers over the years, reacted calmly and offered to cover the check and thought that would be the end of it.

Daniel was instructed to put her on unpaid administrative leave until a complete audit of her department could be conducted. Jamie was shocked and asked Daniel to advocate on her behalf. He was sympathetic but told her his "hands were tied" as the powers to be wanted a full report.

The report was completed. No other discrepancies were found and Jamie was reinstated. Before she returned to work she was called into a meeting with the head of accounting, human relations, and Daniel and was reprimanded harshly for her money-handling practices. From that day on Daniel changed. His management style shifted from laissez-faire to autocratic, but only with Jamie. He would show up several times a week at the center without warning and scrutinize each phase of Jamie's work, including having her balance her cash drawer in front of her co-workers.

The Dysfunctional Behavior

Jamie slid into a severe depression. The entire series of events had shaken her. She admitted that in retrospect it was probably bad practice to use her own funds to help families get the services they wanted and that she was unaware of the policies she was violating. But she could not reconcile the treatment she was receiving after being such a loyal and devoted employee for 16 years. The worst part was Daniel's change in attitude. His cool aloof manner and surprise visits caused her great anxiety and distress. She was a people pleaser and felt now that she could not please anyone. She began to lose sleep, weight, and days of work. Daniel confronted her on her deteriorating work performance. She asked him why he was singling her out and treating her like "a dishonest child." He said he was under pressure from his own bosses to monitor her behaviors closely and that "she brought this on herself." Four weeks after Jamie was reinstated she left work on medical leave because of depression and anxiety.

Assessment and Intervention

With Jamie's permission, the treating mental health provider made contact with the HR director. She told the HR director that Jamie's mental health issues were a direct result of events that had occurred in the workplace and specifically related to conflicts with her supervisor. She suggested that alternatives be explored to create a more supportive work climate for Jamie. The HR director was willing to cooperate. He took the time to read through Jamie's work record including her performance reviews and concluded that she was an exemplary employee. He set a meeting with Jamie. He praised her contributions to the organization over the years and indicated that the county was willing to make accommodations to get her back to work. They agreed that the supervisory relationship with Daniel was too badly tarnished to try to recover. He offered her a parallel position in another community center across town. She would have a new supervisor whose style would be more aligned to her "followership" needs.

The Outcome

Jamie accepted the position and returned to work, and her work performance returned to the same high level it was before the "bounced check." Her new supervisor appreciated having such an experienced employee at the front desk and had no desire to micromanage her activities.

Vignette 3: The Comment

The Story

Allen was in his second year of employment in the marketing department at Allied Electronics. Despite his youth and relative inexperience, he was seen as a "boy wonder" because of his work ethic and skill in gathering consumer information to get lines of products into the best sales outlets. Allen was very excited when his boss told him that he had been assigned to a crossfunctional team at another Allied facility in a different state. The assignment would be for six months and he would join a team of other Allied employees from different parts of the country and with different areas of expertise. Allen would be the "marketing guy."

The first month of meetings went very well. Allen's new project manager, Suzanne, outlined the goals (to develop a new product line that could recapture market share from their chief competitor) and their time lines. There were eight team members and Allen was by far the youngest member and the newest to the organization.

In a key meeting, six weeks into the project Allen made a brief presentation to his team outlining the demographic profile of the customers he believed this new product would attract. Suzanne was not present at the meeting (she was allowing the team to self-manage) but Bill, a 30-year employee with Allied from manufacturing, made this comment: "Allen, you came to this team with strong recommendations. This marketing strategy you outlined flat out won't fly. The product we are developing will never sell to that type of customer but I know who will buy it." Bill was known for his straightforward, blunt communication style and was well respected by other team members. No one said a word for several seconds and finally the meeting continued on to other topics.

The Dysfunctional Behavior

Shortly thereafter, Suzanne sat in on a meeting. She was struck by a distinct change in Allen's behavior in the meeting. He was quiet and displayed none of the enthusiasm and energy he brought to earlier meetings. He seemed preoccupied and distracted. She began to get reports from other team members that Allen was slacking, not carrying his weight, coming to work late, and missing deadlines for work assigned to him. He was slowing the team down and seemed to have no ideas about marketing strategies. Several team members asked that he be replaced.

Assessment and Intervention

Suzanne called Allen into a meeting and laid out the information she had gathered about his abrupt change in behavior on the team. Allen admitted all the information was accurate. She then inquired with curiosity and concern about what had changed to sap his enthusiasm and motivation? Allen hesitated then repeated the comment that Bill had made and that the comment shook his confidence and made him question his worth to the team. He stated that other team members did not speak up on his behalf so obviously they believed Bill had the better marketing plan.

Suzanne asked Allen if he would be willing to repeat the story to the team if she was there to facilitate. She said she could not guarantee outcomes but knew Bill to be a reasonable (albeit formidable) man who responded well to people who "pushed back" on him. Allen agreed. The meeting was held. Allen reminded the team of the comment and the team members realized his "non-team" behaviors had started right after that incident. Several members spoke up about their discomfort when the comment was made. Bill remembered the comment but stated that he had hoped it would inspire Allen to "fight back" and further explicate his plan. When Allen didn't do that, Bill lost some respect for Allen and figured they would need to go forward with Bill's plan.

The Outcome

Allen came back to life in the meeting. He agreed to come back to the team with a new improved version of the marketing plan and to incorporate several of Bill's ideas. Three weeks later he did that. After a lively and sometimes heated discussion, the team adopted his plan and he was praised by his teammates.

Vignette 4: The Piercing

The Story

Melanie had heard the rumor for months. Her organization, the Gannon News Service, was going to be bought out by the multinational conglomerate, Global News and Broadcasting. On Monday, Dave, her manager confirmed that the deal had gone through. There were many changes ahead. Global was a conservative organization and hierarchical in structure. Employees worked standard hours, were tightly supervised, and dress codes were enforced. Melanie had come to work as an editor three years earlier because she fit the culture. Dress at Gannon was informal, supervision was loose, and work hours were flexible as long as the job was done.

The new general manager for Global came to town and called an all-employee meeting. He outlined the changes that were expected in the new Global culture. Melanie sat silently and the more she heard the worse she felt. She loved her work, however, so she made the decision to try to conform.

She arrived at work the following Monday at 8:00 a.m. and wore the basic business informal outfit that would meet the new dress code. At 9:00 a.m. Dave told her the new general manager wanted to see her. She went into his office and he proceeded to tell her that her nose ring had to go. She protested but got nowhere. She left his office, returned to her cubicle, and removed the ring.

The Dysfunctional Behavior

For two weeks she tried to conform to the new culture of working 8 to 5, dressing up, attending countless meetings, and having tight supervision. One day Melanie snapped. Dave found her sitting at her desk just staring into space. He tried to talk to her, but she was unresponsive. Dave was concerned and decided to drive her home. He encouraged her to get some rest and to call him when she could return to work.

Assessment and Intervention

Melanie called Dave three days later and asked if they could meet for coffee. He agreed. Over coffee, Melanie told him that she had spent those days off reflecting on her job situation. Together they concluded that Melanie's attempts to fit into this new culture were akin to hammering a round peg into a recently reshaped square hole. She had lost her drive, spirit, and sense of individuality.

The Outcome

The following Monday, Melanie strode confidently into the office. She went into the general manager's office and handed him her letter of resignation. As she left, Dave noticed that she was wearing the nose ring.

Conclusion

In each of the vignettes, one organizational factor was identified as the most salient issue leading to the employee's dissatisfaction and dysfunctional behavior. The first example featured a disconnection between individual employee and job content, the second example featured a disconnection between individual and boss, the third example was about individual and team, and the fourth example featured individual and organizational culture. The reader will note, however, that each case example involves many layers, all of which are intertwined. Dysfunctional behavior is typically viewed as being about the individual. In fact, dysfunctional behavior is always about interpersonal, group, and organizational dynamics.

SUMMARY

What I attempted to illustrate in the last section of this chapter is the critical role the modern manager must accept in uncovering the interpersonal, group, and organizational factors that are contributing to the onset of an employee's dysfunctional behavior. Something about the work environment is interfering with the employee's satisfaction, enthusiasm, motivation, and the realization of meaningful work. In almost all cases, the first step is to get the employee's story. Until the manager fully comprehends the individual's experience and perspective, he or she cannot initiate some of the accommodations demonstrated in the vignettes or test the organizational waters to see how much flexibility is possible to respond to the situation.

In the case of individual or systemic dysfunction, the manager is the point person in assessing the problem and working with the appropriate key players in and out of the organization to design a plan to minimize or eliminate the dysfunctional behavior and restore the individual's motivation. We live and work in a different era. Individuals matter and in most cases can be retained. In cases of systemic dysfunction, organizations must be willing to examine their part of the relationship when employees' needs are not being met. Brokering this complex and dynamic dance between the interests of the individual and the organization requires a sophisticated level of skills Theory X era managers did not have. It requires leadership.

References

Aditya, R., House, R., & Kerr, S. (2000). Theory and practice of leadership into the new millennium. In C. Cooper & E. Locke (Eds.), *Industrial and organizational psychology* (pp. 130-165). Malden, MA: Blackwell.

Alderfer, C. P. (1972). *Existence, relatedness, and growth.* New York: Free Press.

Argyris, C. (1957). *Personality and organizations.* New York: Harper & Row.

Bernardin, J., & Lee, B. (2002). Mental health and disabilities, the employer and the law. In J. C. Thomas & M. Hersen (Eds.), *Handbook of mental health in the workplace* (pp. 15-29). Thousand Oaks, CA: Sage.

Frew, J. (1992). From the perspective of the environment. *Gestalt Journal, 15,* 39-59.

Hackman, J. R., & Oldham, G. A. (1976). Motivation through the design of work. *Organizational Behavior and Human Performance, 16,* 250-279.

Hunsaker, P., & Alessandra, A. (1986). *The art of managing people.* New York: Simon & Schuster.

Hunter, J. E., Schmidt, F. L., Rauschenberger, J. M., & Jayne, M. E. (2000). Intelligence, motivation, and job performance. In C. Cooper & E. Locke (Eds.), *Industrial and organizational psychology* (pp. 278-303). Malden, MA: Blackwell.

Kouzes, J., & Posner, B. (1995). *The leadership challenge.* San Francisco: Jossey-Bass.

Lowman, R. (1993). *Counseling and psychotherapy of work dysfunction.* Washington, DC: American Psychological Association.

Maslow, A. H. (1954). *Motivation and personality.* New York: Harper & Row.

Maslow, A. H., Stephens, D. C., & Heil, G. (1998). *Maslow on management.* New York: Wiley.

Robbins, S. (2001). *Organizational behavior* (9th ed.). Upper Saddle River, NJ: Prentice Hall.

Robbins, S. (2002). *The truth about managing people.* Upper Saddle River, NJ: Prentice Hall.

Svyantek, D. J., & Brown, L. L. (2002). Dysfunctional behavior in the workplace and organizational design, climate, and culture. In J. C. Thomas & M. Hersen (Eds.), *Handbook of mental health in the workplace* (pp. 477-500). Thousand Oaks, CA: Sage.

Thomas, J. C., & Hersen, M. (Eds.). (2002). *Handbook of mental health in the workplace.* Thousand Oaks, CA: Sage.

Thomas, J. C., & Hite, J. (2002). Mental health in the workplace: Toward an integration of organizational and clinical theory, research, and practice. In J. C. Thomas, & M. Hersen (Eds.), *Handbook of mental health in the workplace* (pp. 3-17). Thousand Oaks, CA: Sage.

Wanous, J. P., & Zwany, A. (1977). A cross-sectional test of need hierarchy theory. *Organizational Behavior and Human Performance, 17,* 79-97.

19

Violence at Work: Causes and Protection

GERALD LEWIS
COMPASS

One cannot truly predict nor prevent violence ... However, one can improve safety and increase protection

Gerald Lewis

N ow that the world and the workplace have moved into the 21st century, there is increasing awareness of changes in individuals, families, communities, countries, and the workplace. Change leads to stress, and stress produces reactions. The majority of people cope quite well with the stresses in their lives; however, some people become overwhelmed and develop reactions that are maladaptive in nature. While there is mounting concern about workplace violence, it should be understood that this is but one way that people evidence pain, anguish, and suffering. Substance or alcohol abuse; marital or familial, financial, or emotional problems; and physical impairments are known to develop if people cannot manage the stresses in their lives. These maladies cause significant turmoil in personal as well as professional life and place the individual (and the workplace) at risk for more severe difficulties.

"Violence in the workplace" has become a familiar phrase in the modern-day employment setting. Reports have been coming fast and furious from a variety of sources citing stories and statistics that increase alarm, anxiety, and apprehension. Statistics are reported in the media that purport a dramatic increase in violence in the workplace. Certainly, one should be concerned about these reports and should make every effort to respond whenever possible. However, this response should be done in an effective and proactive fashion that does not escalate the issue with hype and hysteria. It must be remembered that as tragic as a violent episode may be, it is still a low-frequency occurrence in the workplace. The National Institute of Occupational Safety and Health (NIOSH, 2003, pp. 1-2) reported data indicating that the number of workplace homicides dropped from 929 to 757 between 1980 and 1992. Furthermore, this report indicated that 75 percent of these workplace homicides are committed as part of a robbery by an unknown assailant and that only 4 to 6 percent of homicides in the workplace were committed by co-workers (NIOSH, 2003, p. 11). Finally, NIOSH and the Centers for Disease Control suggested that there are more than one million nonfatal assaults in the workplace each year. However, this represents only about 18 percent of the total acts of violence per year in the United States (Occupational Safety and Health Association [OSHA], 2003, pp. 1-3). The Department of Justice data reported that between 1993 and 1999, the number of nonfatal assaults decreased by 44 percent, while workplace homicides dropped by 39 percent. Eleven percent of these homicides were committed by co-workers, former co-workers, or customers (Bureau of Labor Statistics, 2002). There were 639 homicides in the workplace in 2001, down from the 677 homicides that took place at work in 2000 (Bureau of Labor Statistics, 2002). Although the data may vary as a result of reporting discrepancies and other factors, the numbers indicate that, in fact, the workplace is a relatively safe environment when compared to the streets and homes of America. Compared with feudal systems, slavery, sweatshops, and "preunionized" factories and farms, the worker of today is at much less risk of violence, injury, discrimination, or harassment. The past 50 years have seen laws and policies that have improved the quality, comfort, and safety of most workplaces.

The focus of any workplace should be on maintaining job performance and improving safety and not on managing personality problems. However, the OSHA determined, "Each employer shall furnish to each of his employees employment and a place of employment which are free from recognized hazards that are causing or are likely to cause death or serious physical harm to his employees" (OSHA, 2003 [29 U.S.C. 654(a)]). In recent years, interpretations of this policy have come to include personal safety. It is essential that supervisory personnel be trained to recognize whether an employee is capable of nonhostile civil conduct. The forward-thinking workplace has instituted workplace violence policies that are similar in scope to sexual harassment policies and protocol.

The goal is to have today's work environment continue to provide an increasing level of safety and security. To do so requires that professionals from all walks of life work together to communicate accurate information, to contain and direct the anxiety and apprehension, and to be a proactive and highly visible resource to the total organization. There is no guarantee of one hundred percent prevention, but there is much that can be done to enhance safety and protection.

THE ABILITY TO PREDICT VIOLENCE

Predicting violence can be compared to forecasting tornadoes. We may understand the causes and conditions that precipitate a tornado, but we cannot truly know if, where, or when it may actually occur or how bad the resulting damage may be. However, clinical research and experience have developed a significant body of data that can facilitate a tornado warning or watch. As Michael Miller (2000) wrote in his article "A Model for the Assessment of Violence," "We can identify populations more likely to be violent, but we cannot predict the specific risk for a given individual" (pp. 299-304). Research on individuals who have committed heinous crimes has generated most of the data that we have about predicting violence. By extrapolating from these individuals, researchers have made efforts to develop a series of risk factors. These warning signs or signals may correlate with dangerousness or a propensity for violence; however, there are no absolute predictors. Ultimately, this list of characteristics is expanded into a profile in an effort to gain a clearer sense of who may act out in a hostile or violent manner. Table 19.1 represents the list of warning signs that have been presented in a wide range of documents from respected clinical journals to news magazines, Web sites, and business newsletters (Lewis & Zare, 1999).

As with any profiling, there is valid information that may portend a wide range of extreme and inappropriate behavior including, but not limited to, hostility and violence. However, as with any profiling, it casts too wide a net. People who share some of the characteristics may be included, but they will never act in a violent or hostile manner. Furthermore, many of the characteristics are psychosocial data that are personal and private and may not be known to the workplace. Therefore, while this may be useful information for a clinician to include as part of a comprehensive

---

TABLE 21.1
The Most Often Cited Risk Factors

Thirty-five-years-old or older; male

History of trauma, abuse, neglect

Trouble with the law

Poor school record

Current alcohol or substance misuse, or both

Suicidality

Head injury

Serious mental illness: psychosis or paranoid features, or psycopathy

Familiarity with or ownership of weapons, or both

Recent or past history of violent behavior

Uses denial and projection

Impulsive or compulsive behavior(s): overeating, smoking, drinking

Gambling

"Womanizing"

Excessive buying or spending

Difficulty with authority figures

Frequent job transitions

Feels victimized by the system

Other factors to consider:

    Lower socioeconomic status

    Lower IQ

    Lower formal education

    Unstable living situation

    Significant financial difficulties

evaluation, it should not be oversold as the absolute evaluation. Furthermore, this information, placed in the hands of untrained nonclinical management personnel, may lead to inappropriate administrative actions on their part, or at least it may heighten the state of anxiety that there is a "potentially violent individual" in the workplace. The harsh reality is that any workplace probably has its share of potentially violent individuals who do not evidence any of the "signs or signals." Rather than attempt to profile on the basis of private information, employers can assess someone's risk to act inappropriately by observing his or her daily behavior and relationships. The following mnemonic provides some of the key observational factors.

Characteristics of "TICKED" Individuals

Thought process: Does the individual evidence difficulties with his or her thinking and communication? If so, this could be due to psychosis, personality disorder, paranoia, toxicity, fanaticism, or head injury, which might interfere with the cognitive process.

Isolation: Does the individual evidence a restricted social network with limited contact with family, friends, religion, and work?

Controlled by circumstances: Does the individual talk of feeling trapped legally, financially, or in his or her career, and so forth? Does the individual see others as having power over his or her situation?

Kicks: Is there evidence that the individual uses drugs, alcohol, gambling, or other high-intensity action-oriented or compulsive behaviors to manage anxiety?

Emotionality: Does the individual evidence extreme emotional lability, mood swings, or displays of intense emotions?

Defiance or dysfunction: Does the individual believe that the regular rules of society do not apply to him or her or the situation? Or is his or her lifestyle characterized by chaos and instability?

Once again, one must be cautious not to profile or to overreact but to recognize that these are characteristics of an individual who may be prone to act inappropriately to conflict or stress in his or her life.

Definitions of Nuisance, Conflict, Hostility, and Violence

One of the difficult aspects of dealing with workplace hostility is that terms and phrases are used rather generically with only a superficial understanding of the concepts. I use four different terms when dealing with workplace violence: *nuisance, conflict, hostility,* and *violence.* It is essential to have a basic understanding of each, as they represent different levels of intent. In *Workplace Hostility: Myth and Reality* (Lewis & Zare, 1999), the authors defined behaviors as follows: "*Nuisance* behavior may be annoying and offensive to others but does not have any direct malicious intent to a specific individual or group. Examples might be offensive gestures, swearing, off-color jokes and graffiti. While such behavior may be bothersome and disgusting, it is more a function of immaturity or poor socialization than of violence"

(p. 8). "*Conflict* refers to the normal disagreements that take place in all interpersonal relationships. Whether personal, political or professional in nature, conflicts may be heated and intense, but do not result in permanent damage to the relationship" (p. 8). However, if conflict continues unabated, it may result in damage to the underlying relationship, thus opening the door to the next level of hostility. *Hostility* refers to "acts that are nonphysical but are directed at an individual or group with the intent of inflicting some type of emotional harm." Examples of this are harassment, discrimination, stalking, verbal threats, comments, acts of intimidation, and so forth. The defining characteristic is that there is no bodily contact or destruction of property. However, "*Violence* involves the display of physical force against a person or property with the intention to do personal injury or destruction to property" (p. 8).

While all hostile acts may be viewed as a violation and should certainly not be tolerated, there must be delineation of different types of behavior, rather than lumping them all under one label. Each type of act represents a particular intent, level of control, level of legal or criminal involvement, and potential disciplinary outcome. Although time and space do not permit a full discussion, it is possible to see the distinctions between different types of behavior and different circumstances: writing racial or sexual epithets in the men's room that are not directed to any specific individual is not the same as making a direct slur against a specific employee. Or, as offensive as yelling and swearing at another person may be, it evidences a different level of control than physical assault. Is the behavior overt or is it passive-aggressive in nature? Does the person yell and scream and then leave the workplace, or do they remain and continue to intimidate others? Is an incident a "conflict" between two colleagues with a preexisting positive regard for each other that has escalated into a loud and heated exchange, or is this an escalation between two people whose minimal tolerance for each other has reached a breaking point? The behaviors must be viewed within a multifaceted context that includes social, psychological, and culture factors.

Dynamics in the Workplace

As the preceding discussion suggests, the current tendency is often to look solely at the individual rather than in conjunction with the environment in which he or she works. However, as anyone knows, the U.S. workplace is now and always has been fraught with some degree of tension and turmoil. Religious, ethnic, and gender diversity; organizational transitions; and economic fluctuations create a dynamic environment that is constantly exerting pressures on an ever-changing workforce.

Since World War II, the United States has experienced a significant transition on many levels. The demographics in the workplace have shifted to include women as well as other minority groups working in jobs and at levels that were previously the domain of white men. The development of policies around ethnic diversity, sexual harassment, affirmative action, the Americans with Disability Act (ADA) of 1990, and bilingualism reflect this growing change in the face of the U.S. workforce. With these changes come a variety of issues, conflicts, and concerns that get played out on a daily basis in the workplace and in the courts. Add to this picture increasing demand placed on the individual workers. For many, the 40-hour workweek has been extended, while lunch and personal breaks have been shortened. Downsizing has resulted in a significant increase in the expected volume of work for the individual employee. The social time (chitchats, lunch breaks, water cooler gossip, etc.) that has been the necessary oil that lubricated the human equipment has been dramatically limited. The benefits, workplace social activities, and other aspects that were helpful in mitigating interpersonal stress have been cut back. The use of contract workers, per diem staff, and temporary employees has resulted in a workforce that does not always feel like a coordinated and committed team with a common goal. The advent of new technologies, most notably cell phones, pagers, and e-mail, has blurred the boundaries between work and home and has, in many cases, turned the home or car into a second office. Even on vacations, many people check in with the office to keep up with the flow of work. Most high-level administrative personnel will agree with the aforementioned comments. However, they also will suggest that, with today's economic flux, the reality is that we must continue on the course of running "lean and mean." Be it in the public sector or private industry, schools or banks, or insurance companies or software start-ups, the individual employee is the essential equipment and, in most cases, is working at an intense capacity.

To understand workplace violence one must differentiate between the "at-risk" workplace and the "toxic" workplace (Lewis & Zare, 1999). An at-risk work organization is one that is vulnerable to hostile or violent activities perpetrated from outside the organization. The characteristics of such a work setting are described in Table 19.2. Examples of at-risk workplaces are convenience stores, liquor stores, taxis, and gas stations. The usual types of hostility or violence perpetrated in these types of establishments are robberies. An individual who is unrelated to the workers or the workplace that he or she is robbing usually commits these incidents. Furthermore, if a homicide does result, it is usually not intended or premeditated. The primary motivation is to get cash, drugs, or contraband and to get out of the establishment as quickly as possible. Simply put, the only method to lessen the vulnerability of an at-risk workplace is to improve security (OSHA, 2003. pp. 6-10).

The toxic workplace is one that is vulnerable to hostility and violence generated from within. Characteristics of a toxic workplace are listed in Table 19.3. Many may

---

TABLE 21.2
Characteristics of an At-Risk Workplace

Retail business
Cash on hand
Offers public access
Operates during evening, nights, and holidays
Has no or limited security
Has a small number of customers at any given time
Uses solo employees
Is in an isolated location or near a highway
Handles consumer goods that are valued on the street or are easily fenced

---

TABLE 21.3
Characteristics of a Toxic Workplace

Authoritarian management style
Favoritism
Perceived humiliation
Arbitrary or inconsistent decisions
Poor communication
Increased work demands
Poor working conditions
Minimal management training
Betrayal and abandonment
Feeling trapped

Note. Although these characteristics are often common to most workplaces,
it is the level of perceived intensity of these dynamics that generates toxicity.

---

say that these characteristics are common to most workplaces. Given all of the factors that were discussed in the earlier portion of this chapter, it is true for many organizations that a certain level of dysfunctionality should be expected. Using the metaphor of a chronic medical problem, such as hypertension, may help to illustrate the insidious nature of workplace toxicity. The development of increased blood pressure is often the by-product of aging, heredity, and lifestyle. An elevated blood pressure develops over time and is "quiet," with few obvious symptoms. Hypertension is known to be involved with a wide range of health problems such as headaches, heart disease, strokes, and so forth that may result in grave illness and death. It is recommended that people have their blood pressure monitored and, if it is above a certain level, lifestyle recommendations (diet, exercise, decrease in salt and alcohol, etc.) may be suggested. If these adjustments do not provide the desired remediation, medication often is introduced as a simple and effective method to contain the condition. In much the same way, workplace toxicity may be seen as a chronic condition that might develop in many work organizations. In the workplace, the "aging" factor may reflect issues such as the growth or diminishment of the specific industry, the economy, market fluctuations, and so forth. "Heredity" may be viewed as the workplace demographics and culture and the dynamics that are generated as a result of its unique "gene pool." "Lifestyle" may loosely reflect dynamics and behaviors that result as the organization tries to cope with its aging process and inherited predisposition with events such as relocations, downsizing, demographic shifts, and so forth. Table 19.3 may be viewed as a combination of these heredity and lifestyle characteristics. Continuing to follow the metaphor, the organizational toxicity may begin to elevate in much the same way as an individual's blood pressure, leaving the organization vulnerable to a wide range of serious health risks. Similarly, an organization should be monitoring its own blood pressure; however, it is not as simple as rolling up a sleeve and applying a pressure cuff to one's arm. However, Table 19.4 lists the types of events and incidents that may lead to an increase in

---

TABLE 21.4
Events That May Increase Toxicity in the Workplace

Layoffs, downsizes, or rapid growth in an organization
Significant increase in work demands
Relocation of workplace (regardless of distance)
Demographic changes in the workforce (gender, ethnicity, racial, age, etc.)
Mergers or reorganizations
Strikes or protracted labor disputes
High-visibility (negative) media coverage
Individual termination for disciplinary reasons
Restraining order against an employee by an employer or co-worker

---

toxicity and thus an increase in the potential for a wide range of negative and inappropriate reactions that may include hostility and violence. In much the same way that hypertension is described as a silent killer, most of these events are gradual shifts and changes that may not be acutely noted but rather experienced as a gradual downturn in employee productivity and morale.

SOLUTIONS

Policy and Procedures

As the workplace continues to become increasingly diverse and the customers it serves more varied, and as greater demands are placed on its employees through downsizing, reorganizations, mergers, and such, the pressure and stress often are manifested in inappropriate behaviors. It is essential to set up specific behavioral expectations and guidelines to help employees understand that being cooperative, communicative, and courteous remains a significant component of any job description. Administrative action such as safety regulations, sexual harassment policies, no-smoking rules, drug and alcohol policies, the ADA, and the Family Medical Leave Act have developed over the past twenty-five years in an effort to improve the physical and emotional safety in the workplace. However, these policies often are housed in the human resource department and the employee handbook. So often, they are not discussed again unless an individual has made a significant breach of one of them. It is recommended that adherence to behavioral expectations be included as an essential function of any job description. Currently, most job descriptions focus on technical skills, training, or knowledge and are vaguely worded. Some descriptions include an equally indistinctly formulated statement to the effect that the employee shall perform other duties and responsibilities as delineated by his or her supervisor. This common yet obscure wording of a job description may result in further confusion and conflict. Rather, job descriptions should include as essential duties and responsibilities definitive technical and professional skill as well as components such as the following: "This position requires that the individual be able to abide by the behavioral expectations (codes of conduct) as delineated in the employee handbook. Examples of these behavioral expectations include but are not limited to safety, drug and alcohol, sexual harassment, absenteeism, sick leave policies, and so forth." In addition, it is recommended that the job description also include language to the following effect: "This position requires that the individual be able to comport him- or herself in an appropriate manner, maintaining courteous and effective interactions and communication with other employees and/or customers." Table 19.5 presents a list of behavioral expectations that may be posted in the workplace.

Currently, many organizations tolerate a wide range of behavior that may be considered unsuitable for the workplace. This is usually as a result of it being considered separate and distinct from one's job description and occupational performance. Certainly, as the workplace becomes increasingly diverse, as well as increasingly stressful, there is a need to have very clear guidelines regarding behavioral expectations. Furthermore, employees at all levels need to see that the ability to maintain a certain code of conduct is an essential feature of any job. In addition, including this expectation in a job description would necessitate that supervisors discuss these matters with their supervisees as part of the regular review process. In other words, it keeps the humanistic qualifications of the job description on a par with the technological qualifications.

Some may ask, if this expectation is included as part of a job description, how does it influence or impact the ADA? The ADA has become an increasingly complex issue since it was first implemented. It is not the goal of this chapter, nor is there time or space, to develop all of the intricacies, twists, and turns of the ADA policies (see Chapter 17). However, it would seem that including behavioral expectations (or adherence to codes of conduct) as part of a job description would actually simplify matters regarding what is and is not a "reasonable accommodation." Furthermore, regardless of disability or protected status, tolerance of the aforementioned behavioral expectations would not be considered a reasonable accommodation. As an example, there may be an employee who is suffering from bipolar disorder. This

---

TABLE 21.5
Behavioral Expectations: The Ten Commandments of the Workplace

The following commandments apply to all employees at all levels:

Thou shalt speak in a normal tone of voice (no yelling, raised volume, or sarcasm).

Thou shalt refrain from using profane or vulgar language.

Thou shalt maintain courteous personal space and body language.

Thou shalt work effectively with others to facilitate the completion of their duties and responsibilities.

Thou shalt maintain a suitable dress code as designated by the department head or manager. This dress code may include clothing, makeup, jewelry, tattoos, and so forth.

Thou shalt maintain good personal hygiene.

Thou shalt maintain care and cleanliness of the workspace and equipment.

Thou shalt report to work on time and abide by the specific work schedule.

Thou shalt abide by all company policies (i.e., smoking, sexual harassment, drug and alcohol).

Thou shalt maintain courtesy and cooperation even in the face of discourtesy.

---

illness may be characterized by extreme moodiness, irritability, emotional hypersensitivity, some paranoid ideation, and hyperactivity (American Psychiatric Association, 2000). It is certainly not a reasonable accommodation to tolerate emotional outbursts, hostile behavior, or disruptions in the workplace. In this case, a reasonable accommodation may be to allow for flextime because of side effects of medication or for therapy appointments, or, perhaps, to accommodate through a change in the location of a workspace so as to lessen an employee's stimulation and distraction.

In closing, *professionalism* should be defined as having the training, knowledge, skills, and experience to do the work, as well as the capacity to maintain behavioral expectations relevant to the workplace.

Management Training

As described previously, the modern workplace is often a vibrant living organism with tension and turmoil, agitation and apprehension, and conflict and confusion. This is the norm and to be expected, depending on such factors as economic fluctuations, changes in employee demographics, and myriad other variables. An individual employee often may be under stress as a result of these workplace attributes or due to personal issues in his or her life. Nonetheless, the workplace has requirements and expectations. Supervisors and department heads are key personnel in the functioning of a work department. They are often in the awkward position of having a lot of responsibility with limited authority. They are charged with monitoring the productivity of their supervisees as well as determining their level of compliance with the behavioral expectations as derived from the company policies and procedures, which may be a very daunting task given the current dynamics.

Many supervisors are promoted from within the workgroup and often receive limited supervisory training. Furthermore, they may be in a situation where they are now managing workers who, at a previous time, were colleagues. To further complicate matters, employers roll new administrative policies and procedures down the pipeline with the expectation of comprehensive implementation. Many first- and second-level supervisors do not receive adequate training or understanding of the policies and therefore have a difficult time enforcing the administrative "rules and regs." In addition, the often preferred method of supervision is to practice what this author refers to as the "50 percent rule": If there is a problem and you ignore it, 50 percent of the time it will go away; the other 50 percent of the time it will get worse. Put another way, many supervisors often practice crisis management: wait until a situation becomes a crisis, then try to manage it. Either philosophy may result in many situations escalating to a point of extreme stress for the individual, the supervisor, and co-workers.

The following example provides a demonstration of what typically may occur. Bob was a worker who had been with a small manufacturing company for about three years. His performance was "spotty" and he often came in late or called in sick. On two occasions, he was discovered sleeping in a small storage closet. On more than one occasion, he became very angry and verbally abusive with a co-worker when he was confronted about not "carrying his load." Co-workers in his department felt that he was difficult and would often avoid him at lunch break. Furthermore, he would eat his lunch in his car and often came in with the smell of alcohol on his breath. His supervisor was relatively new to the position, having been promoted about a year earlier. He tried to joke and cajole Bob as a way to try to get him "on track." The significant issue was that the supervisor, along with the rest of the work crew, was afraid of Bob, as he was a rather large man with a history of barroom brawls, arrests for assault and battery, and other types of disruptive incidents. The unspoken rule in the department was to tolerate Bob and try to avoid making an issue of his job performance difficulties. The hope was that he would move on to another job soon. As time went on, Bob's behavior escalated as a result of his (third) wife leaving him. His drinking and absenteeism increased, and he was involved in a car accident. A Breathalyzer test confirmed a high level of alcohol in his system. At this time, the house of cards tumbled and the anger and frustration that had resulted from years of tolerating his behavior surfaced intensely and people were calling for his termination. Fortunately or unfortunately, it was determined that he could not be terminated because (1) the incident occurred on his own time and away from work; (2) he was innocent until proven guilty, and even were he to be convicted and lose his driver's license, he did not need a license to do his work; and (3) none of his job performance difficulties had been documented. He returned to work within two days and was the butt of comments and jokes, which resulted in Bob and another worker getting into a physical altercation. It was determined that were he to be disciplined, the other employee would have to receive the same treatment. By the next day, the entire department was dysfunctional, and crisis management was in operation.

One can only speculate as to what might have happened if the following had occurred:

1. Bob's supervisor had dealt with the abuse of tardiness and absenteeism,
2. Bob had been confronted about the odor of alcohol on his breath and other job performance concerns,
3. the company had an employee assistance program (EAP),
4. the drug and alcohol policies were strictly enforced,
5. the "fear factor" of the supervisor and co-workers had been better managed by the human resources department,
6. the new supervisor had received supportive training and mentoring for his new role, and
7. other co-workers had gone to human resources or other administrative personnel with their concerns.

First- and second-level supervisors need support and training to manage employees. Companies often are not willing or able to devote the time and resources to provide this type of training. Remarkably, an organization often will provide training for a new computer program that is being implemented or a new system to provide service. However, the value of training supervisors about the daunting task of managing a diverse workforce that is under a lot of pressure is not deemed a valuable use of time and resources. Furthermore, the companies that do provide these programs do so in a limited manner, devoting one to two hours a year to a presentation by an outside resource. Often these sessions are of little value, as the presenter will focus the program on the warning signs of potentially violent individuals. The message often creates a sense of profiling and paranoia, leaving the supervisors with the message that they should be able to diagnose which of their employees is about to "go off." Mental health professionals spend years of school and training and are limited in their capacity to determine risk. However, somehow a supervisor with one to two hours of training should be able to make a determination. When I have conducted workshops on topics such as this, the focus is not on diagnosing personality problems but rather on evaluating job performance. The warning signals of an employee should be addressed without the specific concern as to whether the risk is only violent in nature. An at-risk employee is defined as an individual who is evidencing indications of significant difficulties maintaining his or her duties and responsibilities. An at-risk individual is vulnerable to a wide range of personally and professionally disruptive experiences, which may include marital stress, medical problems, and job performance difficulties. Table 19.6 provides a list of signals, signs, and symptoms of an at-risk employee that should be addressed as early as possible (Lewis & Zare, 1999).

A more effective model was implemented by an organization that offers informal monthly lunch meetings with a human resources representative where supervisors can meet and discuss employee issues as a group, giving each other feedback and suggestions. Discussion of policies and procedures, employee issues, and management strategies are the focus of these sessions. Between meetings, supervisors feel free to contact each other to get feedback and guidance. Furthermore, it has helped to improve the often ambivalent relationship between supervisors and the human resources department. This author provided the EAP for this organization and was invited to attend one of the sessions to discuss the EAP and how to help employees who are having difficulty accessing its services. Another organization has an ongoing "university" where supervisors may enroll in a variety of courses that are specifically designed to improve management skills. Another educational system has a mentoring program in which a subordinate is paired with a senior administrative person for a year and spends regular time meeting about management issues and skill building. And finally, there is the concept of executive coaching. This is a training system in which an individual has regular access to an outside professional who may provide phone or face-to-face coaching services. Unfortunately, these services may be quite costly and are therefore usually limited to the senior level of personnel.

In summation, supervisory training of first- and second-level managers is an essential investment in mitigating the impact of stress and therefore the possibility of hostility in the workplace. This training would focus on assisting supervisors in their ability to intervene with employees evidencing job performance difficulties. The focus should not be on just those employees where a fear of violence is the issue but rather be on all employees showing signs of undue stress that affects job performance.

TABLE 21.6
Signs and Symptoms of an At-Risk Worker

Absenteeism
Tardiness
Significant and consistent decrease in job performance
Conflicts with co-workers
Change in personal hygiene
Evidence of physical difficulties: dizziness, slurred speech, incoherence, and so forth
Discussion of serious personal or familial difficulties
Smell of alcohol

Safety Teams

Often a work organization will set up safety teams whose purpose is to look at the physical safety issues within a work environment. Initially the primary motivation for the formation of these teams was to lessen the accidents and injuries that resulted in worker's compensation claims. When empowered and used appropriately, the efforts of these teams have resulted in lowered worker's compensation as well as lowered accidents and injuries. It is the view of this author that the focus of these teams is somewhat restricted and should be broadened to include a wider variety of safety issues. Many of the policies that have been implemented in the workplace over the past 25 years are actually policies that focus on personal and emotional safety. Drug and alcohol, sexual harassment, no-smoking, and racial and religious discrimination policies are all designed to improve the safety of the workplace. Furthermore, it should be remembered that breaches of these policies may be defined as hostile acts within the workplace. With a broader perspective, teams should be formed with representation from all aspects of the workplace, such as human resources, legal, security, EAP, labor, management, and so forth. By meeting regularly, they may keep their thumb on the pulse of the workplace and monitor all aspects of safety: physical, personal, gender, racial, religious, and so on. Increasing safety is a proactive and preventative method of lessening harm from a wide range of sources, including violence and hostility. Focusing on violence is merely a reactive intervention to an incident that has already occurred.

Employee Assistance Programs

EAPs were first used by large and small businesses during the 1980s. Originally designed to provide assistance to employees with substance and alcohol problems, they soon developed a broad brush orientation to a wider variety of emotional, legal, and family-related concerns. A comprehensive EAP should provide the following services:

short-term counseling or clinical consultation to individual employees,
educational and training seminars,
supervisory training and consultation,
on-site crisis intervention, and
administrative consultation.

An EAP should either conduct or have professionals available who may conduct fitness-for-duty evaluations of individuals who evidence severe dysfunction. As indicated earlier in this chapter, the focus should be not just on concerns about potential violence but rather on providing the needed services for any at-risk individual and his or her family. A well-used EAP is an essential feature in (1) responding to stress in the workplace, (2) training supervisors, (3) providing interventions for those employees who are experiencing difficulties, and (4) providing crisis intervention if and when an incident occurs.

At-Risk Assessments: Fitness-for-Duty Evaluations

As work organizations and the mental health field attempt to respond to hostility and violence in the workplace, they often fall back on old methods of intervention. What must be recognized is that the current workplace dynamics require a new response to an increasingly complex milieu. The terminology "fitness for duty," originally taken from the medical model to evaluate physical and medical impairments and illnesses, has been used to assess mental conditions.

Currently, there are a variety of terms used to describe these types of extensive evaluations: *fitness for duty evaluations, forensic evaluations, independent medical evaluations,* and *threat assessments.* A brief review will suggest that these terms no longer have the right fit for the types of evaluations that are being requested or required to determine emotional fitness for duty.

Fitness for duty originally generated from the medical model referring to physical injuries. As an example, an individual may have broken his arm, and a physician determines when the arm will be healed sufficiently and will be fit for duty. Or, as another example, an individual may have suffered a heart attack. In either case, the damage as well as the recovery may be objectively monitored and measured. With broken bones or damaged hearts, it is easier to diagnose and predict the course of treatment and resolution. The vagaries of emotional and psychological disorders are not as easy to formulate and determine. Thus, the medically oriented term *fitness-for-duty evaluation* is not an appropriate label. The label *forensic* is used when pertaining to criminal or legal situations. A forensic investigation is the gathering of evidence at a crime scene by law enforcement personnel. Forensic evaluations may be used to determine guardianship in divorce cases or to evaluate the state of mind of the perpetrator of a crime. An independent medical evaluation is self-descriptive. It usually involves cases where there is a disability or insurance, or both, settlement to be determined. At times, the results of an initial medical evaluation may seem to be biased in favor of either the employee or the employer. In these cases, a mutually agreed-on professional may be called on to make a judgment to resolve the issue. *Threat assessment* is a recent designation that has developed primarily in the workplace when an individual has behaved in a manner that is threatening, violent, or both. It often involves a team or committee of personnel from the workplace who determine if there has been behavior that warrants administrative intervention. Often, this intervention will include an evaluation of the individual. As mentioned earlier, there are many other situations where an individual may have behaved in a significantly inappropriate way, but never uttered or demonstrated any hostile or violent behavior. Nonetheless, an evaluation should be conducted, but it would not be a threat assessment. The term *at-risk assessment* seems to be a more accurate term to describe the individual as well as the process. Furthermore, none of the aforementioned labels apply to an individual who is exhibiting psychotic behavior or mental confusion. Or in the case of someone who has been doing his or her job but makes a veiled threat of violence, none of the terms are a suitable assignation. As is clarified throughout this book, it is our philosophy that a person's inappropriate behavior should be viewed as a sign or symptom of distress and disturbance. Certainly, the workplace cannot tolerate or condone this behavior. These individuals are at risk to themselves as well as others, and intervention is required.

In closing, it is not a simple task to define and diagnose the issues of workplace violence. It is a complex task with multideterminations and factors that require paying attention to the job performance and behavioral expectations of the more than 150 million workers in the United States, the workplace culture and dynamics, the changes in employee demographics, the improved training of supervisors, and the early intervention with employees who are at risk.

References

American Psychiatric Association. (2000). *Diagnostic and statistical manual of mental disorders* (4th ed., text rev.). Washington, DC: Author.

Bureau of Justice Statistics. (2001). *Violence in the workplace, 1993-99*. Washington, DC: U.S. Department of Justice.

Bureau of Labor Statistics. (2002). *BLS survey of occupational injuries and illnesses*. Washington, DC: U.S. Department of Labor.

Lewis, G., & Zare, N. (1999). *Workplace violence: Myth and reality*. Philadelphia: Taylor & Francis.

Miller, M. (2000). A model for the assessment of violence. *Harvard Review of Psychiatry, 7*, 299-304.

National Institute of Occupational Safety and Health. (2003). *Violence in the workplace: Homicide in the workplace*. Retrieved May 30, 2003, from http://www.cdc.gov/niosh/violhomi.html.

Occupational Safety and Health Association. (2003). OSHA Act of 1970. Retrieved May 30, 2003, from www.osha.gov/oshinfo/priorities/violence.html.

20

Promoting Mental Health in the Workplace

CLAIRE A. STEWART
Deakin University

TONY WARD
Victoria University of Wellington

MAYUMI PURVIS
University of Melbourne

INTRODUCTION

*I*n a real sense we are what we do, or at least what we do to make a living. The domain of the workplace can exert a profound influence on the way people view themselves and also constitute a crucial ingredient in the construction of their social identities. A person's choice of occupation can provide him or her with a means of income, valued relationships, opportunities for the development of competence and mastery, a sense of purpose or meaning, and a source of self-esteem and pride. However by way of contrast, unsatisfactory working conditions can lead to alienation, a sense of meaningless, material hardship, profound feelings of inadequacy, and mental health problems. Therefore, work and its component practices and conditions typically exert a powerful effect on the mental health and well-being of individuals. In short, depending on the conditions and nature of work, the well-being of individuals can be enhanced, reduced, or remain unaffected by their work-related experiences. The complex effects work has on our social and personal identity was well described by Hulin (2002, p. 3): "In the United States and other nations in the industrialized world, our work defines us. You are what you do. To do nothing is to be nothing. Just as doing nothing negates our humanity, we are defined privately and socially by our work."

In this chapter we argue that mental health promotion in the workplace has typically proceeded on the basis of the risk management model. In this model risk factors associated with mental health problems are identified and steps are taken to reduce or manage their impact. The concept of risk is complex and contains a number of distinct features. The crucial thing to note is that risk assessment involves an estimate of the likelihood that individuals are likely to be harmed by certain work conditions, experiences, or environments. This estimate strongly points to a value component in the sense that what benefits or harms individuals is a question of specific types of goods and their presence or absence. In addition, this definition suggests that there are a number of risk factors ranging from personal dispositions to environmental factors that should be canvassed in a comprehensive risk assessment. Some of these factors are causally related to mental health problems in a fundamental way while others may simply function as disinhibitors or triggers that precipitate the occurrence of problems.

We argue that instead of relying solely on a risk management approach, the Good Lives Model (GLM) could be used in a complementary manner to enhance the promotion of mental health in the workplace (Ward, 2002a). This model has its origin in the domain of rehabilitation and takes a more holistic approach to mental health and well-being. We suggest that the focus of mental health promotion in the workplace should be on installing strengths or capabilities that will enable an individual to secure valued outcomes rather than on simply removing risk factors. In our model risk factors are usefully seen as internal or external obstacles that compromise an individual's ability to achieve primary goods in personally fulfilling and socially acceptable ways. In other words, risk factors simply denote a lack, or distortion, of the internal and external conditions necessary to live a good life (where "good" refers to the valued aspects of human living such as work, relationships, health, meaning, etc.). A major assumption of the GLM is that a lack of access to primary goods in an individual's life can result in psychological problems and lowered levels of well-being. The existence of conflict between the ways goods are sought also is harmful. Emmons (1999, p. 77) states, "Empirical evidence is continually accruing in support of the notion that conflict is stressful and is associated with both psychological and physical ill-being."

The GLM is essentially a capabilities- or strength-based approach and the aim is to equip individuals with the necessary internal and external conditions (capabilities) to secure primary human goods in socially acceptable and personally meaningful ways. The GLM argues that because human beings are contextual (existing in many, often conflicting, contexts such as social, family, religious, and occupational), an effective approach to mental health promotion in the workplace should take into account the full range of goods people seek in their life. More specifically, the aim should be to ensure that (1) the necessary internal and external conditions required to implement goods in the workplace are installed and (2) that conditions and practices in the workplace do not negatively affect individuals' capacity to realize important goods in their other arenas of their life. In our view, strategies that focus solely on workplace initiatives and interventions are simply too limited to be truly effective and long lasting.

MENTAL HEALTH PROMOTION IN THE WORKPLACE

In the past 40 years there have been some major changes in the nature and structure of the workplace through the constant introduction of new technology commencing in the 1960s and 1970s; a shift toward globalization in the 1980s resulting in mergers, acquisitions, and privatizations, followed by major restructuring and downsizing in the 1990s and 2000s (Sparks, Faragher, & Cooper, 2001). These workplace transitions have arguably affected levels of employee well-being, with the most apparent being increased levels of occupational stress. In addition to the effect on human health, occupational stress is thought to cause huge economic losses, with the United States estimating a loss of more than $150 billion dollars per year (Danna & Griffin, 1999; Neary, 1995). Furthermore, occupational stress represents a portion of workers' compensation claims as well as costs to companies for absenteeism, poor work performance, and staff replacement and retraining. Therefore, there are significant economic and human benefits to be gained from mental health promotion in the workplace, as the effects of employee well-being and health extend far beyond the workplace, affecting workers' families, the wider community, and the economy (Johns, 1995).

Occupational stress and mental health problems can affect any staff member at any time, in any type of work setting. Considering that people who work often spend most of their waking hours in the workplace, there is a real opportunity for organizations to educate employees on mental health issues in order to raise awareness and enable them to make informed judgments regarding their own mental health (Miller, 1998).

Considerable variation exists, however, in the type of meaning attached to the terms *mental health* and *well-being*. As a consequence mental health promotion has been interpreted in several distinct ways. Traditional approaches have focused on the avoidance of disease, illness, and reduced functioning, while recent conceptualizations emphasize health, wellness, and positive functioning. This is not to say there has been a complete transformation, and pathogenic orientations that place health promotion in the context of mental illness rather than mental health can still be found (Pallant & Lae, 2002; Sainsbury, 2000). Past and current approaches to mental health promotion in the workplace have generally been vague, merely stating that the aim of mental health promotion is to increase mental health or prevent mental illness. Furthermore, approaches often have been narrowly designed, with a focus on risk management strategies rather than on mental health enhancement. This has led researchers to identify risk factors that are associated with occupational stress and mental health problems. Once factors that are associated with reduced levels of mental health have been detected the aim is to modify or eradicate them to prevent problems occurring in the future.

Workplace health promotion has been implemented in a domain specific way (i.e., the workplace) with little, if any, consideration of the possibility that satisfactory levels of well-bring might require the realization of goods in all the domains of individuals' life and that what happens in one area can adversely affect the others. For instance, Sparks et al. (2001), in a review of the literature, identified four major factors considered to affect occupational health and employee well-being. These were job insecurity, work hours, control at work, and managerial style. Although these areas were comprehensively discussed, there was almost no mention of the social and personal factors that also have a large impact on employee well-being. There was, however, very limited reference to family problems as a result of long working hours.

This type of conceptualization does not pay sufficient attention to the fact that individuals exist in contexts that are multifaceted, with competing demands from family, social, and work ties (McConkey, 1995). This is a critical consideration for workplace mental health promotion, as the circumstances, pressures, and challenges that people experience in their personal life can greatly influence their mood, involvement, and performance at work (Kelly, 1995). Employees do not leave work matters at the office door, nor do they leave family worries at home. Whether it is the workplace, home, or social environment, people will spend time thinking about their work, family, or personal problems. In certain circumstances a preoccupation with personal or family issues may impair people's functioning in the work domain. Therefore, in recognition that people live their life in multiple contexts, mental health promotion strategies need to acknowledge the complex interactions between people and their surroundings. The identification of risk factors associated with mental health problems remains an important component of mental health promotion. It is suggested, however, that this is an insufficient basis on which to build an approach and a broader perspective that focuses on enhancing and strengthening capabilities, not just avoiding risks, is required.

Mental health promotion has been described in many ways. It has been referred to as "enhancing the life skills and social participation of people with severe mental illness" (Sainsbury, 2000, p. 82) as well as enhancing "general coping skills and mental health of non-clinical populations" with the aim of reducing the likelihood of the development of disorder (Price, 1998, p. 20). However, Moodie (1999, p. 79) described mental health promotion programs as "concerned with strengthening and improving the mental functioning of people who may not be mentally ill (although it doesn't exclude people who are) and may not be particularly at risk of mental illness (more so than we all are). Life can be improved: it does not have to be cured." Intervention, therefore, should not just be about fixing what is broken; it should be concerned with nurturing what is best and right (Seligman & Csikszentmihalyi, 2000).

Thus, it is important to acknowledge that human beings seek a range of primary goods or valued outcomes, and this propensity is based on our common nature. In other words, basic human needs cause us to want and require certain outcomes—for example, relationships, autonomy, food, and warmth—to function in an optimal manner. There is a range of distinct goods and a (good) life requires the presence of all of these elements (see section on the GLM). It is not possible to insulate what happens at work from these other domains, or vice versa.

RISK FACTORS FOR MENTAL HEALTH PROBLEMS

Before outlining the GLM and discussing its application to mental health promotion in the workplace, consideration is given to the variables that have been identified as constituting risk factors for mental health problems. Miller (1998) detailed a comprehensive list of 28 workplace risk factors that are directly associated with occupational stress and poor mental health. The 28 risk factors are grouped into nine broader categories. "Organizational function and culture" refers to a poor problem-solving environment, poor communication, and a nonsupportive culture. "Role in the organization" relates to risk factors such as role ambiguity, role conflict, and high responsibility for people. "Career development" concerns career uncertainty, career plateau, poor pay, and fear of redundancy, and is followed by "decision latitude/control," which refers to lack of decision making and lack of control over work. "Interpersonal relationships at work" concerns risk factors such as social or physical isolation, poor relationships with superiors, interpersonal conflict or violence, and lack of social support. The "home/work interface" refers to the conflicting demands of work and home, low social or practical support at home, and dual career problems. The category "task design" concerns ill-defined work, uncertainty of work, lack of variety or short work cycles, and continual exposure to people, clients, or customers. The eighth category, "workload," is defined by work overload or underload, lack of control over pace of work, and time pressures or tight deadlines, and the last category, "work schedule," is described in terms of shift work and long unsociable work hours.

Miller's identification of workplace risk factors illustrates a typical approach to mental health promotion in the workplace, which seems to assume that identifying risk factors will result in the changes necessary to reduce occupational stress. A problem with most workplace-oriented approaches to mental health promotion is the overriding tendency to identify only aggravating factors. This means that only factors thought to increase the likelihood of poor mental health are presented and are constructed negatively in terms of deficits and problems (e.g., poor pay, poor relationships, role conflict, and lack of social support). This illustrates Ryff and Singer's (1998) assertion that health (and in our view) and health promotion is typically described in negative terms and is measured in terms of disease, illness, and reduced functioning as opposed to rates of wellness and positive functioning. The trouble with simply listing negative factors that contribute to mental health problems is that it really only tells people what they should be avoiding. Research indicates that avoidance goals (goals concerned with decreasing or avoiding a behavior or situation) are much more difficult to achieve than are approach goals and lead to higher levels of psychological distress and lower levels of well-being (Elliot, Sheldon, & Church, 1997; Emmons, 1996; Wegner, 1994). Rather, mental health promotion strategies should be aimed at identifying circumstances that increase one's chance of mental health and psychological well-being (i.e., approach goals); for instance, supporting co-workers, communicating information freely, increasing the opportunity to contribute to decision making, and increasing training for staff. Accordingly, a good lives approach emphasizes strengths rather than deficits and achievement rather than avoidance. The avoidance of a negative situation is implicit in the achievement of a desired one.

Another problem with the risk management approach consists in the narrow way factors affecting mental health are construed. As stated earlier, human beings live their life in multiple contexts and domains, not just in the workplace. While we are not suggesting that employers should be responsible for improving people's life outside of the work environment, they should at least take measures that will reduce the likelihood of work-related matters negatively affecting people's general quality of life, as this can in turn affect their work performance. Put simply, there should be a mutual obligation between employers and employees to make work more positive (Turner, Barling, & Zacharatos, 2002). Furthermore, a successful approach to mental health in the workplace should acknowledge that basic human needs transcend these different domains and their satisfaction is critical for the achievement of general mental health and well-being. In other words, human needs for relatedness, autonomy, and competency should be taken into account in workplace practices as well as in the other arenas of an individual's life (Deci & Ryan, 2000). A workplace focus on building and enhancing strengths and skills, therefore, will enable individuals to fulfill basic human needs, which may lead to improved mental health and well-being and in turn result in happier, better performing workers.

We argue that while risk factors are not sufficient on their own to form the basis of mental health promotion in the workplace, they need to be taken into account. Next we consider how the GLM can be integrated with and supplement the risk management approach to mental health promotion in the workplace.

THE GLM OF MENTAL HEALTH PROMOTION

Unlike traditional approaches to mental health promotion that focus on risk factors and inhibitors of mental well-being, the GLM is essentially a strength-based approach, focusing on factors that comprise a fulfilling or beneficial life for individuals. The term *good lives* as opposed to *good life* endorses the view that for each person there is no singular lifestyle that is ideal or preferred (for stimulating discussions of these issues, see Kekes, 1989, and Rasmussen, 1999). Rather, different people place an emphasis on different primary goods, although all people require the same *set* of primary goods to experience high levels of well-being. For example, some individuals will weight work more highly than relatedness, although all people require elements of both goods if they are to lead a fulfilling life. Primary goods refer to constituents of human functioning and experience that are considered beneficial to human beings and therefore result in higher levels of well-being; for example, relatedness, health, knowledge, and autonomy (Ward, 2002b). The notion that all human beings naturally seek a range of goods is a fundamental assumption of the GLM; all human actions are arguably linked to the seeking of human goods (Ward, 2002b).

The possibility of constructing and translating conceptions of good lives into actions and concrete ways of living crucially depends on the possession of internal (skills and capabilities) and external conditions (opportunities and supports). The specific form that a conception will take depends on the actual abilities, interests, and opportunities of each individual and the weightings he or she gives to specific primary goods. The weightings or priority allocated to specific primary goods is constitutive of an individual's personal identity and spells out the kind of life sought, and relatedly, the kind of person he or she wants to be.

Because human beings naturally seek a range of primary goods or desired states, it is important that all the classes of primary goods are addressed in a conception of good lives; they should be ordered and coherently related to each other. For example, if an individual decides to pursue a life characterized by service to the community, a core aspect of his or her identity will revolve around the primary goods of relatedness and social life. The person's sense of mastery, self-esteem, perception of autonomy, and control will all reflect this overarching good and its associated subclusters of goods (e.g., caring, honesty). The resulting good lives conceptions should be organized in ways that ensure each primary good has a role to play and can be secured or experienced by the individual concerned. A conception that is fragmented and lacks coherency is likely to lead to frustration and harm to the individual concerned, as well as a life lacking an overall sense of purpose and meaning (Emmons, 1996). In addition, a conception of good lives is always context dependent; there is no such thing as the right kind of life for an individual across every conceivable setting.

There is a reasonable consensus (in Western culture at least) regarding the lists of primary human goods noted in psychological research (Cummins, 1996; Emmons, 1999), evolutionary theory (Arnhart, 1998), practical ethics (Murphy, 2001), and philosophical anthropology (Nussbaum, 2000; Rescher, 1990). In our approach, human goods are valued aspects of human functioning and lives that are sought for their own sake; for example, relationships or mastery experiences. Moreover, the GLM is able to clarify the ends individuals seek in their everyday life and can provide specific guidance for employers. It is important to note that all individuals have a GLM, not just those who deliberately pursue a well-thought plan for living that takes into account their strengths, weaknesses, preferences, and circumstances.

On the basis of these considerations, Ward (2002b), drawing on the work of Murphy (2001), offered the following comprehensive list of nine primary human goods: life (including healthy living and functioning), knowledge, excellence in play and work (including mastery experiences), excellence in agency (i.e., autonomy and self-directedness), inner peace (i.e., freedom from emotional turmoil and stress), relatedness (including intimate, romantic, and family relationships) and community, spirituality (in the broad sense of finding meaning and purpose in life), happiness, and creativity. Such a conceptualization fulfills the requirements of a full understanding of human health, as it "encompasses not only physical well-being but also psychological and social flourishing" (Ryff & Singer, 2002, p. 553).

Psychological, work, social, and lifestyle problems emerge when the implicit or explicit models individuals use to structure and plan their life are faulty in some respect. It is hypothesized that there are four major types of difficulties found in the GLM of individuals: (1) problems with the *means* used to secure goods, (2) a lack of *scope* within a good lives plan, (3) the presence of *conflict* among goals (goods sought) or incoherence, or (4) a lack of the necessary *capacities* to construct, implement, and adjust a GLM to changing circumstances (e.g., impulsive decision making).

According to the good lives model, risk factors, such as those outlined previously, are viewed as obstacles that erode an individual's ability to engage in a more fulfilling life. That is, dynamic risk factors are associated with the distortion of the conditions required to achieve primary human goods and can be viewed as internal or external obstacles that prevent basic needs from being met in an optimal manner (Ward, 2002a). A good lives approach thus argues that aiming to simply manage risk is insufficient because minimizing risk factors will not necessarily increase well-being. In fact, Ryff and Singer (2002) reported that when risk factors have subsided but well-being is not fully regained, individuals remain at high risk of relapse. For example, management of workplace risk factors targets only a limited number of factors that can affect mental health, and consequently this context-limited form of mental health promotion will arguably achieve only modest, short-term progress in terms of increasing levels of mental health and well-being (for reasons that are discussed later). Rather, the focus should be on conceptualizing and implementing a good lives approach, as risk factors will be dealt with as a consequence of this. This approach is preferred to merely managing risk, as risk management is necessary but not sufficient for living good lives.

Herrman's (2001) work provided an example of a good lives approach as he described mental health more holistically and identified work-related goals that are more likely to promote mental well-being. He suggested that a number of personal, social, and environmental factors (clustered around a number of distinct themes) will promote mental health and protect against ill health. The first theme concerns the development and maintenance of healthy and safe communities, which among other things includes the provision of good housing, positive educational experiences, employment, good working conditions, and social supports. The consolidation of these factors will in turn facilitate self-determination, a sense of control over one's life, and the satisfaction of the basic needs of food, warmth, and shelter. The second theme relates to each person's ability to deal with the social world, and is associated with the formation of relationships, attachment, and feelings of acceptance. The third theme centers on a person's ability to manage thoughts and feelings (referred to as emotional resilience), which is said to be associated with physical health, self-esteem, conflict management skills, and the ability to learn. This approach to mental health reflects the features of a GLM, as it is centered on the human goods (basic needs) that are required to live a fulfilling and beneficial life.

APPLICATION OF THE GLM TO HEALTH PROMOTION IN THE WORKPLACE

General Comments

Individuals seek a plurality of goods through a variety of means. Each person seeks to live a certain kind of life, and thereby become a certain type of person. Many workers may be unaware of the exact nature of their GLM; however, despite this fact there is always some kind of model that implicitly guides their life choices and is casually implicated in the resulting quality of life and subsequent levels of well-being. A critical issue is that different people will adopt different overarching primary goods and also seek primary goods in a variety of ways and means. For some people, excellence at work will be the most important good and the resultant feelings of competency and esteem most strongly sought. However, for others, while it may be important to perform competently at work, the most important good may reside in cultivating and maintaining intimate relationships or being of service to the community. In other words, it is not wise to assume that all people seek the same degree of satisfaction in the work domain, although all may want to perform competently. For some employees work may provide crucial social contacts, a sense of connectedness to the community, an overall purpose in life, a source of creativity, or simply a chance to get physically healthy. In other words, people may seek quite distinct goods in the work domain and these goods could be crucial to their overall level of well-being. An important assumption of the GLM is that all the primary goods should be realized to some degree although people will vary in terms of exactly what goods are weighted most highly. This means that employers need to be more flexible and appreciate that even for high-functioning employees who perform very well, work may only be a means to other more important ends such as security or leisure time.

We want to stress that it is not the responsibility of employers to devise and implement good lives plans for their employees; that is the responsibility of the individuals. It is unreasonable to expect an employer to function as some kind of paternalistic overseer whose duty is to ensure that every employee is fulfilled in his or her broader life. For one thing, a basic assumption of Western liberal democracies is that each person is responsible for deciding what kind of life he or she wants and then setting out to implement a plan that will make this possibility concrete. However, in view of the assumption (supported by psychological and anthropological research) that human beings are integrated organisms who seek coherence across the domains of their lives and that mental health in the workplace is influenced by and influences the quality of an individual's life in other domains, it makes sense for employers to think more systematically about these issues. Dissatisfied and unhappy workers are unlikely to work effectively and in the end will result in lowered productivity and financial losses to an organization. Performance reviews may be a forum where some of these issues can be addressed and employee goals noted and an implementation plan devised.

Therefore, we argue that employers should address the issue of mental health enhancement in the workplace from a strength-based, good lives approach that moves beyond the obligations of occupational health and safety (which often emphasize physical health) and of managing risk factors. More specifically, the aim should be to ensure that (1) the necessary internal and external conditions required to implement goods in the workplace are installed and that (2) the conditions and practices in the workplace do not negatively affect individuals' capacity to realize important goods in the other arenas of their life.

Risk factors function as markers that there is a problem in the way that an individual is seeking primary human goods in the workplace; a problem that is directly related to his or her lowered levels of well-being. The detection of risk factors merely signals that there is a problem but does not indicate what to do other than to attempt to remove it or weaken its effects. We suggest, therefore, that the risk management approach should be embedded within a GLM, which means that the focus should be on instilling the conditions to achieve human goods in ways that are practically feasible and personally satisfying. Risk analysis only informs employers that there are problems in the way employees seek human goods in the workplace. This does not mean that the concept of risk is irrelevant or that employees should not avoid certain activities (e.g., working without protective equipment, working long hours, etc.). It simply means that the emphasis should be on understanding what primary goods have been sought in the workplace by specific individuals and on designing a style of working that addresses those goods in ways that are personally satisfying, that take account of a person's strengths and interests, and most important, that are realistic in the light of limited resources and practical constraints.

One point of clarification is that the skill demands, opportunities, and goals associated with work will vary according to the type and level of employment. A factory manager will be expected to display greater ability to arrange the deployment of staff to achieve work-related goals and outputs than are shop floor workers. In addition, the capacity to realize the goods of autonomy and mastery will vary according to each employee's degree of responsibility, expertise, and place in the workplace hierarchy. However, to keep our line of argument as clear as possible, we keep our comments relatively general. We now discuss the application of the GLM in the workplace in light of these different tasks, taking into account the distinction between internal and external conditions.

Workplace Practices

It is difficult to detail a detailed good lives approach for mental health promotion in the workplace because, as stated previously, each plan needs to be individualized and realistic, taking into account workers' capabilities, temperaments, interests, personal histories, opportunities, work situations, and settings (Ward, 2002a). Furthermore, as human well-being is a self-directed activity flowing directly from each individual's own choices and effort, the person in question must have personal control over decisions related to his well-being. We attempt, however, to demonstrate how Miller's (1998) identified risk factors can be related to primary goods as outlined in the GLM.

The categories identified by Miller (1998) as organizational function and culture and interpersonal relationships at work can be related to the primary human goods of relatedness and community. This primary good necessitates functional and beneficial relationships, characterized by relatedness, support from people, and the presence of safe, secure environments that enable the development of interpersonal skills such as communication and conflict resolution. Naturally, these goods are necessary for general human functioning and therefore occur and extend beyond the workplace; human goods can and should be fulfilled in a number of contexts, as a greater degree of scope regarding means to accessing goods is preferred over limited options. However, in the workplace, research shows a modest correlation between employee attachment to work groups and commitment to the larger organization, which in turn is related to improved well-being (Turner et al., 2002).

In terms of the internal conditions required to achieve the primary human goods of relatedness and community in the workplace, the primary obligation of the employer is to ensure that workers possess the skills necessary to communicate their work-related needs to their fellow workers and supervisors. This means that adequate training in work-related protocols and practices should be provided. Concerning external (to the individual) conditions, individuals should be allowed adequate periods for breaks and socialization in the workplace. In addition, establishing a company ethos and activities that are partly chosen by employees is critically important, rather than their being imposed from above. The issue of communication breakdowns or relationship conflicts between fellow employees should be addressed by the provision of mediation services and opportunities to air grievances. It also is important to institute procedures that prevent this from happening in the first place; for example, positive practices that promote effective communication.

Role in the organization and workload possibly relate to the primary human goods of excellence in play and work and excellence in agency. The relevant internal conditions include knowledge of the chain of responsibility and a belief that management and other workers value each role in the workplace. Thus attitudes toward each type of worker and his or her specific duties ideally are constructive and result in a sense of overall coherence and mutuality. Concerning the external conditions, work overloads or underloads will negatively affect mastery experiences. For example, having a work underload can lead to a lack of intellectual or physical challenges (depending on work type), resulting in impoverished mastery experiences, whereas work overload indicates that the work or work level is too challenging, which could lead to feelings of helplessness and reduced autonomy (e.g., decreased self-reliance and independence). Similarly, role ambiguity (lack of direction and understanding regarding personal duties and responsibilities) has a similar impact on autonomy and an employee's ability to master challenges. Consistent with these observations, Turner et al. (2002) found that having role clarity (sufficient understanding and predictability of one's work), role agreement (specified set of demands and expectations), and a challenging yet manageable workload affected employee morale and job-related well-being.

Career development and decision latitude and control may relate to the primary goods of knowledge and excellence in play and work. Interest in career development arguably reflects the need to acquire and increase knowledge and skills to avoid problems like career plateau, whereas lack of control and decision-making capacity may relate to knowledge as well as the need to achieve in the workplace through personal decisions and the management of self and personal tasks (e.g., the opportunity to extend knowledge, apply knowledge, and use and develop skills).

In terms of the internal conditions required to achieve these primary human goods, ongoing training schemes and courses can help individuals to regularly improve skills and plan a career course. External conditions including the provision of resources for further training or time off to attend courses are ways in which employers can assist in the realization of these primary goods. In addition, the structuring of tasks in ways that allowed for progressive mastery and appreciation of how individual efforts are related to the finished product are beneficial.

Finally, the risk factor of task design (lack of variety and ill-defined work) may inhibit employees from achieving the primary human goods of creativity and autonomy. The internal conditions required to facilitate the realization of these goods include ensuring that individuals possess the skills necessary to do a range of tasks and allowing them to rotate around different types of jobs. Concerning the external conditions, building in some opportunities for choice in the design of tasks should allow employees to perceive they have some degree of agency. This may help to prevent breaking down tasks into extremely small chunks and ensuring each person has a chance to rotate between related, although distinct, jobs. In addition, having the opportunity to see the finished product is likely to enhance workers' sense of accomplishment, creativity, and autonomy.

While we have not suggested an explicit connection, all of these risk factors are expected to affect the primary human good of happiness. Furthermore, additional risk factors not explicitly mentioned by Miller (1998) include the existence of dangerous work settings and the expectation by some organizations that staff will engage in emotional labor on their behalf (Held, 2002). The term *emotional labor* refers to the deliberate attempt to suppress emotional states that employers regard as inimical to their company ethos or image and to the cultivation of emotional expressions that portray both the workers' experiences and the company in a positive way; for example, cultivating an overly cheerful and expansive demeanor and presenting this face to the public. These risk factors relate to the human goods of life and the need for healthy living as well as inner peace (the need to be free from danger and stress). An example of a situation where emotional labor is expected occurs when employees are the public face of a company or agency and have to bear the brunt of public anger following cuts to services. It is prudent for employers to be aware of the emotional cost of this labor to staff and to institute the appropriate safeguards and supports. For example, debriefing sessions where their concerns and frustrations can be articulated or specialized training to improve workers' ability to manage their stress level. It also should be acknowledged that individuals vary in their capacity to manage negative emotional states and therefore may require distinct and tailored support services.

Thus the necessary internal conditions promoting this good are awareness on the employee's part of the job-related hazards and the corresponding safety practices. Relatedly, workers need to believe that employers are concerned about their welfare and have taken reasonable steps to ensure that the work environment is safe. Concerning the issue of emotional labor, the employee should be free to form his or her attitudes about the company and not be expected to falsify their emotional experience for public relations purposes, although of course it may be necessary for individuals to modify the expression of these feelings in certain employment-related contexts. At this point we are referring to gross distortions of inner experience rather than simply behaving with basic good will toward an employer. The relevant external conditions include the creation of a safe environment by the employer and senior staff, regular equipment and safety audits, mechanisms for allowing reports on dangerous practices, and meetings with staff to hear their safety-related concerns. Finally, there should be no forceful attempts to force employees to adopt false emotional states in order to present the employer in an overly positive (and possibly distorted) light.

Relationship of Workplace to an Individual's Life

The primary relevant risk factors concerning the relationship between the workplace and an individuals' life outside of work are those of the home-work interface and work schedule. The major concern here is that workplace practices might severely frustrate employees' ability to secure goods outside workplace. The home-work interface and work schedule may concern the primary goods pertaining to friendship and community and peace of mind (i.e., emotional equilibrium). Shift work, unsociable work hours, and the conflicting demands of home and work may prevent workers from interacting with family members, friends, and social events. Internal conditions that may help individuals to achieve the primary human goods sought in the domains outside work include allowing workers to place personal items in their workplace, which may help to create a sense of continuity among the various domains of life. Concerning external conditions, the provision of mental health services or schemes may encourage employees to seek help for their problems, no matter what origin of the problem. It also may be helpful to ensure that overtime, work hours, schedules, the work ethos, and cultural practices do not operate to punish those who decline to take up opportunities for additional work. In addition, senior staff should understand that employees may seek distinct goods within and outside of work and therefore should not make it hard for such individuals to seek these goods. For example, certain religious practices may require behavioral commitments on particular days or at specific times. The key issue is that a GLM operates across all the domains of an individual's life and it is not possible, or desirable, to insulate what happens at work from these other arenas. Psychological research suggests that a lack of coherency (i.e., conflict) among goals is associated with lower levels of subjective well-being and less life satisfaction (Emmons, 1999).

CONCLUSION

As stated previously, a good life becomes possible when an individual has access to primary goods, can achieve primary goods, and lives a life characterized by the instantiation of these goods. The identification of risk factors can provide useful information about the workplace, which can be used to develop a more holistic approach to mental health promotion. A risk management approach on its own makes it difficult to derive successful and achievable intervention strategies. If employers keep in mind the primary human goods when dealing with their staff and structure the workplace in a way that gives individuals ample opportunity to achieve these goods (where appropriate), then risk factors will be effectively managed as a consequence of employees' living more coherent and fulfilling lives.

In this chapter we argued that an appropriate approach to mental health promotion in the workplace should keep in mind that people pursue multiple goods in the living of their life and seek these goods in a variety of related domains. Previous and current approaches to mental health promotion have provided us with a good understanding of the range of factors that can affect mental health. However, the conceptual problems associated with these models limits the extent to which they can be used to enhance the mental health of employees. We suggest that a GLM can address these problems and provide organizations with a more comprehensive way of viewing and approaching mental health promotion in the workplace.

References

Arnhart, L. (1998). *Darwinian natural right: The biological ethics of human nature*. Albany: State University of New York Press.

Cummins, R. A. (1996). The domains of life satisfaction: An attempt to order chaos. *Social Indicators Research, 38*, 303-328.

Danna, K., & Griffin, R. W. (1999). Health and well-being in the workplace: A review and synthesis of the literature. *Journal of Management, 25*(3), 357-384.

Deci, E. L., & Ryan, R. M. (2000). The "what" and "why" of goal pursuits: Human needs and the self-determination of behavior. *Psychological Inquiry, 11*, 227-268.

Elliot, A. J., Sheldon, K. M., & Church, M. A. (1997). Avoidance personal goals and subjective well-being. *Personality and Social Psychology Bulletin, 23*, 915-927.

Emmons, R. A. (1996). Striving and feeling: Personal goals and subjective well-being. In P. M. Gollwitzer & J. A. Bargh (Eds.), *The psychology of action: Linking cognition and motivation to behavior* (pp. 313-337). New York: Guilford.

Emmons, R. A. (1999). *The psychology of ultimate concerns*. New York: Guilford.

Held, B. (2002). The trynanny of positive attitude in America: Observation and speculation. *Journal of Clinical Psychology, 58*, 965-992.

Herrman, H. (2001). The need for mental health promotion. *Australian and New Zealand Journal of Psychiatry, 35*, 709-715.

Hulin, C. (2002). Lessons from industrial and organizational psychology. In J. M. Brett & F. Drasgow (Eds.), *The psychology of work: Theoretically based empirical research* (pp. 3-22). Mahwah, NJ: Lawrence Erlbaum.

Johns, G. (1995). Occupational stress and well-being at work. In P. Cotton (Ed.), *Psychological health in the workplace: Understanding and managing occupational stress* (pp. 3-6). Carlton: Australian Psychological Society.

Kekes, J. (1989). *Moral tradition and individuality*. Princeton, NJ: Princeton University Press.

Kelly, S. (1995). The impact of relationship and family stresses in the workplace. In P. Cotton (Ed.), *Psychological health in the workplace: Understanding and managing occupational stress* (pp. 21-29). Carlton: Australian Psychological Society.

McConkey, K. M. (1995). Psychological health issues in the workplace. In P. Cotton (Ed.), *Psychological health in the workplace: Understanding and managing occupational stress* (pp. 13-17). Carlton: Australian Psychological Society.

Miller, D. (1998). Workplaces. In R. Jenkins & T. B. Üstün (Eds.), *Preventing mental illness: Mental health promotion in primary care* (pp. 343-351). Chichester, UK: Wiley.

Moodie, R. (1999). Mental health: A contested standard. *Health Promotion Journal of Australia, 9*, 79-80.

Murphy, M. C. (2001). *Natural law and practical rationality*. New York: Cambridge University Press.

Neary, J. (1995). Challenges of managing the workplace. In P. Cotton (Ed.), *Psychological health in the workplace: Understanding and managing occupational stress* (pp. 7-11). Carlton: Australian Psychological Society.

Nussbaum, M. C. (2000). *Women and human development: The capabilities approach*. New York: Cambridge University Press.

Pallant, J. F., & Lae, L. (2002). Sense of coherence, well-being, coping and personality factors: Further evaluation of the sense of coherence scale. *Personality and Individual Differences, 33,* 39-48.

Price, R. H. (1998). Theoretical frameworks for mental health risk reduction in primary care. In R. Jenkins & T. B. Üstün (Eds.), *Preventing mental illness: Mental health promotion in primary care* (pp. 19-34). Chichester, UK: Wiley.

Rasmussen, D. B. (1999). Human flourishing and the appeal to human nature. In E. F. Paul, F. D. Miller, & J. Paul (Eds.), *Human flourishing* (pp. 1-43). New York: Cambridge University Press.

Rescher, N. (1990). *Human interests: Reflections on philosophical anthropology.* Stanford, CA: Stanford University Press.

Ryff, C. D., & Singer, B. (1998). The contours of positive human health. *Psychological Inquiry, 9,* 1-28.

Ryff, C. D., & Singer, B. (2002). From social structure to biology: Integrative science in pursuit of human health and well-being. In C. R. Snyder & S. J. Lopez (Eds.), *Handbook of positive psychology* (pp. 541-555). New York: Oxford University Press.

Sainsbury, P. (2000). Promoting mental health: Recent progress and problems in Australia. *Journal of Epidemiology and Community Health, 54,* 82-83.

Seligman, M. E. P., & Csikszentmihalyi, M. (2000). Positive psychology: An introduction. *American Psychologist, 55,* 5-14.

Sparks, K., Faragher, B., & Cooper, C. L. (2001). Well-being and occupational health in the 21st century workplace. *Journal of Occupational and Organizational Psychology, 74,* 489-509.

Turner, N., Barling, J., & Zacharatos, A. (2002). Positive psychology at work. In C. R. Snyder & S. J. Lopez (Eds.), *Handbook of positive psychology* (pp. 715-728). New York: Oxford University Press.

Ward, T. (2002a). Good lives and the rehabilitation of offenders: Promises and problems. *Aggression and Violent Behaviour, 7,* 1-17.

Ward, T. (2002b). The management of risk and the design of good lives. *Australian Psychologist, 37,* 172-179.

Wegner, D. M. (1994). Ironic processes of mental control. *Psychological Bulletin, 101,* 453-473.

21

Employee Assistance Program Strategies

DOUGLAS G. MCCLURE
Employee Assistance Services Enterprises

E mployee assistance programs (EAPs) may be one of the more comprehensive
means of addressing psychopathology in the workplace. This chapter provides an overview of EAPs in the United States, including history, types of
programs, prevalence, costs, and some of the issues surrounding use of EAPs by
employees and their dependents. EAP strategies frequently include primary, secondary, and tertiary intervention modalities. Various methods within each modality are
explored.

EAP STRATEGIES

As a software designer, John frequently received accolades from his superiors for
his creativity and willingness to work long hours. It was not at all uncommon for
John to be found working late into the night and, at age 34, he would laughingly
joke with his friends about the similarity of this work to pulling all-nighters in
college when preparing for exams. Sleeping for a few hours on his office couch
restored him and he would be back at the computer early the next morning. John's
co-workers often perceived him as somewhat eccentric, but this was not unusual for
persons doing the work he did. He had always had occasional bouts of irritability
and when these bouts began to increase, they were attributed to the stress of his
workload. His supervisor encouraged him to take time off, but John resisted, saying
he had too much work to do.

Over time, John's performance began to suffer. He missed deadlines, he was
playing computer games more frequently with office mates, and his supervisor
noticed that he seemed to be staring at his computer for long periods of time yet
accomplishing little. This went on for several months before John's supervisor
confronted him. John readily acknowledged that his performance had slipped and
admitted that it was likely due to some problems he was having in his marriage.

Furthermore, while he appreciated his supervisor's concern, he felt that he had his situation under control and that he was addressing the problems. He told his supervisor that he would refocus his efforts and get back on track. The supervisor again expressed concern for John, encouraged him to talk with her at any time, and urged him to take care of himself. John was a good employee, vital to their company, and she hoped and believed that he would do better, both personally and professionally.

Three weeks later, the human resources manager notified John's supervisor that John would be on medical leave until further notice. She was surprised and wondered if there might have been anything she could have done to prevent this. If John's company had an EAP, there might have been many resources available to John and his supervisor that may have helped address the difficulties John was having.

As we have seen from the previous chapters in this book, the workplace is not immune to employees having difficulties that affect their performance. Employees, like everyone else, occasionally have issues in their life that create difficulties for them. Some of the time, those difficulties interfere with their ability to perform their jobs. EAPs are designed to be a resource to employees (and often their immediate family members), managers and supervisors, human resource personnel, and upper management as a key strategy in maintaining a sound workforce (Dickman, 1988). In this chapter, we review basic elements of the EAP and common strategies they use in preventing and addressing employee problems.

EAPS: AN OVERVIEW

The Employee Assistance Professionals Association (EAPA, 2003) defined the EAP as a "worksite-based program designed to assist (1) work organizations in addressing productivity issues and (2) 'employee clients' in identifying and resolving personal concerns, including, but not limited to, health, marital, family, financial, alcohol, drug, legal, emotional, stress, or other personal issues that may affect job performance." Although it varies by industry, as of 1996 EAPs were part of the benefit package provided by approximately 33 percent of all private, nonagricultural work sites in the United States with 50 or more full-time employees, covering about 55 percent of all U.S. employees in private industry (Hartwell et al., 1996). These figures likely fell short of the actual prevalence rates because the majority of private employers in the United States employ fewer than 50 people and this data also did not include public employers. A 2002 survey conducted by Open Minds (Naughton-Travers, 2002) revealed that more than 80 million workers are enrolled in EAPs and that this reflected a 3 percent increase from the previous year.

A Brief History of the EAP

As surprising as it may seem, it was not uncommon for workers in the nineteenth century to drink alcohol on the job. Often this was done at specified times, lunch for example, and frequently at the expense of the employer. As employers became more focused on profits and efficiency, there became an increasing concern regarding the use of alcohol in the workplace. Compensation laws, which held the employer responsible for most job-related injuries regardless of who was at fault, exacerbated their concern that employees under the influence of alcohol might be more prone to injure themselves or others (Brody, 1988). There became a financial incentive for the employer to address potential problems with employees who were abusing alcohol.

Alcohol programs in the workplace began to emerge in the 1940s. Alcoholics Anonymous (AA) was an early self-help program that was founded in 1935. By 1944, there were 300 AA groups with more than 10,000 members. Many of the groups met at the work site and were supported by a variety of sources, including industrial physicians and upper management (Brody, 1988).

In 1970, Congress passed the Hughes Act, which established the National Institute on Alcohol Abuse and Alcoholism (NIAAA) the following year. Its initial goal was to promote programs for problem drinkers in the public and private workforce, and it was subsequently amended to include drug abuse in order that the problem drinker or drug user could again become productive in the workplace. The NIAAA sought to address the significant percentage of alcoholics and drug users who were employed and mandated that treatment programs be a part of all federal agencies and military installations. Although the programs often were informal and staffed by employees with no formal training who were recovering alcoholics themselves, they were frequently successful (Brody, 1988). Supervisors were taught to identify problems in performance and how to confront their employees. Workplace policies were written to include procedures for responding to alcohol- and drug-abuse problems.

The EAPs emerged about this same time as a more broad-based approach. Not only were these programs equipped to respond to the employee with chemical-abuse and dependency issues but also they were prepared to deal with a broader range of mental health issues. Unlike some of the earlier approaches, employers offered EAPs to employees as part of the fringe benefit package, allowing employees and their family members to access the EAP services at no charge to the employee or employee's family. Today, EAPs frequently provide a broad range of services, including mental health assessment, short-term counseling, work-life programs, training for management and employees, crisis interventions, twenty-four-hour response, critical incident stress debriefings (CISD), management consultation, workplace policy advising, and more.

The effectiveness of the EAP depends on several factors: it has to have the endorsement and support of high-level management and organized labor, it needs to have clear policies and procedures outlining the intent and purpose of the program, and it must maintain strict confidentiality (Dickman, 1988). This is not as simple as it might seem, as we see later.

Types of EAPs

EAPs typically are defined as either internal or external, part-time or full-time, on-site or off-site. There is not universal agreement about these definitions (Leong & Every, 1997). Early EAPs were typically found solely in large companies. The EAP staff was hired by the company management and had offices on company premises. Later, private enterprises offered to provide this service to a particular company, but the EAP staff was not composed of employees of the company to whom the services were being provided. The original model became known as an internal EAP and the distinguishing characteristic is that the EAP personnel are employees of the same company as are those they are serving. The other model is generally referred to as an external EAP because the EAP personnel are not company employees. Both models may provide their services on a part-time or full-time basis to the company and may provide those services either on company premises (on-site) or at another location (off-site). Many, if not most, EAPs will provide both on-site and off-site services, depending on the need of the company and its employees.

There has been considerable discussion and research attempting to ascertain whether the internal or external EAP model is better. The answer may depend on the question that is being asked. If employee use of the EAP is the primary criteria, some of the research suggests that use by employees of an internal EAP may be as much as one-third higher than that with an external EAP (Collins, 2000). Internal EAPs also generally provide more services than an external EAP (French, Zarkin, Bray, & Hartwell, 1999) and may provide additional benefits such as familiarity with a company's culture and policies and more visibility to employees than an external program (Leong & Every, 1997). If cost is a primary concern, an external EAP may be a better choice. In their 1993 and 1995 national surveys, French et al. found that across all work sites, the average annual cost per eligible employee for an internal EAP was more than $5.00 higher than the per employee cost for an external program.

As noted previously, confidentiality is critical in developing and maintaining an effective EAP. However, it is not always easy for the EAP professional or the employee to determine whether it is an *employee* assistance program or an *employer* assistance program. After all, whether the EAP professional is employed directly by the company in an internal EAP or by an enterprise specializing in EAP services that has a contract with the company, it is the company that is paying for the service. It is inherent upon management and the EAP, whether internally or externally based, to define the limits of confidentiality prior to the onset of services.

Perception of the EAP as confidential is a critical factor in use by employees. In a study of an internal EAP, Harlow (1998) found that less than 50 percent of the employees surveyed agreed that the EAP protects confidentiality. Actual use of the EAP is a key factor in perception of confidentiality (French, Dunlap, Roman, & Steele, 1997) and yet nearly two-thirds of employees believe that, while the EAP is a good benefit, they would not be likely to use it (Butterworth, 2001). This is particularly true for men, who are less likely to use the services of the EAP when compared with women (French et al., 1997).

Additional factors that influence employees' attitudes toward the EAP include perceived support by upper management and supervisors. Perceptions of the EAP as accessible also influence attitudes, particularly if the EAP is perceived to be more responsive than providers on the employees' health plan and if the location of the EAP office is conveniently located. Nevertheless, encouraging employee use is an ongoing challenge for EAPs in most work settings.

INTERVENTION STRATEGIES

The EAP uses a variety of strategies to reduce the incidence, prevalence, and extent of psychopathology in the workplace. These strategies often are referred to as primary, secondary, and tertiary prevention, or intervention, strategies. Primary prevention attempts to prevent a disorder from occurring. Secondary interventions in EAP settings seek to identify specific populations who may be at risk to have personal problems and have them seek help as soon as possible to minimize possible factors that might inhibit employees from working to their fullest capacity. Tertiary interventions seek to address a disturbance that has already occurred, with the goal of helping the employee address the distress, impairment, or handicap in as an efficient manner as possible. Most would consider tertiary interventions as the bulk of EAP work, but those are not the only ways that EAPs try to help employees and employers.

Primary Interventions

As noted earlier, one of the ongoing tasks of EAPs is familiarizing employees and their families with the EAP and all that the EAP has to offer. Frequently this is done in a variety of ways. Many EAPs provide explanatory brochures, posters to be placed around the work site, business cards, and payroll envelope stuffers as means of providing information about the EAP. These mediums seek to repeatedly emphasize to the employee that the EAP is available as a confidential resource. Furthermore, many EAPs provide on-site orientations to employees during which the presenter explains how the EAP works and how the employees may access its services. During the orientation, confidentiality and accessibility are again emphasized while the notion that one must have a diagnosable disorder or other major problem before accessing the EAP's services is disputed. The on-site orientation also serves the purpose of familiarizing the employees with at least one person from the EAP, thus potentially removing a psychological barrier for an employee who might be hesitant to access the EAP.

Newsletters, both paper and electronic, are another way that many EAPs seek to provide primary intervention. Topics are generally focused around the maintenance of emotional and physical health. Sample topics might include recognizing problem-drinking behaviors, keys to better communication, the importance of maintaining good physical health through exercise, anger management strategies, the signs and symptoms of depression, personality factors that contribute to resiliency, and many more. The EAP's Web site serves as an additional resource for the employee to learn more about the EAP and potentially gain valuable information on a variety of topics. Most Web sites also include links to additional resources.

A third area of primary intervention is through the use of wellness presentations by the EAP to the employees at their place of work. Also known as lunchtime or brown-bag topics, these presentations usually last 45 minutes to an hour and often are presented, not surprisingly, during the lunch hour. These presentations frequently focus on issues pertaining to the employee in the workplace, but they are not limited to that. Wellness presentations addressing issues in the workplace may include effective communication skills in the workplace, coping with the stresses of change, keys to resiliency, dealing with difficult people at work, skills for managing anger, and effective strategies for responding to the difficult customer. Wills and estate planning, effective parenting, couples' communication, balancing work and family, and financial management are some of the topics that might be available that do not pertain directly to work. The value of these latter topics arises from the belief that employees are apt to be more productive if they are aware of and addressing possible issues in their personal life.

Some EAPs also are offering work-life or work-family programs. Whereas the EAP has an official definition, as noted earlier (EAPA, 2003), work-life and work-family programs do not enjoy the same clarity (Herlihy, 2000; Peck, 2001). These programs may include assisting with workplace policy in matters such as parental leave, flextime, job sharing, and working part-time. Perhaps more commonly these programs are associated with assisting employees and their families by way of consultation, referral, or education in a wide range of topics including, for example, "working during pregnancy, choosing a daycare facility, father support groups, summer camps, choosing a private school, college planning, managing money, caring for older relatives, and planning for retirement" (Herlihy, 2000, p. 35).

In our opening case example, had John's company had an EAP he would have had information available to him that could have helped him address some of the issues in his life before they became problematic in the workplace. Had he attended some wellness programs, or perhaps availed himself of work-life opportunities, he might have altered his behavior or thinking processes before his problems arose, thus preventing the onset of his difficulties altogether. Of course, that is the goal of primary interventions.

Secondary Interventions

Recently, the Substance Abuse and Mental Health Services Administration (Wright, 2002) released reports indicating that between 4 and 11 percent of all persons in the United States ages 12 years and older had reported some form of illicit drug use during the previous month in the years 1999 and 2000. "Among full-time workers aged 18 to 49 years in 2000, 8.1 percent reported past month heavy alcohol use, and 7.8 percent reported past month illicit drug use. In the past year, 7.4 percent of these workers were dependent or abusing alcohol, and 1.9 percent were dependent or abusing illicit drugs" (SAMHSA, 2002b). In their review of substance abuse in the workplace, Bush and Autry (2002, p. 14) cited an earlier SAMHSA report that indicated, "77% of the population 18 years old and over reporting current illicit drug use were employed."

This use is in spite of the fact that more than three-quarters of employees in this same age group are aware that their companies have written policies pertaining to employee substance abuse (SAMHSA, 2002a). Furthermore, when compared with those not reporting problematic alcohol or illicit drug use in the past year, workers abusing these substances were about twice as likely to have worked for more than three employers in the past year and more than three times as likely to have skipped work more than two days in the past month. Illicit drug users also were more likely to have missed more than two days in the past month because of illness or injury (SAMHSA, 2002b).

However, substance abuse is not the only factor affecting workers' productivity in the workplace; emotional and psychological distress also has a significant impact.

"Mental illness is the number one cause of disability for American business and industry today and is second only to cardiovascular disease in total disability costs" (Marlowe, 2002, p. 17).

In their analysis of a large manufacturing firm, French and Zarkin (1998) found that employees who reported emotional and psychological problems had higher absenteeism and lower earnings when compared with otherwise similar co-workers. As might be anticipated, women in this study reported a significantly higher prevalence of emotional and psychological symptoms than did their male co-workers. These findings were robust even when potentially confounding variables such as alcohol and illicit drug use were included, suggesting that mental health issues play an important role in productivity.

Depression may be the most widespread mental disorder affecting productivity in the workplace (Johnson & Indvik, 2001; Marlowe, 2002). In any given year, 20 percent of workers experience symptoms of mild to major depression and the majority of those persons go undiagnosed and untreated. Depression's financial impact on the workplace rivals that of hypertension, heart disease, diabetes, and back problems (Marlowe, 2002). In examining the short-term disability costs for one of their Fortune 500 clients, Marlowe (2002, p. 17) found that "15% of all [short-term disability] events for this company cited depression as a primary diagnosis," which ultimately resulted in a "33% increase in wage replacement costs." Furthermore, short-term disability claims are growing by about 10 percent annually.

The direct costs through disability are easily seen. Indirect costs of emotional and psychological distress are not so easily observed but may include such things as reduced workplace performance, loss of profit, increased numbers of accidents, and on-the-job absenteeism, recently referred to as presenteeism. "Presenteeism occurs when a worker shows up for work but is less productive due to an underlying problem. Most experts agree that presenteeism accounts for greater indirect costs than absenteeism" (Marlowe, 2002, p. 18).

Given that the vast majority of managers and supervisors is not trained in mental health assessment and diagnosis, they are ill equipped to assess whether their employees might be experiencing a mental disorder or the effects of substance abuse. However, they are in a prime position to attend to workplace performance among their employees, which may indicate an underlying mental or substance disorder, and the ways in which they intervene with their employees makes a difference (Dunnagan, Peterson, & Haynes, 2001). It is for this reason that EAPs frequently place significant emphasis on secondary interventions to train managers and supervisors to recognize the occurrence of performance problems in the workplace and how they might intervene with the worker in a timely, sequential process of interventions.

Training of management in responding to employee problems in the workplace often involves reorienting them to the role of the EAP as a confidential resource that may be used at various steps in a disciplinary process. The goal is to adequately acquaint them with the EAP so that they have the confidence to use it for themselves as well as refer other employees to it. Management will have many opportunities to refer their employees to the EAP without there being any performance problems, as many, if not most, employees talk at least occasionally about situations that are causing them some level of distress, even when their work is not being adversely affected. Alert managers can remind their employees about the EAP while leaving it entirely to the employee to decide whether to contact the EAP.

A second area of focus in management training is to equip managers with the ability to recognize problematic behavior in the workplace. Generally, this component addresses two areas. First, managers must learn to identify behaviors that are problematic. Absenteeism through excessive sick leave or unauthorized absences is a commonly recognized problem for most managers, as are workplace accidents. As noted previously, however, absenteeism may not be the most problematic area that most managers will encounter. Much more common is presenteeism, which may manifest itself in ways many managers will miss, perhaps in part because everyone occasionally has an "off" day. Furthermore, co-workers often are remiss to complain about an employee who is having performance difficulties, especially if they are long-time employees, arrive and leave on schedule, and appear to be trying hard. Co-workers often assist these employees in staying abreast of their work or in catching up, again under the belief that this might happen to them someday and they would hope for a similar response. In the last section of this chapter, I provide a sample checklist of behaviors that management can use in identifying employees having performance problems.

Recognition, however, is only the first step. Managers must also make the time to record in writing when an employee is identified as having a performance difficulty, as well as what steps are taken to address it. This documentation provides managers with a written history that is less susceptible to the vicissitudes of memory and allows them to differentiate between an isolated event and a pattern of problematic behavior. Some training in effective confrontation may be helpful for managers, as many have received no previous training in this area.

A third focus of this managerial training is progressive disciplinary procedures. Here the EAP trainer seeks to inform managers on the steps of progressive discipline; that is, from an informal intervention with an employee to a mandated referral and the possibility that this final step will be a condition of continued employment. Throughout this component of training, managers are encouraged to consider their EAP as a resource for both the manager and the employee. Managers are discouraged from attempting to ascertain the causes of performance difficulties (other than those that appear to be due to inadequate training, equipment, or some other work-related factor). Instead they are to respond to the employees' performance and use the EAP as a resource in seeking to understand potential causality. In early steps of the progressive discipline process, the manager offers the EAP as an optional resource in the hopes that employees will address any underlying issues that may be affecting their workplace performance. In this phase of discipline, the manager usually will not know whether the employee has followed through with the EAP referral.

The EAP also may serve employees and their companies when a referral is mandated because of a disciplinary action. In these situations, EAP counselors are keenly aware of the line they tread between meeting the needs of the company and its employees and the importance of maintaining confidentiality (Brody, 1988). In assessing an employee who has been mandated to the EAP, the counselor seeks to ascertain what, if any, causes there may be that are contributing to the employee's current problematic performance. If the etiology is a mental health or substance-abuse issue, the counselor may refer the employee to an outside resource for education or treatment. If appropriate, usually this referral will be made to a provider on the employee's health plan.

In our opening example, John had been having significant difficulty at work for some time. His performance was erratic and it was likely that others were covering for him. His manager had observed some of John's difficulties, but she did not take the necessary steps to make an appropriate intervention. Had her company used the management training that the EAP offered in recognizing and responding to performance problems, she might have learned some ways to effectively intervene with John when she first noticed that his difficulties were not sporadic but regular and unrelenting. Had her interventions been progressive in nature, John's company may have abetted John's addressing his problems before they became overwhelming for him, while also saving the trouble of finding a temporary replacement and the expense of an employee on short-term disability.

Tertiary Interventions

The most commonly perceived purpose of EAPs is their tertiary intervention strategies: confidential assessment, referral and short-term counseling of employees and their family members, management consultation, and CISDs. In many EAPs, these interventions are offered on a 365-day, 24-hour basis, at least by phone.

While the EAP began as a tool to help employers combat their employees' alcohol problems, today's EAPs do far more. They provide assessment, short-term counseling, and referral for a variety of mental health issues and various other problems encountered in life at no cost to the employee or family member. An abbreviated list of some of the issues that an EAP counselor might address include depression, anxiety, work-related and general stress, relationship issues, family concerns, grief, adjustment disorders, career concerns, addictions (including alcohol and illicit substances but not limited to them), financial and legal difficulties, physical health concerns, skill building, and many more. In a confidential setting, the EAP counselor meets with the employee or family member in an effort to determine the areas of concern and the most effective means to address those concerns. Usually this initial assessment lasts 45 to 60 minutes, although it may be longer or shorter. Contrary to the frequently long delays in accessing a mental health counselor in today's marketplace, the EAP counselor seeks to schedule an initial face-to-face appointment as quickly as possible. In many EAPs the goal is to see clients within 72 hours after their initial call. If a follow-up appointment is appropriate, it will most likely be scheduled at the end of the initial appointment. If a referral to another health care provider is suggested, the EAP counselor will assist the employee client in arranging an appointment with a provider on the employee's health plan. Accessing one's health plan may mean an outlay of money for the employee, either for co-pay or to meet insurance deductibles. EAP counselors usually have free or low-cost community resources available for employees who are uninsured or unable to afford the costs of their insurance-covered provider.

There is a growing body of literature that suggests that counseling is an important tool in responding to the distressed employee and that work may be an important resource in helping the employee through a difficult time ("Managing Emotional Fallout," 2002; Marlowe, 2002; Mitka, 2002). Thus, our fictional employee John could have availed himself of his EAP benefits. It would have been confidential, accessible, and at no cost to him. There he would have found a trained, understanding counselor who could have provided the resources to help him respond appropriately to the issues that he was facing. As a result, he may have found that he had an increased desire to return to work in a productive fashion, and he may have been able to use work as a means of coping appropriately with the other stressors in his life, rather than having work become an additional burden.

Simultaneously, John's supervisor could have used the EAP for a management consultation. Management consultations are an additional means of tertiary intervention available to companies through which problems in the workplace may be addressed. By consulting with an EAP counselor who was versed in personnel issues, John's manager may have recognized that, while her concern for John's welfare was genuine, she had more resources for intervention available to her than she was using. The EAP could have helped her assess the various problems in performance that John was exhibiting and worked with her toward developing a strategy for intervention. A follow-up call with the manager might be arranged to provide additional consultation on John's performance and the outcome of her interventions.

A third, if usually infrequent, area of tertiary intervention for EAPs is the CISD. Arising from a desire to provide brief, immediate intervention to trauma survivors (Plaggemars, 2000), the CISD has evolved to include structured interventions following disasters of all kinds, either natural caused (floods, earthquakes, etc.) or human caused (shootings, accidents, terrorist attacks, etc.). EAPs typically respond to a workplace tragedy with immediate phone access and, depending on the nature of the situation and the desire of the company, may arrange for counselors to be available at the workplace for formal group debriefings, informal employee meetings, or both, as either a group or individually. Those experienced in CISD recognize that group interventions are not for everyone and may even cause some people harm (Griepentrog, 2001). Whether as a group or individually, formal or informal, CISDs can be a useful resource for helping distressed employees normalize their reactions to a stressful event.

Looking to the Future

In providing primary, secondary, and tertiary intervention strategies, the EAP provides one of the most comprehensive strategies of response for employees with emotional and psychological problems. Even with a downturn in the economy at the time of this writing, the number of companies providing EAPs for their workers continues to grow (Naughton-Travers, 2002). Given the growing recognition by companies of the financial impact of emotional and psychological problems, it seems that providing resources for their employees through entities such as EAPs would be a profitable decision by management.

For those readers interested in a career as an EAP professional, it is important to know that job satisfaction is generally high (Sweeney, Hohenshil, & Fortune, 2002). This is especially true for persons who enjoy variety and opportunities to be creative in their job and for those who have a high need for providing social service. For those who have strong desire for career advancement and higher salaries, the EAP profession may be less to their liking. Sweeney et al. found that EAP professionals in "externally located programs rated themselves as significantly more satisfied than did those employed in internal programs" (p. 58). Because the number of externally located programs is growing, the future looks good for EAP professionals who seek a career that is challenging and satisfying on many levels and one that uses diverse skills in a variety of domains.

IDENTIFYING TROUBLED EMPLOYEES THROUGH PERFORMANCE EVALUATION

Think about the employees you supervise. Do any of them have any of the following characteristics? Go through the following list and place an *X* next to each characteristic or change you have noted in any of your staff members.

1. Absenteeism
    _____a. Multiple instances of unauthorized leave
    _____b. Excessive sick leave
    _____c. Frequent Monday and/or Friday absences
    _____d. Repeated absences, especially if following a pattern
    _____e. Excessive tardiness, especially on Monday morning or after lunch
    _____f. Early work departure
    _____g. Peculiar and increasingly improbable excuses for absences
    _____h. Higher absenteeism rate than other employees for colds, flu, gastritis, etc.
    _____i. Frequent, unscheduled, short-term absences (with or without medical explanation)

2. On-the-Job Absenteeism ("presenteeism")
    _____a. Continued absences from post, more than job requires
    _____b. Frequent trips to the water fountain or restroom
    _____c. Long coffee breaks
    _____d. Physical illness on the job

3. High Accident Rate (consequently, more accident claims)
    _____a. Accidents on the job
    _____b. Accidents off the job

4. Difficulty in Concentration
    _____a. Work requires greater effort
    _____b. Jobs take more time

5. Confusion
   _____a. Difficulty in recalling instructions, details, etc.
   _____b. Increasing difficulty in handling complex assignments
   _____c. Difficulty in recalling or recognizing own mistakes

6. Spasmodic Work Patterns
   _____a. Alternate periods of high and low productivity

7. Reporting to Work
   _____a. Coming to or returning from work in obviously abnormal
   condition

8. Generally Lowered Job Efficiency
   _____a. Missed deadlines
   _____b. Mistakes due to inattention or poor judgment
   _____c. Bad decision making
   _____d. More material wasted
   _____e. Complaints from users of product
   _____f. Improbable excuses for poor job performance

9. Poor Employee Relationships on the Job
   _____a. Overreaction to real or imagined criticism
   _____b. Wide swings of mood
   _____c. Borrowing of money from co-workers
   _____d. Unreasonable resentment or hostility
   _____e. Complaints from co-workers
   _____f. Withdrawal from co-workers

10. Other
    _____a._____
    _____b._____

References

Brody, B. E. (1988). Employee assistance programs: An historical and literature review. *American Journal of Health Promotion, 2,* 13-19.

Bush, D. M., & Autry, J. H., III. (2002). Substance abuse in the workplace: Epidemiology, effects, and industry response. *Occupational Medicine: State of the Art Reviews, 17,* 13-25.

Butterworth, I. E. (2001). The components and impact of stigma associated with EAP counseling. *Employee Assistance Quarterly, 16,* 1-8.

Collins, K. (2000). EAPs: Better onsite or offsite? *Behavioral Health Management, 20,* 42-46.

Dickman, F. (1988). Ingredients of an effective employee assistance program. In F. Dickman (Ed.), *Employee assistance programs: A basic text* (pp. 110-121). Springfield, IL: Charles C. Thomas.

Dunnagan, T., Peterson, M., & Haynes, G. (2001). Mental health issues in the workplace: A case for a new managerial approach. *Journal of Occupational and Environmental Medicine, 43,* 1073-1080.

Employee Assistance Professionals Association. (2003). *What's an EAP?* Retrieved March 3, 2003, from http://www.eapassn.org.

French, M. T., Dunlap, L. J., Roman, P. M., & Steele, P. D. (1997). Factors that influence the use and perceptions of employee assistance programs at six worksites. *Journal of Occupational Health Psychology, 2,* 312-324.

French, M. T., & Zarkin, G. A. (1998). Mental health, absenteeism and earnings at a large manufacturing worksite. *Journal of Mental Health Policy and Economics, 1,* 161-172.

French, M. T., Zarkin, G. A., Bray, J. W., & Hartwell, T. D. (1999). Cost of employee assistance programs: Comparison of national estimates from 1993 and 1995. *Journal of Behavioral Health Services and Research, 26,* 95-103.

Griepentrog, W. (2001). The role of EAPs in disaster response. *Behavioral Health Management, 21,* 14-18.

Harlow, K. C. (1998). Employee attitudes toward an internal employee assistance program. *Journal of Employment Counseling, 35,* 141-151.

Hartwell, T. D., Steele, P., French, M. T., Potter, F. J., Rodman, N. F., & Zarkin, G. A. (1996). Aiding troubled employees: The prevalence, cost, and characteristics of employee assistance programs in the United States. *American Journal of Public Health, 86,* 804-808.

Herlihy, P. A. (2000). Employee assistance and work/family programs: Friends or foes? *Employee Assistance Quarterly, 16,* 33-52.

Johnson, P. R., & Indvik, J. (2001). The boomer blues: Depression in the workplace. *Public Personnel Management, 26,* 359-365.

Leong, D. M., & Every, D. K. (1997). Internal and external eaps: Is one better than the other? *Employee Assistance Quarterly, 12,* 47-61.

Managing emotional fallout: Parting remarks from America's top psychiatrist. (2002, February). *Harvard Business Review, 80,* 55-60.

Marlowe, J. F. (2002). Depression's surprising toll on worker productivity. *Employee Benefits Journal, 27,* 16-21.

Mitka, M. (2002). Business learns wisdom of treating employees with psychaiatric disability. *Journal of the American Medical Association, 287,* 2933-2934.

Naughton-Travers, J. P. (2002). *Industry statistics.* Gettysburg, PA: Open Minds.

Peck, R. L. (2001). EAP vs worklife: What's the difference (and does it matter?)? *Behavioral Health Management, 21,* 14-17.

Plaggemars, D. (2000). EAPs and critical incident stress debriefing: A look ahead. *Employee Assistance Quarterly, 16,* 77-96.

Substance Abuse and Mental Health Services Administration. (2002a). Awareness of workplace substance use policies and programs. *The NHSDA Report.* Retrieved September 27, 2002, from http://www.DrugAbuseStatistics.samhsa.gov.

Substance Abuse and Mental Health Services Administration. (2002b). Substance use, dependence or abuse among full-time workers. *The NHSDA Report.* Retrieved September 6, 2002, from http://www.DrugAbuseStatistics.samhsa.gov.

Wright, D. (2002). *State Estimates of Substance Use from the 2000 National Household Survey on Drug Abuse: Volume I. Findings* (DHHS Publication No. SMA 02-3731, NHSDA Series H-15). Rockville, MD: Substance Abuse and Mental Health Services Administration, Office of Applied Studies.

Sweeney, A. P., Hohenshil, T. H., & Fortune, J. C. (2002). Job satisfaction among employee assistance professionals: A national study. *Journal of Employment Counseling, 39,* 50-60.

Index